Human capital and empire

Manchester University Press

STUDIES IN IMPERIALISM

General editors: Andrew S. Thompson and Alan Lester
Founding editor: John M. MacKenzie

When the 'Studies in Imperialism' series was founded by Professor John M. MacKenzie more than thirty years ago, emphasis was laid upon the conviction that 'imperialism as a cultural phenomenon had as significant an effect on the dominant as on the subordinate societies'. With well over a hundred titles now published, this remains the prime concern of the series. Cross-disciplinary work has indeed appeared covering the full spectrum of cultural phenomena, as well as examining aspects of gender and sex, frontiers and law, science and the environment, language and literature, migration and patriotic societies, and much else. Moreover, the series has always wished to present comparative work on European and American imperialism, and particularly welcomes the submission of books in these areas. The fascination with imperialism, in all its aspects, shows no sign of abating, and this series will continue to lead the way in encouraging the widest possible range of studies in the field. 'Studies in Imperialism' is fully organic in its development, always seeking to be at the cutting edge, responding to the latest interests of scholars and the needs of this ever-expanding area of scholarship.

To buy or to find out more about the books currently available in this series, please go to:
https://manchesteruniversitypress.co.uk/series/studies-in-imperialism/

Human capital and empire

Human capital and empire

Scotland, Ireland, Wales and British imperialism in Asia, c.1690–c.1820

Andrew Mackillop

MANCHESTER UNIVERSITY PRESS

Copyright © Andrew Mackillop 2021

The right of Andrew Mackillop to be identified as the author of this work has been asserted by them in accordance with the Copyright, Designs and Patents Act 1988.

Published by Manchester University Press
Oxford Road, Manchester M13 9PL

www.manchesteruniversitypress.co.uk

British Library Cataloguing-in-Publication Data
A catalogue record for this book is available from the British Library

ISBN 978 0 7190 7072 3 hardback
ISBN 978 0 7190 7073 0 paperback

First published 2021
Paperback published 2023

The publisher has no responsibility for the persistence or accuracy of URLs for any external or third-party internet websites referred to in this book, and does not guarantee that any content on such websites is, or will remain, accurate or appropriate.

Typeset by
Servis Filmsetting Ltd, Stockport, Cheshire

To Carol, Coll and Ruth

Contents

List of tables	viii
Acknowledgements	x
Naming conventions and currencies	xiii
Abbreviations	xiv
Maps	xv
Founding editor's introduction	xviii
Introduction: Complicating the coloniser: Scottish, Irish and Welsh perspectives on British imperialism in Asia	1
1 Beginnings: London and early links with the English East India companies	29
2 The brokers of human capital: shareholders and directors	57
3 Civil servants and mariners	83
4 The military: economies of high- and low-value human capital	119
5 Circuits of human and cultural capital: medicine and the knowledge economy in Asia	157
6 The free traders: connecting economies of human and monetary capital	192
7 Returns: realising the human capital economy	220
Conclusion: 'Poor' Europe's pathways to empire and globalisation	254
Appendices	268
Bibliography	276
Index	312

List of tables

1.1	London-Scots securities and the EIC, 1690–1775	47
2.1	Scottish, Irish and Welsh EIC stockholders, 1790	62
2.2	Scottish, Irish and Welsh directors, 1754–1794	67
2.3	David Scott of Dunninald's patronage, 1788–1799	74
3.1	Scottish, Irish and Welsh EIC civil servants, 1690–1813	90
3.2	Civil servants: regional, social and educational backgrounds	95
3.3	Scottish, Irish and Welsh merchant marine officers, 1690–1813	105
3.4	Merchant marine officers: regional, social and educational backgrounds	107
4.1	Military officers, 1690–1749	128
4.2	Scots, Irish and Welsh military officers in Asia, 1690–1813	131
4.3	Military officers: regional, social and educational backgrounds	136
4.4	Military profits: Bengal, Bombay, Madras wills, 1753–1813	143
4.5	Irish, Scots and Welsh senior officers, Asia, 1747–1813	145
4.6	Irish, Scots and Welsh military profiteering	146
5.1	Educational backgrounds, EIC surgeons, 1764–1800	163
5.2	Metropolitan provincial surgeons: directorate minutes and Probate Court of Canterbury wills, 1690–1800	168
5.3	Irish, Scots and Welsh medical personnel in Asia, 1690–1813	170
5.4	East India Company assistant surgeon appointments, 1805–1813	171
5.5	East India Company surgeons: regional and social backgrounds	175
6.1	Official free merchants and mariners, 1690–1780	194
6.2	Irish, Scots and Welsh free merchants and mariners, Calcutta and Madras, 1778–1812	196
6.3	Scots, Irish and Welsh free merchants and mariners, 1690–1813	196
6.4	Private traders: occupational profiles	198
6.5	Transnational remittance networks	207

7.1	The Eastern Empire in metropolitan provincial politics	225
7.2	The proceeds of human capital: metropolitan provincial fortunes, *c*.1730–*c*.1820	231
7.3	Asia-derived wealth relative to landed rents	233

Acknowledgements

The nature of historical investigation generates such a range of obligations, both practical and intellectual, that it is impossible to thank all concerned. The bulk of research for this book occurred at the National Records of Scotland (NRS), the National Library of Scotland (NLS), and the British Library as well as a number of other archives in Scotland, Ireland and the USA. The staff at these repositories help make research an enjoyable as well as thought-provoking process and I would like to thank them for all their assistance. Dr David Brown at the NRS not only provided insights on Henry Dundas and the East India Company but also imparted crucial knowledge on searching the vast resource that is the post-1781 abridgements of Scottish sasines. Beyond the public repositories I would like to express my appreciation to Mr Grant of Monymusk, The Brodie of Brodie, and the earl of Balcarres for permission to use their family papers, held either in the NRS, the NLS or privately.

This book has been a long time in the making. It began as a much smaller project exploring Scottish military officers in the East India Company and was funded by a Glenfiddich Fellowship in Scottish History at the University of St Andrews. Arts and Humanities Research Council (AHRC) funding while at Aberdeen enabled the phased development of what is now the Scottish, Irish & Welsh in Asia, 1690–1820 database (SIWA). It currently enumerates 6,129 individuals and details their cycle of departure and return from Asia. These people were among the most powerful migrants in the history of the early modern British and Irish Isles. In charting their backgrounds, careers, profits and lifecycles, SIWA forms the key foundation for the ideas offered here. A Trinity Long Room Fellowship at Trinity College Dublin enabled me to explore some of the great untapped resources relating to Irish society's substantial engagement with the English East India Company. As with all great research experiences, the fellowship left me conscious of how much more there is to do and how fascinating the contrasts are between Ireland and Scotland in the long eighteenth century.

Acknowledgements

London also looms large in this study. Involvement in a series of workshops on the theme of Scots in early modern England organised by Professor Keith Brown's AHRC research project at the University of Manchester provided much food for thought on how the links between societies like Ireland and Scotland and the metropolis are best conceived.

This book will appear with my professional affiliation listed as the University of Glasgow. However, all the research and the completion of a rough (and excessively long) draft occurred during my time in the Department of History at the University of Aberdeen. My warm thanks to my former colleagues there: to Marjory Harper, who taught me much about the Scottish Diaspora; Jackson Armstrong for his unfailing collegiality and for getting me into Scottish legal history; Aly Macdonald for reminding me more than once in the Machar that 'Jock spotting' has limited appeal; Ben Marsden for telling advice on empire and knowledge; and Andrew Dilley for many a productive exchange on the nature of British imperialism and the state of the UK's contemporary constitutional politics. And of course to Bill Naphy for all his friendship and advice, most of which he knew I wouldn't take!

Over the years I have been lucky to supervise a number of PhDs from whom I learned much: Steffi Metze, Anne Crerar, Aisling MacQuarrie and latterly Eloise Grey kept me on my toes when thinking about empire. I owe a special thanks to 'slow history man', Thomas Brochard for many illuminating exchanges on Highland history. I still miss our mutual support sessions at O'Neills on the Back Wynd when enduring the tribulations of following the Scottish and French rugby teams. It was at Aberdeen that I met a number of colleagues, all now in Ireland, to whom I owe an immense amount: Tom Bartlett, for many valuable lessons on Ireland and the Empire; to David Ditchburn for his all characteristically forthright encouragement and advice, as well as his willingness to indulge in unscheduled pit stops in the Machar and hostelries in Dublin and in Edinburgh. Many thanks, too, to Éamonn Ó Ciardha and Micheál Ó Siochrú for more pints than is advisable, for all their insights on Ireland and especially for their humour and friendship over the years.

Colleagues at Glasgow have been warmly welcoming and forgiving of a newbie distracted by the task of editing down an inordinately long draft manuscript. To Jamie Kelly, my neighbour on the top floor of Number 9, my grateful thanks for being a patient graphics guru for the maps. Arrival at Glasgow has led to many intellectually exciting discussions, not least with Nigel Leask and Jim Tomlinson, scholars with very different specialisms but who have done much ground-breaking work in helping us think about the historical significance of connections between Scotland and Asia. Jim kindly read draft sections of this work and provided much-needed advice regarding a stubbornly over-length draft.

Jelmer Vos and Christine Whyte put up with my constant tendency to ask how Scottish evidence fits into their frameworks and have responded by giving me much to think about in terms of comparisons between the Atlantic and Asian spheres of European colonialism. Julia McClure's seemingly endless energy and enthusiasm is matched by her fascinating insights on poverty, property and capital accumulation in early modern empires, themes which lie at the heart of this study. Besides his wicked line in bulk-buying of rum (invariably 5 minutes after last orders in Tennents), Stephen Mullen has taught me a huge deal in a short time about the impact of the Atlantic Empire upon post-union Scottish society. Aonghas MacCoinnich, Martin MacGregor and Dauvit Broun have provided collegiality and insight in equal measure. Their critical yet empathetic appraisals of Scottish society and its links with the wider world over many centuries helped me clarify (and edit down) my fuzzy thinking on questions of locality and of nation in a global empire.

My final intellectual debt is to John MacKenzie, a scholar whose generosity and patience need no restatement from me. Beyond his amazing knowledge of the central themes at the heart of this book, there is his inexhaustible enthusiasm, his ability to mix gentle encouragement with pointed 'get on with it' advice and simple human generosity. Like many in the field I owe him a huge debt and completing this book pays back but a very small amount. I need hardly add that any mistakes of fact or interpretation are mine alone.

To Wills (and Hec the cat), many thanks for being an accommodating landlord during my extended relocation from Aberdeen to Glasgow. Along with Wills, Joe and Coobs, my Hearaich friends (Nom, Calum, James and Murch) have been steadfast in their scepticism concerning the value of my endeavours and loud in their assessments of its boring nature – usually while demanding another round. I wouldn't have it any other way.

My last and most important thanks go to my family. My mum, brother and sister have put up with me venting about progress (or more usually the lack of it) on 'the book' through more years than they would care to remember. My deepest thanks of all go to Carol, Coll and Ruth, who have weathered with patience, encouragement and love my tendency to exist in the eighteenth century rather than the twenty-first century. Dedicating this book to them with all my love seems a very small return, but it is a heartfelt one.

Naming conventions and currencies

Colonialism and associated processes of expansion have left many tangled and controversial legacies that need a clear and early acknowledgement in a study such as this. One area where such aftermaths are obvious is in place names. Many of the geographic labels used by the English and later British in Ireland and by Europeans in Asia during the early modern period are no longer in common usage. However, to maintain continuity with the contemporary English language sources and much of the terminology used by the secondary literature, this study retains these older 'anglicised' forms. It does so while acknowledging that many such names are no longer recognised by the people and communities of these places and may indeed carry negative or offensive connotations. The alignment with the Company's records alone explains why the Iranian, Indian, Indonesia and Chinese cities of Bandar Abbas, Chennai, Srirangapatna, Kolkata, Bardhaman, Mumbai, Tiruchirappalli, Bengkulu, Jakarta and Guangzhou are referred to as Gambroon, Madras, Seringapatam, Calcutta, Burdwan, Bombay, Trichinopoly, Benkulen, Batavia and Canton respectively.

The same principle is applied to some counties in Ireland. County Derry is listed as Londonderry while the counties of Laois and Offaly are referred to by their previously anglicised titles of Queen's and King's.

The primary currencies used throughout this study are:

Pounds sterling (£): 1 £=20 shillings (/-); 1 shilling=12 pence (d)
Pounds Scots: all £ Scots and subset values such as merks are converted into £ sterling unless otherwise indicated.
Pagoda: Key currency in the Madras presidency. Converted at a value of 8/- per pagoda.
Rupees: Bombay and Sicca Rupees are converted on a sliding scale of 2/-2d to 2/-6d
Spanish dollar ($): converted on a value of 5/- per $.

For discussion and tabulation of currencies see K. N. Chaudhuri, *The Trading World of Asia and the English East India Company, 1660–1760* (Cambridge: Cambridge University Press, 1978), p. 471.

Abbreviations

ACA:	Aberdeen City and Shire Archives, Aberdeen
AUL:	Aberdeen University Library, Aberdeen
BC:	Brodie Castle, Forres
CSAS:	Centre for South Asian Studies, Cambridge
DCA:	Dundee City Archive, Dundee
DCM:	Dunvegan Castle Muniments, Isle of Skye
EIC:	English East India Company
EUL:	Edinburgh University Library, Edinburgh
GCA:	Glasgow City Archive, Mitchell Library, Glasgow
GHL:	Guildhall Library, London
GUL:	Glasgow University Library, Glasgow
HAC:	Highland Archive Centre, Inverness
HL:	Huntington Library, Pasadena, CA, USA
IOR:	India Office Records, Asia, Pacific and Africa Collections, British Library, London
KH:	Kinross House Papers, Kinross
LMA:	London Metropolitan Archives, London
NAI:	National Archive of Ireland, Dublin
NLI:	National Library of Ireland, Dublin
NLS:	National Library of Scotland, Edinburgh
NRS:	National Records of Scotland, Edinburgh
PKA:	Perth and Kinross Archive, A. K. Bell Library, Perth
PRAI:	Property Registration Authority of Ireland, Dublin
PRONI:	Public Record of Northern Ireland, Belfast
RRCPG:	Records of the Royal College of Physicians and Surgeons of Glasgow, Glasgow
SIWA:	Scots, Irish, and Welsh in Asia, 1690–1820
TCD:	Trinity College Dublin, Library (Manuscripts and Archives)
TNA:	The National Archives, Kew, London

Maps

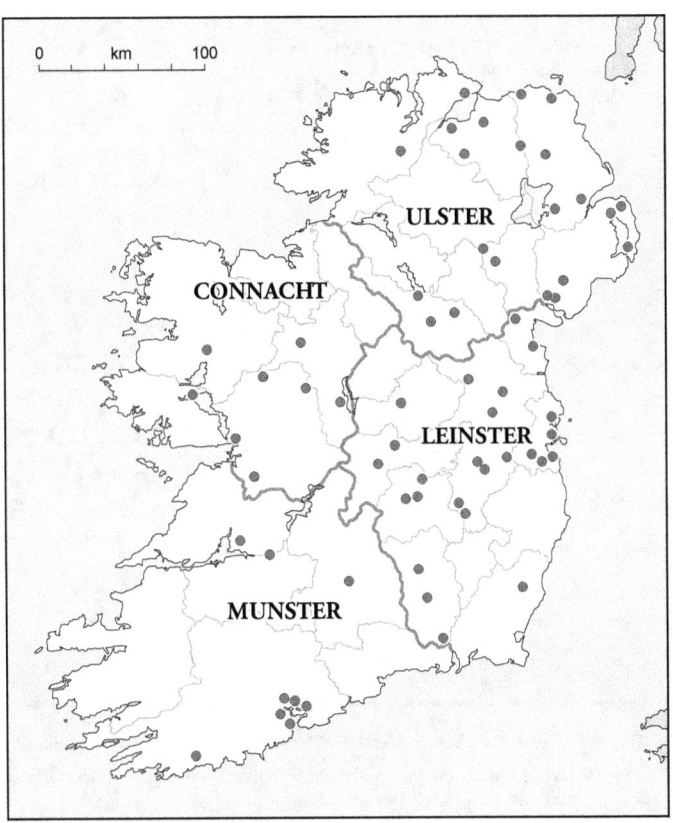

Map 1 Estates with Asia-linked ownership, Ireland, *c*.1760–*c*.1820
Connacht: Mayo; Galway; Leitrim; Roscommon; Sligo;
Leinster: Carlow; County Dublin; Longford; Louth; Kildare; Kilkenny; Meath; West Meath; Queen's; King's; Wexford; Wicklow (NB: two additional unnamed estates are linked with West Meath but cannot be plotted);
Munster: Clare; Cork; Kerry; Limerick; Tipperary; Waterford;
Ulster: Antrim; Armagh; Cavan; Donegal; Down; Fermanagh; Londonderry; Monaghan; Tyrone (NB: one unnamed estate in Fermanagh and one in Tyrone cannot be plotted)

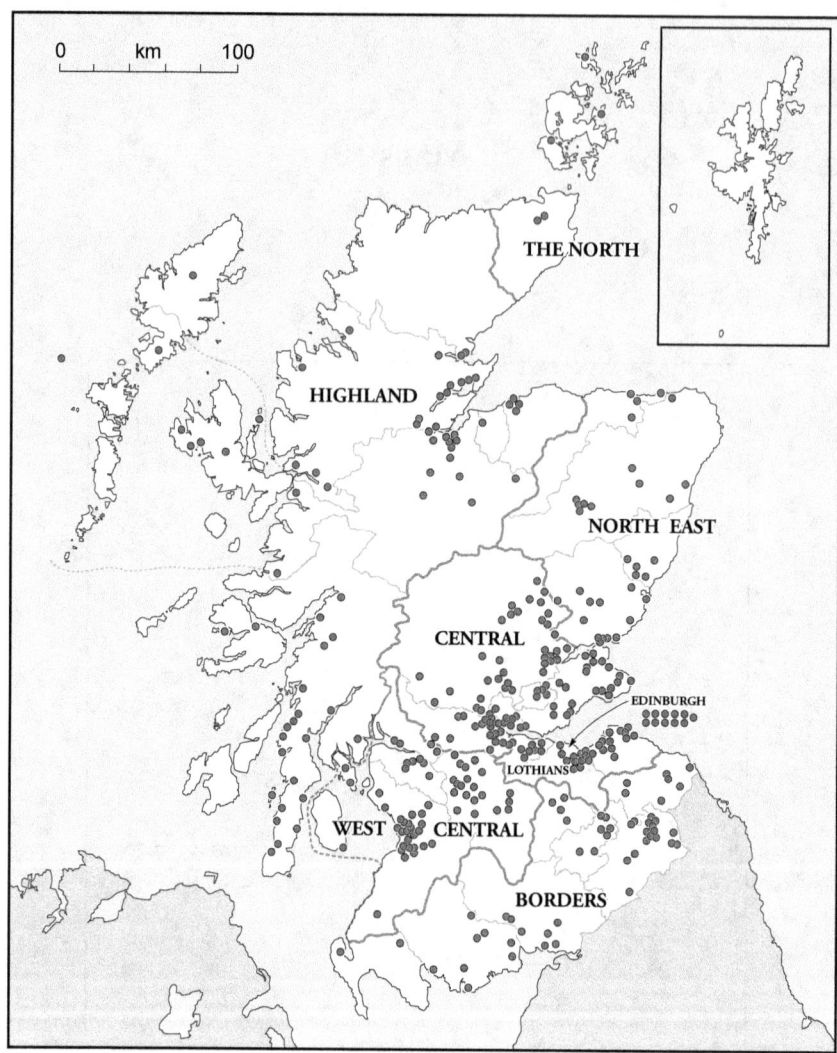

Map 2 Estates with Asia-linked ownership, Scotland, c.1740–c.1820

Borders: Berwick; Dumfries; Kirkcudbright; Peebles; Roxburgh; Selkirk; Wigton;
Lothians: Edinburgh city; Haddington; Linlithgow; Lothian;
West Central: Ayr; Bute; Dunbarton; Lanark; Renfrew;
Central: Clackmannan; Fife; Kinross; Perth; Stirling;
North East: Aberdeen; Angus; Banff; Kincardine;
Highland: Argyll; Inverness; Moray; Nairn; Ross and Cromarty; Sutherland (NB: For the purposes of this map the island of St Kilda in the county of Inverness is placed c.25 miles east of its actual location, c.50 miles west of the Isle of Harris, the Western Isles parish to which it was attached);
The North: Caithness; Orkney; Shetland

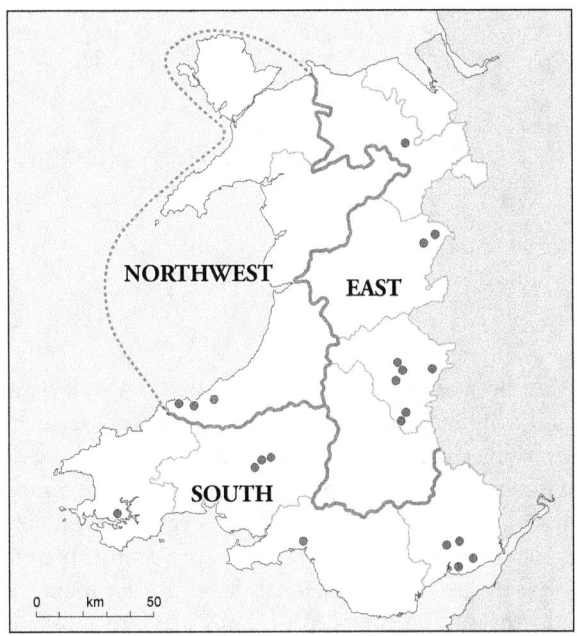

Map 3 Estates with Asia-linked ownership, Wales, c.1760–c.1820

East Wales: Brecon; Denbigh; Flint, Montgomery; Radnor;
South Wales: Monmouth, Carmarthen, Glamorgan, Pembroke;
West/North Wales: Anglesey; Cardigan; Merioneth; Caernarvon.

Founding editor's introduction

The relationship between the 'metropolitan provinces' of Ireland, Scotland and Wales and empire received very little attention until comparatively recently. Migration, particularly transatlantic migration, was the one area that has been intensively studied, particularly when such migration was connected with major socio-economic disasters in the domestic setting, whether the Highland Clearances or Irish Famine. Such movements of migrants have been analysed with growing sophistication, with the focus extended both backwards into the seventeenth century and forward into the key volume period of the late nineteenth and twentieth centuries. But the structural social and economic relationships between the societies of Ireland, Scotland and Wales and Asia, notably the operations of the East India Company, have received much less attention. When such connections have been discussed there has been a tendency to deal in impressionistic terms, with more or less confident assertions often lacking in foundational quantification. The metropolitan provinces were certainly known to have been instrumental here with famous literary allusions by Sir Walter Scott or Rudyard Kipling, but a close and particularly statistical analysis has been absent.

In the case of Scotland, the relationship between the West-Central region, notably the city of Glasgow, and the sugar and tobacco economies of the Caribbean and North America has received close study. Turning to the Scottish Highlands, some recent books of essentially family history have turned the spotlight on significant regional and social connections with India. These include Alistair Mutch's *Tiger Duff: India, Madeira and Empire in Eighteenth-Century Scotland* (2017) and Alexander Charles Baillie's *Call of Empire: From the Highlands to Hindostan* (also 2017). Familial traditions and influences in career choice are certainly significant. But now we have in Andrew Mackillop's book the first really authoritative study of the connection of the East India Company not only with Scotland, but also with Ireland and Wales during the long eighteenth century from 1690 to 1820. As any reader can discern, this has been the work of many years' intensive research, utilising a tremendous range of sources and developing all manner of statistical techniques and theoretical notions to appraise the effects of the Asian connection with these three so-called provincial societies.

Mackillop develops the concepts of the involvement of poorer parts of Europe and of the investment of human rather than finance capital. The metropolitan provinces were richer in such manpower capital and they were able to enter into the imperial relationship through its deployment in the East, its conversion (when successful) into monetary value and its consequent effects upon domestic local economies. The study seeks to highlight the distinctions and contrasts among the three chosen regions by utilising the notions of high-volume/low-value and low-volume/high-value forms of human capital. These ideas are developed in terms of the key areas of employment in the East – as bureaucrats, merchants and mariners, in the military, in medical services, and as free traders. But these are examined in terms of the manner in which the personnel secured positions in the Company by means of forms of patronage and networking through the operations of directors and shareholders at the imperial heartland in London. The results demonstrate the relatively low involvement of Wales and the reasons for its comparative decline from the early period, the famously high participation of the Irish, notably in the rank and file of the military, and the strikingly strong entryism of the Scots, particularly into the bureaucratic structures of the company and the officer corps. Not the least of the significance of the study lies in the manner in which Mackillop identifies the micro-, meso- and macro-networks (that is local, those connecting with the levers of the metropolis and the principal interconnections of operations between Britain and Asia), illuminating the ways in which these relationships are both articulated and are strikingly instrumental. And finally he provides fascinating data on the manner in which the fortunes which are made in India (in the midst of the failures of many) return to Wales, Ireland and Scotland for reinvestment in land, stock or the creation of further networks of clientage. In all these he also pays attention to the cultural capital which operates, for example, to create environmental improvements, educational and medical opportunities that draw attention away from the ways in which wealth made in Asia had already developed dubious resonances.

There can be little doubt that this is one of the most significant studies of the relationship of provincial societies with Asia in the eighteenth century. The appendices and maps are particularly valuable, complementing the many tables that run through the book. It is a study which should certainly stimulate more research, not least in terms of familial connections, local dimensions and further cultural phenomena in the embracing of the imperial opportunities in Asia.

John M. MacKenzie

Introduction
Complicating the coloniser:
Scottish, Irish and Welsh perspectives
on British imperialism in Asia

This book is about Scottish, Irish and Welsh involvement in the English East India companies that controlled official contact between the British and Irish Isles and Asia throughout the early modern era.[1] It uses three societies not usually considered central to Europe's eastward expansion to consider the multiple pathways into empire and to reflect on the ways in which links to Asia changed colonising countries in profound and often contrasting ways. The central contention is that Scotland, Ireland and Wales's engagement with the English East India companies between c.1690 and c.1820 provides a case study of the mutually constitutive interaction of global, imperial, national, corporate, regional, local and familial dynamics during the age of 'proto-globalisation'.[2]

Increasing participation in one hemisphere of England and later Britain's worldwide empire is here conceptualised as a cycle of human mobility and human capital. The focus is not on the formal corporate, financial and economic structures of English and British colonial power in Asia.[3] The emphasis is on people moving across oceanic distances and considering what this mobility meant for the individuals involved, their families and communities. Once they arrived in Asia, Scots, Welsh, Irish and their fellow English employees associated with a cosmopolitan set of Europeans: French, Dutch, Danes, Portuguese, Spaniards, Austrians and Swedes. They worked with, lived with and exploited local people before returning home or dying in Asia and leaving whatever fortune they made to travel back instead of them.[4] Understanding these developments involves recapturing the scale of human movement to and from Asia between c.1690 and c.1820. This timeframe not only aligns with the last phase of proto-globalisation but also marks two turning points in the history of the English East India Company (EIC). The 1690s were the last occasion when a non-English corporation, the Company of Scotland, attempted to break London's monopoly of British and Irish Isles contact with Asia. In 1813, by contrast, the Company lost exclusive control of the trade to India, heralding the beginning of the end of the *ancien régime* nature of Britain's empire in that part of the world.[5]

The chronology and quantity of Irish, Scottish and Welsh participation in the commercial, merchant marine, military and medical divisions of the pre-1815 corporation are outlined in detail for the first time. The survey extends to the free merchants and free mariners licensed to conduct trade in Asia while being forbidden to interfere in the Company's monopoly of international commerce between East and West. The approach treats migration as more than a social reaction to the transformations and displacements created by an increasingly capitalist economy. Human movement is considered here as a substitute method of investment in the proto-global economy by those parts of Europe that were 'poor' in terms of surplus monetary capital. Conceptualising people and social networks as an important form of wealth involves remaining sensitive to familial and regional perspectives as well as issues of professional status and local, national and supranational identities. Yet the sociology of Irish, Scottish and Welsh mobility is not viewed in isolation but is linked to the patronage networks in London that facilitated the acquisition of elite and often lucrative employment.

The cycle of people sojourning to and capital returning from Asia might appear a simple exchange. It was not. At the start of this period Scotland, Ireland and Wales lacked their own autonomous means of contact with that part of the world. The first chapter considers the growing connections to London which enabled an initially halting access to the English East India Company during the last decade of the seventeenth and first four decades of the eighteenth centuries. These developments are the subject of Chapters 1 and 2. Employment and material prospects altered radically in the 1740s and 1750s as the corporation underwent major change in both London and South Asia. Given the longer-term significance for Asian, British, imperial and world histories arising from this transformation, it is understandable that its nature remains much debated.[6] The Company's rise as a territorial and colonial power is treated as an evolving framework of opportunity into which the less affluent parts of the British and Irish Isles sent substantial numbers of middling social order migrants. Chapters 3, 4 and 5 analyse how, when, in what numbers and from which regions Scots, Irish and Welsh joined the civil service, the merchant marine, the military officer corps and the medical service. Chapter 6 completes coverage of the main sojourning activities by analysing the free merchants and mariners licensed to conduct private trade. The final chapter completes the cycle by assessing the scale and impact of sojourners and their monetary capital returning to Ireland, Scotland and Wales.

Integrating these dimensions of human mobility with the Company's trade and empire necessitates engagement with a series of historiographies and methodologies. These range from relevant trends in global history, South Asian and British imperial studies, British history, East India Company studies, Scottish, Irish, Welsh, regional and familial histories. They all provide pertinent frameworks for different aspects of the book. Much of the current dynamism in British imperial history arises from the introduction of and reaction to a range of theoretical positions that blur the boundaries between previously demarcated themes. Among the most significant of these are the strictures against established historical approaches emanating from post-colonial and post-modernist scholarship.[7] One result has been the emergence of a synthesis of methodologies that seeks to combine the best of critical discourse perspectives with a rigorously historicised understanding of imperialism. This confluence is known as the new imperial history, although as an idea it is no longer particularly 'new'.[8] The post-colonial injunction to 'decentre' empire provides new interpretative space and relevance for societies such as Ireland, Scotland and Wales that participated in global expansion through different trajectories when compared to the better-known examples of Portugal, Spain, France, the Netherlands or England.[9]

If less centralised frameworks provide an opportunity to rethink the nature and consequences of early modern imperialism, the importance of Ireland, Scotland and Wales should not be overexaggerated. These were (and still are) small countries with limited populations and economies. Investigating their increasing connections to Asia needs to be sensitive to the charge that such an approach risks a form of 'metropolitan parochialism', which reaffirms the metropole as the privileged subject of study.[10] One means of addressing this concern is to avoid essentialising these countries into unproblematic national categories. All three societies are conceived of as 'metropolitan provinces'. Province in no way denotes marginality. It is simply a unit of analysis that balances an emphasis on integration and ongoing distinctiveness. As such it is an apt framework for those areas of the British and Irish Isles that retained distinguishing political, economic, social, cultural and even national characteristics while integrating into Anglo-Britain to a greater or lesser extent.[11] The varying degrees of integrated but ongoing difference are one reason why Scotland, Ireland and Wales offer fresh ways of thinking about the configurations of early modern empire and global expansion.[12] Yet any emphasis on incorporation into empire is not about resurrecting concepts of 'internal colonialism' or of viewing these societies only as subordinated to external, metropolitan forces. Dichotomous models of 'English' centre and 'Celtic' periphery are reconfigured by factoring in dynamic interactions between the metropolis and the vibrant regional economies that reshaped Britain and Ireland.[13] The aim is to use the eastern hemisphere of the Empire to multicentre rather than atomise the British and Irish Isles in the long eighteenth century.

The critiques of the new imperial history partially explain the current vitality of empire studies. However, they do not sufficiently acknowledge the extent to which new lines of analysis have continually reshaped interpretative possibilities. Human mobility is now considered a vital component of Britain's economic, financial and cultural 'expansion', which in turn facilitated formal military control and 'imperialism'.[14] While the British Empire was understood primarily through its political, legal and military structures or the influence of London's financial markets, Scotland and Ireland were easily marginalised. But once the role of population mobility is considered these two societies move to the foreground of any assessment of British imperialism. Sojourning to and from Britain and Ireland to Asia was only one of a number of migration streams that sustained the Empire's expansion.[15] While this outward movement has been the subject of exhaustive scholarship, return migration remains a relatively neglected theme.[16] One of the central aims of this study is to better chart the return of personnel, wealth and ideas from Asia and to explore their impact upon Irish, Scottish and Welsh society.

Other relevant historiographical trends include the reinterpretation of imperial spaces, boundaries and interactions through Atlantic, British World and global frameworks.[17] Running parallel to these expansive models has been the return to smaller-scale levels of analysis. The family unit now provides a lens through which themes of economic motivation, concepts of public service in colonial contexts and enduring anxieties over social status, gender and race can be reconsidered.[18] All these perspectives have reconfigured the British Empire as a global and interdependent entity that cannot be understood primarily through the prism of national histories.[19] Yet these reformulations have not rendered the 'national' obsolete. As the cultural politics of reaction and resistance to historic forms of globalisation receive greater attention, the national paradigm has retained and even enhanced its value. Global history practitioners now seek to intertwine supranational, national, regional, local, micro- and familial levels of investigation.[20]

It is in this decentred and multilayered analytical framework that an exploration of the metropolitan provinces of Britain and Ireland can contribute to wider debates on the nature of early modern European colonialism. They offer excellent case studies of the imprecise category of 'semi-periphery' used in World Systems theory to divide the European 'core' into zones of development and expansion and underdevelopment and dependency. Explanations of this early modern 'core' and its imperialism stress the slow emergence of key comparative advantages over non-European societies. These led eventually to a 'Great Divergence' from Asia after about

1800. Prior to this date, structural similarities rather than differences were the norm. One consequence of this rightly influential conceptualisation is the reimagining of Europe itself. Moving away from the 'core' (North-West Europe) and 'periphery' (Eastern and Central Europe) binary used in World Systems explanations, the continent is reconceived as a mosaic of internal zones. Although all of Europe benefited directly or indirectly from access to the Americas, certain regions are taken to be endowed with crucial developmental traits or 'comparative advantages'. England, the Low Countries and northern France evolved legal and state structures that protected accumulated property, production capacities, flexible labour practices, 'industrious' economies of consumption, better access to energy sources and surplus capital. These characteristics enabled certain areas of 'rich Europe', as opposed to differently configured 'poor Europe', to eventually outcompete similarly well-developed parts of the globe such as Gujarat, Bengal or the south-east of China.[21]

While persuasive as an overarching explanation of Europe's emergence to global dominance after about 1800, this configuration does not convincingly explain how the 'semi-peripheral', 'comparative disadvantaged' or 'poor' zones participated in empire. As exemplars of financially constrained societies neighbouring England, one of the richest and most aggressively expansionist countries, Ireland, Wales and Scotland's interaction with Asia enables an exploration of precisely this question. As case studies they can facilitate an evaluation of Europe's pre-1815 globalisation as a diverse and polycentric phenomenon shaped to a substantial degree by the continent's heterogeneity as much as its homogeneity. A better understanding of the potential for multiple routes into empire resonates with assessments that stress the 'plural pathways' and 'multiple modernities' that marked out proto-globalising trends between about 1600 and 1820.[22] Exploring the engagement of countries such as Ireland, Wales and Scotland with expansion and empire in Asia tests how such plurality existed and developed across the British and Irish Isles. Their example points to the underexplored pathways used by Europe's seemingly 'semi-peripheral' and monetarily 'poor' regions to participate in early modern empire and globalisation.

Debate over the character of pre-1815 Europe's expansion and the new imperial history's reconfiguring of British imperialism provide the book with two of its key historiographical rationales. But it also addresses other themes. One of the most prominent of these is the controversy over the Empire's impact upon the British and Irish Isles. Opinion on this question has been described as 'minimalist' or 'maximalist', although the two camps do not divide neatly along theoretical lines.[23] Post-colonial informed scholarship broadly favours a maximalist interpretation, downplaying any structural demarcations between nation and empire and stressing instead the tangled exchanges between metropole and colony.[24] Minimalists, by contrast, argue that definitions of empire and colonialism are often too vague, that evidence is compiled out of proportion and out of context and insufficient care is taken to properly historicise imperialism and other forms of expansion.[25]

Scotland, Ireland and Wales provide manageable case studies for exploring the maximalist and minimalist positions. All three societies retained distinctive characteristics, although all were clearly part of the metropole in the broadest sense. Their politics, economies, social structures and cultures developed important structural similarities to that of England.[26] However, they were also distinguished from their neighbour by substantial economic, social and linguistic differences as well as institutional separation in law, banking, religion, education, poor relief, landholding structures and electoral systems. The implications for British imperialism arising from this diversity are widely acknowledged but still need further excavation.[27] Analysing the Asia connection in Scottish, Irish and Welsh society can facilitate a reimagining of the British and Irish Isles less as the site of an inevitable nation-state and imperial 'core' but as an accretion of expanding regional, national and supranational communities and cultures. Adopting this decentred perspective enables a less deterministic assessment of the Empire's capacity to efface Britain and Ireland's internal differences. This interest in the coloniser's ongoing heterogeneity does not constitute the reinvention of metrocentric history in a Scottish, Irish or Welsh guise. Substantive differences within the expanding society are no more important than the complexities and diversities that characterised the peoples and the territories on the receiving end of British imperialism in Asia; but understanding metropolitan diversity and its role in shaping colonial expansion is also a crucial objective.

Convergence and divergence:
Scotland, Ireland, the British union and the Empire

It is axiomatic that the Empire shaped Scotland and Ireland's differing experiences of Britain and British identity. Its impact on the timing and pattern of Scottish integration into the United Kingdom was fundamental and yet remains a matter of intense debate.[28] Assumptions that overseas expansion operated only to erode domestic difference and facilitate Britishness are no longer taken for granted.[29] Further study is required into whether imperial expansion as a whole, and not just its Atlantic hemisphere, facilitated a linear form of assimilation or irruptive patterns of integration sandwiched between periods when Scotland's distinctiveness remained largely intact or was even enhanced. Interpreting the participation of metropolitan provinces like Scotland in one of the Empire's major hemispheres provides a global evidence base with which to address the issue of whether imperialism's centripetal influence was always consistent.

If Scotland's experience was one of partial assimilation, Ireland's relationship with Britain and the Empire emerges as one of partial exclusion and 'aborted integration'.[30] That British political culture ultimately lacked the constitutional flexibility to reconcile large parts of Irish society has not prevented productive discussion of what role empire played in shaping the trajectory of British-Irish relations.[31] Given Ireland's central constitutional and demographic role in British expansion, it is unfortunate that some of the most cogent theories relating to the eighteenth-century phase of empire avoid that kingdom's experience. Both Linda Colley's seminal work on British identity and Peter Cain and Anthony Hopkins's influential model of the 'gentlemanly capitalist' economy shy away from a systematic analysis of Ireland. Exclusion is explained in terms of the kingdom constituting 'a problem', and the 'dauntingly complex' character of Anglo-Irish relations.[32]

Yet rather than an 'Irish problem' historians need to think equally in terms of the 'British problem'. One reason why eighteenth-century Ireland's experience is so valuable is that it challenges deeply embedded historical assumptions about an automatically constructive dynamic between empire and British nation. This approach tends to exceptionalise Ireland's trajectory rather than using its example to rethink how metropolitan provincial integration generated new domestic divergences as well as integrative tendencies. Including Ireland in such a framework is not an attempt at reincorporation into a 'new British history' via the back door of imperial studies.[33] The aim is to compare and contrast Scottish, Irish and Welsh participation in the East India Company to better understand the Empire's clear successes and its clear limitations in binding together the component parts of the British and Irish Isles.

London's empire:
the English East India Company and the metropolitan provinces

The character of early modern imperialism and its impact on the metropolitan provinces could be explored using any geographic part of Britain's worldwide empire. But particular reasons exist for focusing on Asia. From the viewpoint of Irish, Welsh and Scottish historical studies, the eastern half of the British Empire can seem a distant and disconnected world; this is meant in a historiographic as opposed to geographic sense. East India Company studies constitute a discrete and noticeably vibrant branch of British imperial history with its own set of controversies.[34] Characterisations of the corporation as a largely commercial entity until the 1750s and its rapid transformation thereafter into a territorial power have met with persuasive criticism. Analysis increasingly stresses the organisation's status as an early modern corporate sovereignty and as an institution profoundly influenced by the Asian contexts in which it operated.[35]

This book contributes to these debates by comparing for the first time the scale and nature of metropolitan provincial involvement and by showing how the Company projected Britain and Ireland's internal heterogeneity outwards into Asia. Understanding this process involves grasping the organisation's development in London. The corporation's status as a metropolitan institution is well known.[36] Yet the Company and its world can still seem like an empire apart, impinging upon Britain largely through high-profile impeachment trials, financial crises in London, and above all through enabling patterns of mass commodity consumption.[37] This sense of separation is fast disappearing as the variety of political, economic and cultural influences upon the British and Irish Isles arising from the connection with Asia become clearer.[38] However, the process still has some way to go. This point can be best illustrated by a comparison with the Atlantic world. The western half of the Empire forms an integral part of any history of eighteenth- and early nineteenth-century Scotland, Ireland and increasingly, Wales.[39] Asia is seen as far less central to the experience of all three societies in this period. The apparent lack of importance manifests itself in far lower levels of publications on the subject compared to output on the Atlantic. Most studies on the British in Asia do acknowledge the disproportionate number of Scots and Irish, particularly in the Company's military,[40] but a robust understanding of numbers, social backgrounds, networking patterns and the impact on Scots, Welsh and Irish society arising from growing connections to the East Indies remains elusive. Given the importance of Ireland's manpower there are remarkably few comprehensive studies of Irish military elites and soldiers in pre-1815 India, although impressive work does exist on social and professional networks for the post-1830 period.[41] Asia is in fact the last major sector of the eighteenth-century Empire lacking a detailed analysis of the Scottish, Irish and Welsh contribution and the resultant domestic consequences.

A productive effort has been made to explore the parallels between Ireland and India as colonies during the mid- to late nineteenth and the twentieth century. For all their geographic, social and cultural differences, both countries were exposed to similar processes of British imperialism, stymied industrialisation, nationalist reaction and eventual partition and protracted decolonisation.[42] In Ireland, resistance to and involvement in empire went hand in hand, one of the many reasons why the country provides such a crucial lens on the nature of British imperialism. One influential conceptualisation envisages the kingdom as a 'sub-metropole', interacting with India through a web of 'Irish imperial networks'.[43] Work on Wales similarly tends to concentrate on the post-1830 period. For the pre-1815 empire, Company demands for copper and the evolution of a small number of Welsh networks within the corporation linked that society in limited but definite ways to developments in Asia.[44]

The participation of Scots has received greater attention. Surveys summarise the connection with Asia in different ways. One approach stresses socio-economic, materialist factors, while the other emphasises the significance of Enlightenment ideas.[45] Both types of analysis exemplify the tendency of the 'Scots in empire' method to engage only partially with wider debates in British imperial studies. The importance of Company patronage in Scotland has received attention, as has the political and commercial networking of Scots in Asia. The capacity of the Eastern Empire to shape aspects of landed society in Scotland has begun to reveal the surprisingly pervasive presence of the East Indies connection.[46] But Scots are invariably viewed in isolation, an approach which distorts and exaggerates their numbers while implying exceptional ethnic cohesion and financial success.[47]

One reason why the empire in the east remains a poor cousin compared to output on the Atlantic is the distinctive nature of migration to the different destinations. Unlike the tens of thousands involved in transatlantic mobility, the volume of movement to Asia can appear trivial.[48] Yet a numeric evaluation alone is highly misleading: the EIC's administrative, military and commercial communities in Asia attracted substantial levels of professional and artisanal migrants. Many of these sojourners came from affluent backgrounds and formed a service cohort who travelled east for a limited time before (hopefully) returning to Europe.[49] This objective was in contrast to the majority of migrants heading to North America. Transatlantic movement is primarily understood in terms of landlordism and depressed economic conditions for the artisan, tenant and labouring classes. Stereotypes of the poor agrarian migrant have been modified to take account of the numerous professional, mercantile and artisanal transients who departed to areas like the Chesapeake and the Caribbean.[50] Nevertheless, transatlantic mobility retains a high profile in both national histories because of its enduring links to well-known and culturally contentious events such as the Highland Clearances, religious discrimination in Ireland and the Irish and Highland famines.[51] The British communities in Asia, by contrast, are long gone and appear to have left no obvious inclusive legacy or enduring human connections.

The semi-detached relationship between Scottish, Welsh and Irish history and East India Company studies also reflects the distinctive institutional basis of expansion. Contact between the British and Irish Isles and Asia for most of the period between 1690 and 1820 was the exclusive right of the United English East India Company.[52] The Company's monopoly is such a familiar aspect of British imperialism that it can easily be taken for granted. Given this regulatory framework it is easy to see why the Asia connection can appear to be a London venture rather than an inclusive English or British-Irish enterprise. As 'the most impressive overseas manifestation of the alliance between land and finance in the eighteenth century', the Company exemplifies the gentlemanly capitalism thesis.[53] Yet the extent to which London dominated eighteenth-century British expansion and imperialism is a matter of debate. Cain and Hopkins have been challenged for their excessive concentration upon the metropole and for marginalising the English regions and Ireland and Scotland, not least during the long eighteenth century.[54] One particularly effective rethinking of the original conception stresses the idea of 'gentry capitalism'. This reformulation shifts attention from London-based merchants to regional families and kin groups already possessing landed resources. The enterprise undertaken by these commercially minded gentry connected the English provinces with London in new ways. The profits, credit and leverage arising from Atlantic trades, particularly enslavement-based production, helped entrench and expand local status. Gentry capitalism helpfully rebalances the dynamic intersections between province and metropole through its emphasis on English locality and expansive Atlantic Empire.[55] Its utility to historians of Ireland, Scotland and Wales is obvious.

In the context of these historiographical disconnections and innovations, Scots, Welsh and Irish movement into the English Company furthers consideration of how imperialism in Asia reconfigured links between the metropolitan provinces and the metropolis. Doing so involves adapting the premise of gentry capitalism in three ways. The first of these is geography. Rather than provincial England, Ireland, Scotland and Wales are foregrounded, but in ways that emphasise connections rather than separations. The second adjustment involves the encompassing of a wider range of groups beyond landed gentry. Included here are clerical, medical, burgh and even leading tenant families aspiring to greater material and social status through empire. The final modification of gentry capitalism shifts consideration away, at least initially, from the conventional forms of monetary finance used to participate in empire. Because their societies faced relative material and financial constraints, the examples of Ireland, Scotland and Wales draw attention to the tactics used to surmount a lack of venture capital and credit. They exemplify how 'poor' regions accessed empire and commerce through the use of proxy forms of capital. The aim is to chart the effectiveness of what might be called metropolitan provincial gentry capitalism in the Asian as opposed to western hemisphere of the Empire.

Localising empire: the metropolitan provinces and imperial impacts

Though the book connects with a number of historiographies, it is in the end a history of Scotland, Ireland and Wales in the early modern British Empire. These countries might not seem to make for an obvious comparison. Eighteenth-century Scotland and Ireland certainly differed as much from each other as their bigger neighbour. A defining distinction was religion. Scotland was an overwhelmingly Protestant country: only around 2 to 3 per cent of the population professed Catholicism in the 1750s. Ireland was roughly 80 per cent Catholic. Protestant communities there were disfigured by the acrimonious relationship between the established Anglican Church of Ireland and the dissenting Presbyterians. Religious politics played a major role in shaping Irish expansion in the Atlantic. Whether this was similarly the case for Asia is far less clearly understood. The sectarian bar on Catholics in key walks of public life constituted a major failure of British political imagination which stymied the potential for the majority community to integrate into the evolving British nation-state and empire before and after the 1800 union.[56] Yet this exclusion did not operate with the same degree of force across what was a markedly *ancien régime* empire characterised by a patchwork of jurisdictions, privileges and liberties.[57] Faced with crippling mortality rates, the EIC never fully implemented England and Britain's discriminatory policies and indeed formally tolerated Catholicism in settlements such as Bombay as early as the 1660s.[58] If viewed as an employer of manpower rather than as an institution of state and empire, the Company emerges as an ambivalent organisation. It was a privileged metropolitan corporation infused with all of British society's religious prejudices. Yet it was also receptive to certain groups such as Jewish and Quaker communities that could facilitate its operations. This pragmatism has profound implications, particularly in the case of the Irish. The Company can be analysed as an *ancien régime* 'estate' with substantial commercial, professional and military privileges. In this organisation Catholics might, with the right financial and social connections, carve out opportunities not easily possible elsewhere in the Empire until at least the 1780s to early 1800s.[59]

Comparative analysis can also uncover how the different political cultures of Scotland and Ireland shaped engagement with the Eastern Empire. With its own parliament and extensive Protestant electorate, Ireland sustained a vibrant public sphere, albeit one which excluded the bulk of the population on sectarian grounds. While formal politics in Ireland focused on the Dublin parliament, Scotland's political culture was noticeably more corporate and characterised by a range of social interests with extensive privileges and liberties.[60] Post-union Scotland's *ancien régime* configuration has not been sufficiently related to its experience of the pre-1815 empire. The 1707 settlement entrenched a number of 'estates', including the nobility, the lawyers, the Kirk, the royal burghs and the universities. These retained lobbying institutions such as the General Assembly, the Convention of Royal Burghs and the Faculty of Advocates. These organisations and patron–client networks, as much as electoral enfranchisement, enabled middling elites to pursue their political objectives.

Scotland and Ireland differed in one other vital respect. Scottish politics focused on London to a greater degree than was necessary in Ireland until the 1800 union. Both countries maintained distinctive managerial regimes, where patronage and clientage played an important if not necessarily decisive role.[61] The capacity of provincial patronage networks to forge links with London and the EIC is a central theme in Chapters 1 to 6 for the simple reason that securing imperial opportunities had substantial repercussions for both societies. Any variations in this regard threatened rising social expectations and political attitudes among the aspiring middling orders. Growing access to overseas expansion undoubtedly assuaged key interest groups in Scotland; meanwhile, Irish middle-class alienation at political and religious exclusion at home risked insufficient displacement into enterprise abroad.[62] These dynamics mean that the differing reaction of provincial societies to the legitimacy of the British state cannot be separated from the simultaneous influence of empire.[63] Until Irish numbers in one half of the Empire are better understood, a holistic assessment of the internal and external factors working for and against British-Irish integration will remain elusive.

The focus so far has been on Scotland and Ireland as national entities, but overly centralised characterisations of both societies, and indeed Wales, are best avoided. Yet another reason why the metropolitan provinces have a wider usefulness is that they subdivide into clear regions and localities. The Scottish Highlands and Lowlands, or the Gaelic west of Ireland, east Ulster and 'the Pale' are the most obvious examples. Wales too fits this regional approach. Its southern counties formed a developed agricultural and manufacturing zone not unlike the central belt of Scotland or the linen districts of east Ulster. The north and west of Wales were more akin to the Scottish Highlands or Connacht; all were characterised by linguistic distinctiveness, low levels of urbanisation and a dependency on pastoral economies.[64]

Irish, Welsh and Scottish society undoubtedly engaged with empire through regional pathways. Ports like Cork and Belfast participated in the Atlantic economy, while towns like Waterford and Dundee remained focused on Europe. Immersion in the imperial framework took place on a far more systematic scale in Scotland yet was still characterised by pronounced local variation. Glasgow became a major emporium of colonial goods while the Highlands evolved export economies in primary products like cattle and manpower.[65] These patterns explain why the chapters break the Irish, Scots and Welsh profiles down into their regional origins. Not only does this approach reflect the complexity of these societies but it better facilitates an understanding of how provincial diversity was projected outwards into the eastern half of the Empire.[66]

Human capital and meso-networks: connecting the imperial, national and local

Having considered the relevance of this study to different strands of the historiography, it is important to define key concepts and methodologies. Understanding the Irish, Welsh and Scottish presence in Asia involves inter-relating a number of analytical frameworks, ranging from the idea of empire as a global process, to the corporate nature of expansion in Asia and the impact of the East Indies upon Britain, Scotland, Ireland, Wales, their regions and localities. All these perspectives necessarily overlap. This 'glocal studies' approach advocates 'tack[ing] back and forth between and among various territorial levels to examine the ways in which the local, regional, national, trans-national and global are mutually implicated'.[67]

One way of combining the different levels while avoiding excessive localism, national exceptionalism or ahistorical concepts of globalisation is to utilise theories of human and social capital. Definitions of human capital centre upon the qualities, aptitudes and characteristics acquired by, or believed by others to be invested in, a given individual. This socially imagined asset is enhanced through the accumulation of 'embodied cultural capital', usually by means of education, professional training, personal and familial reputations. The inculcation of knowledge and behavioural codes as well as an accompanying specialised vocabulary act as valuable resources which confirm an individual's trustworthiness and indicate their actual or potential social status.[68] Crucially, not all human capital holds the same value. A surgeon or experienced maritime officer embodied greater potential for wealth generation (high value) than a common soldier or seaman (low value). There is considerable disagreement over how best to define human, cultural and social capital, not least when assessing their interaction at the individual and collective, social level.[69] There is however a consensus that human, social and cultural capital can, like the monetary equivalent (referred to as physical, finance or economic capital), be extremely valuable and transferred easily by means of migration.[70]

If human capital refers to individual characteristics, social capital is defined as 'positions and relationships that can serve to enhance an individual's access to opportunities, information, material resources, and social status'.[71] In other words, social capital is the means by which the latent value of its human equivalent is mobilised and realised.[72] These socially constructed and validated forms of wealth accumulate through kin, local, regional, professional or other civic affiliations and are heavily dependent on the reciprocity and trust inherent in networks. Networks constitute a 'commodity similar to money' and form a vitally important source of wealth in their own right. This is because they act as enabling or bridging mechanisms which facilitate the mobilisation through migration of human and social capital.[73] Both historic and contemporary networks come in all shapes and sizes and serve a bewildering array of purposes. Critics of social network theory claim that definitions have become so multitudinous that their explanatory force is threatened. Nevertheless, a number of features define nearly all networks. Informal associations usually originate around 'closed' and 'vertical' relationships. These 'strong' family, kinship, fictive kinship and kith links often provide the initial organising principle. But networks invariably evolve into 'open' or 'horizontal' connections that encompass a greater number of non-kin associates.[74]

Network theory emphasises that these social webs operate at and between the macro-, meso- and micro-level.[75] These conceptual gradations are applicable to the history of how individuals, localities, regions and nations interacted with expansion and empire in Asia. Micro-networks form around family and kinsmen and are anchored by strong vertical bonds of association and trust. A persistent characteristic of micro-networks is that they embed themselves in official institutions and profitable sectors of the economy. At the other extreme, macro networks equate to generic, conventional patterns of political, social and cultural behaviour or standard practices within markets and the agencies of state and empire such as parliament, the army, navy and the EIC.[76] This combination of 'closed' and 'open' characteristics enable networks to remain responsive and flexible. They expand to include individuals and incorporate smaller, micro-networks or contract back to the original membership and primary function. Uninhibited by spatial barriers, such webs of affiliation facilitate trust and mutually beneficial action across short distances – such as Edinburgh and Dublin to London – or over oceanic spaces. The value of focusing on networks lies in recovering their role as informal bridging mechanisms that enabled kin and regional interests to access the Empire's formal institutions and markets via social as well as monetary means.[77]

Network theory is a now staple methodology for understanding British expansion and empire.[78] What has not yet been sufficiently explored, at least within an eighteenth-century British imperial context, is the vital significance of meso-networks that connected the micro (individuals, family and kin) to that of the macro (the British fiscal-military state and the English East India Company). Meso-networks are the intermediate stages of associative behaviour and social organisation that extend beyond micro-affiliations by means of a greater number of 'horizontal' links. This open-ended arrangement increases the social and political scope and the geographic reach of the meso-level network as well as its operational effectiveness and potential shelf life.[79] Active at a familial, regional, national and transnational level, and incorporating a malleable set of political, professional and economic connections, meso-networks are central to understanding how metropolitan provincials accessed the macrostructures of British imperialism. Scottish, Welsh and Irish society's capacity to create meso-networks is a central concern of this study. The benefit of this framework is that it avoids prioritising or exceptionalising any one facet of networking activity. Familial, local, region, national, imperial and global are all encompassed within the human-social capital analysis and related to each other in a holistic way. The unofficial nature of micro- and meso-networks can be evaluated as an embedded complement to the formal macro structure of the EIC.

However, concentrating only on the character and operation of networks misses a deeper, more significant attitude towards the accumulation and deployment of human and social capital. The importance of these non-monetary assets has yet to be incorporated into understandings of pre-1815 British imperialism and proto-globalisation. Too much focus on the personnel, scope and function of networks means concentrating on the mechanisms that moved and realised human capital rather than exploring the deeper implications arising from a reliance on this form of wealth. Effect (network) has been prioritised over cause (mobilisation of human capital). Social networks are treated in this study as merely an outward symptom or manifestation of a deeper, structural reliance on non-monetary forms of capital. If viewed as an exercise in resource mobilisation, a better awareness of human capital has profound implications for understanding how 'provincial' societies like Scotland, Ireland and Wales participated in global imperialism.[80] This perspective enables an exploration of a Europe comprised of zones where differently constituted forms of capital were available in different degrees and mobilised accordingly. In the case of early modern Ireland and Scotland, they exhibited finance-'poor' but human capital-'rich' characteristics. Historicising and analysing these differences can facilitate a critical understanding of how societies responded to proto-globalisation in distinctive national, regional and localised ways and with a variety of forms of capital.

Human and socially constructed resources were productive, transferable forms of proxy assets which Irish and Scottish elites possessed in abundance – often in marked contrast to their limited monetary reserves. Faced with a relative lack of enterprise finance and a preponderance of static sources of landed wealth, Scottish and Irish society had every reason to develop a pronounced reliance upon non-monetary forms of capital. Aspects of Scottish civic society promoted the accumulation of human and social, as opposed to monetary, wealth. The country's system of parochial schooling and its surplus capacity of university education gave Scots a competitive advantage in the process of enhancing human, cultural and social modes of capital.[81] The ability to manufacture and deploy higher-value forms of human wealth through this civic infrastructure is an underappreciated reason why Scots could maximise benefits from empire and globalisation. In terms of the capacity to generate human wealth and the social networks required to mobilise it, early modern Scotland was actually a 'rich' European society.

The accumulation and realisation of human and social wealth in Ireland was partly determined by the kingdom's fractured political, economic, social and cultural condition. The existence, nature and scope of 'underground' Catholic gentry networks remains a matter of controversy.[82] However, if the marshalling of human-social wealth by the Catholic majority occurred in ways that differed significantly from that of their English, Welsh, Scots and Protestant Irish equivalents, or was impaired in any way, then the implications for empire involvement are profound.[83] Understanding how Ireland's political and social structures might have nurtured extensive and successful microconnections while stymieing the consistent emergence of meso-level networks aligned to imperial opportunities is a central concern of this study.

Be they in London, in cash-straitened Scotland and Ireland, or operating in Asia, all individuals relied upon social networks of one sort or another. In societies where liquidity remained scarce, however, a dependence on networks that mobilised human and social assets became necessarily greater. Evidence of this imperative can be glimpsed in the persistent commentary on the migratory character of Irish and Scottish society and especially the tendency of Scots to practice various forms of diasporic 'clannishness'.[84] This stereotyping was less evidence of national loyalties at work as an indication of contemporaries attempting to articulate the heavy reliance on social and human forms of capital.[85] London merchants or gentry in the Home Counties were no less likely to construct effective kin and professional networks; but in Scotland and Ireland there was a greater reliance on these socially reproduced and non-monetary forms of wealth.[86] The difference is one of degree, but it was a vitally important difference. Disproportionate Scottish and Irish deployment of human capital through high-risk, high-return forms of migration constituted a compensatory tactic designed to counter poverty in the orthodox financial sense. For Europe's 'poor' regions, human capital played a defining role in how they experienced and exploited proto-globalisation. The implications for global history are that the financial and economic characteristics of what constituted supposedly 'advanced' or 'comparatively advantaged' societies need to be recalibrated.

The political and social (as opposed to economic or financial) leverage exerted by Scottish and Irish networks means that the metropolitan provinces did not exist automatically in a dependent, subordinated relationship to the metropolis. In contrast to the underdeveloped, impoverished peripheries portrayed by the gentlemanly capitalism and World Systems theses, both countries had impressive reserves of human and social-networked assets. Indeed, Scotland and Ireland offer a neglected but productive way of recovering an alternative dynamic between capital and empire, one where human and social wealth acted as a substitute investment strategy designed to secure a return of conventional capital surpluses. This exchange was a key operating principle of metropolitan-provincial gentry capitalism.

Ideas of human and social capital provide the conceptual framework for thinking about Ireland, Scotland and Wales's experience of the pre-1815 empire in Asia. The overall aim is to demonstrate that models of proto-globalisation need to better appreciate the ways in which finance-'poor' regions of Europe used human mobility and social capital as highly productive pathways into global empire and expansion. The metropolitan provinces of the most successful European power in Asia can help reveal in new ways the use of people as substitute capital in the processes of empire and early modern globalisation. Such a re-evaluation is attempted in the spirit of what one historian of globalisation called 'connective and comparative histories'.[87] It investigates the reciprocal interactions between the familial, local, region, national, imperial and the global that shaped the character of British expansion in Asia. Regional differences within the British and Irish Isles are not assessed in isolation but in relation to the centripetal influence of London and the EIC. Balancing this metrocentric emphasis involves recognising that empire created and entrenched new forms of national, regional and local distinctions within the colonising society. In this sense the book is as much about Asia's centrifugal impact on Britain and Ireland as about dynamics of uncomplicated integration or assimilation through common involvement in imperialism.

Notes

1 The term 'British and Irish Isles' denotes the archipelago of England, Ireland, Scotland and Wales. 'United Kingdom' and 'Britain' are used interchangeably for the polity created in 1707. 'Ireland' describes both the island and the kingdom that entered into political union with the United Kingdom in 1800. 'East Indies' and 'Asia' are used interchangeably for the area east of the Cape of Good Hope and west of Cape Horn demarcated as the monopoly of the various incarnations of the English East India Company. The terms actually reflect the corporation's main centres of activity in South Asia, the Indian Ocean, the Gulf, South East Asia and China. Philip J. Stern, *The Company State: Corporate Sovereignty and the Early Modern Foundations of the British Empire in India* (Oxford: Oxford University Press, 2011), pp. 41–2.
2 This study draws on an important articulation of the historic phases of globalisation and the distinctive early modern characteristics of proto-globalisation. See A. G. Hopkins, 'Introduction: Globalisation – An Agenda for Historians' and 'The History of Globalisation – and the Globalisation of History?', both in A. G. Hopkins (ed.), *Globalisation in World History* (London: Pimlico, 2002), pp. 5–7, 25–8.
3 C. A. Bayly, *Imperial Meridian: The British Empire and the World, 1780–1830* (London: Longman, 1989); N. Canny (ed.), *The Oxford History of the British Empire, I: The Origins of Empire* (Oxford: Oxford University Press, 1998); P. J. Marshall (ed.), *The Oxford History of the British Empire, II: The Eighteenth Century* (Oxford: Oxford University Press, 1998).
4 P. J. Marshall, 'British Society in India under the East India Company', *Modern Asian Studies*, 31 (1997), 90–1, 101; Idrani Chatterjee, 'Colouring Subalternity: Slaves, Concubines, and Social Orphans in Early Colonial India', in Ranajit Guha, Partha Chatterjee and Gyanendra Pandey (eds), *Subaltern Studies, X: Writings on South Asian History and Society* (Delhi: Oxford University Press, 1982), pp. 51–63; Durba Ghosh, *Sex and the Family in Colonial India: The Making of Empire* (Cambridge: Cambridge University Press, 2006), pp. 39–47.
5 A. Mackillop, 'A Union for Empire? Scotland, the English East India Company and the British Union', *The Scottish Historical Review*, 87 (2008), 116–34; W. D. Rubinstein, 'The End of "Old Corruption" in Britain 1780–1860', *Past & Present*, 101 (1983), 55–86.
6 Philip J. Stern, 'History and Historiography of the English East India Company: Past, Present, and Future!', *History Compass*, 7 (2009), 1146–80; Phillip J. Stern, 'Seeing (and Not Seeing) Like a Company-State: Hybridity, Heterotopia, Historiography', *Journal of Early Modern Cultural Studies*, 17 (2017), 105–20.
7 Catherine Hall, 'Culture and Identity in Imperial Britain', in Sarah Stockwell (ed.), *The British Empire: Themes and Perspectives* (Oxford: Blackwell, 2010), p. 200; R. W. Winks, 'The Future of Imperial History', and D. A. Washbrook, 'Orients and Occidents: Colonial Discourse Theory and the Historiography of the British Empire', in R. W. Winks (ed.), *The Oxford History of the British*

Empire, V: Historiography (Oxford: Oxford University Press, 1998), pp. 596, 601–2, 659–65.
8. J. M. MacKenzie, *Orientalism: History, Theory and the Arts* (Manchester: Manchester University Press, 1995), pp. 4–30; C. A. Bayly, 'The Second British Empire', in Winks, *Oxford History of the British Empire*, V, pp. 70–1; F. A. Nussbaum, 'Introduction', in F. A. Nussbaum (ed.), *The Global Eighteenth Century* (Baltimore, MD: Johns Hopkins University Press, 2003), pp. 7, 11.
9. Catherine Hall, 'Introduction: Thinking the Postcolonial, thinking the Empire', in Catherine Hall (ed.), *Cultures of Empire: Colonisers in Britain and the Empire in the Nineteenth and Twentieth Centuries* (Manchester: Manchester University Press, 2000), pp. 15–24; K. Wilson, 'Introduction: Histories, Empires, Modernities', in K. Wilson (ed.), *A New Imperial History: Culture, Identity, and Modernity in Britain and the Empire, 1660–1840* (Cambridge: Cambridge University Press, 2004), pp. 1–3, 17; K. Wilson, 'Empire, Gender, and Modernity', in Philippa Levine (ed.), *Gender and Empire* (Oxford: Oxford University Press, 2004), p. 16.
10. Antoinette Burton, 'Who Needs the Nation? Interrogating "British" History', *Journal of Historical Sociology*, 10 (1997), 227–48.
11. Bernard Bailyn and Philip D. Morgan, 'Introduction', in Bernard Bailyn and Philip D. Morgan (eds), *Strangers within the Realm: Cultural Margins of the First British Empire* (Chapel Hill, NC, and London: University of North Carolina Press, 1991), pp. 20–31; H. V. Bowen, *Elites, Enterprise and the Making of the British Overseas Empire, 1688–1775* (London: Palgrave Macmillan, 1996), pp. 154–5; K. Wilson, *The Sense of the People: Politics, Culture and Imperialism in England, 1715–1785* (Cambridge: Cambridge University Press, 1998), pp. 13, 32–41.
12. The book's use of 'province' owes much to the work of Ned Landsman and Huw Bowen. N. C. Landsman, 'The Provinces and the Empire: Scotland, the American Colonies and the Development of British Provincial Identity', in Lawrence Stone (ed.), *An Imperial State at War: Britain from 1689–1815* (London: Routledge, 1994), pp. 260–3; Bowen, *Elites, Enterprise*, pp. 153–5.
13. M. Hechter, *Internal Colonialism: The Celtic Fringe in British National Development, 1536–1966* (London: Routledge and Kegan Paul, 1975); Tony Dickson, *Scottish Capitalism: Class, State and Nation from before the Union to the Present* (London: Laurence & Wishart, 1980), pp. 86–99; Alex Murdoch, *British History, 1660–1832: National Identity and Local Culture* (Basingstoke: Macmillan, 1998), p. 47.
14. The definition of 'expansion' and 'imperialism/empire' used throughout the book draws directly on P. J. Marshall, *The Making and Unmaking of Empires: Britain, India and America c.1750–1783* (Oxford: Oxford University Press, 2005), pp. 4–6, 13–16, 25–33, 57–8.
15. E. Richards, *Britannia's Children: Emigration from England, Scotland, Wales and Ireland since 1600* (London: Hambledon & London, 2004), pp. 87–90; James Belich, *Replenishing the Earth: The Settler Revolution and the Rise of the Anglo-World, 1783–1939* (Oxford: Oxford University Press, 2011), pp. 58–60.

16 J. F. Codell and D. S. Macleod, 'Orientalism Transposed: the "Easternisation" of Britain and Interventions to Colonial Discourse', in J. F. Codell and D. S. Macleod (eds), *Orientalism Transposed: The Impact of the Colonies on British Culture* (Aldershot: Ashgate, 1998), pp. 1–4; M. Harper, 'Introduction', in M. Harper (ed.), *Emigrant Homecomings: The Return Movement of Emigrants, 1600–2000* (Manchester: Manchester University Press, 2005), pp. 1–14; Mario Varricchio (ed.), *Back to Caledonia: Scottish Homecoming from the Seventeenth Century to the Present* (Edinburgh: John Donald, 2012).

17 C. A. Bayly, 'The First Age of Global Imperialism, c.1760–1830', *Journal of Imperial & Commonwealth Studies*, 26 (1998), 28–47; D. Armitage and M. J. Braddick, 'Introduction', in D. Armitage and M. J. Braddick (eds), *The British Atlantic World, 1500–1800* (Basingstoke: Palgrave, 2002), pp. 3–5; C. A. Bayly, *The Birth of the Modern World, 1780–1914* (Oxford: Blackwell, 2004), pp. 27–83; P. J. Stern, 'British Asia and the British Atlantic: Comparisons and Connections', *William and Mary Quarterly*, 63 (2006), 693–712; H. V. Bowen, Elizabeth Mancke and John G. Reid, 'Introduction: Britain's Oceanic Empire', in H. V. Bowen, Elizabeth Mancke and John G. Reid (eds), *Britain's Ocean Empire: Atlantic and Indian Ocean Worlds, c.1550–1850* (Cambridge: Cambridge University Press, 2012), pp. 1–11.

18 David Veevers, '"Inhabitants of the Universe": Global Families, Kinship Networks, and the Formation of the Early Modern Colonial State in Asia', *Journal of Global History*, 10 (2015), 101–3; Margot Finn, 'Anglo-Indian Lives in the Later Eighteenth and Early Nineteenth Centuries', *Journal for Eighteenth-Century Studies*, 33 (2010), 49–65; Margot Finn, 'Family Formations: Anglo-India and the Familial Proto-State', in David Feldman and Jon Lawrence (eds), *Structures and Transformations in Modern British History* (Cambridge: Cambridge University Press, 2011), pp. 100–17; Emma Rothschild, *The Inner Lives of Empires: An Eighteenth-Century History* (Princeton, NJ: Princeton University Press, 2011), pp. 1–58.

19 David Armitage, 'Greater Britain: A Useful Category of Historical Analysis', *American Historical Review*, 102 (1999), 444; Bayly, *The Birth of the Modern World*, pp. 8–9; Marshall, *The Making and Unmaking of Empires*, pp. 1–9.

20 Richard Drayton and David Motade, 'The Futures of Global History', *Journal of Global History*, 13 (2018), 1–15; Neus Rotger, Diana Roig-Sanz and Marta Puxan-Oliva, 'Introduction: Towards a Cross-Disciplinary History of the Global in the Humanities and the Social Sciences', *Journal of Global History*, 14 (2019), 326–7.

21 Immanuel Wallerstein, *The Modern World-System I: Capitalism Agriculture and the Origins of the European World-Economy in the Sixteenth Century* (Berkeley and Los Angeles, CA: University of California Press, 2011), pp. 112–29; Immanuel Wallerstein, *The Modern World-System II: Mercantilism and the Consolidation of the European-World Economy, 1600–1750* (Berkeley and Los Angeles, CA: University of California Press, 2011), pp. xix, 37, 75–91, 131–43; Kenneth Pomeranz, *The Great Divergence: China, Europe, and the Making of*

the *Modern World Economy* (Princeton, NJ, and Oxford: Princeton University Press, 2000), pp. 5, 7–8, 31–107.
22 Prasannan Parthasarathi, *Why Europe Grew Rich and Asia Did Not: Global Economic Divergence, 1600–1850* (Cambridge: Cambridge University Press, 2011), pp. 5–7; Karin Bowie, 'Cultural, British and Global Turns in the History of Early Modern Scotland', *The Scottish Historical Review*, 92 (2013), 48; Andrew Phillips, 'The Global Transformation, Multiple Early Modernities, and International Systems Change', *International Theory*, 8 (2016), 481–8.
23 Burton, 'Who Needs the Nation?', 140–1; C. Hall, *Civilising Subjects: Metropole and Colony in the English Imagination, 1830–1867* (Cambridge: Polity Press, 2002), p. 4; P. J. Marshall, 'Imperial Britain', *Journal of Imperial & Commonwealth History*, 23 (1995), 380; Andrew Thompson, *The Empire Strikes Back? The Impact of Imperialism on Britain from the Mid-Nineteenth Century* (Harlow: Pearson Longman, 2005), p. 5.
24 Kathleen Wilson, *The Island Race: Englishness, Empire and Gender in the Eighteenth Century* (London: Routledge, 2003), pp. 5, 27–8, 52; Hall, *Civilising Subjects*, pp. 4, 11–12; Catherine Hall and Sonya Rose, 'Introduction: Being at Home with the Empire', and Laura Tabili, 'An Homogeneous Society? Britain's Internal "others", 1800–present', both in Catherine Hall and Sonya O. Rose (eds), *At Home with the Empire: Metropolitan Culture and the Imperial World* (Cambridge: Cambridge University Press, 2006), pp. 13–14, 32–4, 51–2.
25 B. Porter, *The Absent-Minded Imperialists: Empire, Society and Culture in Britain* (Oxford: Oxford University Press, 2004), p. 147; B. Porter, 'Further Thoughts on Imperial Absent-Mindedness', *Journal of Imperial and Commonwealth History*, 36 (2008), 102.
26 Keith Wrightson, 'Kindred Adjoining kingdoms: an English Perspective on the Social and Economic History of Early Modern Scotland', in R. A. Houston and I. D. Whyte (eds), *Scottish Society, 1500–1800* (Cambridge: Cambridge University Press, 1989), pp. 250–9.
27 J. M. MacKenzie, 'On Scotland and the Empire', *International History Review*, 15 (1993), 714–24; J. M. MacKenzie, 'Empire and National Identities: The Case of Scotland', *Transactions of the Royal Historical Society*, sixth series, 8 (1998), 215–31; J. M. MacKenzie, *Empires of Nature and the Nature of Empires: Imperialism, Scotland and the Environment* (East Linton: Tuckwell Press, 1997), pp. 64–5; J. M. MacKenzie, 'Irish, Scottish, Welsh and English Worlds?' A Four-Nation Approach to the History of the British Empire', *History Compass*, 6 (2008), 1244–63.
28 R. J. Finlay, 'Caledonia or North Britain? Scottish Identity in the Eighteenth Century', in D. Brown, R. J. Finlay and M. Lynch (eds), *Image and Identity: The Making and Remaking of Scotland through the Ages* (Edinburgh: John Donald, 1998), pp. 143–53; A. Murdoch, 'Scotland and the Idea of Britain in the Eighteenth Century', in T. M. Devine and J. R. Young (eds), *Eighteenth-Century Scotland: New Perspectives* (East Linton: Tuckwell Press, 1999), pp. 106–16; T. Brotherstone, A. Clark and K. Whelan, 'Rethinking the Trajectory of Modern British History: An Ireland–Scotland Approach', in T. Brotherstone, A. Clark

and K. Whelan (eds), *These Fissured Isles: Ireland, Scotland and British History, 1798–1848* (Edinburgh: John Donald, 2005), pp. 10–23.
29 MacKenzie, 'Empire and National Identities: The Case of Scotland', pp. 220–31; Eliga H. Gould, 'A Virtual Nation: Greater Britain and the Imperial Legacy of the American Revolution', *The American Historical Review*, 104 (1999), 476–7; Joseph Sramek, 'Rethinking Britishness: Religion and Debates about the "Nation" among Britons in Company India, 1813–1857', *Journal of British Studies*, 54 (2015), 822–43.
30 Bayly, *Imperial Meridian*, pp. 86–9.
31 S. J. Connolly, 'Varieties of Britishness: Ireland, Scotland and Wales in the Hanoverian State', in Alexander Grant and Keith J. Stringer (eds), *Uniting the Kingdom? The Making of British History* (London: Routledge, 1995), pp. 107–14.
32 P. J. Cain and A. G. Hopkins, *British Imperialism: Innovation and Expansion, 1688–1914* (London: Longman, 1993), p. 8; L. Colley, *Britons: Forging the Nation, 1707–1837* (London: Pimlico, 1992), p. 8.
33 G. Burgess, 'Introduction: The New British History', in G. Burgess (ed.), *The New British History: Founding a Modern State, 1603–1715* (London: I.B.Tauris, 1999), pp. 8, 12–17; S. J. Connolly, 'Introduction', in S. J. Connolly (ed.), *Kingdoms United? Great Britain and Ireland since 1500: Integration and Diversity* (Dublin: Four Courts Press: 1998), p. 9.
34 Stern, 'History and Historiography', 1146–80; Stern, 'Seeing (and Not Seeing)', 105–20; P. J. Marshall, *Bengal: The British Bridgehead: Eastern India, 1740–1828* (Cambridge: Cambridge University Press, 1990), pp. 93–146; S. Alavi, 'Introduction', in S. Alavi (ed.), *The Eighteenth Century in India* (New Delhi: Oxford University Press, 2002), pp. 1–22.
35 C. A. Bayly, 'The British Military-Fiscal State and Indigenous Resistance: India, 1750–1820', in Stone, *An Imperial State at War*, pp. 324–5; D. Washbrook, 'South India, 1770–1840: The Colonial Transition', *Modern Asian Studies*, 38 (2004), 479–506.
36 L. Sutherland, *The East India Company in Eighteenth-Century Politics* (Oxford: Clarendon Press, 1962), pp. 50–179; P. J. Marshall, *Problems of Empire: Britain and India, 1757–1813* (London: George Allen and Unwin, 1968), pp. 102–4; H. V. Bowen, 'British India, 1765–1813: The Metropolitan Context', in Marshall, *Oxford History of the British Empire*, II, pp. 530–50.
37 N. B. Dirks, *The Scandal of Empire: India and the Creation of Imperial Britain* (London: Harvard University Press, 2006), p. 26; Bowen, *Elites, Enterprise*, p. 9.
38 P. J. Marshall, 'Empire and Authority in the Later Eighteenth Century', *Journal of Imperial and Commonwealth History*, 15 (1987), 113–20; P. Lawson, *The East India Company: A History* (London: Longman, 1993), pp. 165–6; H. V. Bowen, *The Business of Empire: The East India Company and Imperial Britain, 1756–1833* (Cambridge: Cambridge University Press, 2006); Jonathan Eacott, *Selling Empire: India and the Making of Britain and America, 1600–1830* (Williamsburg, VA: University of North Carolina Press, 2016), pp. 3–5, 137–52,

168–226; Margot Finn and Kate Smith, 'Introduction', in Margot Finn and Kate Smith (eds), *The East India Company at Home, 1757–1857* (London: University College London Press, 2018), pp. 1–23.
39 B. Bailyn, *Voyagers to the West: Emigration from Britain to America on the Eve of the Revolution* (London: I.B.Tauris, 1987), pp. 44–95; L. M. Cullen, 'The Irish Diaspora of the Seventeenth and Eighteenth Centuries', and T. C. Smout, N. C. Landsman and T. M. Devine, 'Scottish Emigration in the Seventeenth and Eighteenth Centuries', in N. Canny (ed.), *Europeans on the Move: Studies in European Migration, 1500–1800* (Oxford: Clarendon Press, 1994), pp. 98–104, 140–1; D. J. Hamilton, *Scotland, the Caribbean and the Atlantic World, 1750–1820* (Manchester: Manchester University Press, 2005), p. 23; Chris Evans, 'Wales, Munster and the English South West: Contrasting Articulations with the Atlantic World', in H. V. Bowen (ed.), *Wales and the British Overseas Empire, 1650–1830* (Manchester: Manchester University Press, 2011), pp. 40–61.
40 Marshall, *Bengal*, p. 31; Marshall, 'British Society in India', 90–1.
41 P. Cadell, 'Irish Soldiers in India', *The Irish Sword*, 1 (1949–53), 75–6; T. G. Fraser, 'Ireland and India', in K. Jeffery (ed.), *An Irish Empire? Aspects of Ireland and the British Empire* (Manchester: Manchester University Press, 1996), pp. 77–80; Thomas Bartlett, 'The Irish Soldier in India, 1750–1947', in Michael Holmes and Denis Holmes (eds), *Ireland and India: Connections, Comparisons, Contrasts* (Limerick: Blackwater Press, 1997), pp. 12–28; Barry Crosbie, *Irish Imperial Networks: Migration, Social Communication and Exchange in Nineteenth-Century India* (Cambridge: Cambridge University Press, 2012), pp. 68–98.
42 C. A. Bayly, 'Ireland, India and the Empire: 1780–1914', *Transactions of the Royal Historical Society*, sixth series, 10 (2000), 377–97; Michael Holmes and Denis Holmes, 'Ireland and India: A Distant Relationship', in *Ireland and India*, pp. 1–7; S. Ryder, 'Ireland, India and Popular Nationalism in the Early nineteenth Century', in T. Foley and M. O'Connor (eds), *Ireland and India: Colonies, Culture and Empire* (Dublin: Irish Academic Press, 2006), pp. 12–25.
43 Jane Ohlmeyer, 'Eastward Enterprises: Colonial Ireland, Colonial India', *Past & Present*, 240 (2018), 83–118; Crosbie, *Irish Imperial Networks*, pp. 17–23.
44 A. Mackillop, '"A Reticent People?": The Welsh in Asia, 1700–1815' and H. V. Bowen, 'Asiatic Interactions: India, the East India Company and the Welsh Economy, *c.*1750–1830', both in Bowen, *Wales and the British Overseas Empire*, pp. 143–67, 168–92; A. L. Rees, 'Welsh Sojourners in India: The East India Company, Networks and Patronage, *c.*1760–1840', *The Journal of Imperial and Commonwealth History*, 45 (2017), 165–87.
45 M. Fry, *The Scottish Empire* (East Linton: Tuckwell Press, 2001); T. M. Devine, *Scotland's Empire, 1600–1815* (London: Allen Lane, 2003), pp. 250–70; T. M. Devine, 'Scottish Elites and the Indian Empire, 1700–1815', in T. C. Smout (ed.), *Anglo-Scottish Relations, 1600–1900* (Oxford: Oxford University Press, 2005), pp. 213–29. For the most effective combination of these perspectives

see M. McLaren, *British India and British Scotland, 1780–1830* (Akron, OH: Akron Press. 2001), pp. 1–12.
46 J. G. Parker, 'Scottish Enterprise in India, 1750–1914', in R. A. Cage (ed.), *The Scots Abroad: Labour, Capital, Enterprise, 1750–1914* (London: Croom Helm, 1985), pp. 191–219; B. R. Tomlinson, 'From Campsie to Kedgeree: Scottish Enterprise, Asian Trade and the Company Raj', *Modern Asian Studies*, 36 (2002), 769–91; J. Riddy, 'Warren Hastings: Scotland's Benefactor?', in G. Carnall and C. Nicolson (eds), *The Impeachment of Warren Hastings* (Edinburgh: Edinburgh University Press, 1989), pp. 30–57; G. K. McGilvary, *East India Patronage and the British State: The Scottish Elite and Politics in the Eighteenth Century* (London: I.B.Tauris, 2011), pp. 48–229; A. Mackillop, 'Europeans, Britons and Scots: Scottish Sojourning Networks and Identities in Asia, *c*.1700–1815', in A. McCarthy (ed.), *A Global Clan: Scottish Migrant Networks and Identities since the Eighteenth Century* (London: I.B.Tauris, 2006), pp. 19–47; T. M. Devine and Angela McCarthy, 'Introduction: The Scottish Experience in Asia, *c*.1700 to the Present: Settlers and Sojourners', in T. M. Devine and Angela McCarthy (eds), *The Scottish Experience in Asia, c.1700 to the Present: Settlers and Sojourners* (Cham: Palgrave Macmillan, 2017), pp. 1–21; G. J. Bryant, 'Scots in India in the Eighteenth Century', *The Scottish Historical Review*, 64 (1985), 22–41.
47 McGilvary, *East India Patronage*, pp. 203–29; T. M. Devine, 'A Scottish Empire of Enterprise', in *The Scottish Experience in Asia*, p. 43.
48 Smout, Landsman and Devine, 'Scottish Emigration in the Seventeenth and Eighteenth Centuries', pp. 90–104.
49 P. J. Marshall, *East Indian Fortunes: The British in Bengal in the Eighteenth Century* (Oxford: Clarendon Press, 1976), pp. 9–16; E. I. Burley, *Servants of the Honourable Company: Work, Discipline, and Conflict in the Hudson's Bay Company, 1770–1870* (Oxford: Oxford University Press, 1997), p. 71.
50 Alan Karras, *Sojourners in the Sun: Scottish Migrants in Jamaica and the Chesapeake, 1740–1800* (Ithaca, NY, and London: Cornell University Press, 1992), pp. 1–15; Hamilton, *Scotland, the Caribbean and the Atlantic World*, p. 23.
51 J. Hunter, *'A Dance Called America': The Scottish Highlands, the United States and Canada* (Edinburgh: Mainstream, 1994), pp. 82–6, 245–52; P. Griffin, *The People with No Name: Ireland's Ulster Scots, America's Scots Irish and the Creation of a British Atlantic World, 1689–1764* (Princeton, NJ: Princeton University Press, 2001), pp. 16–19, 90–1.
52 P. J. Marshall, 'The English in Asia to 1700', in Canny, *Oxford History of the British Empire*, pp. 266–83; P. J. Marshall, 'The Eighteenth-Century Empire', in J. Black (ed.), *British Politics and Society from Walpole to Pitt* (Basingstoke: Palgrave, 1990), pp. 181–2.
53 Cain and Hopkins, *British Imperialism*, pp. 321–2.
54 A. Porter, '"Gentlemanly Capitalism" and Empire: The British Experience since 1750', *Journal of Imperial and Commonwealth History*, 18 (1990), 270–8; Bowen, *Elites, Enterprise*, pp. 18–19; R. E. Dumett, 'Exploring the Cain/

Hopkins Paradigm. Issues for Debate; Critique, and Topics for New Research', in R. E. Dumett (ed.), *Gentlemanly Capitalism and British Imperialism: The New Debate on Empire* (London: Longman, 1999), pp. 5–9, fn. 18, 39.
55 S. D. Smith, *Slavery, Family, and Gentry Capitalism in the British Atlantic: The World of the Lascelles, 1648–1834* (Cambridge: Cambridge University Press, 2006), p. 9.
56 C. G. Brown, *The Social History of Religion in Scotland since 1730* (London: Methuen, 1987), pp. 34–40; T. Barnard, *A New Anatomy of Ireland: The Irish Protestants, 1649–1770* (New Haven, CT: Yale University Press, 2004), p. xvii; Thomas Bartlett, '"This Famous Island Set in a Virginian Sea": Ireland in the British Empire, 1690–1801', in Marshall, *Oxford History of the British Empire*, II, pp. 272–4.
57 Lauren Benton, 'Colonial Law and Cultural Difference: Jurisdictional Politics and the Formation of the Colonial State', *Comparative Studies in Society and History*, 41 (1999), 563–88.
58 H. Furber, *Rival Empires of Trade in the Orient, 1600–1800* (Minneapolis, MN: University of Minnesota Press, 1976), pp. 299–305; Stern, *The Company State*, pp. 102–3, 113.
59 Cadell, 'Irish Soldiers in India', p. 76; Ohlmeyer, 'Eastward Enterprises', 88, 93.
60 J. C. D. Clark, *English Society, 1688–1832* (Cambridge: Cambridge University Press, 1985), pp. 6–7.
61 J. S. Shaw, *The Political History of Eighteenth-Century Scotland* (Basingstoke: Macmillan, 1999), p. 32; E. M. Johnston (ed.), *History of the Irish Parliament, 1695–1800*, 6 vols (Belfast: Ulster Historical Foundation, 2002), vol. II, p. 382; P. McNally, *Parties, Patriots & Undertakers: Parliamentary Politics in Early Hanoverian Ireland* (Dublin: Four Courts Press, 1997), pp. 118–47.
62 L. M. Cullen, 'Scotland & Ireland, 1600–1800: Their Role in the Evolution of British Society', in Houston and Whyte, *Scottish Society, 1500–1800*, pp. 231–43; Bartlett, '"This Famous Island Set in a Virginian Sea"', pp. 258, 272.
63 James Livesey, *Civil Society and Empire: Ireland and Scotland in the Eighteenth-Century Atlantic World* (New Haven, CT, and London: Yale University Press, 2009), pp. 9–23; Alvin Jackson, *The Two Unions: Ireland, Scotland and the Survival of the United Kingdom, 1707–2007* (Oxford: Oxford University Press, 2012), pp. 127–36, 207–12.
64 Murdoch, *British History*, pp. 6–9, 76–8; G. A. Williams, *When Was Wales?: A History of the Welsh* (London: Penguin, 1991), pp. 143–5; Evans, 'Wales, Munster and the English South West', pp. 40–61; C. A. Whatley, *The Industrial Revolution in Scotland* (Cambridge: Cambridge University Press, 1997), pp. 1–3, 27–38.
65 Eric Richards, 'Scotland and the Uses of the Atlantic Empire', in Bailyn and Morgan, *Strangers within the Realm*, pp. 67–114.
66 For the regional divisions used in this study see Maps 7.1, 7.2 and 7.3.
67 D. Armitage, 'Three Concepts of Atlantic History', in Armitage and Braddick, *The British Atlantic*, pp. 21–3; Nussbaum, 'Introduction', p. 10; Bayly, *The Birth of the Modern World*, pp. 2–3; Hall, *Cultures of Empire*, p. 16.

68 Pierre Bourdieu, 'The Forms of Capital', in John G. Richardson (ed.), *Handbook of Theory & Research for the Sociology of Education* (New York: Greenwood Press, 1986), pp. 243–8; G. S. Becker, *Human Capital: A Theoretical and Empirical Analysis* (Chicago: University of Chicago Press, 1993), pp. 11–24; J. Field, *Social Capital* (London: Routledge, 2003), pp. 5–7, 13–14.

69 A. Portes, 'The Two Meanings of Social Capital', *Sociological Forum*, 15 (2000), 2–4; James Farr, 'Social Capital: A Conceptual History', *Political Theory*, 32 (2004), 6–10.

70 Jean-Pierre Vidal, 'The Effect of Emigration on Human Capital Formation', *Journal of Population Economics*, 11 (1998), 589–600; Nan Lin, 'Building a Network Theory of Social Capital', in Nan Lin, Karen Cook and Ronald S. Burt (eds), *Social Capital: Theory and Research* (New Brunswick, NJ: Aldine Transaction, 2005), pp. 5–6; C. Wetherell, A. Plakan and B. Wellman, 'Social Networks, Kinship and Community in Eastern Europe', *Journal of Interdisciplinary History*, 24 (1994), 643–5.

71 Bourdieu, 'Forms of Capital', p. 248; H. Rose Ebaugh and M. Curry, 'Fictive Kin as Social Capital in New Immigrant Communities', *Sociological Perspectives*, 43 (2000), 190; Jelle van Lottum and Jan Luiten van Zanden, 'Labour Productivity and Human Capital in the European Maritime Sector of the Eighteenth Century', *Explorations in Economic History*, 53 (2014), 90–8; Jelle van Lottum, Aske Brock and Catherine Sumnall, 'Mobility, Migration and Human Capital in the Long Eighteenth Century: The Life of Joseph Anton Ponsaing', in Maria Fusaro, Bernard Allaire, Richard Blakemore and Tijl Vanneste (eds), *Law, Labour, and Empire: Comparative Perspectives on Seafarers, c.1500–1800* (London: Palgrave Macmillan, 2015), pp. 158–61, 172–6.

72 J. S. Coleman, 'Social Capital in the Creation of Human Capital', *American Journal of Sociology*, 94 (1988), 98–100, 109–10, 118–19; B. Fine, *Social Capital versus Social Theory* (London: Routledge, 2001), pp. 26–9, 34. For a historicised reading of human-to-social capital, see Sebouh Aslanian, 'Social Capital, "Trust" and the Role of Networks in Julfan Trade: Informal and Semi-Formal Institutions at Work', *Journal of Global History*, 1 (2006), 384–8.

73 Farr, 'Social Capital', 9; D. Halpern, *Social Capital* (Cambridge: Polity, 2003), pp. 1–29; S. M. Koniordos, 'Introduction', in S. M. Koniordos (ed.), *Networks, Trust & Social Capital: Theoretical and Empirical Investigations from Europe* (Aldershot: Ashgate, 2005), pp. 3–6; D. J. Saddle, 'Migration as a Strategy of Accumulation: Social and Economic Change in Eighteenth-Century Savoy', *Economic History Review*, 50 (1997), 3–20; C. Tilly, 'Transplanted Networks', in V. Yans-McLaughlin (ed.), *Immigration Reconsidered: History, Sociology, and Politics* (Oxford: Oxford University Press, 1990), pp. 84–9.

74 Nan Lin, *Social Capital: A Theory of Social Structure and Action* (Cambridge: Cambridge University Press, 2003), p. 38; D. Hancock, 'Combining Success and Failure: Scottish Networks in the Atlantic Wine Trade', in D. Dickson, J. Parmentier and J. Ohlmeyer (eds), *Irish and Scottish Mercantile Networks in Europe and Overseas in the Seventeenth and Eighteenth Centuries* (Ghent: Academia Press, 2007), pp. 5–8, 20–4.

75 Randall Collins, 'The Micro Contribution to Macro Sociology', *Sociological Theory*, 6 (1988), 242–53; J. H. Turner, 'Toward a General Sociological Theory of the Economy', *Sociological Theory*, 22 (2004), 230.
76 Lin, 'Building a Network Theory', pp. 6–15; J. H. Turner, 'The Formation of Social Capital', in P. Dasgupta and I. Serageldin (eds), *Social Capital: A Multifaceted Perspective* (Washington, DC: World Bank, 2000), pp. 95–7.
77 N. Glaisyer, 'Networking: Trade and Exchange in the Eighteenth-Century British Empire', *The Historical Journal*, 47 (2004), 451–75; Gary B. Magee and Andrew S. Thompson, *Empire and Globalisation: Networks of People, Goods and Capital in the British World, c.1850–1914* (Cambridge: Cambridge University Press, 2010), pp. 15–19, 45–63.
78 D. Hancock, *Citizens of the World: London Merchants and the Integration of the British Atlantic Community, 1735–1785* (Cambridge: Cambridge University Press, 1995), pp. 20–1, 41; Z. Laidlaw, *Connecting Colonies: Metropole and Professions, 1815–1845* (Manchester: Manchester University Press, 2003), pp. 13–38; Hamilton, *Scotland, the Caribbean and the Atlantic World*, pp. 5–6; Alan Lester, 'Imperial Circuits and Networks: Geographies of the British Empire', *History Compass*, 4 (2006), 124–41.
79 For definitions of a meso-network, see P. Hedström, R. Sandell and C. Stern, 'Meso-Level Networks and the Diffusion of Social Movements: The Case of the Swedish Social Democratic Party', *The American Journal of Sociology*, 106 (2000), 145, 154–5; Turner, 'Toward a General Sociological Theory', pp. 230–2; Helmut K. Anheier, Jurgen Gerhards and Frank P. Romo, 'Forms of Capital and Social Structure in Cultural Fields: Examining Bourdieu's Social Topography', *The American Journal of Sociology*, 100 (1995), 860–6.
80 Hopkins, 'The History of Globalisation', pp. 5–7, 25–8.
81 L. Stone, 'Literacy and Education in England, 1640–1900', *Past & Present*, 42 (1969), 135; J. M. MacKenzie with N. R. Dalziel, *The Scots in South Africa: Ethnicity, Identity, Gender and Race, 1772–1914* (Manchester: Manchester University Press, 2007), p. 11.
82 K. Whelan, 'An Underground Gentry? Catholic Middlemen in Eighteenth-Century Ireland', *Eighteenth-Century Ireland/Iris an dá chultúr*, 10 (1995), 7–17, 37–40; T. C. Barnard, 'The Gentrification of Eighteenth-Century Ireland', *Eighteenth-Century Ireland/Iris an dá chultúr*, 12 (1997), 144–6, 150, 155.
83 Michael J. Braddick and John Walter, 'Introduction. Grids of Power: Hierarchy and Subordination in Early Modern Society', in Michael J. Braddick and John Walter (eds), *Negotiating Power in Early Modern Society: Order, Hierarchy, and Subordination in Britain and Ireland* (Cambridge: Cambridge University Press, 2003), p. 31.
84 For commentaries on Irish and Scottish society which can be read as evidence that contemporaries understood the reliance on human capital and its mobilisation, see BL, Richard Newton, 'Progress of a Scot' (London: William Holland, 1794): www.britishmuseum.org/collection/object/P_1868-0612-1247; Richard Newton, 'Progress of an Irishman (London: n.p., 1794): www.britishmuseum.org/collection/object/P_1948-0214-372; Joseph Price, *Some Observations and*

Remarks on a Late Publication Entitled Travels in Europe, Asia and Africa (London: n.p., 1783), pp. 113–17.
85 Paul Langford, 'South Britons' Reception of North Britons, 1707–1820', in Smout (ed.), *Anglo-Scottish Relations*, pp. 143–69.
86 D. Cressy, 'Kinship and Kin Interaction in Early Modern England', *Past & Present*, 113 (1986), 38–69. For durable English kin networks in the East India Company, see Jean Sutton, *The East India Company's Maritime Service, 1746–1834: Masters of Eastern Seas* (Woodbridge: Boydell Press, 2010), pp. 11–19; Margot Finn, 'The Female World of Love & Empire: Women, Family & East India Company Politics at the End of the Eighteenth Century', *Gender & History*, 31 (2019), 9.
87 Bayly, 'Ireland, India and the Empire', 377.

1

Beginnings: London and early links with the English East India companies

Asia does not loom large in assessments of early modern Ireland, Wales or Scotland, and for good reason. Although a highly attractive commercial destination for small, relatively underdeveloped north-west European societies, Asia's economies were notoriously difficult to access. Entering the service of one of the European powers offered a possible solution to this problem. The Ostend and French East India companies attracted a range of Irishmen into its financial and military echelons while the Dutch East India Company (VOC) and its Swedish counterpart hosted a number of Scots acting as either directors, captains or merchants.[1] But involvement in these organisations was never especially large. Neither did the European avenues prove to be as long lasting nor as significant as participation in the English East India Company (EIC). Political and economic developments from the late 1680s to the 1740s hastened the likelihood that the English corporation would emerge as the main conduit for metropolitan provincial contact with Asia. This outcome, however, was far from inevitable and it remains unclear when and by what means Scottish, Irish and Welsh individuals and networks first became substantively embedded in the EIC. The current understanding highlights the significance of Scots joining the Company's directorate from the 1720s. How Scots began exploiting the Eastern Empire has at least been addressed in some detail: the Irish and Welsh have been far less well served. Beyond evidence that Irishmen benefited from the influence of Laurence Sulivan from county Cork, a prominent director and chairman of the Company between 1755 and 1786, networks of London-based lawyers and the patronage of the lord lieutenants, the timing and extent of early links remain unclear. Scholarship relating to the Welsh has similarly yet to establish overall patterns of involvement, although a number of prominent social networks have received revealing attention.[2]

Participation in one whole hemisphere of England and then Britain's global empire was shaped by the existence and patronage capacities of expatriate communities in London.[3] Although the subject of increasing research, the topic of Irish, Scots and Welsh migration to early modern London remains noticeably understudied. The de-emphasis arises from a combination of factors, ranging from political sensitivities over the nature of British history and indeed Britishness itself, to a desire on the part of historians of Ireland, Wales and Scotland to understand what makes their countries distinctive as opposed to marginalised entities within frameworks inevitably dominated by England.

Another reason is the perceived importance of distance within the process of migration. Exotic and far-removed locations attract greater attention than seemingly mundane forms of mobility involving a journey of no more than 300–500 miles and a couple of weeks at most. Innovative case studies have appeared intermittently since the early 2000s on the Welsh, Irish and Scots in eighteenth-century London. Historians of Wales and Ireland have led the way although some important research now exists on Scottish migration to and assimilation in the metropolis.[4] The Irish presence in London was large and multifaceted enough by the 1750s to generate influential webs of association that stretched across the entire empire.[5] The depth and sophistication of these metropolis-based networks have forced major reconsiderations of the timing, extent and means by which Ireland participated in British imperialism.[6] Yet without comprehensive evidence of how London–Irish interests interacted with the eastern sphere of expansion, it cannot be said with certainty that Ireland's links with the metropolis worked to negate the growing constitutional frictions generated by the link with Britain. A similar lack of coverage applies to the flow of Scots migrants through London to destinations overseas. Until the nature of the metropolis connection is sufficiently excavated, assessments of Scotland, Wales and Ireland in the pre-1815 empire remain incomplete.[7]

How Scottish, Irish and Welsh social networks infiltrated the English East India Company is a useful case study in another important respect. Because so few metropolitan provincials had ventured to Asia by the early 1700s, the origins, timing and scale of more sustained involvement is relatively easy to track. This clarity is in stark contrast to conditions in the Atlantic, where the considerable pre-1700 activities of migrants and merchants from Ireland, Wales and Scotland muddy attempts to trace key continuities and discontinuities across the seventeenth and eighteenth centuries. The Asia hemisphere of British expansion can be conceptualised as a clean slate upon which the arrival of new groups from the metropolitan provinces can be better identified, traced, tracked and understood.

Open or closed:
the corporate culture of the English East India Company

There can be no meaningful study of the provinces' contact with Asia without understanding the English East India companies. Their importance is such that their histories frame the chronology of this book. At the start of the 1690s the Company of Merchants of London Trading to the East Indies (the 'Old' Company), which had been established in 1600, held the monopoly of trade between England and Asia. Its privileges, though extensive, were far from secure.[8] In 1695 the Scottish Parliament challenged the assumption that England alone in the British and Irish Isles was entitled to participate in oceanic commerce with Asia. Yet for all its ambition the Company of Scotland trading to Africa and the Indies marked an end rather than a beginning. Liquidated under the terms of the 1707 union, the Scots Company was the last serious effort before the early 1790s by one of the non-English kingdoms to break London's monopoly.[9]

The second challenge to the established company in the 1690s arose from a group of City merchants frustrated by its restrictive control of a key branch of world trade.[10] Lobbying by these disaffected interests ensured that on 5 September 1698 the Company of England trading to the East Indies (the 'New' Company) obtained a charter in return for a £2 million loan to the Crown.[11] The advent of this new company raised hopes of a relaxation in the highly restricted nature of contact between the British and Irish Isles and Asia. However, in March 1700 such expectations received a major blow when William of Orange indicated his preference for a corporate union between the competing organisations. The parallels between the Anglo-Scottish settlement and the amalgamation of the old and new companies are striking and confirm that models of economic rationalisation were gaining credence within English political culture.[12] The process of company union was finalised in March 1709 with the creation of the 'United Merchants of England trading to the East Indies'.[13] This organisation existed until its dissolution in the aftermath of the rising of 1857 in South Asia, and is hereafter referred to as the EIC. Although its monopoly charter was subject to periodic parliamentary review, the corporation controlled official trade between Britain, Ireland and India until 1813. This date, rather than the traditional emphasis on 1707 and 1780 or 1800 marked the point when the domestic Welsh, Irish and Scottish economies gained unrestricted access to colonial commerce across most of Asia. Even then, the remnants of monopoly persisted in the China trade until 1833.[14] The United English East India Company was the corporate entity that all British and Irish subjects must access or else forego the legal opportunities arising from one whole hemisphere of Britain's expansion. The 1690s formed a period of flux which enabled new commercial interests to access the two India companies while 1813 heralded the end of the corporation's exclusive control of connections with Asia. These dates mark the start and end points of a transformative phase of growing interaction between the Company and a host of individuals and networks from Ireland, Wales and Scotland. They represent neglected chronological watersheds in the trajectories of these provincial societies within the wider phenomenon of proto-globalisation.

Viewed from the metropolitan provinces of the British and Irish Isles, the EIC presented a mixture of monopoly corporatism and a complex tangle of informal London-based social and financial networks.[15] Its structure and activities in the metropolis and in Asia are well known. For those with the requisite venture finance it was an attractive investment option. What is far less clear is the extent to which the EIC was accessible to human capital from the provinces. An assessment of the corporation's receptiveness towards the non-London regions of the British and Irish Isles cannot rely purely on an institutional analysis; any evaluation must include social and cultural perspectives. Historians have noted how the organisation's elaborate hierarchy masked a permeable structure. This interpretation sees the Company as a protective canopy or enabling mechanism that allowed its own civil servants, military officers, the shipping interest and free merchants to facilitate their private business interests in Asia.[16]

The EIC's status as one of London's premier civic and financial corporations moulded its employment ethos.[17] It evolved a set of prescriptions regarding the ideal employee or 'honourable servant'. Hiring conditions were infused with a strong emphasis on morality, even of semi-sacred obligation and explain why new civil servants were required to sign a 'covenant' with their employers.[18] This recruitment culture ensured that human, cultural and social capital were vital collateral when applying for posts. The EIC existed as a combination of aggressive venture capitalism and apparently archaic social assumptions about gentlemanly honour and character.[19] Its currencies were many, and it traded freely in the human as well as in the monetary forms of wealth. That it did so provided a crucial opportunity to the under-resourced, in venture-capital terms, metropolitan provinces. Here was an organisation receptive to the human and social assets that constituted a disproportionately important resource for cash-poor societies like Ireland, Wales and Scotland.

Questions of probity and personal character infused the ethos of all the guilds and corporations of London. But such concerns operated with an unusual degree of force in the EIC. The physical distances involved meant that the directors could not control decision-making processes in Asia. A great degree of latitude had to be granted to servants on the spot. A key stage of the Company's recruitment process involved applicants nominating two people to act as security for their good character and behaviour.[20] Considerable significance was attached to those who in effect guaranteed the human capital of new employees. The name, status and residence of these 'securities' were noted assiduously in the directors' minutes. No similar effort was made to list the personal details of those appointed to the post of factor, merchant or writer. Only from 1749, when the first writers' applications survive, is it possible to chart with certainty the geographic and social backgrounds of those entering the EIC's elite civil service.[21] Prospective Company servants were acutely aware of the importance of using the right people as securities. Writing from Madras in 1731 to his uncle John Drummond of Quarrell, Alexander Wedderburn from Fife noted that; 'I am obliged to Messrs Andrew Drummond and John Crawford who stood my security to the Honourable Company'.[22] The social networks that initiated an EIC career had to be robust and capable of commanding credit on an impressive scale.

The key problem facing Scots, Irish and individuals from the English and Welsh regions was that opportunities were most readily available to those with entrenched financial and social connections in the capital. In addition, metropolitan prejudices could facilitate or hinder the drift of provincials into employment. On the positive side, Presbyterians maintained a high profile within the guilds and business elite of late seventeenth-century London. Protestant dissenters facing a religious test when contemplating a career in the army and navy could expect a reasonably sympathetic reception in some of the metropole's key civic institutions, including the Company. In October 1696 the directors authorised oaths of loyalty that consolidated Quaker access to the corporation. Alexander and Abraham Hume of Ayton in Berwickshire rose to prominence in the late 1730s as a director and an influential figure in the shipping interest respectively. Both were of Quaker stock. John Drummond of Quarrell, another early example of a Scot on the directorate, used the marriage of a kinsman into Quaker circles to entrench his social and business affiliations in London during the 1730s.[23]

The EIC's receptiveness towards socio-religious groups facing discrimination in other walks of British and Irish life should not be overexaggerated. But a case can be made that the corporation was more accessible than other sectors of the fiscal-military state like the army and navy.[24] Few examples exist of the English East India companies systematically excluding Scots or Irish Protestants, even during the seventeenth century. When exclusion did occur it was usually the result of overly aggressive lobbying. In December 1698 the new company finalised arrangements for sending its first ship to China. The senior supercargo charged with responsibility for both the safety and sale of the £25,000 cargo was a London-based Scot called Robert Douglas. His appointment demonstrates that Scots could acquire high-ranking positions within the English companies prior to 1707. However Douglas's experience also reveals the limits of corporate receptiveness. Not satisfied with his own status, Douglas asked that another Scot, a Mr Henderson, be made junior supercargo. Despite pondering their decision on Christmas Eve the directors demonstrated little festive goodwill, ordering that 'the China ship be forbidden carrying any of the Scotch nation except Mr Douglas'.[25]

This explicit bar on Scots was highly unusual. But the lack of formal discrimination is deceptive. It was corporate cultures rather than explicit policies of systematic exclusion that slowed the progress of non-London personnel and networks. The name of the new company established in 1709 exemplifies the predicament facing metropolitan provincials. 'The United Merchants of England trading to the East Indies' reflected the priorities of London rather than those of the fledgling British union, still less the wider British-Irish monarchy. Although there is considerable truth in the argument that the Empire quickly became a British entity after, if not before, 1707, this interpretation reflects certain geographic assumptions. England's global empire tends to get equated with the Atlantic system of commerce and settlement made legally accessible to Scots by means of union in 1707 and by the concession of free trade to Ireland in 1780 and full access through union in 1800.[26] In the western hemisphere the Scots and Welsh (though not the Irish) participated by virtue of their Britishness. In Asia the rhetoric and concept of corporate Englishness remained central.[27] At no time was the EIC ever formally referred to as 'British'. Under the terms of the new charter of 1698 (which formed the constitutional template for the EIC's post-1709 monopoly) a director had to be 'a natural born Englishman'. The bylaw was not revoked at the 1707, 1709 or 1800 union: instead, an unwritten convention evolved by which individuals of non-English origin were granted all the requisite rights and liberties. Scots, Welsh and Irish in Company service became in effect honorary Englishmen.[28]

The Company's anglicised rhetoric and metrocentric rules might appear to be merely obscure technicalities that did little to prevent full participation. Yet the lack of an overtly British tone to the EIC's self-regulation indicates how slowly it evolved from its origins as a City corporation into a genuinely British imperial institution. Its ethos comes across clearly in the procedures for appointing personnel. Obtaining two securities was only the first step in a delicate process that required an insider's knowledge of business sensibilities in London. In 1714, and again in 1731, the EIC ordered that no employment applications be considered unless accompanied by the support of two directors. The directors concerned were expected to 'inform themselves of the sufficiency of the persons proposed to be their [the applicant's] securities, and represent the same to the court'. The bylaw was reiterated in 1751 with the added stipulation that those standing surety were to be 'substantial persons'.[29]

Finding two sympathetic directors and two suitable securities constituted a major challenge for Irish, Welsh and Scottish families residing hundreds of miles away from London. The crux of the problem involved winning the support of a small group of men whose financial, social and mental horizons predisposed them towards the sons and clients of their fellow London elites and associates.[30] The challenge facing metropolitan provincials during the early decades of the eighteenth century lay well beyond simply having sufficient venture finance. They had to develop and then deploy human, social and cultural capital to operate effectively in the metropole. The scale of the potential obstacle is revealed by a survey of those acting as securities. Between 1700 and 1710 nearly two-thirds of all securities with a clear kinship link to applicants obtaining civil service posts were individuals listed as London residents.[31]

By contrast, bonds of surety from the metropolitan provinces were conspicuous by their absence. Of the hundreds accepted by the directors between 1690 and 1750, only thirteen came from Ireland, Scotland and Wales. The majority (six) were lodged by Welsh gentry from the counties of Flint, Denbigh and Glamorgan. This pattern reflects the established nature of political, social and cultural links between Wales and London.[32] At the beginning of the eighteenth century the Welsh held a real advantage in terms of the social assets and cultural capital required to access the corporation. It is telling, too, that in the early 1700s there were more securities from Ireland than from Scotland. Three of the four Irish securities were from the Dublin merchants, John Lovett, Charles Brouchier and Michael Harrison. The links forged between the English and Irish metropoles through insular trade, as well as professional and financial exchanges, helped to expedite Irish contact with the Company beyond the courtly and aristocratic contacts exemplified by Gerald Aungier, brother of Francis, first earl of Longford. The first Scottish-based security did not appear until 1725 and was supplied by Sir Gilbert Elliot of Stobbs. It would be another twenty years before the next securities from Scotland were accepted, those of Sir William Dalrymple of Cousland and Sir John Gordon of Invergordon.[33]

The strong bias towards established London connections was symptomatic of deeper, underlying tensions between the corporation and the metropolitan provinces. Although the Company's servants and directors often demonstrated a sophisticated understanding of conditions in Asia, they could exhibit a distinctly parochial attitude towards their own British and Irish hinterlands. The provinces more than reciprocated. A virulent strain of anti-metropolitan prejudice characterised political attitudes and culture in the English regions and found vocal expression in resentment of the Company's monopoly privileges.[34] The same was true in Scotland and in Ireland, though for different reasons. Relations between the English East India companies and the Scottish political nation had never been cordial. As early as 1617 the old Company used its influence at the Stuart court to quash the establishment of a Scottish East India Company. The corporation took a similarly hostile attitude towards the formation of the Company of Scotland in 1695.[35]

Once the question of a Scottish East India Company was resolved to the EIC's satisfaction under the terms of the 1707 union, the directors had no reason to concern themselves with northern Britain until forced by ministerial influence to service demands from Scottish MPs for patronage. Calls for the Equivalent to be paid by the EIC rather than by national taxation did little to make Scottish political agendas welcome at Leadenhall Street during the first two decades of the Union. The consolidation of the United Company's monopoly in 1709 rankled in Scotland. In that year John Gordon, MP for the Aberdeen burghs, was among a number of Scots parliamentarians who petitioned against corporate commercial privilege on the grounds that it constituted a breach of the national as opposed to the corporate union. More broadly, the role of the English organisation in the demise of the Company of Scotland left a legacy of bitterness that was still evident as late as the 1780s.[36]

Ultimately, however, the northern half of Great Britain was decidedly marginal to the EIC's domestic agenda. Ireland was not. The kingdom's substantial population made it the second most important British and Irish Isles market for the Company's textile imports. Questions of import and export put Irish commercial and political interests at loggerheads with Leadenhall Street. Much like Scotland, Ireland invested substantial economic and symbolic importance in its linen manufactory. With its parliament still intact, the Irish political nation could defend the island's textile interests in ways no longer available to the Scots.[37] In 1704, 1710 and again in 1734 it imposed heavy duties on Bengal calicos, silks and other EIC imports. The Company responded by mobilising its influence with Westminster politicians like Thomas Pelham-Holles, first duke of Newcastle, who in turn put pressure on the Irish legislature to limit the scope of its protectionist policies.[38]

It is hardly surprising that some shades of political and popular opinion in Ireland viewed the EIC as an institution at the cutting edge of the country's constitutional subordination to Britain.[39] This did little to enhance its reputation there or make overt Irish political influence especially welcome at East India Company House. To middling elites from outside the metropolis the EIC must have sparked a deeply ambivalent set of emotions. It offered lucrative employment opportunities, yet its corporate culture did not bode well for easy involvement.

Unlocking the Company: the London-Scots, -Irish and -Welsh

Increasing participation in the EIC can be traced directly to the development in London of meso-level political, mercantile, professional, regional and kin networks with connections back to the metropolitan provinces. The city had attracted Scots, Welsh and Irish migrants for centuries.[40] While these shared many characteristics in common, the profile of the different nationalities varied over time and from each other. Such differences played an important part in the variable profiles within the EIC that marked the Irish, Welsh and Scots out from each other. Trade was an obvious common dominator driving human mobility into the city. In 1700, 42 per cent of Ireland's export trade lay with England, rising to over 85 per cent by 1800. Although Bristol, Chester and Liverpool played a crucial role, London was the undisputed centre of commerce between the two kingdoms. London–Irish merchant houses emerged to service the substantial flow of Irish textiles and agrarian produce into England and to access financial services for clients back in Ireland. By the early eighteenth century, mercantile dynasties like the Cantillons, Kirwans, Cairnes and Nesbitts were well established. This commercial bridgehead grew substantially over the century, with no fewer than 135 Irish merchant houses identified for the years between 1736 and 1796.[41] Their presence in the metropolis represented a major extension of Irish social and networked capital beyond Ireland and constituted a central mechanism for expediting broader involvement in all areas of the Empire.

Trade was similarly crucial to the timing, scale and nature of Scottish migration to London. The free trade initiated across Britain in 1707 accelerated economic trends that had emerged during the seventeenth century. The conventional analysis of Scotland's post-union economy emphasises the rise of the west of Scotland and the transatlantic trades rather than deepening domestic links with London and the rest of the English and Welsh economy.[42] The result is a noticeable neglect of the east coast tramping trades which linked places like Inverness, the Moray coast ports, Aberdeen, Montrose, Dundee, the Forth burghs, Leith and Dunbar to the British capital. The North Sea coasting trade can seem mundane when compared to involvement in Atlantic commerce. But the commodities involved were absolutely central to Scotland's development and its place within the Union and the Empire. Linen, oats and barley were vital staples. Angus, Kincardine and Perthshire produced large quantities of these products for English markets, while coal from the Fife and Forth mines shaped the expansion of shipping and mercantile links.[43] These connections ensured that Scotland's North Sea-facing burghs played a far more important role in the trade to London than they were ever to do in the Atlantic. The deepening of contact with the metropolis had a significant impact in determining the timing and nature of Scottish movement into the English Company.

Although Welsh, Irish and Scottish links to London shared some basic similarities, there were important differences. As the finishing school for those intending to practise English law, the Inns of Court shaped patterns of middling-sort migration from Ireland and Wales. Welsh patronage networks were well established within Gray's Inn by the seventeenth century, while the Irish became strongly associated with Trinity Inn, forming over 45 per cent of the annual intake by the 1730s.[44] Scotland's distinctive legal system and church government ensured there was no equivalent reliance on London or the Oxford and Cambridge colleges for the purposes of professional education. Aspiring Scots lawyers trained mainly in the Netherlands and in universities north of the border, although the British capital always retained a central importance for medical training and other professional opportunities. Merchants, financiers, educationalists and doctors formed a significant percentage of the Scottish middle-class migrants in London during the later seventeenth and eighteenth centuries.[45] These groups would go on to forge enduring links between Scottish society and the EIC.

Evolving patterns of Scottish mobility generated a number of formal and semi-formal institutions which facilitated lobbying and mutual support among expatriates. In 1615 King James VI and I created the office of Master of Requests to regulate applications from Scots seeking patronage at the new British court.[46] The delivery of poor relief for unsuccessful immigrants was initiated by the creation of a Scottish poor box as early as 1613. The process of self-help was put on a surer footing between the 1660s and the early 1680s by the foundation of the Scotch (Founders') Hall and Blackfriars kirks in London. Something of the scale of migration from north of the border over the course of the eighteenth century can be gleaned from the fact that as well as the Founders' and Scots Church at Swallow Street in Westminster, another eleven Presbyterian congregations attracted a substantial minority Scottish presence.[47] This expanding demographic bridgehead was officially consolidated during the Restoration by the creation of the Scottish Corporation in London in 1665. A similar Welsh organisation, the Society of Ancient Britons, first met in 1715, and by 1718 managed a school and poor relief centre for Welsh children. The subscription lists of these two organisations give a clear indication of the increasing volume of middling and elite movement from Wales and Scotland into the city. By 1800 the Welsh society had over 312 subscribers: the Scots Corporation had 558 members who donated more than £5 to its coffers between 1665 and 1737. Membership rose to 1,130 by 1808, making it one of the largest migrant associations in London.[48]

It is tempting to draw parallels between the émigré Scots in the United Provinces and in the English capital. Although there were similarities, there were also crucial differences. By the end of the seventeenth century no European city could match the number and overlapping nature of Scottish organisations and networks in London.[49] The density of informal and formal charitable institutions, church congregations, political clubs, coffee and merchant houses nurtured the development among expatriate Scots of insider knowledge and strong webs of lobbying, social and financial credit.[50] The formal organisations were supplemented by the 1760s with a number of boarding houses run by Scots which specialised in taking Scottish lodgers. Charles Stuart, the son of the ninth earl of Blantyre, who journeyed to London to complete his training before joining the EIC, was among those benefiting from this informal web of social provision.[51] The development of this reception capacity facilitated the mobilisation of Scottish human capital through social networking.

Mutual assistance did not aim at preserving an exclusive form of Scottish-ness, separate from the mainstream of London society. By creating civic infrastructure like the poor box, the Scottish Corporation and the Society of Ancient Britons, expatriate Scots and Welsh mirrored ideals of communal responsibility and sociability that permeated the city's political culture. This hastened acculturation and created bonds of association that linked migrants more securely into metropolitan society. These connective and integrative processes generated forms of cultural capital and ensured that a number of routes into the EIC slowly became available. Scottish elites could lobby at court from 1603, and, after 1707, via the country's forty-five MPs. Besides the formal channels of politics there were the Scots kirks, the Scots clubs of London and Westminster and the Scottish Corporation. In their different ways they all constituted entry points into the social, financial and business milieu of London's guilds and corporations, including the EIC. The émigré organisations enabled micro-networks based in Scotland to access meso-level associations in the capital in ways that facilitated a surer navigation of the world of EIC patronage.

Influence in London was the vital springboard for step and chain migration into the Eastern Empire. However, the process varied over time and in scale. Influence at the Stuart court facilitated Scottish and Irish involvement in the Old East India Company almost from the moment of its inception. The Aberdonian cleric Patrick Copland was appointed chaplain to the Company's tenth voyage in 1612, before going on to have an oceanic career that encompassed the western and eastern spheres of England's new empire.⁵² As befitted an elite with more courtly, religious and cultural connections to England than their Scottish (although not their Welsh) equivalents in this period, the Anglo-Irish gentry and nobility were clearly if intermittently prominent in Company service by the Restoration. Robert Boyle, a son of the first earl of Cork sat as a director in the 1660s and 1670s. Kinship links with the courtier, Francis Annesley, earl of Anglesey assisted the career of Gerald Aungier who went on to be a highly successful governor of Bombay between 1669 and 1676.⁵³ Their careers demonstrate how, with the right social and political connections, Ireland's Protestant aristocracy reached the top of the English Company's hierarchy 130 years before the Wellesleys.

No scion of a Scottish family matched Aungier's high rank during the pre-union period. Yet the example of William Fraser, governor of Madras between 1709 and 1711, confirms how middling Scots exploited career opportunities in English Asia before 1707. William was from Petty in Inverness-shire; by the mid-1670s his brother James was tutor to one of Charles II's numerous natural and ennobled sons. He also had a powerful patron in the person of Henry Hyde, second earl of Clarendon. Through these links James acquired considerable status in London's civic circles. He was secretary of the Chelsea Hospital from 1682 and during the 1690s was licenser at the Stationer's Hall. As Clarendon's man of business he became intimately acquainted with East India affairs and maintained close contacts with company officials.⁵⁴ Ten years of financial and social networking enabled James to place William at Madras by 1685. William rose steadily through the old Company's civil service to become a factor and councillor in the 1690s: by 1700 he was governor of Fort St. David. His reappointment to the council of Madras in 1704 involved the usual securities. Listed in the court minutes as 'Mr James Fraser of Chelsea', his brother offered a bond of security for £1,000, with a second provided by another London associate.⁵⁵ In their different ways Aungier and Fraser profited from the courtly imperialism that characterised the era of Charles II and James VII and II. The later Stuarts used empire, including settlements in the Carolinas, East New Jersey and patronage in the Hudson's Bay Company to nurture centres of extra-parliamentary loyalty.⁵⁶ What has not been fully appreciated is the global extent of the Restoration monarchy's manipulation of England's overseas possessions to reward Irish and Scottish clients.

As with many aspects of Stuart policy, however, there was a yawning chasm between ambition and reality. Monarchical patronage was neither consistent nor strong enough to insert supporters from Ireland or Scotland into the English Company in large, self-replicating numbers. Other links emerged which would eventually play a major role in shaping sustained patterns of participation during the eighteenth century. As the coastal tramping trade between Scotland and England expanded, seamen such as William Young from Prestonpans found employment on East Indiamen by the 1680s and 1690s.[57] At the higher levels of the corporation the picture is not impressive in numeric terms. Men like John Archer, a burgess maltman from Perth and John Innes, son of an Aberdeen burgher, both of whom died in the Company's service in the early 1700s, were exceptions.[58] Involvement was still characterised by a piecemeal drift of individuals to Asia, with micro-networks of association underpinning individual career trajectories. If Fraser had ended up in Madras through kin influence at court, religion provided the motive for the Reverend James Stirling of Paisley. He left Scotland in the 1670s in reaction to the Restoration regime's ecclesiastical policies and in an effort (unappreciated it seems) to bring Presbyterianism to Bombay.[59] These isolated examples underscore the reality that Scotland and Ireland's mercantile and maritime networks still lacked the capacity to deliver large-scale opportunities in Asia.

Between 1700 and 1710 only four Scots and two Irishmen can be positively identified from a total of 178 factor and writer appointments.[60] The figures are almost certainly an underestimate: John Forbes, elected a factor for Benkulen in 1709, was in all probability a Scot. Thomas MacBurny, appointed a writer in 1701, had securities supplied by James MacBurny of Westminster and was most likely an Irishman. But even if a number of individuals obscured by the Company's metrocentric bureaucratic methods is allowed for, it is striking how 'English' the English East India Company remained in the era of the British union. The Atlantic was already a far more 'British-Irish' world by 1700, with substantial and sustained Scottish and Irish participation in trade and migration. No point of access into the English old and new East India companies as yet delivered a large influx of personnel from the metropolitan provinces. It took the slow build-up over decades of multiple and overlapping political, financial and mercantile networks among London-Scots, -Irish and -Welsh expatriates to generate the sort of influence which could successfully secure EIC patronage.

Brokering human capital: credentialism and the London-Irish, -Scots and -Welsh

Gaining influence in East India circles could be a remarkably convoluted process. Apparent failures led to success in the longer term while initial progress did not automatically produce a sustained presence within the organisation. The attempt by the London-Scots James Foulis, Robert Douglas, Walter Stuart, David Nairn and William Paterson to acquire English finance for the Company of Scotland is usually viewed as a failed prelude to the even greater disaster of Darien.[61] But this analysis misses the longer-term significance of the short-lived London phase of the Scots Company. These men point to the emergence of the London-Scots as an interest group which remained acutely aware of and responsive to affairs north of the border. Of the eleven individuals identified by the Scottish parliament as representatives of the Scots Company in London, six were also involved in the establishment of the Bank of Scotland. South of the border these men were prominent players in the émigré institutions: eight of the Scottish Company's eleven London agents were subscribers to the Scots Corporation.[62] In facilitating meso-level networks between the metropolis and Scotland the expatriates performed one of their most vital if still under-researched functions. The same was true of their Welsh and Irish counterparts.

The initial success of Foulis, Douglas, Nairn and others in gaining the support of English merchants disgruntled with the 'old' Company facilitated the growth of Scottish influence among City interests which would later set up the 'new' Company. This co-operation demonstrates that Scots expatriates were never inclined towards ethnic exclusivity. Instead they branched out into the wider financial, mercantile and social world of the English capital well before union. The experience of James Foulis was typical. While lobbying for the Scots Company in late 1695 he became acquainted with shareholders and directors of the old Company keen to diversify their trading options.[63] These contacts gave him a profile at East India Company House. By April 1701, barely a year after the loss of the Darien colony, Foulis secured the appointment of his son John as factor and deputy governor of Saint Helena. The London-Scots merchant and subscriber to the Scots Corporation, William Graham, acted as John's security.[64] Robert Douglas, another agent of the Company of Scotland, became known in both old and new English Company circles. In early 1697 he and William Stewart acted as security for Charles Douglas, who was appointed as a factor to one of the old Company's settlements in India; a year later Robert himself became the supercargo on the first new Company ship to China.[65] These contacts reveal how the failure of the Scots Company nevertheless enabled patterns of commercial association in London just as surely as it influenced constitutional politics in Edinburgh. The Scots Company's spectacular implosion in Central America has distracted historians from its role in creating a number of productive links between London-Scots and the English Company during the mid-1690s to the early 1700s.

Another apparent Company of Scotland failure was the *Speedwell*. Owned by a cartel of London-Scots, the vessel sailed from the Clyde to Asian waters in 1701 and conducted a successful country trade before being wrecked in the Strait of Malacca in 1704. The proceeds of her voyage

(£6,300) were deposited at the old Company's Bombay and Surat factories. In 1711 the owners, Sir David Nairn, Sir James Gray and William Elliot lobbied the EIC's directors for repayment. The sum was duly remitted to Elliot (as agent for the owners) between 1711 and 1718. It is ironic that the *Speedwell*'s loss was the means by which a small but important number of London-Scots became familiar faces at EIC House. Sir Gilbert Elliot of Stobbs used William Elliot as security for his son's successful application for a Bengal writership in 1725 largely on the basis of William's earlier business dealings with the directorate.[66]

Another individual who exemplifies the incremental but crucial process of interaction with the Company was William Stuart of Shambellie from New Abbey in Kirkcudbright. A merchant in London, he and his brother, Walter, were active in the Scots Corporation. Walter played a prominent role in soliciting subscriptions on behalf of the Scots Company in 1695. These activities ensured that both brothers developed business associations with the City merchants who founded the 'new' East India Company, a set of contacts that resulted in William's appointment as one of the new Company's first directors in 1698. Influence within the new organisation was matched by William's election as an alderman of London in 1711, and then as mayor in 1721. In 1716 he sponsored the appointment of his nephew, Walter Browne, to the council of Bombay and that of another relation, Stuart Browne as a writer, again at Bombay.[67] The experience of Foulis, Douglas, Elliot and Stuart illustrate that the London phase of the Company of Scotland in late 1695 is in need of a major reappraisal. Contacts generated at this time increased the capacity of London-Scots to embed social contacts and networks within the two English companies.

While the origins of more sustained Scottish involvement in the East Indies are associated with the appointment of John Drummond as a director in 1722, interaction had been gradually intensifying since the 1690s. Drummond's role in facilitating the movement of clients to Asia in the 1720s and 1730s is undeniable, but there is a need to move beyond explanations which focus only on trends in the directorate.[68] Engagement with the corporation was not the work of two or three prominent individuals, important though these men undoubtedly were. The influence wielded by the likes of Drummond or Alexander Hume of Ayton was part of a much wider and denser web of contacts between the EIC, the London-Scots and elites in Scotland that evolved from the 1680s to the 1740s.

This process mirrored the growing importance of London. While European destinations like Rotterdam and Danzig continued to attract migrants throughout the eighteenth century, the English and then British capital increasingly attracted a greater number and variety of Scots.[69] Not surprisingly, there emerged in Scotland a widespread belief that the English metropolis now hosted a discernible Scottish community. Prior to the Union, English politicians spoke of 'ye Scots in town'.[70] It was commonly believed in Scotland that expatriates remained in a reciprocal relationship with their native country. Whether relations between Scots north and south of the border ever operated in this idealised way is unlikely. One of the main points of tension was the expectation that kinsmen and patrons in the metropole could and should deliver up jobs and patronage at will.[71] Episodic disagreements notwithstanding, the belief persisted that London-Scots ought to work with and in the interest of their kith and kin, if not necessarily their countrymen in general. In 1762 George Bogle of Daldowie celebrated this perception when writing to his brother, John, in Virginia regarding their sibling, Robert, a merchant in London. He noted; 'whenever a Glasgow person (or I may say anybody that he is acquainted with), comes down from London they rave upon the civilities they receive'.[72]

Bogle's observation highlights the importance ascribed by contemporaries to maintaining active links between Scotland and London and, through such connections, the wider empire. Most histories of the eighteenth century portray London as the dominant imperial centre.[73] In formal political, financial and economic terms this assessment is undeniable. But Scottish, Irish and Welsh migrants complicate such an interpretation and suggest that the relationship between the City and the provinces of Britain and Ireland was far from one sided. Although London-based finance colonised the domestic regions, the metropolis was in turn colonised through internal migration. As monetary capital moved out of London, large reserves of social and human capital moved in. The London-Scots and their Irish and Welsh equivalents formed a reception and hosting mechanism for those journeying to the city in search of opportunities in England and further afield. In this growing economy of human mobility other types of capital besides those of a financial nature were significant. Yet the influence of these social resources is not sufficiently acknowledged in assessments of how the metropolitan provinces exploited overseas expansion.

The connections that evolved between the British and Irish regions, London and Asia are an historicised case study of the mobilisation of human capital through social networks. This perspective not only underlines the ongoing importance of older forms of social wealth but points to the ways in which proto-globalisation involved more than the intensifying flow of monetary resources or exchanges of key commodities. Redefining what constituted start-up wealth points to how those areas of Europe less well equipped with comparative advantages nevertheless carved out niche avenues of participation in the emerging world economies. This broader definition of venture capital can be illustrated by the way in which the EIC recruited its elite civil servants. Theorists of the relationship between human and social capital point to the importance of 'credentialism'. This is a process for conveying 'information about underlying abilities, trustworthiness and other valuable traits'.[74] The system of securities demanded by the EIC is a historic example of 'credentialism' in action. This arrangement was more than simply a patron–client relationship or a mechanism for confirming educational and professional qualifications. It constituted a flexible means of quantifying, formalising and embedding the value of human capital. In order to perform the vital function of underwriting human capital, credentialism developed different social, financial, educational, professional and political forms. Yet regardless of the specific circumstances or patronage arrangements that enabled it, credentialism's key function lay in deploying the social capital inherent in networks to mobilise the value of human capital. By tapping into the sociocultural assumptions that shaped the EIC's recruitment system, metropolitan provincial interests used London as a brokerage centre where human and social capital could be traded for access to imperial service. Viewed in this way, the City emerges not so much as a hegemonic centre of financial power but as a Catherine wheel dispersing human capital into the Empire in the form of professional migrants and sojourners.

Realising the latent value of human resources through migration to Asia was already underway before 1707, albeit on a small scale. In 1702 the London-Scots merchants James Bruce and James Graham helped George Drummond, the brother of John Drummond of Quarrel, secure the fifth mate's post on the *Josiah* East Indiaman.[75] Contacts made at a London Presbyterian congregation as well as kin and business networks secured for Henry Clerk, son of Sir John Clerk of Penicuik a place on the *Stretham* in 1700. Henry's appointment was also an act of British political patronage. As a prominent member of the Scottish parliament, Sir John had become acquainted with Wriothesley Russell, second duke of Bedford, whose part ownership of the *Stretham* provided the decisive influence on Henry's behalf.[76] As with the example of William Fraser, imperial patronage presaged the advent of Britain itself.

Welsh and Irish individuals sought EIC posts using the same tactics. There is evidence that at the beginning of the eighteenth century Irish and Welsh interests were better placed in terms of influence and networks in the capital than their Scottish equivalents. Historians of urban society have noted how Welsh families were already well tied into the capital's guild and apprenticeship networks by the 1660s.[77] When the Welshman William Kyffin was made an old Company writer in January 1696 his securities were fellow countrymen whose membership of Lincoln's Inn confirmed their and his social and financial standing with the directors.[78] The movement into London of Irish professionals for the purposes of legal training similarly generated support, credit and patronage networks. These connections ensured that notaries like Mr Fitzgerald, who transferred £500 in EIC stock for the Jackson family of Cork in November 1711, were ideally placed to handle financial and human brokerage business from Ireland.[79]

Irish merchants in London played a crucial role in facilitating early contact with the EIC, usually by acting as securities for other Irishmen. As early as January 1714 Patrick Macky of the Navy Office and Henry Cairnes provided security for Robert Macky, appointed to Benkulen. Originally from Ulster, Robert went on to have a successful career before returning to Ireland during the 1730s as one of the kingdom's first nabobs.[80] 'Nabob' was the derogatory term used to describe a wealthy but morally tainted Company official, soldier or merchant who had returned home from Asia.[81] The willingness of Irish merchants to provide securities increased as the century progressed. Albert and Arnold Nesbitt underwrote the careers of three Irishmen appointed as writers to Bengal and Madras in 1750 and 1751, committing £1,500 in surety in the process. This was patronage as credentialism on a significant scale. Their clients included Thomas Bury and Henry Brooke from Dublin.[82] This sponsorship role can be seen in the Ulster connections that bound together the Macky, Alexander and Boyd merchant houses: Robert Boyd stood surety with William Alexander of Cateaton Street in the City for John McClintock from Strabane, appointed as a writer to Madras in 1766.[83]

Evidence sifted from the granting of securities between the 1690s and 1740s show that Irish elites were initially more prominent than their Scottish counterparts. Yet the credentialism undertaken by the Nesbitts or Boyds focused more consistently on bonds of security which facilitated entry into key London institutions like the Inns of Court.[84] These performed exactly the same function as standing surety for an individual at East India Company House: they confirmed and formalised an person's perceived human capital. Irish social networks evolved in response to close financial, legal and educational links between Dublin and London in ways that shaped the alignment of credentialism activities. The result was a considerable focus on the capital's legal and domestic institutions. This emphasis was a matter of degree rather than absolute but becomes easier to discern through a contrast with the London-Scots. It is possible to track the scope of contact between London-Scots and the EIC with a greater degree of certainty compared to the Welsh and Irish. The reason for this difference lies in the membership lists of the Scots Corporation covering the later seventeenth century and the whole of the eighteenth century. These identify prominent mercantile, political, financial and social elites from Scotland (or with clear links to Scotland) present and active in the metropolis. If these lists are cross-referenced with

Table 1.1 London-Scots securities and the EIC, 1690–1775[85]

Scots Corp. Members, 1665–1737	EIC Links 1690–1737	Scots Corp. Members, 1738–1775	EIC Links 1738–1775
557	51 (9.1%)	309	103 (33.3%)
Securities	Amount	Securities	Amount
William Stewart = 3	£2,500	Ninian Ballantyne = 7	£2,400
Alexander & George		Hugh Ross = 7	£4,200
Ouchterlony = 3	£5,000	Andrew Moffat = 14	£13,000

(Source: *Summary of the View of the Rise, Constitution, and Present State*, pp. 9–27; *A Supplemental List of Benefactors, for 38 Years* (London: n.p., 1775), pp. 37–58; IOR, B/40–B/91).

the securities recorded in the court of directors' minutes the results are striking.

The evidence demonstrates conclusively that the brokering of human capital by an array of Scottish merchants and financiers in London was, alongside the arrival of Scots on the directorate, the defining factor in early participation in the Company by other Scots. The figures in Table 1.1 show the number of Scots Corporation members with links to the EIC, either as securities or as attorneys acting on behalf of associates in Asia. The figures offer a new way of understanding the origins of Scottish engagement with Britain's expansion and empire in Asia. The dearth of securities from Scotland during the early decades of the eighteenth century did not indicate a failure to connect with the Company. Few financial bonds from Scotland were required because London-Scots fulfilled the directors' preference for guarantees from among their metropolitan peers.

The Irish and Welsh had no comparable mass of prominent expatriates in London lobbying consistently at Leadenhall Street to this extent. The real significance of Table 1.1 is that it reveals the scale of metropolitan-based meso-networks that connected micro-networks in Scotland to the macro-institution of the EIC. The reach and effectiveness of these intermediate-level links are central to understanding when and how British Asia became accessible. Credentialism by William Stewart and the Ouchterlony brothers provided financial and social underwriting to Scots from the 1710s to the 1730s; in the 1740s to the 1760s they were followed by the likes of Hugh Ross. In standing security for the human capital value of his clients, Ross's credentialism exemplifies how London-Scots operated multilayered kin, local and regional patronage networks that traded in different forms of wealth. Although originally from Ross-shire, Hugh's familial links to Ayrshire explain his sponsorship of Daniel Gordon, appointed a writer to

Benkulen in 1761. Hugh also supported his own nephew, Andrew Ross, who became a free merchant in Madras in 1751.[86] Others who benefited included the Orientalist James Fraser of Reelig, made a factor at Surat in 1742, and Kenneth Mackenzie, the son of Mackenzie of Scatwell, made a free mariner in 1752.[87]

Ross was only one of a growing number of London-Scots prepared to endorse the step migration of fellow countrymen to Asia. Andrew Moffat provided security for Robert Erskine from Carnock in Fife, appointed a Bombay writer in 1749. He also sponsored William Maxwell from Dumfries and Charles Stuart for Bengal writerships in 1761 and 1763 respectively.[88] Moffat's credentialism at East India Company House operated on an impressive scale: he stood security for at least fourteen Scots, committing £13,000 in bonds of credentialism in the process. The strategy demonstrates the productive linking of economies in human and monetary capital. His reliable underwriting of human resources materially enhanced his cultural capital at Leadenhall Street. As his standing in East India Company circles improved he was able to help his brother, James, who entered the merchant marine in 1748. Through their involvement in marine insurance, Andrew and James became acquainted with Laurence Sulivan. Along with Andrew's good name among the directors, this connection secured James the command of an East Indiaman in 1759. The benefits of kin, social and financial status worked both ways. James's growing prominence in shipping made Andrew's securities ever more acceptable to the directorate. The brothers fed off each other's influence, mutually reinforcing their social and financial standing. This culminated in James's election to the directorate on four occasions between 1768 and 1790.[89] Human and social capital always operated most effectively when aligned with the financial equivalent. But as the example of the Moffat brothers demonstrates, monetary resources were best mobilised and maximised through strong, durable social networks and personal bonds of mutual trust and obligation. For undercapitalised provincials, the social forms of capital, mobilised via meso-networks, amplified what financial resources were available.

Although the Moffat brothers were unusually successful, their example illustrates why so many London-Scots acted as brokers of human capital. The figures in Table 1.1 show a steep rise in the number of expatriates dealing in human credentialism. The sum of 557 is the total of these gifting the Scots Corporation more than £5 between 1665 and 1737. As such it includes an indeterminate number of individuals active before 1689 who should not strictly be equated against the fifty-one London-Scots who provided securities from 1690 to 1737. Given that the relevant total membership for the period under consideration was less than 557, it is reasonable to conclude that over 10 per cent of Scots Corporation subscribers had links to the EIC during the 1690s and early decades of the eighteenth century. The figures for the 1740s to the 1770s are compelling. In this period fully one-third of the Corporation's elite membership were involved in credentialism with the Company. It was these London-Scots who slowly but surely embedded other Scots in and across the EIC's various branches.

Conclusion

The 1690s to the 1740s remain a neglected era in Irish, Welsh and Scottish social and economic history. This holds true for both domestic and overseas developments and means that early provincial links to the EIC have never received sufficient attention, especially when compared with the crucial connections already evident in the Atlantic world. Reviewing early eighteenth-century contacts with the corporation suggests an apparent conundrum: on the face of it not much appeared to change. The United English East India Company remained an overwhelmingly English organisation both in its institutional ethos and in its personnel. The noticeable increase in Glasgow's transatlantic commerce from the 1720s to 1740s or Cork's growing prominence in the provisioning trade simply had no equivalent in the Asia sphere of expansion.[90] Gradual Scottish and Irish involvement, which had commenced decades before the early 1700s, still had some way to go by the 1740s. This lack of progress supports assessments of early eighteenth-century Scotland and Ireland that stress hesitant economic and social change and the partial nature of the countries' integration into Anglo-Britain and its overseas colonial systems.[91]

However, this conclusion is partial at best. The decades between the 1690s and the 1740s were in fact hugely important. Their significance does not lie in any conspicuous breakthrough into the EIC: no dramatic upsurge in Irish, Scots or Welsh involvement occurred. What happened was far less obvious and much closer to home. It was during these decades that provincial migrants in London slowly consolidated multiple avenues of contact with the Company. This crucial process happened organically and unspectacularly. Far more eye-catching population movements across the North Channel and the Atlantic explain the persistent underestimation of migration from Ireland and Scotland to the metropolis from the 1690s to the 1740s. Likewise, participation in the Atlantic was possible without working through London. However, the city was unavoidable for any individual or social network contemplating involvement in the Asia trades. Unless posts were obtained in one of the European organisations, prospective sojourners had to take their chances in the metrocentric world of East India Company House. To succeed at Leadenhall Street they needed insider knowledge and patrons who commanded substantial monetary and social capital with the shareholders and with the directorate. These realities explain why expatriates in London were central to the timing, success and limitations of metropolitan provincial involvement.

Only once sufficient influence had been built up at Leadenhall Street could a sustained breakthrough occur into the elite sectors of employment. The Welsh and Irish had some initial and distinct advantages over the Scots in this respect. The legal and religious training of Welsh and Protestant Irish middling and professional migrants focused on London to a far greater extent than was the case with their Scottish counterparts. Nevertheless, by the 1720s and 1730s Scottish migrants in the metropole were increasingly supporting their countrymen's lobbying activities. From the 1740s to the 1770s alone approximately one hundred London-Scots sponsored the EIC careers of other Scots. The genesis of a substantial Scottish profile in key sectors rested on the willingness of these metropolitan expatriates to facilitate step and chain emigration to Asia. The seminal importance of these brokers of human capital has been missed in established histories of Scotland in the British Empire, with attention focusing instead on one or two prominent individuals. Compared to the small number of Scots on the directorate, there were always far more London-Scots willing to act as securities, agents or trustees for those in the East Indies. Their pivotal role sprang from a capacity to form meso-networks that unlocked the EIC for a range of micro-networks from north of the border. Their patronage via credentialism is a revealing historical example of social capital's productive capacity to mobilise human capital.

It is clear from the Company's records that London-Irish and London-Welsh interests, which were more than capable of replicating the connective function of Scottish networks, did not do so to the same extent. As a result, applicants lacked the same critical mass of city-based patrons that facilitated the growing drift of Scots to Asia. This had nothing to do with an inability to forge such links, simply that Irish and Welsh webs were aligned to exploit London's domestic patronage in the areas of church, learning and law to a greater degree. This difference was to have a major impact on wider patterns of Scottish, Irish and Welsh participation in British Asia.

Notes

1 M. A. Lyons, 'The Emergence of an Irish Community in Saint-Malo, 1550–1710', and J. Parmentier, 'Irish Mercantile Builders in Ostend, 1690–1790', in T. O'Connor and M. A. Lyons (eds), *Irish Communities in Early-Modern Europe* (Dublin: Four Courts, 2006), pp. 120–5 and pp. 367–78; S. P. Sen, *The*

French in India, 1763–1816 (New Delhi: M. Manoharlal, 1971), pp. 39–43; L. M. Cullen, 'Merchant Communities Overseas, the Navigation Acts and Irish and Scottish Responses', in L. M. Cullen and T. C. Smout (eds), *Comparative Aspects of Scottish and Irish Economic History, 1600–1900* (Edinburgh: John Donald, 1977), p. 169; A. Mackillop, 'Accessing Empire: Scotland, Britain, Europe and the Asia Trade, c.1690–1750', *Itinerario*, 29 (2005), 15–17; L. Müller, 'Scottish and Irish Entrepreneurs in Eighteenth-Century Sweden', in Dickson, Parmentier and Ohlmeyer, *Irish and Scottish Mercantile Networks*, pp. 149–63.

2 McGilvary, *East India Patronage*, pp. 12–67; Fraser, 'Ireland and India', pp. 79–80; Crosbie, *Irish Imperial Networks*, pp. 44–57; Mackillop, '"A Reticent People?"'; Bowen, 'Asiatic Interactions'; Rees, 'Welsh Sojourners in India', 165–87.

3 Andrew Mackillop, 'Locality, Nation and Empire: the Scots in Asia, c.1695–1813', in John M. MacKenzie and T. M. Devine (eds), *The Oxford History of the British Empire: Scotland and the British Empire* (Oxford: Oxford University Press, 2011), pp. 62–3; Craig Bailey, *Irish London: Middle-Class Migration in the Global Eighteenth Century* (Liverpool: Liverpool University Press, 2013), pp. 5, 17.

4 J. Taylor, *A Cup of Kindness: The History of the Royal Scottish Corporation, 1603–2003* (East Linton: Tuckwell, 2003); E. Jones (ed.), *The Welsh in London* (Cardiff: University of Wales, 2001); D. Hancock, *Citizens of the World*, passim; C. Bailey, 'Metropole and Colony: Irish Networks and Patronage in the Eighteenth-Century Empire', *Immigrants & Minorities*, 23 (2005), 161–81.

5 C. Bailey, 'The Nesbitts of London and Their Networks'; L. M. Cullen, 'The Two Fitzgeralds of London, 1718–1759'; T. M. Truxes, 'London's Irish Merchant Community and North Atlantic Commerce in the Mid-Eighteenth Century', all in Dickson, Parmentier and Ohlmeyer, *Irish and Scottish Mercantile Networks*, pp. 231–309; Bailey, *Irish London*, passim.

6 Crosbie, *Irish Imperial Networks*, pp. 17–23, 253–62.

7 Colley, *Britons*, pp. 124–5.

8 H. Horwitz, 'The East India Trade: The Politicians and the Constitution: 1689–1702', *Journal of British Studies*, 17 (1977), 10–15.

9 R. Mackenzie, *A Full and Exact Account of the Proceedings of the Court of Directors and Council-General of the Company of Scotland Trading to Africa and the Indies with Relation to the Treaty of Union now under Parliament's Consideration* (Edinburgh, n.p., 1706), pp. 7–20; Mackillop, 'A Union for Empire?', 116–34; Stern, *The Company State*, pp. 159–62.

10 Furber, *Rival Empires of Trade*, pp. 98–100; D. W. Jones, *War and Economy in the Age of William III and Marlborough* (London: Blackwell, 1988), pp. 334–5; Lawson, *East India Company*, pp. 53–5.

11 W. J. Barber, *British Economic Thought and India, 1600–1858* (Oxford: Clarendon Press, 1975), pp. 36–9, 45–6; IOR, B/40, pp. 77, 88, 195; IOR, B/42, p. 1.

12 J. Robertson, 'Empire and Union: Two Concepts of the Early Modern European Political Order', in John Robertson (ed.), *A Union for Empire: Political Thought and the British Union of 1707* (Cambridge: Cambridge University Press, 1995), pp. 34–6; Mackillop, 'A Union for Empire?', 130–1.
13 IOR, B/43, pp. 228, 259; B/45, pp. 49–50, 169; B/47, pp. 1–3; B/50A, pp. 1–64.
14 T. Webster, 'The Political Economy of Trade Liberalization: the East India Company Charter of 1813', *Economic History Review*, 43 (1990), 404.
15 K. N. Chaudhuri, *The Trading World of Asia and the English East India Company, 1660–1760* (Cambridge: Cambridge University Press, 1978), p. 19; Lawson, *East India Company*, p. 165.
16 N. Steengaard, 'The Companies as a Specific Institution in the History of European Expansion', in L. Blussé and F. Gaastra (eds), *Companies and Trade: Essays on Overseas Trading Companies during the Ancien Régime* (Leiden: Leiden University Press, 1981), pp. 245–64; Bowen, *The Business of Empire*, pp. 21–2.
17 J. R. Woodhead, *The Rulers of London, 1660–1689* (London: Arrowsmith, 1965), pp. 15–181; IOR, B/61, pp. 261, 409; P. Withington, *The Politics of Commonwealth: Citizens and Freemen in Early Modern England* (Cambridge: Cambridge University Press, 2005), pp. 127–30.
18 IOR, H/78, pp. 681–732; B/62, p. 478; J/1/8, p. 386; O/1/1: Bonds and Agreements, 1741–91; NLS, Acc 9769/30/4/372.
19 Cain and Hopkins, *British Imperialism*, pp. 30–1, 60–1; J. Smail, 'Credit, Risk and Honor in Eighteenth-Century Commerce', *Journal of British Studies*, 44 (2005), 439–45; Stern, *The Company State*, p. 18.
20 IOR, B/41, p. 47; B/43, pp. 212–13; B/56, pp. 236–6; B/62, pp. 546–7.
21 IOR, J/1/1–28.
22 NRS, GD24/1/464 (n) 33–4, 86.
23 G. K. McGilvary, 'East India Patronage and the Political Management of Scotland, 1720–1774' (PhD dissertation, The Open University, 1989), p. 209; IOR, B/49, p. 209; J. G. Parker, 'The Directors of the East India Company, 1754–1790', 2 vols (PhD dissertation, University of Edinburgh, 1977), vol. I, pp. 73–5; NRS, GD24/1/495/42–3.
24 Stern, *The Company State*, pp. 102–3.
25 IOR, B/42, pp. 96, 128–9.
26 Devine, *Scotland's Empire*, p. xxiii; D. Allan, *Scotland in the Eighteenth Century* (London: Longman, 2002), p. 165; A. I. Macinnes, *Union and Empire: The Making of the United Kingdom in 1707* (Cambridge: Cambridge University Press, 2007), pp. 5–6, 325–6.
27 Marshall, 'British Society in India', 101; Anon., *Administration of Justice in Bengal. The Several Petitions of the British Inhabitants of Bengal ...* (London: n.p., 1780), pp. 46, 107; NRS, RH4/51, 'Letter Book of Sir John Lindsay, 1770–71', pp. 18–19, 32–7.
28 Lawson, *East India Company*, p. 56; *An Act for assuring to the English company trading to the East-Indies, on account of the united stock, a longer time in the fund and trade* (London: n.p., 1707) pp. 306–7.

29 IOR, H/78, p. 107; B/53, pp. 164, 223; B/71, p. 347.
30 Nicholas Rogers, 'Money, Land and Lineage: The Big Bourgeoisie of Hanoverian London', *Social History*, 4 (1979), 437–54.
31 Mackillop, 'Accessing Empire', 15.
32 Mackillop, '"A Reticent People?"'.
33 IOR, B 41, pp. 109, 113; B/43, pp. 463–5, 697–8; B/48, pp. 822, 840; B/49, p. 827; B/51, p. 276; B/55, p. 229; B/58, p. 219; B/67, pp. 497–8, 511.
34 Wilson, *Sense of the People*, p. 153; Linda Colley, *Captives: Britain, Empire and the world, 1600–1850* (London: Jonathan Cape, 2002), pp. 254–5.
35 Lawson, *East India Company*, p. 33; Joseph Wagner, 'The Scottish East India Company of 1617: Patronage, Commercial Rivalry, and the Union of the Crowns', *Journal of British Studies*, 59 (2020), 582–607; IOR, B/41, pp. 72–4, 81–4, 90; *The Scots Magazine*, 2 (1740), pp. 377, 419.
36 *Reasons why the East-India Company ought to pay the equivolent agreed to be paid the Scots Company by the articles of union: and also some cautions offer'd with respect to the renewal of their grant* (London: n.p., 1708), pp. 1–4; *Scots Magazine*, 50 (1788), pp. 281, 567.
37 *Scots Magazine*, 1 (1739), pp. 139, 361–3, 623; C. A. Whatley, *Scottish Society, 1707–1830* (Manchester: Manchester University Press, 2000), pp. 60–1, 105–8; R. B. McDowell, *Ireland in the Age of Imperialism and Revolution, 1760–1801* (Oxford: Clarendon Press, 1991), pp. 313–14.
38 IOR, B/47, p. 238; B/51, p. 85; B/62, pp. 529–31; HL, Stowe Collection, ST 58/4, p. 171.
39 L. M. Cullen 'Economic Development, 1750–1800', in T. W. Moody and V. E. Vaughan (eds), *A New History of Ireland* (Oxford: Clarendon Press, 1986), pp. 173, 193; Martyn Powell, *The Politics of Consumption in Eighteenth-Century Ireland* (London: Palgrave Macmillan, 2005), passim.
40 D. Ditchburn, *Scotland and Europe: The Medieval Kingdom and Its Contacts with Christendom, c.1215–1545* (East Linton: Tuckwell, 2000), pp. 245, 256; Williams, *When Was Wales?*, pp. 122, 140–1; P. Jenkins, *The Making of a Ruling Class: The Glamorgan Gentry, 1640–1790* (Cambridge: Cambridge University Press, 1983), pp. 22, 239–41; E. Jones, 'The Age of Societies', in Jones, *The Welsh in London*, pp. 54–5.
41 L. M. Cullen, *Anglo-Irish Trade, 1600–1800* (New York: A. M. Kelley, 1968), pp. 16, 43–5; Bailey, *Irish London*, p. 164.
42 T. M. Devine, *The Scottish Nation, 1700–2000* (London: Penguin, 1999), pp. 56–7; T. M. Devine, 'The Union of 1707 and Scottish Development', *Scottish Economic and Social History*, 5 (1985), 32.
43 NRS, GD24/1/464/D/47; Whatley, *Scottish Society*, pp. 24–5, 36, 53–55; Eric J. Graham, *A Maritime History of Scotland 1650–1790* (East Linton: Tuckwell, 2002), p. 239; Taylor, *A Cup of Kindness*, pp. 8–11; A. Mackillop, 'Dundee, London and the Empire in Asia', in Christopher Whatley, Charles MacKean and Bob Harris (eds), *Dundee: A History* (Dundee: Dundee University Press, 2009), pp. 160–86.

44 Jenkins, *Making of a Ruling Class*, pp. 225–6; Barnard, *A New Anatomy of Ireland*, pp. 16–17; Bailey, 'Metropole and Colony', 164–5.
45 J. H. McCulloch, *The Scot in England* (London: Hurst & Blackett, 1935), pp. 74–94, 121–5; R. A. Cage, 'The Scots in England', in R. A. Cage (ed.), *The Scots Abroad: Labour, Capital, Enterprise, 1750–1914* (London: Croom Helm, 1985), pp. 39–43; Stana Nenadic, 'Introduction', in Stana Nenadic (ed.), *Scots in London in the Eighteenth Century* (Lewisburg, PA: Bucknell University Press, 2010), pp. 9–13.
46 G. P. Insh, *Scottish Colonial Schemes, 1620–1686* (Glasgow: Maclehose, Jackson & Co., 1922), p. 47.
47 LMA, LMA/4365/A/001–2: Session Books of the Scots-Church in Swallow St., Westminster, 1735–1806; George G. Cameron, *The Scots Kirk in London* (Oxford: Becket, 1979), pp. 19, 30–9.
48 *An Account of the Rise, Progress and Present State of the Most Honourable and Loyal Society of Ancient Britons* (London: n.p., 1800), pp. 7–8, 23–32; *A Summary of the View of the Rise, Constitution, and Present State of the Charitable Foundation of King Charles the Second, commonly called the Scots Corporation* (London: n.p., 1738), pp. 9–27; *An Account of the Institution, Progress, and Present State of the Scottish Corporation in London* (London: n.p. 1806), pp. 15–43.
49 D. Catterall, 'At Home Abroad: Ethnicity and Enclave in the World of Scottish Traders in Northern Europe c.1600–1800', *Journal of Early Modern History*, 8 (2004), 319–36.
50 Taylor, *A Cup of Kindness*, pp. 52–3; NRS, GD24/1/464/E/49.
51 CSAS, Hunter-Blair Papers, Box 1/1/32.
52 Canny, 'Introduction', in *Oxford History of the British Empire*, I, p. 18; S. Vance, 'A Man for all Regions – Patrick Copland and Education in the Stuart World', in Allan I. Macinnes and Arthur H. Williamson (eds), *Shaping the Stuart World, 1603–1714. The Atlantic Connection* (Leiden: Brill, 2005), pp. 58, 62–3.
53 J. H. Ohlmeyer, 'A Laboratory for Empire? Early Modern Ireland and English Imperialism', in K. Kenny (ed.), *Ireland and the British Empire* (Oxford: Oxford University Press, 2004), pp. 52–6; Ohlmeyer, 'Eastward Enterprises', pp. 83–118; Stern, *The Company State*, pp. 113–14.
54 GUL, MS Hunter 73 (T.3.11.), fo. 59.
55 H. D. Love (ed.), *Vestiges of Old Madras, 1640–1800*, 3 vols (London: John Murray, 1913), vol. I, pp. 483, 496; vol. II, pp. 66–70, 103; IOR, B/41, p. 712; B/44, pp. 11, 284; B/46, p. 70; B/47, pp. 375–6.
56 A. Mackillop and S. Murdoch, 'Introduction', in A. Mackillop and S. Murdoch (eds), *Military Governors & Imperial Frontiers, c.1600–1800: A Study of Scotland and Empires* (Leiden: Brill, 2003), pp. xxxvi–vii; A. I. Macinnes, 'Union Failed, Union Accomplished: The Irish Union of 1703 and the Scottish Union of 1707', in D. Keogh and K. Whelan (eds), *Acts of Union: The Causes, Contexts, and Consequences of the Act of Union* (Dublin: Four Courts, 2001), pp. 74–8.

57 TNA, PROB 11/371, p. 32; ACA, Propinquity Book, 1637–1705, fo. 152; Propinquity Book, 1706–1733, fo. 16; NRS, CC8/8/84, p. 874.
58 NRS, CC8/8/83, pp. 780–2; ACA, Propinquity Book, 1706–1733, fos. 29, 40.
59 R. Woodrow, *Analecta: or, materials for a History of Remarkable Providences; mostly relating to Scotch Ministers and Christians*, 3 vols (Edinburgh: Maitland Club, 1843), vol. III, pp. 23–4, 36.
60 IOR, B/43–B/49. See B/49, pp. 320, 840, 860.
61 Devine, *Scotland's Empire*, pp. 42–6; D. Watt, *The Price of Scotland: Darien, Union and the Wealth of Nations* (Edinburgh: Luath, 2007), pp. 39, 210–11.
62 G. P. Insh, 'The Founding of the Company of Scotland Trading to Africa and the Indies', *The Scottish History Review*, 22 (1924), 289–95; T. Thomson (ed.), *The Acts of the Parliaments of Scotland*, 9 (Edinburgh: n.p., 1822), pp. 377–8; *A Summary of the View of the Rise, Constitution, and Present State*, pp. 9–27.
63 Woodhead, *Rulers of London*, p. 72; IOR, B/41, pp. 81–4.
64 IOR, B/43, pp. 413, 423; *A Summary of the View of the Rise, Constitution, and Present State*, p. 14; HL, Stowe Collection, ST 58/1, p. 12.
65 IOR, B/41, pp. 299, 306; B/42, pp. 128–9; Watt, *The Price of Scotland*, pp. 58, 120–1.
66 IOR, B/51, pp. 172, 305, 507, 517; B/54, p. 557.
67 *A Summary of the View of the Rise, Constitution, and Present State*, p. 24; IOR, B/42, p. 1; B/54, pp. 2, 275, 469–70, 481; B/57, p. 570; TNA, PROB 11/592, pp. 344–6; PROB 11/604, pp. 48–9.
68 McGilvary, *East India Patronage*, pp. 38–67; Mackillop, 'Accessing Empire', 22–3; T. M. Devine, 'Scottish Elites and the Indian Empire', in Smout, *Anglo-Scottish Relations*, pp. 223–9.
69 NRS, GD345/1157/1/3; GD345/1155/2/14; GD 345/1155/5/6; GD345/1155/7/25; GD345/1155/8/5; GD345/1155/9/16; GD345/1155/10/15, 18, 24, 32, 35, 43; NLS, MS16526, fos. 65–6; MS16549, fos. 231–2.
70 NLS, MS16536, fo. 50; HL, Stowe Collection, ST 57/vol. 1, pp. 94–6.
71 Hancock, *Citizens of the World*, pp. 52–7.
72 GCA, Bogle Papers, Bo. 7/2.
73 E. A. Wrigley, 'A Simple Model of London's Importance in Changing English Society and Economy 1650–1750', *Past & Present*, 37 (1967), 44–70; Cain and Hopkins, *British Imperialism*, pp. 321–2.
74 P. Bourdieu, 'The Forms of Capital', pp. 248–9; L. N. Rosenband, 'Social Capital in the Early Industrial Revolution', *Journal of Interdisciplinary History*, 29 (1999), 436.
75 A. Farrington, *A Biographical Index of East India Company Maritime Service Officers, 1600–1834* (London: British Library, 1999), p. 231; NRS, GD24/1/464/D/5; GD 24/1/463/45, 47–8, 93.
76 NRS, GD18/5218/35–8, 40–2, 49, 52, 56.
77 C. Brooks, 'Apprenticeship, Social Mobility and the Middling Sort, 1550–1800', in J. Barry and C. Brooks (eds), *The Middling Sort of People: Culture, Society and Politics in England, 1550–1800* (London: Macmillan, 1996), p. 60.
78 IOR, B/41, pp. 99, 110–11.

79 IOR, B/51, p. 635.
80 IOR, B/52, pp. 595, 602; B/70, p. 95; Barnard, *A New Anatomy of Ireland*, p. 282.
81 P. Lawson and J. Philips, '"Our Execrable Banditti": Perceptions of Nabobs in Mid-Eighteenth Century Britain', *Albion*, 16 (1984), 226–40.
82 Bailey, 'The Nesbitts of London', pp. 231–49; IOR, B/70, pp. 539, 542–3; B/71, pp. 262, 267, 611–12; J/1/1, pp. 139–42.
83 IOR, B/82, p. 365; J/1/6, pp. 370–72; Bailey, *Irish London*, pp. 62, fn. 16, 162–4.
84 Bailey, *Irish London*, pp. 54–86.
85 The list of Scots Corporation members includes only those giving more than £5.
86 NLS, MS1328, fo. 254; MS1367, fo. 82; IOR, J/1/4, pp. 68–70; B/76, pp. 203–4, 271; O/5/30, fos. 210–13.
87 NLS, MS1367, fo. 6; IOR, B/67, pp. 148, 152.
88 IOR, B/72, p. 281; B/73, pp. 529, 537; B/76, pp. 271, 367; B/77, pp. 188, 271; B/79, pp. 246, 305; J/1/1, pp. 53–6; J/1/4, pp. 233, 282–5.
89 G. McGilvary, *Guardian of the East India Company: The Life of Laurence Sulivan* (London: I.B.Tauris, 2006), pp. 27–30; Parker, 'Directors of the East India Company', vol. I, pp. 182–6; Farrington, *Biographical Index*, p. 550.
90 Douglas Hamilton, 'Scotland and the Eighteenth Century Empire', in T. M. Devine and Jenny Wormald (eds), *The Oxford Handbook of Modern Scottish History* (Oxford: Oxford University Press, 2012), pp. 424–6; David Dickson, *Cork: Old World Colony: Cork and South Munster 1630–1830* (Cork: Cork University Press, 2005), pp. 149–69.
91 Devine, *The Scottish Nation*, pp. 16–17, 24, 54–7; Whatley, *Scottish Society*, pp. 50–64, 100–108; D. Dickson, *New Foundations: Ireland 1660–1800* (Dublin: Criterion Press, 1987), pp. 102–3; L. M. Cullen, *An Economic History of Ireland since 1660* (London: Batsford Press, 1987), p. 52.

2

The brokers of human capital: shareholders and directors

The emergence from the 1690s to the early 1740s of sustained links between the EIC and expatriate social networks in London constituted a vital prerequisite for wider involvement in the corporation and its operations overseas. That demonstrable influence in the city was required for metropolitan provincial participation in one whole hemisphere of the Empire provides cogent support for the concept of gentlemanly capitalism and its focus on the central role of London. Yet the extent and nature of the city's control remains a matter of debate. Although there has been a recalibration of the metropole's power to one of 'relative' rather than absolute hegemony, not least through the articulation of ideas of gentry capitalism, this important revision has yet to be tested in detail against the distinctive conditions of the pre-1815 empire in Asia.[1] This lack of coverage is because debates over gentlemanly capitalism remain rooted in the nineteenth and early twentieth centuries. What studies do exist of the long eighteenth century tend to accept the basic premise, viewing even major Company settlements like Madras and Calcutta as financial extensions of London.[2]

Besides this skewed temporal coverage there is the question of how the capital's links with its own domestic provinces are best characterised. Understanding Scottish, Irish and Welsh society's interaction with the gentlemanly capitalist economy remains a work in progress and has implications for more than just the national histories of the three countries.[3] The changing basis of Britain's expansion, for example, can be considered in a different light. How England's empire evolved as a consequence of greater metropolitan provincial engagement has developed into two distinct strands of thought. One perspective is that the growing presence of Irish and Scottish individuals and networks simply meant a diversification of personnel rather than a fundamental modification of England's pre-existing forms of empire.[4]

Set against this reading is the proposition that the early to mid-eighteenth century marked the end of the seventeenth-century empire forged largely, although by no means exclusively, through English expansion. In its place there evolved a genuinely British and even multinational enterprise.[5] While much of the outward institutional, legal and financial structure remained resolutely English in character, the imperial project became far more heterogeneous as the century progressed. Analysis of this crucial development emphasises its excentric character, with the most dramatic manifestations of growing provincial participation occurring overseas. Large numbers of Irish and Scots, but not it seems Welsh, appeared in the transatlantic provisioning trades, in the slavery-based economies in the Caribbean, commerce in Chesapeake tobacco and Hudson's Bay furs and in the navy and army. They also constituted an increasingly disproportionate component of the mass migration to North America which underpinned coercive settler colonialism. Welsh participation was defined less by the movement of people and instead involved South Wales's economic integration into the British Atlantic.[6] The metrocentric aspects of this provincialisation of empire are less well understood, although Irish, Welsh and Scots migration into the city is receiving increasingly effective attention.[7] Recovering patterns of shareholding and the patronage strategies of Scots, Irish and Welsh in the EIC helps place the metropole more fully into an understanding of how English imperialism became a broader British and Irish phenomenon.

The emergence in the Company of shareholders and directors from Irish, Scottish and Welsh backgrounds also provides a historicised case study of the interaction of human and social capital with a monetary-intensive sector of Britain's globalising imperial economy. Acquiring EIC shares or a directorship required the deployment of what were by contemporary standards vast amounts of finance. It is hardly surprising that the EIC is taken to exemplify gentlemanly capitalism's command over unprecedented levels of money and credit.[8] In this context, possession of corporate stock and access to the directorate were vital if senior figures were to act as brokers of human capital on a larger and more consistent scale.

Not enough is known about the sequence in which the differently constituted forms of wealth interacted: did finance capital have to be deployed before the human or social variants could be successfully mobilised, or could the latter help generate the former? If monetary assets constituted the only real means of realising the human and social equivalents, and not the other way around, then the implications for the metropolitan provinces were profound. A lack of venture capital might well impair the full use of human and social resources as proxy wealth and so inhibit access to expansion and the Empire's more lucrative sectors. Both this eventuality and the alternative scenario, where human and social networks generated conventional forms of profits, can be explored through an analysis of shareholders and directors linked to the metropolitan provinces. This focus on how provincial gentry capitalism intersected with City gentlemanly capitalism better reveals the timing and methods by which individuals and networks from Ireland, Scotland and Wales accessed one of London's key imperial institutions. This province-to-City alignment also enables a recalibrating of the pre-1815 gentlemanly capitalist economy by both recentring and partially decentring London's regulation of the imperial project. Surveying these perspectives offers new insights into the extent to which empire enabled start-up strategies based upon non-monetary forms of assets and socially constructed wealth.

Shareholding

Writing from Calcutta on 26 December 1770 to his brother Robert in London, the Company civil servant, George Bogle observed: 'I hope you are so intimate with the great people in the Direction that it may rather be of service to me.'[9] Better known for his later travels in Tibet and his empathetic association with the Panchen Lama, Lobsang Palden Yeshe, Bogle's injunction draws attention to the constant networking that framed his time in Asia.[10] Although Bogle would later benefit from the patronage of Governor-General Warren Hastings, his instinct to look for leverage in London was a trait common to all connected with the Company.[11] For human capital to operate effectively it needed constant supplementation. This necessitated the nurturing, adaptation and deployment of network influence in Scottish, Irish and Welsh localities, in London and between these locations and the Company's power centres in Asia.[12] A fundamental precondition for success involved either direct participation in EIC shareholding or, for those lacking the requisite monetary reserves, the forging of connections with those with the wealth to purchase stocks. This blending of social and financial resources underlines how the EIC functioned as a corporation in which multiple forms of capital – monetary, human and social – were deployed as viable currencies.

Viewed in this light, the Company can be conceived of as a permeable monopoly. Its court of shareholders exemplifies this aspect of its character. From its inception in 1709 the nominally sovereign body of the United English East India Company was the General Court of Proprietors. Anyone possessing £500 in stock could attend and vote on its deliberations, including their choice of directors: under the terms of the 1773 Regulating Act the voting qualification was raised to £1,000.[13] For those with the requisite means, the proprietary court was an open door into the heart of the organisation. It is not necessary to support the characterisation of England as an intrinsically *ancien régime* society to nevertheless view the Company's court as a distinctive 'estate', with its own privileges and liberties. It formed part of a highly corporatised English polity and political culture.[14] Interpreting the Company in this way draws attention to its role as a site of extra-parliamentary patronage lobbying. The existence in the metropolis of this corporate forum shaped the political dynamic between London and the metropolitan provinces. The exclusion of Ireland from British parliamentary politics until 1801 and the structural underrepresentation of Scots at Westminster after 1707 might have restricted influence in London to a privileged few with direct connections to MPs.[15] An important reason why this eventuality did not occur was that the metropolis had more than one major political forum: there were multiple entry points into the City's gentlemanly capitalist politics, economy and empire. The amount of people with a stake, however nominal, in the EIC's internal decision-making was surprisingly high. By 1700 the number of shareholders stood at 928: ninety years later those entitled to vote numbered 1,792.[16] By the mid-eighteenth century more people were enfranchised as EIC shareholders than could vote in all of Scotland's burghs during a parliamentary election.[17] The court of stockholders constituted one of the most porous political institutions in the United Kingdom and Ireland and was understood as such in the metropolitan provinces.[18]

Many of the general characteristics of this shareholding group are well known.[19] However, forming even a reasonably accurate assessment of the number of Irish, Scottish, Welsh and regional English stockholders is problematic. The Company's culture of record keeping meant that investors invariably listed London addresses rather than their place of origin in Scotland, Wales and Ireland.[20] Foregrounding their metropolitan credentials proclaimed their genteel status and enabled the Company to demonstrate the confidence it commanded among the capital's monied and investor interests. A published list from 1790 contains at least fourteen Scottish landlords, including Robert Drummond of Megginch, Sir Archibald Campbell of Inverneil, George and Thomas Graham of Kinross-shire and Sir Archibald Edmonstoune. However, all listed their London residences or in the case of Megginch his status as a former commander of the *General Elliot* East Indiaman.[21]

The publishing conventions that shaped the public representation of EIC stockholding served to underplay the number of individuals with connections to the metropolitan provinces. Despite these problems of identification, it is clear that the volume of provincial shareholding increased during the eighteenth century.[22] This upward trajectory developed from a noticeably low starting point. The conventional emphasis on Scottish precociousness within the eighteenth-century empire needs to be tempered by the fact that initial involvement in the Company's finances was minimal. Between 1710 and 1730 the directors' minutes show only one stockholder clearly listed as a Scot, George Mackenzie of Stonehaven, British consul in Moscow, who authorised a transfer of shares (in his case £500). There were others, however. An indication of the possible scale of early investment can be seen in the examples of Major James St Clair and William Fraser in Madras who between them held £3,500 of shares in 1710: neither were listed with any indication of their Scottish origins.[23]

If those noted as living in Scotland were conspicuous by their absence, the directors' minutes do record individuals in Wales transferring £2,814 in stock between 1710 and 1730.[24] Compared to the tentative nature of both Welsh and Scottish shareholding, the scale of Irish involvement in the early decades of the century is noticeable.[25] In the 1720s persons with links to Ireland were involved in transfers registered in the directors' minutes to a greater extent than Scots resident north of the border; ten transfers totalling £9,316 are recorded by people with clear Irish connections between 1710 and 1730. Such transactions reveal some of the kingdom's early links to the Company. Huguenot immigration not only generated important economic ties between Ireland and London but clearly acted as a vital conduit into East India circles.[26] Between the mid-1710s and the 1720s these connections enabled stock trading by Josias de Robillard of Portarlington in Queen's County and Theodore La Caultiere and John Delamer, both of Dublin. The Anglo-Irish aristocracy held considerable investments, far more at this stage than their Scottish counterparts. Shareholders included the baroness of Coleraine, the countess of Leinster, the earl of Orrey and Lord Londonderry.[27] The extent to which these elites perceived themselves to be Irish is debatable. Prior to the emergence of a heightened sense of patriotism among the kingdom's Protestants after the 1720s, these aristocratic and gentry families could just as likely view themselves as the 'English of Ireland'.[28] Nevertheless, their example warns against assumptions that Irish society was somehow predestined for marginalisation within the world of gentlemanly capitalism generated by British imperialism. It looked likely between the 1710s and the 1730s that Irish Protestants rather than Scots would emerge as the main metropolitan-provincial investors in the EIC.

It was from the 1730s to the 1750s that Scots seem to acquire a greater volume of stock. During these decades the directors' minutes show share transfers by individuals in Ireland totalling £9,000. For whatever reason Irish investment levelled off, perhaps being drawn instead into the generally buoyant domestic economy.[29] At the same time, a crucial shift in the Scottish profile intensified as aristocrats such as the dukes of Atholl and Argyll, Rotterdam-based merchants like Adam Duncan from Lundie in Angus and the directors of the Bank of Scotland began committing capital to the eastern wing of British expansion. The result between 1730 and 1750 was share transfers by Scots totalling at least £25,000.[30] This pattern of

Table 2.1 Scottish, Irish and Welsh EIC stockholders, 1790[31]

Total	Nationality (%)	Total Votes
1,792	Scots = 69 (3.8)	91
	Irish = 18 (1.0)	21
	Welsh = 7 (0.33)	9

(Source: *Names of those Members of the United Company ... 13th April 1790*, pp. 1–75).

greater Scottish involvement held true for the rest of the century. The totals in Table 2.1 show investors with at least £1,000 in stock living Scotland, Ireland or Wales, or who originated from those countries that can be securely traced to London or Asia.

As with other findings from the corporation's archive, these figures are symptomatic rather than conclusive. They underestimate overall Irish, Welsh and Scottish involvement. While the incidence of surnames associated with the metropolitan provinces would inflate the total for all three groupings, this is not a robust method. An indeterminate number of Scots, Irish and Welsh residing in London cannot be identified definitively and so are not included. The numbers that can be confirmed do however reveal important differences between the three provincial societies. There were over three times as many Scottish shareholders as there were Irish, with this ratio rising to nearly a factor of ten in the case of the Welsh comparison.

However, it is the overall percentages in Table 2.1 that are most revealing. Even taking into account the disguising effect of the preference for London addresses, the figures show a substantial metropolitan provincial underrepresentation within the shareholders.[32] This marginal profile indicates how Scots, Irish and Welsh, or at least those resident outside of London, were far less involved in one of the most finance-intensive branches of gentlemanly capitalism. This was especially the case when compared to the increasing role of Ireland and Scotland in the demography and commerce of the Atlantic colonies. If people rather than money represented the primary route into the western empire, the same pattern was to hold true in relation to Asia.[33]

While constraints on venture finance made relying on human capital more realistic, the solution created its own problems. The lack of stockholders could become a major barrier to a more generalised involvement in the EIC. Insufficient numbers threatened a lack of influence at the proprietary court which in turn would inhibit a trickle-up and trickle-down effect. Shareholders elected the twenty-four directors, each of whom was required to hold at least £2,000 in stock to qualify for office.[34] Not surprisingly, directors constantly curried the favour of stockholders and vice versa. Charles Boddam's comments in 1778 to a fellow director confirm how proprietors exerted upward pressure for favours and places. Writing on behalf of the London merchants, Charles and David Webster, originally from Dundee, he noted:

> You know the importunes of friends here for letters of recommendation abroad, and such is my case ... from the two brothers Webster, both staunch proprietors always in my interest. Their nephew, the bearer, Mr Charles Wedderburn, being brought up a surgeon, has leave to go out to Bengal. I give him this address to you just to introduce him to your notice.[35]

Investors from Ireland acted in much the same manner. In 1780 James Alexander from Londonderry, a retired Bengal civil servant who later became first earl of Caledon, informed an associate that he intended retaining his stock to protect friends still in India.[36] The London-based merchants and financiers, Sir William and Robert Mayne, who originated from Stirlingshire, mirrored Alexander's actions exactly (see Appendix 6.1). In 1775 they informed their Kinross kinsman John Graham, in Bengal: 'We have for many years held each of us a qualification, tho' a considerable loss, to serve our friends on your side [Asia] and to enable us now and again to provide for a relation.'[37] Stockholding acted as a political lever as well as a conventional financial asset. It was a form of corporate enfranchisement which facilitated the close links between patronage and credentialism that enabled the mobilisation of human capital. Viewed in this light, Table 2.1 shows that Scots held a real advantage when lobbying proprietors and directors for posts or for advancement once in Asia.

EIC patronage also had a higher profile in Scottish political culture when compared with conditions in Ireland. To a greater degree than Edinburgh, eighteenth-century Dublin functioned as the centre of a substantial civil, clerical, revenue and military establishment. For Ireland's Protestant elite, though not for the disenfranchised Catholic majority, there were simply more domestic options when seeking posts and offices.[38] A comparison of the patronage available to the Scottish political manager, Henry Dundas with that dispersed by the lord lieutenant of Ireland, William Grenville, first marquis of Buckingham, demonstrates this crucial distinction. From 1782 to 1799 Dundas's own papers show him dispersing 168 offices from the Scottish customs and excise, the universities, judiciary and the Kirk – an average of nine per annum. In 1787 alone Buckingham allocated thirty-eight posts, mainly staff commissions in the army's Irish establishment, places in the Church of Ireland or employment in the barrack and linen departments.[39]

A constricted domestic infrastructure in Scotland displaced familial, local and regional interests into London. Imperial patronage played a growing role in the political culture of both kingdoms and Wales. But it loomed larger in Scotland. The EIC developed as a focal point for familial and social networks reacting to the straitened conditions of patronage north of the border. The highly corporatised nature of post-union Scotland's political culture chimed with that of the EIC in ways not so readily evident in the other two metropolitan provinces. The corporation's ethos of shareholder politics mirrored franchise practice (and malpractice) in Scotland. Well used to dividing their landed superiorities to generate additional voters, Scottish elites would have immediately recognised the tactic of splitting stock to generate additional leverage in the court of proprietors. These methods of vote creation in London and in the Scottish counties diversified access to influence while maximising the productivity of investor capital and landed estates in exactly the same manner.[40] The negative and positive pressures driving networks into the metropolis have implications for understanding the patterns in Table 2.1. These were less the result of greater Scottish financial resources than evidence of a pronounced reliance on metropolitan and imperial avenues of employment.

Whichever factors generated the larger Scottish profile among the shareholders, the longer-term implications were significant. William Johnstone-Pulteney from Westerhall in Dumfriesshire, a well-connected proprietor at the heart of an imperial-familial network that exemplifies provincial gentry capitalism, demonstrates what just one shareholder could attempt.[41] Between 1764 and 1784 he received at least twenty-two requests from kinsmen and associates in the Scottish Borders, Lanarkshire, Edinburgh and Inverness-shire to use his influence with the directors.[42] Not all these applications were successful. Yet Johnstone-Pulteney's investor status created a robust conduit into one of the Empire's key institutions. His lobbying reveals that it did not take a large number of shareholders to act as an access point to the corporation's metropolitan elite and the large reserves of employment they controlled. Possession of sufficient monetary capital to acquire stock expedited credentialism and brokering of its social and human equivalents. Crucially, Scotland had greater numbers of these brokers than either of the other two metropolitan provinces.

The directors: commercial lords of men

Proprietors not only lobbied directors – some aspired to the directorate. This was an understandable ambition. The director Joseph Hume, originally from Montrose, used a striking analogy in 1813 when he likened an EIC directorship to 'a sort of Commercial Peerage in the City [of London]'.[43] These men presided at East India Company House on Leadenhall Street and played a fundamental role in the corporation's initial phases of expansion and colonialism. Although the Crown increasingly co-opted their political and military authority after 1773, a wide range of posts remained within their gift. By the early 1700s the main presidencies – Calcutta, Madras and Bombay – operated as sophisticated commercial, financial and governmental outposts, mirroring in miniature the corporate world of the Company in London.[44] From these settlements emanated the tangled processes of informal commercial expansion and formal political, military and economic imperialism that characterised relations with South Asian successor states from the 1740s to 1850s. Smaller factories like Tellicherry, Masulipatam, Patna or Dacca served as subsidiaries for the main ports. Other bases like Gambroon on the Gulf or Benkulen in South-East Asia functioned as entrepôts for the inter-Asia 'country' trade. In the case of Saint Helena, the settlement secured transhemispheric lines of communication.[45] The most unusual Company bridgehead was at Canton. With settlement strictly regulated by the Chinese authorities, a seven-strong council of supercargoes negotiated one of the EIC's most dynamic sites of commerce.[46]

It was to these settlements and onboard the outward and homeward fleets of East Indiamen that the directors sent the vast majority of their civil, maritime, medical and military appointees. Already substantial by the 1690s, the pool of offices increased rapidly as the EIC acquired greater political, military, fiscal and administrative power in South Asia from the later 1740s. The Company employed approximately 1,000 civil and medical servants in the East Indies at any one time by 1800, in addition to some 35,000 military and marine officers, rank-and-file European soldiers and sailors.[47] No other non-state organisation in Britain, Ireland or the Empire employed anything like this number of people. As with the VOC, the EIC was a voracious consumer of human resources. While histories of the organisation emphasise its financial sophistication, its constant drive for new markets and its innovative mixed-sovereignty colonialism, its need for human capital was no less significant. The rapid turnover in personnel through mortality and return to Europe kept numbers in Asia at any one time deceptively low, disguising the large overall volume of appointments. For those provincial regions of Britain and Ireland which relied to a greater degree on the deployment of human and social assets, the EIC's incessant and predictable demand for a range of high- and low-value manpower made it an ideal prospect. Human capital, just as surely as its monetary equivalent, played a key role in the complex balance of political, economic, cultural, racial and demographic factors that shaped the character of the Company's emerging empire.

There is general agreement among historians of pre-1815 British imperialism that the Atlantic hemisphere was of greater political, economic and cultural importance, at least until the 1780s.[48] If viewed in terms of British exports, settler colonialism and a sense of cultural and religious connection, this assessment is indisputable. But as a source of offices suitable for middling-sort sojourners, the Asian hemisphere of empire easily stood comparison with its Atlantic equivalent by the 1750s at the latest and surpassed it thereafter. A list from the early 1790s of colonial offices available to the Crown in New South Wales and in what remained of the Atlantic Empire totalled 157. By contrast, between 1788 and 1792 EIC directors appointed 583 civil servants, cadets and surgeons (an average of 116 per annum) – a total which excluded the large annual hire of at least 100 maritime officers. Conditions in Asia meant the directors knew they would recruit a similar number again over the next five years.[49] There was also a qualitative character to East India patronage. As part of the 1784 Pitt Act reforms that sought to end the endemic corruption and graft of the Company's early raj, civil servants were denied the right to involvement in commerce. In return they had their salaries enhanced as compensation.[50] The attraction of the rapid fortunes made during the initial phase of predatory imperialism from the 1740s to the 1780s gave way to the less dramatic but no less significant appeal of secure and well-paid genteel office holding. In 1785 the Bengal presidency government consisted of 393 civil servants, the lowest paid of which received £150 to £250 per annum; 167 officials received more than £1,000 per annum, a level of remuneration that placed them at the upper reaches of the British social order. Together with the salary of the judiciary (£58,042), a 134-strong staff of surgeons costing £78,830, and a limited number of Crown appointments, the entire Bengal presidency's pay bill stood at over £1 million per annum.[51] Smaller establishments also existed in Madras and Bombay. The EIC's governments in India generated a pool of offices that rendered insignificant the patronage available in Scotland and even outstripped the resources commanded by the lord lieutenant of Ireland. As a commercial project the Company was always of global significance: as an empire of patronage its importance is equally difficult to exaggerate.

Election to the directorate opened up this substantial and annually renewed pool of employment. It was precisely for this reason that Henry Dundas constantly reminded those applying to him that the directors, and not the Board of Control, made the large majority of appointments.[52] But the lack of a strong Irish, Scottish or Welsh profile among the shareholders who chose the directors threatened to impair access to such patronage. A key reason why metropolitan provincials struggled to acquire posts in the early eighteenth century lay partly in the lack of directors with strong links to Scotland, Wales or Ireland. The apex of the corporation remained firmly in the hands of London's established mercantile and financier interests for decades after 1707. The numbers in Table 2.2 illustrate the known Scots, Irish and Welshmen elected to the directorate from the 1750s to 1790s.

Table 2.2 Scottish, Irish and Welsh directors, 1754–1794

Total	Scots (%)	Region	Irish (%)	Region (%)	Welsh (%)	Region (%)
138	11 (7.9)	Borders = 2 Lothians = 2 Edinburgh = 2 NE = 3 Highland = 1 Unknown = 1	4 (2.8)	Ulster = 2 Munster = 1 Unknown = 1	3 (2.1)	S. Wales = 2 Unknown =1

(Source: Parker, 'The Directors of the East India Company', vols I and II, passim).

The overall number of directors was surprisingly small: only 138 individuals held the office from 1754 to 1794, with a further 110 between 1784 and 1834.[53] These totals underline the restrictive nature of the corporation's upper echelons. The metropolitan provincial share was well below each country's percentage of Britain and Ireland's population, but, significantly, well above their presence among the stockholders. This disparity partly reflects the artificially low percentages in Table 2.1, but also points to the need to understand how provincials acquired a greater share of directorships than the minimal shareholder presence might suggest was possible. The distribution trends in Table 2.2 do have some important similarities with Table 2.1: there were significantly more Scots compared to Irish and Welsh. This profile was to have crucial repercussions further down the Company's chain of offices and opportunities.

Regional origins are included where these can be ascertained. The marked bias towards the east coast among the Scottish directors points to how insular links to London shaped wider global connections. Glasgow and the west coast may have cornered the bulk of Scotland's Atlantic enterprise but EIC evidence reveals how other parts of the country and to a lesser extent Ireland developed their own regional pathways into global imperialism. Burghs like Edinburgh, Montrose, Dundee and Aberdeen are not strongly associated with Scottish participation in the eighteenth-century empire.[54] Yet directors like David Scott from Montrose, Sir James Cockburn from Eyemouth, Hugh Inglis from Edinburgh and Simon Fraser from Inverness stand equivalent to Glasgow's tobacco lords. Regionalism characterised the Irish presence too, with Ulster maintaining a high profile among the small number of directors with identifiable Irish origins.

The higher percentage of directors over shareholders shown in Tables 2.1 and 2.2 arose in the context of the corporation's evolution in Asia. The greater (if still insignificant) share of directorships was the direct result of individuals with quite different backgrounds to the established City elite appearing in the court of proprietors in growing numbers. They were returnees who used their success in Asia to access London rather than the other way around, and who saw stockholding as the culmination of their career rather than as an entry point into the EIC.[55] A significant number of the Scots, Welsh and Irish elected to the directorate after 1750 came from these backgrounds. Laurence Sulivan from Cork, the Company's most powerful eighteenth-century director, made his fortune in Bombay in the 1740s, while David Scott operated as a Bombay free merchant between 1763 and 1786.[56] Colonel Sweny Toone from Tipperary, Robert Gregory from Galway, William Wigram whose family came originally from Wexford, John Michie from Aberdeenshire, William Fullerton-Elphinstone from Stirlingshire, Sir William Jones from Pembrokeshire, and Charles Grant from Inverness-shire had successful military, marine, mercantile or administrative careers in Bengal, Madras or Bombay. Upon returning to Britain they were all elected at various times between the 1770s and 1820s.[57]

These returnees illustrate how influence forged at the frontiers of empire gravitated back into the metropolis, blurring and blending the nature of power relationships between putative 'core' and 'periphery'. Their careers point to the mutually constitutive dynamic between human and monetary forms of capital, with the migration of the former into the Empire facilitating the acquisition of the latter at the metropolis. The phenomenon of returning imperial personnel challenges the view of London as the uncomplicated centre from which financial, economic and mercantile power diffused out into the Empire. Viewed in terms of conventional monetary resources, this conception has much to commend it. It is far less effective when attempting to assess the role of human mobility in the creation of conventional wealth. Interaction between the metropolis and Asia operated in multiple and reciprocal ways that challenge the characterisation of the presidency settlements as mere adjuncts to London's financial, social and cultural hegemony.[58] The trajectory of these individuals reveals how high-risk and high-return human mobility constituted an effective and realisable alternative to the lack of finance capital which might otherwise have inhibited the build-up of stockholding. Strategies of human mobility and human capital could, if deployed successfully in Asia, circumvent the lack of financial power that stymied direct access to East India Company House.

Growing provincial engagement was further assisted by the fact that it did not take a large number of directors to disperse employment. John Drummond of Quarrell is the prime example of the early impact made by just one individual. Quarrell's role was hugely significant, especially given his contacts with other London-Scots such as his kinsman, the banker Andrew Drummond of Charing Cross and a wide range of other City financiers.[59] His dispersal of posts to fellow countrymen was widely acknowledged: Thomas Hope of Hope Park noted in 1732 that Drummond was 'the father of all our young countrymen'.⁶⁰ The precise number of those he helped is unclear, with some estimates suggesting at least fifty posts, including thirty civil servant appointments.⁶¹ The directors' minutes and his own correspondence confirm that in the twelve years after 1722 he assisted (at a conservative estimate) thirty-eight Scots in obtaining Company appointments or free mariner and merchant licences.⁶² The influence of a director, or a small group of directors, could be out of all proportion to their number. It is significant in this context that Drummond and Alexander Hume between them served on the directorate from the early 1720s to later 1750s, except when Company bylaws prevented them standing for election.⁶³ By the 1760s and 1770s two or even three Scots could be found on the directorate in any given year, while Sulivan and Robert Gregory were the longest-serving Irishmen consistently elected during these decades. The figures in Table 2.2 actually underestimate the Scottish profile towards the latter decades of the century. By 1794 the presence of Hugh Inglis, William Fullerton-Elphinstone, Simon Fraser, Charles Grant and David Scott meant Scots routinely held one in five places on the directorate.⁶⁴ Individuals from Irish and Welsh backgrounds never acquired this sort of critical mass and so involvement from these areas developed accordingly.

Patronage as credentialism: investing in human capital

While clearly a prestigious office, acting as a director was never easy. As Charles Boddam observed, there was a constant barrage of requests for patronage and promotion. This province-to-metropolis pressure was one of the great engines driving the development of an integrated British-Irish politics, economy and society. Yet it also generated pressures which tested even the well-known patience of John Drummond of Quarrell. Writing to his brother in 1731 after yet another wave of solicitations, he complained; 'I am plagued by your clients ... Frank Pringle knows nothing about how such places are to be obtained or he would not write as he does, for I cannot get posts for everyone that wants them ....'⁶⁵ The chasm between expectations in Scotland, Ireland and Wales and what London-based brokers of human capital could deliver threatened to disrupt the webs of reciprocal trust and obligation that underpinned micro- and meso-networks. Expatriates could and did become alienated by such demands and sever or minimise contact with their home localities.⁶⁶ Growing access to imperial employment ironically generated new tensions and complications even as they solved old problems. The Empire created metropolitan-based and thoroughly assimilated British-Irish elites who made available to their home regions the overseas gentlemanly capitalist economy. But the pressure from the provinces which arose from a heavy reliance on human capital induced disruptive tensions that strained the connective function of networks even as they expanded. Dynamism and fragility lay at the heart of the social capital connections that facilitated Irish, Scottish and Welsh movement into the Eastern Empire.

There is clear evidence that EIC directors tried hard to meet demands from kinsmen and local clients. However, their political horizons and strategies necessarily transcended regional and national chauvinisms. One reason for aligning with other metropolis-based interests lay in the configuration and routine operation of Company patronage. Although the overall volume of posts available was impressive, each director's annual quota of patronage was limited. The EIC leadership developed an intricate and hierarchical system of allocating directors a percentage of the available jobs. Each normally had only a writership, a couple of cadetships and one medical office within his gift.[67] Faced with these constraints, wider alliances with other directors could diversify access to patronage. Sharing and exchanging nominations enabled a consistent dispersal of favours while generating stronger webs of obligation and trust among the peer group. This metropolitan culture of mutual reliance resulted in convoluted arrangements as directors from Scottish or Irish, Welsh and English backgrounds asked colleagues with available patronage to sponsor their clients on the basis of a previously granted favour or on the understanding they would reciprocate at a later date.

These placements occurred in large numbers every year. Once applications for civil service posts become extant from 1749 they reveal this economy of obligation in action. From 1750 to 1759 a total of 244 successful candidates are listed, including twenty-six Scots, six Irish and four Welsh. English directors such as Roger Drake, Thomas Phipps and William Mabbott sponsored individuals from across the metropolitan provinces. Phipps acted as patron for John Molesworth from Stephen's Green in Dublin in 1752 and William Shewin from Swansea in 1755.[68] Alexander Hume asked Drake to nominate Alexander Callander from Stirlingshire and David Carnegie from Haddington in 1758, having already in October 1753 secured Mabbott's willingness to add John Drummond, the son of Drummond of Megginch to his director's list.[69] This action created an expectation that Hume would in the future use one of his spaces to place Drake and Mabbott's clients or had already done so.

Such transactions were more than the routine graft of Namierite-style patronage politics. They reveal the directorate's sophisticated use of economies of credentialism. These were socio-economic as much as political exchanges and generated dense webs of British-Irish reciprocal obligation that belie the Company's official 'English' title. The corporation's records after c.1750 reveal the complexity of such arrangements and how they criss-crossed the British and Irish Isles in definite if ephemeral ways. Typical in this respect is the deal agreed between the Scots director Hugh Inglis and the Irish representative peer, Du Pré Alexander, second earl of Caledon. On 14 February 1813 Inglis used one of his nominations to place Arthur Crawford, the son of a retired Madras army officer from Hollywood, County Down, and a client of Caledon's. Earlier in 1809 it was Colonel Sweny Toone who provided one of his vacancies to a Scottish director, George Cumming. On the latter's recommendation, Toone, despite having no substantive interest in that part of Britain, sponsored the commissioning as a cadet in the Bombay army of John Sutherland, the son of a tenant farmer from Duffus in Moray.[70]

Through such brokerage local interests connected with the metropolis-based meso-networks that facilitated the step migration of clients to Asia. These province-to-metropole dynamics show the directors functioning as a genuinely integrated elite at a time when the British-Irish union, hastily inaugurated in 1801, suffered from a range of political, religious and cultural barriers that inhibited its success and its long-term legitimacy.[71] In this respect the English East India Company was a far more effective and connective British-Irish institution than the union nation-state.

Yet despite the need to form inclusive intra-corporate alliances, the extent to which directors remained connected to their metropolitan provincial origins is striking. Henry Dundas's favouritism toward his fellow Scots is well known; but he was far from alone in this respect. As the Edinburgh lawyer Thomas Tod noted of Sir James Cockburn in 1780 'to give him his due, he has always been very friendly disposed to his countrymen, and has provided for many of them'.[72] Laurence Sulivan did the same for clients from Ireland. His high status in London did not displace his Cork and Munster affiliations, it globalised them. He sponsored the careers in South Asia of at least four Sulivan family members and formed alliances in the 1770s and early 1780s with other countrymen active in the Company, including his fellow director, Robert Gregory, and the Dublin Castle politician Lord George McCartney from Antrim.[73] His connections with Thomas Allan, a major Company shareholder and the MP for Killybegs and Naas in the 1760s to the early 1780s, linked London-corporate and Dublin-political power.[74] The Sulivan-McCartney nexus represented only the most obvious manifestation of over forty years of growing Irish participation in the corporation. Between 1780 and 1785, 39 per cent of applications for EIC patronage listed in McCartney's private correspondence were from fellow Irishmen and included clients of George Beresford, second earl of Tyrone, Thomas Allan, and the lord lieutenant.[75]

The connection was more than just a micro-level set of linkages. Sulivan's sponsorship of McCartney's governorship of Madras in 1780 provides a significant example of a meso-network forged around discernibly Irish affiliations. The web of connections stretched from Ulster, through Dublin and London to Madras and serviced a range of individual and familial interests from across Ireland. The evolution of this transhemispheric network underlines how Protestant Irishmen felt no sense of contradiction between involvement in the Empire and the maintenance of strong, well-defined Irish associative tendencies. Sulivan is one of the eighteenth-century empire's most important figures, yet he retained an obvious awareness of and responsiveness to his provincial origins. Irish interests and personnel loomed large in his calculations, revealing how Irishness (of the Protestant variety at least) combined with corporate imperialism in subtle but unmistakable ways.

The persistence of provincial associationalism has significant implications for how best to understand the Empire's impact on identities across the British and Irish Isles. Too often the emphasis is on the creation or reinforcement of new racial demarcations overseas and the generating of British identities at 'home'.[76] This interpretation is in many respects correct of course, but only partially so. The new imperial identities were always protean, contingent and composite. Company expansion in Asia nurtured far more than just a one hegemonic sense of identity, be that 'White', 'European' or 'British'. It modernised and gave a pressing new relevance to a host of familial, local, regional and older national loyalties, none more so than that of Ireland's Protestants. This is not, as Colley's famous thesis would have it, Irishness disassociated or 'othered' from empire. Sulivan and McCartney's connections reveal disproportionate involvement by Irish interests but in ways that embedded a form of working Irishness in the metropole and drove engagement with a major theatre of global expansion.[77]

A key characteristic of the Scots and Irish individuals who rose to the directorate is what might be described as their metropolitan-regionalism. This hybridity arose because integration into London society did not mean assimilation, at least not for the first generation.[78] The formation of close alliances with fellow directors always operated in conjunction with the servicing of regional horizons. Patronage strategies, if viewed as the brokering of human capital, show the fusion of the global and the local in action. This persistence of the provincial reveals the EIC directors to be an important example of early modern glocalism. Appendix 2.1 indicates this dynamic at work. It compares the profile of clients sponsored by a sample of Scottish, Irish and Welsh directors and government ministers between the late 1790s and the 1810s. It covers only commission-level posts in the civil, military and medical establishments in Asia dispersed to their fellow metropolitan provincials by William Fullerton-Elphinstone, Charles Grant, Sweny Toone and Robert Stewart, first viscount Castlereagh. Like Sulivan, McCartney, Cockburn or Drummond before them, they all clearly favoured their own countrymen. But national-level attachments are not the most obvious feature. Regional connections played a key role. Castlereagh's willingness to serve Ulster-based clients is obvious: fully 67 per cent of those from Ireland benefiting from his influence hailed from his home province. This was a higher percentage than Scots directors gave to their own regional dependents. While acting as a senior government official, Castlereagh clearly remained responsive to the familial and regional interests of his place of origin. What these trends underline is the surprisingly intimate and local horizons of some of the metropole's most prominent 'commercial lords' and influential empire officials.

However, these dynamics did not operate with equal force across the different metropolitan provinces. While Scots increasingly acquired a range of civil, maritime, military and medical posts, two key trends impaired the growth of a similarly qualitative and diverse Irish and Welsh presence. The first of these relates to differing patterns of favouritism. If Toone exhibited a clear tendency to assist fellow Irishmen (and, in the case of Castlereagh, Ulstermen) both still gave lower ratios of posts to their own countrymen than was the case with directors from Scottish backgrounds. The figures in Appendix 2.1 show Fullerton-Elphinstone and Grant gave over 90 per cent of all offices dispersed to metropolitan provincials to fellow Scots. This was a marginally higher rate than Castlereagh and significantly more than that of Toone.

This pattern of preference is confirmed in Table 2.3, which traces the management of human capital by the director David Scott of Dunninald at the height of his influence at East India Company House. As with others at the corporation's apex, Scott catered to a range of alliances at Leadenhall Street. Given this imperative, the figures in Table 2.3 are heavily regional and Scottish in character; 50 per cent of all Scott's Asia-based offices went to fellow Scots. This was a considerably larger share than the 39 per cent dispersed by McCartney to Irish clients in the early 1780s. These figures reveal that McCartney acted as a British governor in Madras to a greater extent than Scott acted as a British director in London. But Scott's partiality was highly selective, with 54 per cent of posts given to fellow countrymen going to kinsmen and clients in the north east and central regions encompassing Scott's parliamentary constituency.[79]

The eighteenth-century stereotype of blatant Scottish privileging of fellow Scots was not all crude metropolitan prejudice. In the case of David Scott and other directors it had a definite basis in fact.[80] The reuse of local and regional connections to access global empire has been described as a form of 'archaic cohesion'.[81] Yet if too much emphasis is placed on the

Table 2.3 David Scott of Dunninald's patronage, 1788–1799[82]

Total	Type	Scots	Social/Regional Origins
97*	Writers = 20	11 (55%)	Kinsmen = 10 (18%)
	Cadets = 44	30 (68%)	Central = 11 (20%)
	Assistant surgeons = 16	9 (56%)	NE = 9 (16%)
	Bombay Marine = 5	2 (40%)	Henry Dundas = 5 (9%)
	Free mariners = 12	4 (33%)	Other Scots = 21 (37%)

(Source: IOR, MS Eur. D.1087, pp. 3–13).

'archaic' nature of these patterns there is a risk of underestimating the adroit redeployment of old connections to exploit new opportunities. Scott's actions confirm that EIC directors practised a historical form of glocalism, with transnational, imperial and metropolitan horizons intermingling with the immediate and the intimate, one circle of priorities influencing the other.

While both acted on clear regional loyalties, Scott's strategy contrasts with that of Castlereagh. The latter's background and career exemplifies the underappreciated influence of the Eastern Empire in pre-1815 Ireland. His family's rise to regional and then national prominence owed much to the arrival back in the 1730s of the nabob Robert Cowan.[83] Castlereagh served as president of the Board of Control from 1802 to 1806. Alongside Richard Wellesley, Governor-General from 1798 to 1805, he formed part of a significant Protestant Irish presence at the top of the EIC's London and South Asia hierarchies in the early 1800s. This was twenty years after the era of Sulivan and McCartney and a generation before another spike in Irish involvement in the 1840s and 1850s.[84] Patronage lists for those years reveal his supervision, although not direct dispensing, of 169 posts. The vast majority were military cadets but with a sprinkling of writerships and medical appointments. Despite the obvious prioritising of his Ulster connections evident in Appendix 2.1, this larger sum of patronage makes Castlereagh's priorities look similar to that of McCartney: approximately 31 per cent of the posts he regulated in the early 1800s went to Irishmen.[85] This assessment may hide less obvious Irish associations in London, but the pattern still suggests Castlereagh's connections were more genuinely British and Irish Isles in scope than those of David Scott.

The varying degree of willingness to promote fellow countrymen was compounded by a second, more significant factor: there were simply a greater number of directors from Scotland. Throughout the period from the 1790s to the 1810s Hugh and John Inglis, Thomas Reid, Simon Fraser and Campbell Marjoribanks from the Borders joined Scott, Fullerton-Elphinstone and Charles Grant on the directorate. At a conservative estimate the first five men on this list dispersed 168 writerships, military and maritime officer commissions as well as surgeoncies to fellow Scots between 1791 and 1813. This is over and above the numbers in Appendix 2.1.[86] Alongside the high-profile metropolitan brokers like Dundas and Scott, the influence of these lesser-known directors helps to explain why Scots obtained a significantly higher per capita percentage of commissioned posts than either Irishmen or Welsh over the course of the late eighteenth and early nineteenth centuries.

When the two trends are considered together, what is revealed is a substantively different pattern of interaction between Irish, Welsh and Scottish society and one of the Empire's key institutions. A survey of the directors' minutes for writer, cadet and medical appointments between 1740 and 1813 has recovered 484 individual acts of patronage for Irishmen and 1,388 for Scots. These totals do not represent 484 and 1,388 separate patrons. As Appendix 2.1 demonstrates, a single director or government official could support a large number of clients over a number of years. The figures relate to acts of sponsorship traceable to an identifiable patron. Non-Irish individuals provided 259 of these 484 instances of assistance to Irishmen – 53.5 per cent: 509 acts of patronage were from non-Scots to Scots – 36.6 per cent.[87]

The difference is considerable and significant. The percentages reflect the distinctive degrees of connection that evolved between the metropolitan provinces and the EIC. They make possible the conclusion that significantly more Scots accessed the Asian hemisphere of the Empire through the actions of their own countrymen than did their Irish or Welsh counterparts. These difficult-to-reconstruct trends have major implications for understanding the interplay between Britain, Ireland, Wales, Scotland and imperialism. Elite Irish involvement was initiated through noticeably Anglo-British connections, especially when compared to the greater role of metropolitan-regionalism in shaping the contours of Scottish engagement. In the case of Welshmen the numbers are too small to be statistically significant although there is evidence that directors with Welsh connections provided openings for their countrymen. William James, for example, sponsored David Price from Brecon into the Bombay army in 1780.[88] This type of patronage mirrored the actions of Scott or Castlereagh; the difference lay in the scope and scale of the linkages into Leadenhall Street. There were simply more Scottish directors willing to cater to demands from their home localities and at a greater rate than their Irish and Welsh counterparts. The combination is a key reason why the profiles of metropolitan provincials in Asia diverged from each other.

Conclusion

The growing intersection between the EIC and Scottish, Irish and Welsh shareholders, directors and their clients offers new perspectives on the dynamics between London and the metropolitan provinces. Movement into the corporation relied heavily on patron credentialism as a means of underwriting the value of human capital and reveals a diversified, decentred version of both the gentlemanly and gentry capitalist economies. London remained the defining political and financial node, but the nature of its influence and its connections to the provinces of the British and Irish Isles need to be reconsidered. The City emerges more as a regulating site for a diverse tangle of integrative, complementary regional economies and local interests. It functioned less as a singular, hegemonic centre controlling one dominant form of capital than as a clearing house where disparate forms of monetary and social wealth were brought together, exchanged and transferred to Asia and back again.

A heightened awareness of this diversity of capital enables a better appreciation of how wealth flowed into and out of the metropolis from different directions. Wealthy former EIC employees or free merchants returning from Asia proved an especially effective means by which metropolitan provincials accessed the corporation's higher reaches from a position of strength.[89] Here London was not the gateway to empire: empire was the key to London. This development meant that meso-networks created by the likes of Sulivan and Scott could combine local agendas with new levels of influence in the City. These interests embedded themselves in the Company's shareholding, in its directorate, and ultimately in its maritime, mercantile, military and medical corps. Brokering both monetary and human currencies drove this entryism. Potential obstacles created by lower reserves of venture capital were bypassed by deploying human, social and cultural forms of wealth as alternative modes of investment.[90] This exchange mechanism explains the apparent paradox by which very few metropolitan-provincial shareholders and directors could produce a substantially greater number of post-holders overseas, especially in the case of Scots.

General assessments of Britain's imperial economy and the character of its proto-globalisation have not sufficiently recognised the existence and importance of this provincial form of political economy. London's regulatory control was not lessened, but it did mean Irish, Scottish and to a lesser extent Welsh society helped diversify the City's economy through their deployment of differently constituted forms of capital. The commerce in human wealth was not of course restricted to these three countries: it was a general feature of Britain, Ireland and indeed the rest of early modern Europe.

The metropolitan provinces simply relied upon this mode of economy to a greater extent and in ways that complemented and supplemented London's pre-existing exchange systems centred around monetary capital.

The brokering of human capital via corporate employment prompts questions about the nature of the EIC and its status as an exemplar of early modern imperialism and global expansion. Assessments of the Company need to incorporate the resilient metropolitan regionalism of some of its most significant mid- to later eighteenth and early nineteenth-century directors. Individuals like Sulivan, Scott and Grant remained highly sensitive to the concerns of kith and kin and local webs of clientage. Their maintenance of such perspectives reinforces the argument that regionalism was a key factor shaping the nature and the limits of British integration and was equally vital in processes of global imperialism.[91] One of the EIC's most intriguing characteristics is the way it functioned as a modern, supranational, capital-intensive institution while hosting traditional, paternalistic networks that were often centred upon local allegiances, obligations and identities. Foregrounding the role of human capital in expansion into Asia supports interpretations which reconfigure empire into a more familial and intimate light.[92] Suggestions that a key feature of proto-globalisation involved cannibalising older social formations rather than their direct replacement find a strong resonance in the manner in which metropolitan provincials moved out to Asia.[93] Reliance on human assets, and the receptiveness of the EIC to these forms of socially imagined wealth, underscores the sophistication of the metropolitan provinces' response to empire and the enduringly *ancien régime* character of the Company. If these structural characteristics seem less than fully 'modern' they were still highly effective and point to the enduring role of kinship, region and localism in the Company's metropolitan and global forms of imperialism.

Notes

1 Cain and Hopkins, *British Imperialism*, pp. 61–3; P. J. Cain and A. G. Hopkins, 'Afterword: The Theory and Practice of British Imperialism', in Dumett, *Gentlemanly Capitalism*, pp. 96–199; Smith, *Slavery, Family and Gentry Capitalism in the British Atlantic: The World of the Lascelles, 1646–1834* (Cambridge: Cambridge University Press, 2006), p. 9.
2 Søren Mentz, *The English Gentleman Merchant at Work: Madras and the City of London 1660–1740* (Copenhagen: Museum Tusculanum Press, 2005), pp. 46–81; Anthony Webster, *The Twilight of the East India Company: The Evolution of Anglo-Asian Commerce and Politics, 1790–1860* (Woodbridge: Boydell, 2009), pp. 6–9.

3 Porter, '"Gentlemanly Capitalism" and Empire', 265–95.
4 Belich, *Replenishing the Earth*, pp. 58–62; Dumett, 'Exploring the Cain/Hopkins Paradigm', pp. 5–11, 39.
5 Stephen Conway, *Britannia's Auxiliaries: Continental Europeans and the British Empire, 1740–1800* (Oxford: Oxford University Press, 2017), pp. 3–19; N. C. Landsman, 'The Legacy of the British Union for the North American Colonies: Provincial Elites and the Problem of Imperial Union', in Robertson, *A Union for Empire*, pp. 297–317.
6 P. J. Marshall, 'A Nation Defined by Empire', in Grant and Stringer, *Uniting the Kingdom?*, pp. 209–11; Marshall, *The Making and Unmaking of Empires*, p. 15; Bowen, *British Enterprise*, p. 151; Evans, 'Wales, Munster and the English South West', pp. 54–5.
7 Hancock, *Citizens of the World*, passim; Nenadic, *Scots in London*, passim; Bailey, *Irish London*, passim; K. M. Brown and A. Kennedy, "Their Maxim is Vestigia nulla restrorsum": Scottish Return Migration and Capital Repatriations from England, 1603–c.1760', *Journal of Social History*, 52 (2018), 1–25; Keith M. Brown and Allan Kennedy, 'Land of Opportunity? The Assimilation of Scottish Migrants in England, 1603–c.1762', *Journal of British Studies*, 57 (2018), 709–35; Keith M. Brown and Allan Kennedy, 'Becoming English: The Monro Family and Scottish Assimilation in Early-Modern England', *Cultural and Social History*, 16 (2019), 125–44.
8 Cain and Hopkins, *British Imperialism*, pp. 321–2; Bowen, *The Business of Empire*, pp. 84–117.
9 Riddy, 'Warren Hastings', pp. 47–8; Michael Fry, *The Dundas Despotism* (Edinburgh: Edinburgh University Press, 1992), p. 112; Devine, *Scotland's Empire*, pp. 251, 269. GCA, Bogle Papers, Bo. 2: Letter Book of George Bogle of Calcutta, p. 62; HL, Pulteney Papers, Box 3, Calcutta, 24 December 1761.
10 Kate Teltscher, *The High Road to China: George Bogle, the Panchen Lama and the First British Expedition to Tibet* (London: Bloomsbury, 2007), passim.
11 IOR, MSS Eur. E276, Vol. I: No. 5, No. 29; NRS, GD51/3/14/10; GD51/3/53/1; NRS, GD128/1/3: September 1776; NRS, GD29/2055/2; TCD, MS3551, fos. 29–30, No. 42; GCA, T-SK/11/2/67: Calcutta, 10 February 1750.
12 NLS, MS1367, fo. 82; NRS, GD29/2057/13; GD29/2063/7; NRS, GD110/975; NRS, GD137/1136; GCA, T-SK/11/2/67.
13 Sutherland, *The East India Company*, pp. 15–16; H. V. Bowen, '"The Little Parliament": The General Court of the East India Company, 1750–1784', *The Historical Journal*, 34 (1991), 860–3.
14 Clark, *English Society*, pp. 423–45; Stern, *The Company State*, pp. 6–11.
15 W. Ferguson, *Scotland: 1689 to the Present* (Edinburgh: Mercat, 1997), pp. 133–7; Connolly, 'Varieties of Britishness', pp. 201–2; Shaw, *Political History of Eighteenth Century Scotland*, pp. 23–37; R. Harris, 'The Scots, the Westminster Parliament and the British State in the Eighteenth Century', in J. Hoppit (ed.), *Parliaments, Nations and Identities in Britain and Ireland* (Manchester: Manchester University Press, 2003), pp. 124–6.

16 Anon., *A List of the Names of those Members of the United Company of Merchants of England, Trading to the East Indies who stood qualified as voters on the Company's Books the 13th of April 1790* (London: n.p., 1790), pp. 1–75; H. V. Bowen, 'Investment and Empire in the late Eighteenth Century: East India Stockholding, 1756–1791', *Economic History Review*, second series, 42 (1989), 187.
17 D. J. Brown, 'Henry Dundas and the Government of Scotland' (PhD dissertation, University of Edinburgh, 1989), p. 11.
18 *Scots Magazine*, 14 (1754), pp. 533–4.
19 Furber, *Rival Empires of Trade in the Orient*, p. 195; Bowen, '"The Little Parliament"', 857–72; Bowen, 'Investment and Empire', 201; Bowen, *The Business of Empire*, pp. 96–112.
20 Bowen, 'Investment and Empire', 201; Bowen, *The Business of Empire*, pp. 109–13.
21 *A List of the Names of those Members of the United Company of Merchants of England ... 13th of April 1790* (London: n.p., 1790), pp. 1–75; NRS, Registers of Sasine (Perth) (1744) (3614) (3641) (4649).
22 Bowen, *The Business of Empire*, pp. 110–13.
23 IOR, L/AG/14/5/1: East India Stockholders, 1710; *A list of the names of the members of the United-Company of Merchants of England, Trading to the East-Indies, who are also members of the general society, the 7th of April, 1709* (London: s.n., 1709), p. 3.
24 IOR, B/53, p. 90; B/56, p. 432; B/60, pp. 19, 254.
25 McDowell, *Ireland in the Age of Imperialism and Revolution*, p. 137.
26 S. J. Knox, *Ireland's Debt to the Huguenots* (Dublin: Alexander Thom, 1959), pp. 12–14, 24–30; H. G. Roseveare, 'Jacob David: A Huguenot London Merchant of the Late Seventeenth Century & His Circle', in I. Scouloude (ed.), *Huguenots in Britain and Their French Background, 1550–1800* (Basingstoke: Macmillan, 1987), pp. 74–7, 84.
27 IOR, B/54, pp. 57, 443; B/55, p. 11; B/56, pp. 93, 610; B/57, p. 247; B/58, p. 105; B/60, p. 412.
28 T. Bartlett, '"A People Made Rather for Copies than Originals": The Anglo-Irish, 1760–1800', *International History Review*, 12 (1990), 15–25; S. J. Connolly, *Religion, Law and Power: The Making of Protestant Ireland* (Oxford: Clarendon Press, 1995), p. 122.
29 IOR, B/64, p. 370; Dickson, *New Foundations*, pp. 96–116; Connolly, *Religion, Law and Power*, pp. 44–54.
30 IOR, B/61, p. 541; B/63, pp. 66, 410; B/64, pp. 52, 370, 538; B/65, pp. 99, 144; B/66, p. 523; B/68, pp. 63, 95, 449; B/69, p. 363; B/70, pp. 95, 315, 467; NRS, GD24/1/464 (c) 154–5; NLS, MS16549, fos. 100–1.
31 The list only includes those with at least £1,000 in shares and so able to vote at the court of proprietors.
32 Bowen, *The Business of Empire*, p. 111.
33 A. Mackillop, 'Military Scotland in the Age of Proto-Globalisation', in David Forsyth and Wendy Ugolini (eds), *A Global Force* (Edinburgh: Edinburgh

University Press, 2016), pp. 16–20; A. Mackillop, '"Subsidy State" or "Drawback Province": Scotland and the British Fiscal-Military Complex', in Aaron Graham and Patrick Walsh (eds), *British Fiscal Military States, 1660–1783* (London: Routledge, 2016), pp. 79–199.
34 IOR, B/40, p. 212; B/43, p. 89; B/54, p. 270; B/63, p. 211; B/85, pp. 221–2.
35 DCA, GD131/30: London, 24 June 1778; IOR, J/1/9 [1778], p. 246.
36 PRONI, D/2433/A/3/2, 5 March 1780: James Alexander to the earl of Bristol.
37 IOR, MSS Eur. Photo 109, pp. 7–8; NRS, GD29/2112/4; GD29/2057/13. For the Bogles of Daldowie, see GCA, Bo 12/5: Calcutta, 26 December 1770.
38 HL, Stowe Collection ST/71, 'Irish Civil Establishment, August 1788'; ST/74: 'List of persons seeking preferment and the answers they received from the Duke of Rutland, late Lord Lieutenant'; Patrick Walsh, 'The Fiscal State in Ireland', *Historical Journal*, 56 (2013), 629–56; Charles Ivar McGrath, *Ireland and Empire, 1692–1770* (London: Pickering & Chatto, 2012), pp. 79–179.
39 NLS, MS1078, fos. 22–31; HL, Stowe Collection, ST/68, 'List of persons recommended to him as Lord Lieutenant for preferment in army, church and state in Ireland, George Grenville, 1st Marquis of Buckingham, 1787–88'.
40 Riddy, 'Warren Hastings', pp. 6–41; R. Sunter, *Patronage and Politics in Scotland, 1707–1832* (Edinburgh: John Donald, 1986), pp. 2–21; NLS, MS1368, fo. 177.
41 Rothschild, *The Inner Lives of Empires*, pp. 4–53.
42 HL, Pulteney Papers, Boxes 4–26; NRS, GD30/1597; NRS, GD248/227/295.
43 Bowen, *The Business of Empire*, p. 125.
44 Stern, *Company State*, pp. 19–40; Mentz, *English Gentleman Merchant*, pp. 68–70; H. V. Bowen, 'A Question of Sovereignty? The Bengal Revenue Issue, 1765–67', *Journal of Imperial and Commonwealth History*, 16 (1988), 156–71.
45 Marshall, 'The English in Asia', p. 265; D. K. Basset, 'Early English Trade and Settlement in Asia, 1602–1690', in P. Tuck (ed.), *The English East India Company, 1600–1858* (London: Routledge, 1998), pp. 1–18.
46 IOR, B/47, pp. 193–4; B/56, p. 496; B/57, p. 123; B/61, pp. 388, 403.
47 Bowen, *The Business of Empire*, p. 272.
48 P. J. Marshall, 'The Caribbean and India in the Later Eighteenth Century: Two British Empires or One?', in P. J. Marshall (ed.), *'A Free though conquering people': Eighteenth-Century Britain and Its Empire* (Aldershot: Ashgate, 2003), p. 37; Richard Drayton, *Nature's Government: Science, Imperial Britain and the 'Improvement' of the World* (New Haven, CT: Yale University Press, 2000), p. 67; Giorgio Riello, *Cotton: The Fabric that Made the Modern World* (Cambridge: Cambridge University Press, 2013), p. 89.
49 NLS, MS11041, fos. 7–14, 161; HL, Stowe Collection, ST 80: 'List of Colonial Officers, *c.*1790'; NRS, GD51/3/16; GD51/4/4, 43, 88, 89, 167; Brown, 'Henry Dundas', pp. 29–30.
50 Dirks, *The Scandal of Empire*, pp. 188–9; Jon E. Wilson, *The Domination of Strangers: Modern Governance in Eastern India, 1780–1835* (London: Palgrave Macmillan, 2008), pp. 57–9; NLS, MS1060, fos. 205–9; MS10919, fos. 100–1.

51 *A List of the Hon and United East India Company's civil and military servants on the Bengal establishment, 1785*. (Calcutta: n.p., 1785), pp. 3–105; NRS, GD51/3/16: 'Civil Offices in Bengal, List of February 1785'; GD51/3/3/28.
52 NRS, GD51/3/99; GD51/4/2/1, GD51/4/88; GD51/17/69, p. 19; NLS, MS1060, fos. 131–2; MS1062, p. 66–8; MS3387, pp. 13–5, 163–5; Brown, 'Henry Dundas', pp. 30–1.
53 C. H. Phillips, *The East India Company, 1784–1834* (Manchester: Manchester University Press, 1961), p. 8.
54 T. M. Devine, *The Glasgow Tobacco Lords* (Edinburgh: John Donald, 1976), pp. 171–3; Devine, *Scotland's Empire*, pp. 70–87; Andrew Mackillop, 'Dundee, London, and the Empire in Asia', p. 161.
55 Huw Bowen, *Revenue and Reform: The Indian Problem in British Politics, 1757–1773* (Cambridge: Cambridge University Press, 1991), p. 34; Bowen, *The Business of Empire*, pp. 127–31.
56 McGilvary, *Guardian of the East India Company*, pp. 10–19; Webster, *Twilight of the East India Company*, pp. 26–7.
57 Parker, 'Directors of the East India Company', vol. I, pp. 73–5, 114–16, 122–5, 146–9, 175–8; vol. II, pp. 241–2; V. C. P. Hodson, *List of the Officers of the Bengal Army, 1758–1834*, vol. IV (London: Longman, Orme, Brown & Co., 1927), pp. 291–2; IOR, B/76, pp. 170, 248; IOR, MSS, Eur. F164/55/98.
58 Mentz, *English Gentleman Merchant*, pp. 40–9.
59 George McGilvary, *East India Patronage*, pp. 1–89.
60 NRS, GD24/1/463 (c) 193, 203, 212; GD24/1/464 (e) 54 and 146; NLS, MS16538, fos. 176–7.
61 McGilvary, *East India Patronage*, p. 62.
62 IOR, B/57, p. 378; B/58, pp. 219, 447; B/59, p. 425; B/60, pp. 146, 354–8, 374, 420; B/61, pp. 157, 219, 223, 233–7; B/62, p. 576; B/63, p. 546; B/64, p. 501; B/67, p. 416; NRS, GD24/1/464 (c) 49, 58, 75, 79, 83, 204, 176; GD24/1/464 (d) 148; GD24/1/464 (n) 3, 7, 11, 23, 41, 49, 67–70; GD24/3/302, 304–5, 313, 337, 346/2, 360, 362/6.
63 IOR, B/57, pp. 2, 308; B/58, pp. 2, 302; B/59, pp. 2, 232; B/60, pp. 2, 244; B/61, p. 280; B/62, p. 2, 310; B/64, p. 308; B/65, pp. 2, 324; B/66, p. 1; B/67, pp. 2, 286; B/68, p. 2, 262; B/69, p. 266; B/70, pp. 2, 297–8.
64 IOR, MSS Eur. F164/55/98; NRS, GD51/4/167. For a similar percentage in 1791, see GD51/4/89.
65 GCA, T-LX3/16/1; NRS, GD24/1/484/62, 121.
66 Hancock, *Citizens of the World*, pp. 56–7.
67 NLS, MS1367, fo. 86; NLS, MS10872: fos. 86, 200; NRS, GD248/226/5/31.
68 IOR, J/1/1–3; J/1/1 [1752], pp. 356–9; J/1/2 [1755], pp. 309–13. See also, NLS, MS1328, fo. 244.
69 IOR, J/1/2 [1753], pp. 29–32 [Drummond]; J/1/3 [1758], pp. 178–81[Callander]; J/1/3 [1758], pp. 186–9 [Carnegie].
70 IOR, J/1/28, pp. 227–32; L/MIL/9/119, No. 21.
71 L. M. Cullen, 'Alliances and Misalliances in the Politics of The Union', *Transactions of the Royal Society*, X (2000), 221–41; Thomas Bartlett, *Ireland*:

A History (Cambridge: Cambridge University Press, 2010), pp. 236–43; Jackson, *The Two Unions*, pp. 183–7.
72 Fry, *The Dundas Despotism*, pp. 106–8; Gordon Pentland, 'We Speak for the Ready': Images of Scots in Political Prints, 1707–1832', *The Scottish Historical Review*, 90 (2011), 89–90; NLS, MS14439, fo. 79.
73 IOR, J/1/5, pp. 310–17; B/80, p. 232; B/80, pp. 232, 248; B/85, pp. 257–9, 323; PRONI, D/572/19/73, 84, 87, 91; Crosbie, *Irish Imperial Networks*, pp. 51–7.
74 Johnston, *History of the Irish Parliament*, vol. III, p. 80.
75 PRONI, D/572/19/15, 40, 64, 72–3, 79, 88, 91, 94–5, 103, 110–12, 124; T. Bartlett (ed.), *McCartney in Ireland, 1768–1772* (Belfast: PRONI, 1978), pp. 71–6, 110–11, 275.
76 Kathleen Wilson, *Sense of the People*, pp. 32–41; Kathleen Wilson, *The Island Race*, pp. 27–52.
77 Bailey, *Irish London*, pp. 150–6; John McAleer, 'This "Ultima Thule": The Cape of Good Hope, Ireland and Global Networks of Empire, 1795–1815', *Eighteenth-Century Ireland/Iris an dá chultúr*, 29 (2014), 63–84.
78 For an important analysis of how metropolitan provincials assimilated into London society over three generations, becoming English rather than British in the process, see Brown and Kennedy, 'Becoming English', 125–44.
79 Sunter, *Patronage and Politics*, pp. 134–7.
80 Colley, *Britons*, pp. 121–8; Langford, 'South Britons' Reception of North Britons', pp. 152–68.
81 Bayly, *Imperial Meridian*, p. 84.
82 Only postings to Asia are included.
83 PRAI, Registry of Deeds, Vol. 115, pp. 84–91, No. 79488; IOR, B/63, p. 409.
84 Scott B. Cook, 'The Irish Raj: Social Origins and Careers of Irishmen in the Indian Civil Service, 1855–1914', *Journal of Social History*, 20 (1987), 507–29.
85 IOR, MSS Eur. F/5/19, pp. 1–22; NLI, MS14337: Camp near Saulnah: 9 March 1809.
86 IOR, B/65–B/95; L/MIL/9/107–125; L/MIL/12/86; L/MIL/9/358–365; IOR, MSS Eur. D.1087; MSS Eur. F/5/19; NRS, GD51/3/3; GD51/4/1–2, 16, 89–91, 168–169; PRONI, D572/19.
87 IOR, B/65–B/95; J/1/13–28; L/MIL/9/107–125; L/MIL/12/86; L/MIL/9/358–365; Bailey, *Irish London*, pp. 54–86, 161–214.
88 Bowen, 'Asiatic Interactions', pp. 171–2.
89 Crosbie, *Irish Imperial Networks*, pp. 44–51; Bowen, *The Business of Empire*, pp. 127–32.
90 Philips, *East India Company*, pp. 15–16.
91 Murdoch, *British History, 1660–1832*, pp. 76–87; Tony Ballantyne, 'Empire, Knowledge and Culture: from Proto-Globalisation to Modern Globalisation', in Hopkins, *Globalisation in World History*, p. 116.
92 Finn, 'Family Formations: Anglo-India and the Familial Proto-State', pp. 100–17.
93 C. A. Bayly, '"Archaic" and "Modern" Globalisation in the Eurasian and African Arena, c.1750–1850', in Hopkins, *Globalisation in World History*, p. 50.

3

Civil servants and mariners

Long after they developed a large and sophisticated colonial regime in South Asia, the English East India Company's leadership still portrayed the corporation as an essentially mercantile and maritime entity.[1] The desire to retain an idealised Protestant and commercial vision of its presence in Asia may have increasingly diverged from reality, but the impulse had practical consequences. Offices relating to merchant and shipping activities remained among the most prestigious and remunerative not only in the corporation but across the entire empire.[2] Yet the sociology of this elite remains understudied partly because the Company is understood primarily in institutional, ideological, governmental and economic terms, rather than as a lived system of individuals working within and between the London and Asian spheres of operation.[3]

After 1750, however, it is possible to recover in considerable detail the social and geographic backgrounds of employees as well as traces of the kin, educational and metropole-based networks that facilitated careers in Asia. People and their social capital lay at the heart of much the organisation's bureaucratic gaze. These priorities shaped the nature of the resultant archive in ways that make the concept of human capital a particularly useful lens through which to understand the movement of metropolitan provincials into the EIC. The directors accumulated copious amounts of biographical data in order to ascertain the character and competences of their prospective civil servants. Information ranged from the applicant's age, education, their father's occupation, to their parish of birth: no other long eighteenth-century imperial elite are as well documented. In the case of the commercial and administrative cadre, known as civil servants, the best qualitative source is the annual series of petitions that list 2,068 successful applications between 1749 and 1813.[4]

The auditing of human capital spanned the whole workforce and encompassed tens of thousands of European soldiers and sailors. This bureaucratic mentality evolved over time into the racial stratifying of South Asians and the use of 'caste' as a social enumerator.[5] The volume of information is such that only the marine, mercantile-administrative, military and medical officers are analysed in detail. One feature of this culture of record keeping is of vital importance in the context of exploring Scottish, Irish and Welsh involvement. While social and financial standing were the overriding criteria in selecting senior personnel, after about 1740 EIC bureaucrats began recording the nationality of seamen, soldiers and later the free merchants and mariners. They did so by listing employees as 'English', 'Irish', 'Scot' and 'Welsh' rather than as 'Britons'.[6] The use of these national labels greatly facilitates this study. The individuals traced here can be confidently assigned a place of origin because the records were often explicit on this point. It is for this reason that the EIC archive is one of the best resources for recovering the migratory and social-networking dimensions of Britain and Ireland's long eighteenth-century expansion and imperialism. New insights on national patterns can be reconstructed alongside otherwise difficult-to-recover regional and local nodes of involvement. The full diversity of metropolitan-provincial economies of human capital can be traced in the Company more easily than in any other major sector of the pre-1815 empire.[7]

Although the extant records make possible a detailed reconstruction of key aspects of the sojourning elite, coverage has been uneven to date. Assessment of participation in the merchant marine has not progressed much beyond individual case studies, with little sense of overall numbers or when and how the shipping sector was accessed in a meaningful way.[8] More is known about trends in the civil service. The underrepresentation of Irishmen prior to the introduction of competitive examinations in the mid-1850s has been acknowledged, even if the reasons are not well understood.[9] Meanwhile, historians of the Company are rightly sceptical of suggestions that some areas of the corporation were little more than Caledonian fiefdoms by the era of Henry Dundas.[10] The tendency to exaggerate the Scottish presence is a by-product of using diaspora history as a vicarious form of national history. From this emphasis has sprung a fixation on disproportionate numbers and uncritical assumptions about national as opposed to familial and regional forms of identity at work in the Empire.[11] Focusing on broad trends rather than individuals reduces any tendency to exceptionalise. There are also wider benefits to a better understanding of the Scots, Irish and Welsh within the upper echelons of the mercantile and marine workforce. The timing and nature of their participation offers new insights into the means by which undercapitalised societies adopted human-capital strategies to exploit lucrative sectors of global expansion.

A dance called India: sojourning economies in Company Asia

No other sector of the EIC matched the prestige and remuneration potential of the covenanted civil service. The most sought-after posts were the merchant, factor and writer's offices at the apex of the employment hierarchy.[12] Something of the extensive power and profit capacity of these offices is captured in John Johnstone of Westerhall's description of his responsibilities as a Bengal civil servant. Made chief collector (revenue official) in 1762 for Burdwan, Johnstone noted that his annual tax target of £75,000 was raised from among approximately two million people.[13] Even if exaggerated as part of a lobbying campaign for reinstatement after his dismissal by Robert Clive, these statistics reveal the authority wielded by senior personnel during the formative decades of the Company's raj. Scotland's land tax at this time stood at £48,000, its entire receipts from customs at £78,654 and the population around 1.25 million.[14] The material gains to be derived from exploiting the large reserves of public revenue and private commerce of the sort outlined by Johnstone ensured that Asia exercised a powerful pull on the imaginations of metropolitan provincials, just as it did across the rest of Europe.

Yet for all its attractions Asia was not the most obvious choice for those contemplating enterprise abroad. A dearth of venture finance impaired the ability of many gentry and middling order families to pay apprentice fees among the merchant houses specialising in international trade.[15] This hindered the placement of younger sons in mercantile forms of employment. Participation in the notoriously capital-intensive Asia trades might seem a counter-intuitive response when faced with such constraints. Yet the East Indies' reputation for under-utilised wealth and the availability of local credit from Asian merchant-financiers or other Europeans offered an increasingly well-understood solution. Distance also changed the value of capital. Those with limited monetary reserves could utilise oceanic mobility to make their assets more productive. Exactly this thinking motivated Sir Peter Halket of Pittfirrane's recommendation of a client to John Drummond in 1725: 'his stock is soe small he cannot make anything of it in this countrie, it is just £2,000 (Scots) [*c*.£166.13.0 sterling]. He would gladie be in the East Indies.'[16] The belief that migration enhanced liquidity and gave access to otherwise unattainable reserves of credit drove thousands to consider Asia as a destination.

Most Europeans, including Scots, Welsh and Irish, journeying eastwards were sojourners. These migrants moved to a destination with the intention of returning home at a later date with enhanced material resources and social status. Many of course did not return. Asia's environment and associated diseases killed large numbers regardless of rank, function and social standing. Some sojourners also turned imperceptibly into permanent settlers. Many stayed and lived out their lives in places like Calcutta, Madras or Bombay either because of limited financial success, the creation of new personal and familial relations or simply through acculturation to their new surroundings. Regardless of the eventual outcome, the intention to return was a vital factor in determining career, commercial and associational strategies.[17] Sojourning is a well-studied subset of early modern migration history, however, the phenomenon in an Irish, Welsh and Scottish context is much better understood in relation to the Atlantic world when compared with movement to Asia.[18] Recovering the scale and sociology of sojourners in the upper echelons of the Company addresses a major lacuna in the migration and empire histories of all three metropolitan provinces.

It took a considerable time for Asia to be viewed as a realistic or preferable option. Nor was the decision to venture eastwards always a happy one. With increased knowledge came the realisation that the 'Orient' was never the financial nirvana of popular perception. Writing home from Fort St David in 1749, Lieutenant John Grant from Strathspey voiced a common disillusionment: 'A great many in Brittain [sic] imagine that there is money to be hade in the East Indies for the taking of it up … but of ten that go to the Indies for that purpose seldom one gets back to their own country with a fortune.'[19] The dangers of climate, disease and mortality were compounded by violent cycles of commercial boom and bust or the phases of economic underperformance that wracked the Company's world in Asia during the period of the 1730s to the 1740s, in the late 1760s and early 1770s and again in the 1800s.

India's reputation for offering quick fortunes was undermined further by parliamentary policy in the 1780s and 1790s. Part of the purpose of the 1784 India Act was to rein in the corruption endemic among Company personnel. The result by the 1790s was that families like the Elliots of Minto, Brookes of Leinster or Coles of Enniskillen were far less sanguine about Asia than those from similar backgrounds had been in the 1770s.[20] Many parents were horrified at the prospect of sending their sons and, increasingly, daughters to such remote and alien locations. Separation was made all the more poignant by the high likelihood of death and the near certainty of no reunion with older family members.[21] The Grants of Grant, Camerons of Locheil and the Cochranes of Rochsoles, or the Carnacs in Dublin and the Anglo-Irish Maxwell-Stones either refused to let a scion depart or needed to be persuaded of the necessity. Sir Archibald Mackenzie of Coul in Ross-shire noted in 1759 of his son's plans for a Company writership: 'I prefer [him] a Scotchman to an Englishman and much more to an Indian. If my son will be a merchant let him be a merchant in Britain, not out of it.'[22] Joining the Company's ranks was for many a gamble born of limited economic options. Families turned to Asia after they failed to obtain for a scion a place in London merchant houses, Edinburgh legal firms, a placement in Europe, the Caribbean or in the army and navy.[23] Asia's growing prominence as a sojourning destination did not necessarily denote an enthusiasm for relocation to the other side of the world.

In the end, however, the attractions outweighed the perceived negatives. The individuals studied here chose to risk their lives by exercising a degree of personal freedom, economic agency and racial privilege which was not available to many millions of people on the receiving end of the Empire's expansion. The opposition of parents and fears over alterations in the EIC's conditions of employment were never enough to undermine Asia and particularly India's reputation as the best place in the Empire to make a fortune quickly. A family friend in Ulster in 1802 informed Arthur Cole, then a recently arrived writer in Bengal, that there were many young boys in their home locality who enthusiastically believed they were destined for the East Indies and riches (see Appendix 6.1).[24] This imagining of Asia involved a heady amalgam of the modern and the mythic. As early as the 1730s metropolitan-provincial periodicals such as the *Scots Magazine* listed EIC stock alongside shares in the City's other premier financial institutions. In this way the East Indies came to represent a natural even routine place where virtuous and 'liberty'-enhancing Protestant commerce might be practised. Yet in the very same publication the eastern hemisphere was portrayed as the 'Orient', a place of prodigious wonders, vicious tyrants, sexual profligacy, exotic religions, cannibals and mermaids. This was a construction of the 'Orient' deeply encoded in European culture and associated with vast wealth and commerce.[25] As a Scot writing in 1773 observed: 'one would really imagine that the golden age reigns with universal sway on the other side of the Cape and that in these regions it rains silver rupees'.[26] Though partly tongue in cheek, the comment reveals the profound hold that ingrained stereotypes of Asia exerted over the imagination of British and Irish sojourners.

Whether such wealth was ever anything more than wishful thinking is beside the point. As with the mental horizons of the boys in Ulster, the expectation developed across the British and Irish Isles that Asia offered accessible and lucrative employment.[27] One feature of the civil service seemed especially suited to provincial regions lacking large reserves of venture capital. Promotion prospects were largely although never exclusively based upon seniority rather than financial resources.[28] Some of the defining aspects of human and embodied cultural capital – education, language skills, experience, reputation and professional longevity – determined routine progress in the civil service. These intangible but vital social assets were embodied in the prestige of a writer's post. Holding such an office made it much easier to acquire credit from South Asian financiers. Calcutta 'Banians' or Madras 'Dubashes' lent to Europeans who were increasingly viewed not as individual commercial risks but as government officials with guaranteed access to secure forms of repayment income.[29]

That the corporation's occupational hierarchy magnified human capital can be seen clearly in the 1771 comments of George Bogle:

> the advantages that a Company servant enjoys after he has been some little time in the country [are] that nobody can carry on trade to so good purpose, the numbers of posts and appointments to which he, and he only, is entitled and last of all that he is rising in the service every year and getting up by steps to that situation which must ensure him an independent fortune.[30]

Arriving in Asia with surplus capital obviously facilitated career progress and commercial advantage. But a lack of hard cash could be circumvented. To under-resourced genteel and middling families in Ireland, Wales, Scotland and the English regions, a defining attraction of Company service was that it offered an entrée to the vast credit reserves held by Asia's 'portfolio capitalists'.[31] Relocation to the East Indies was nothing less than a solution to liquidity constraint through transhemispheric migration. While 'the rage' for emigration to North America in the 1760s and 1770s has received detailed attention from historians of Ireland and Scotland, there existed a hugely important equivalent to Asia. Just as the 'Dance called America' hastened the permanent departure of tens of thousands of Scots and Irish artisans and tenants, so a parallel Dance called India gripped the middling and gentry classes from the late 1740s onwards. Brigadier-General David Wedderburn from Fife, who arrived in Bombay in 1770, observed the same culture of human mobility that seemed to drive developments in the Atlantic world. He noted: 'Since the disease of getting out anyhow to India became epidemical, some well educated, pretty young men, who could not get to Madras, or Bengal, have come here, rather than not be in India at all.'[32] The characterisation of sojourning as a form of social distemper is ironic. The 1760s and 1770s witnessed Scottish and Irish elites struggle to come to terms with what they saw as the irrational craze for emigration among the rural and urban labouring populations of their respective countries.[33] Yet at exactly the same time far riskier forms of mobility were pursued by their own family members and social peers.

The rush for socially appropriate and potentially profitable employment resulted in acute competition for civil service posts which only intensified as the eighteenth century wore on. The deputy governor of Bombay, Robert Cowan from Ulster, stressed the difficulty of obtaining openings for associates as early as 1728.[34] By 1775 the Grants of Grant estimated that without a director's influence a writer's office cost £1,500 to secure; by the 1790s and 1800s the price stood at between £3,675 to £5,250. In the absence of social capital deployed through connections with shareholders and directors in London, substantial finances were required to initiate a career in this branch of the corporation. These realities shaped the profile of successful applicants and ensured that the effectiveness of province-to-metropole networks became more and more important. In 1790 Hugh Macleod of Geanies, son of the sheriff-depute of Ross-shire was one of 1,000 applicants for the sixty-three writerships available in that year. It took the intervention of the Prince of Wales to secure Macleod the post.[35] Even this level of cut-throat competition did not lessen the attraction of the civil service. Scots, Irish, Welsh and English families were drawn to the Company by a heady cocktail of rational, commercial calculation and the stubbornly persistent myth of the 'Orient' and its riches.

The sociology of an imperial elite: the civil servants

The timing and scale of participation in the civil service is summarised in Table 3.1. These figures and those in the chapters that follow are drawn from an AHRC-funded database, 'The Scots, Irish and Welsh in Asia, c.1690–c.1820' (SIWA). Compiled from Company records, wills and private archival collections, it currently contains information on 6,129 individuals traced to the commissioned echelons of the civil, merchant marine, military and medical services between 1690 and 1813. Also included are metropolitan provincials identified as free merchants and mariners for the same period. The survey produces overall, but by no means definitive, totals of 4,013 Scots, 1,796 Irish and 320 Welsh across the various occupations. These may not seem large numbers over 123 years, especially when compared to the tens of thousands crossing the Atlantic. Yet the timing of deepening connections with the Company was such that 5,994 of the 6,129 left for Asia after 1740, compressing the timescale and the increasing average annual rate of departure. It is also important to restate the power, influence and profit potential available to these sojourners. They joined a civil, military, maritime and commercial elite responsible for one of the most significant acts of territorial conquest in the entire history of Western imperialism. The assault upon South Asia alone lasted over a century from the late 1740s to the 1840s and eventually brought several hundred million people under the Company's and then Britain's formal rule.[36] At the same time, free merchants and mariners developed the 'country trade' across South Asia into the Gulf, South-East Asia and China, reshaping transformative global capital and commodity flows in the process. The database only includes senior personnel. It excludes thousands of seamen and soldiers and

Table 3.1 Scottish, Irish and Welsh EIC civil servants, 1690–1813

Years	1690–1709 B-ser	1710–1729 B-ser	1730–1749 B-ser	1750–1769 J-ser/B-ser	1770–1789 J-ser/B-ser	1790–1813 J-ser only	Total
Total	285	369	346	592/785	385/538	1,070	3,393
Scots	5 (1.7%)	15 (4%)	22 (6.3%)	69 (11.6%)/96 (12.2%)	35 (9%)/74 (13.5%)	227 (21.2%)	439 (12.9%)
Irish	3 (1%)	5 (1.3%)	3 (0.8%)	18 (3%)/30 (3.8%)	9 (2.3%)/18 (3.3%)	69 (6.4%)	128 (3.7%)
Welsh	8 (2.8%)	0	2 (0.5%)	12 (2%)/14 (1.7%)	3 (0.7%)/5 (0.9%)	14 (1.3%)	43 (1.2%)

(SIWA. Sources: IOR, J/1/1–29; B/40–B/95; P/328/60–64; P/416/77–98; L/AG/34/29/4–22, 185–210, 341–343; TNA, PROB 11/549–1903; IOR, MSS Eur. F. 128/12; NRS, CC1/6/56, 59, 74, 133; CC3/3/12, 15; CC3/4/32; CC3/5/2, 5–6; CC8/8/84, 90, 105, 110, 112–13, 116, 118–19; 120–36, 138–39, 140–42, 144–46; CC97; CC10/5; CC16/4; CC18/4; CC20/7/4, 7; CC21/7/9; SC36/38/1; SC36/48/6–7; SC70/1/3–4, 6–7, 12–14, 17, 22–23; SC70/1/12; CC8/8/125, 132, 141; *The East India Kalendar, or, Asiatic register for … 1791 to 1800. …* (London: J. Debrett, 1791–1800); V. C. P. Hodson, *List of the Officers of the Army of Bengal, 1754–1834*, I–IV (London: Longman, Orme, Brown & Co., 1927)).

the large number of corporals and sergeants (NCOs – non-commissioned officers) employed in the three presidency armies or by the British army and Royal Navy units deployed into the eastern half of the Empire.[37]

The database mirrors the structure of the Company's surviving records. Yet even an archive as comprehensive as that of the EIC has gaps. No full applications for writerships survive prior to 1749. The totals shown in Table 3.1 for 1690 to 1750 are drawn from civil service posts approved in the directors' minutes (the B-series). This enables a partial reconstruction of the rate of formal appointments before 1750.

The utility of civil servant numbers derived from this method is confirmed once a comparison is drawn between the B-series and the more detailed J-series, which is available from 1749 onwards. While comprehensive on individual submissions, the J-series underestimates the rate of civil servant appointments by 24 per cent to 28 per cent; the discrepancy is due to a combination of partial recording in London and the absence of details on 'country' promotions in Asia.[38] The practice of appointing unofficial writers means that arriving at a definitive total of civil servants is difficult. It is also the case that the J-series has partial gaps in the mid-1770s and the 1780s. After 1790, however, applications survive in a comprehensive form.[39] These features of the extant record mean that the B-series give a better indication of overall numbers while the qualitative data in the J-series provides crucial insights on regional and social backgrounds. This explains why a double set of figures using both sets of records are listed for the decades between 1750 and 1789, with the fuller J-series providing robust evidence for the 1790s onwards.

Only persons definitively traced to Scotland, Ireland or Wales or with fathers from these countries are listed in Table 3.1. Second-generation individuals with a father of Irish origin residing in London, elsewhere in the United Kingdom or in Asia numbered twenty-seven: this equates to 21 per cent of the known Irish civil servant total. The prominence of London-based families is the first indication that Irish civil servants were drawn from a rather narrow circle of well-connected Anglo-Irish interests and those already in Company service. Four scions of Laurence Sulivan's family obtained high-ranking civil posts between 1769 and 1806; Francis Hastings Toone and Henry Toone, the sons of Colonel Sweny Toone followed in 1804 and 1807.[40] Those born in England, in India or elsewhere in the Empire with a Scottish father totalled fifty-seven (13.1 per cent of the Scots total). In comparison to the Irish situation, access for Scots was less restricted to service families with existing links to the Company. Yet if the Scottish intake was less socially circumscribed, some families did develop a tradition of intergenerational employment. Claud, George, John, William and Charles, the sons of Claud Russell from Lothian, a prominent Madras civil servant in the 1750s to the 1770s, followed in their father's footsteps.[41] A similar profile characterised Welsh appointees: eight out of forty-three (18.6 per cent) were born outside Wales but with traceable links to that part of the United Kingdom. Among them were James, Wigram and Septimius Money, sons of Captain William Money, an EIC merchant marine commander from Carmarthen.[42] These second-generation scions typify the way the Company's empire generated an assimilated Anglo-British elite.

Where clear geographic origins cannot be confirmed individuals are not included. Surname evidence alone is discounted. The overall results are undoubtedly conservative but represent the first comparative survey of Irish, Scots and Welsh participation in the highest commercial and administrative levels of the pre-1815 empire in Asia. The nature of the surviving record means that the Scottish total is augmented in comparison to those of the Irish and Welsh. This is because the wills and testaments of civil servants can also be traced in the records of the Scottish commissary and sheriff courts. The absence of a comparable set of searchable sources for Ireland and Wales lowers recoverable numbers for these groups both in relation to the overall and the Scottish totals.

The purpose of Table 3.1 is to set metropolitan provincial numbers against the total volume of appointments rather than viewing participation trends in isolation. This wider comparison reveals the decidedly marginal place of these nationalities in the elite echelons for the first half of the eighteenth century. The tiny percentage in this period underline the Company's London-centred hiring preferences. It is equally clear that variations between the different groups existed from the start. Initially, the Welsh share was the most substantial, with the long-established expatriate presence in London delivering a ratio of posts in the 1690s and early 1700s proportionate to the country's population. Yet across the whole eighteenth century the overall picture is one of declining involvement and, eventually, statistically marginal Welsh numbers.[43]

Ireland fits the same pattern of sustained underrepresentation. The kingdom's growing profile in the Atlantic world from the 1700s to the 1750s found no parallel in this crucial sector of the EIC.[44] The increase from less than 1 per cent to over 3 per cent in the 1750s to the 1770s continued into the 1790s and 1800s. Yet even the later rate of employment is minimal compared to Ireland's substantial share of the British and Irish Isles' population. This conclusion needs qualifying in one vital respect. Analyses of social and regional origins in Table 3.2 confirm that the majority were from regions with the largest concentrations of Church of Ireland and dissenting Protestant communities.[45] These groups made up only 18–20 per cent of the kingdom's population, which equates to approximately 5 to 6 per cent of the British-Irish total. If viewed in this context, the 6.4 per cent of civil service jobs secured in the 1790s and 1800s point to Ireland's Protestants obtaining elite employment at a rate which paralleled almost exactly with their weight of population. But achieving this parity occurred at a time when political strategies had already begun the protracted and always partial process of making public office available to Catholics.[46] There is no evidence that recruitment from the majority religious community occurred in the EIC's civil service to any meaningful extent in this period. These divergent trends mean that while Protestant Ireland gained a proportionate share of employment, the overall Irish profile remained markedly underdeveloped before, during and immediately after union with Great Britain.

The Scottish profile shared some important characteristics with that of the Irish in the early decades of the eighteenth century. Despite the argument that Robert Walpole, Archibald Campbell, earl of Ilay (later the third duke of Argyll) and John Drummond delivered 'startling' levels of patronage in the 1720s and 1730s, the acquisition of civil offices was actually well below the country's share of population until the 1750s.[47] The established emphasis on excessive Scottish involvement in the EIC's civil service for most of the century is simply not borne out when confirmable numbers are set against total recruitment levels. The most detailed assessment to date proposes a total of 243 Scots in the civil service between 1720 and 1780. The totals in Table 3.1 are configured in different time scales but give an aggregate of 183 for the same period.[48] The disparity becomes less important when set against overall rates of appointment, a contextualisation which serves to make both totals appear as marginal percentages. Only in the 1750s and 1760s did participation reach the 12 per cent mark, which equated to Scotland's demographic weight inside the British and Irish monarchy. As with Ireland, participation in the Asian half of the Empire was noticeably slower than in the Atlantic. The key divergence from Irish and Welsh trends was that Scots acquired a proportionate per capita share by the 1750s. The 1790s and 1800s marked a major breakthrough, with the Scottish rate climbing to 21 per cent, just under twice the amount relative to its share of population. The steep upward movement points to the need for a major reappraisal of Henry and Robert Dundas's time at the India Board of Control from the 1780s to the 1800s. The stereotype of Henry Dundas as the creator of an exceptionally influential web of patronage has been the subject of major revision and should not be resurrected uncritically: but it does have some basis in fact.[49] The trends shown in Table 3.1 confirm that Henry and Robert Dundas presided over an era of conspicuous Scottish success.

Understanding the slow emergence of this overrepresentation should not rely on monocausal explanations. The figures represent the slow working out of longer-term trends, with the facilitating role of the expatriate community in London matched by a growing and consistent Scottish presence on the directorate. This confluence of factors eventually, and uniquely among metropolitan-provincials in this period, enabled the number of Scots in the civil service to expand to a considerable minority percentage. However, the process occurred over an extended timescale. Substantial engagement with empire could take decades to develop and depended on a range of organic dynamics that were as significant as supposedly watershed moments like the unions of 1707 and 1800.

The regional and social class characteristics of those entering the civil service provide new insights into the ways in which engagement with empire played out differently across the British and Irish Isles. Existing regional disparities were reshaped but also perpetuated and deepened. Drawing on the bibliographical information in the J-series and wills registered in South Asia and in London, Table 3.2 summarises the sociology of Irish, Scots and Welsh civil servants. In Ireland and Wales certain districts supplied large ratios while other localities were noticeably underrepresented. The provinces of Leinster and Ulster contained the largest concentration of Protestant populations and provided the bulk of appointees (59.8 per cent) with traceable origins. Connacht, the least anglicised part of Ireland, secured only 3 per cent. However flexible its hiring practices may have been further down the employment ladder, the higher reaches of the English East India Company remained overwhelmingly Protestant. Another effect was the reinforcement of the socio-economic dominance of Dublin. Excluding the rest of the surrounding county, the city supplied thirty-one (24 per cent) of the country's 128 confirmed civil servants.[50] Such a significant profile is testimony to the city's role as a key subsidiary metropole connecting Irish society to the pre-1815 empire. In the case of Wales, the eastern and southern counties supplied much higher ratios than the west and north: families from the county of Glamorgan provided 18 per cent of all verifiable Welsh civil servants; by contrast only one individual can be traced to Merioneth in the north-west.[51]

Scotland offers a significant contrast to the uneven patterns of participation that characterised Ireland and Wales. Involvement was spread across the country's regions in a broadly uniform way, other than in the north (Caithness, Orkney and Shetland). The combined total of 22 per cent of high-value patronage secured by families from Highland and north-eastern counties belies the supposedly underdeveloped economy and marginal political status of these areas. The outcome is less surprising if the terms of reference shift from conventional yardsticks of monetary wealth and political leverage towards an analysis predicated on the deployment of human and social capital. The east-coast counties of Aberdeen, Angus and Fife acquired a much larger number (sixty-seven in total) than districts usually

Table 3.2 Civil servants: regional, social and educational backgrounds

Nationality	Region	Social Origins	Education
Irish 128	Leinster = 37 (28.9%) Ulster = 33 (25.7%) Munster = 17 (13.2%) London = 12 (9.3%) Asia = 11 (8.5%) Connacht = 4 (3.1%) England = 3 (2.3%) Unknown = 11 (8.5%)	EIC = 17 (13.2%) Clergy & legal = 15 (11.7%) Merchant = 12 (9.3%) Gentry = 11 (8.5%) Aristocracy = 8 (6.2%) Govt & municipal = 5 (3.9%) RN & military = 4 (3.1%) Mariner = 2 (1.5%) Unknown = 54 (42.1%)	London = 33 (25.7%) Dublin = 17 (13.2%) England = 9 (7%) Ulster = 4 (3.1%) Munster = 2 (1.5%) Leinster = 2 (1.5%) Connacht = 1 (0.7%) Ireland = 1 (0.7%) Europe = 1 (0.7%) Unknown = 58 (45.3%)
Scots 439	Central = 63 (14.3%) Edinburgh = 49 (11.1%) Highlands = 48 (10.9%) NE = 48 (10.9%) Borders = 47 (10.7%) West Central = 42 (9.5%) Lothians = 38 (8.6%) London = 27 (6.1%) Asia = 18 (4.1%) Misc. = 14 (3.1%) The North = 6 (1.3%) Unknown = 39 (8.8%)	Gentry = 155 (35.3%) Clergy & legal = 43 (9.7%) EIC = 42 (9.5%) Merchant = 35 (7.9%) Aristocracy = 23 (5.2%) Misc. = 24 (5.4%) RN & military = 19 (4.3%) Govt & municipal = 19 (4.3%) Caribbean = 7 (1.5%) Unknown = 72 (16.4%)	London = 84 (19.1%) Edinburgh = 79 (17.9%) Scotland = 37 (8.4%) Aberdeen = 12 (2.7%) England = 12 (2.7%) Glasgow = 8 (1.8%) Dundee = 5 (1.1%) Inverness = 4 (0.9%) Perth = 3 (0.6%) Europe = 2 (0.4%) Unknown = 193 (43.9%)
Welsh 43	South Wales = 17 (39.5%) East Wales = 14 (32.5%) London = 5 (11.6%) W/N Wales = 4 (9.3%) England = 1 (2.3%) North America = 1 (2.3%) Unknown = 1 (2.3%)	Gentry = 10 (23.2%) Clergy = 4 (9.3%) Misc. = 4 (9.3%) Merchant = 2 (4.6%) Medical = 1 (2.3%) Manufacturer = 1 (2.3%) Unknown = 21 (48.8%)	England = 12 (27.9%) London = 5 (11.6%) South Wales = 2 (4.6%) Unknown = 24 (55.8%)

(SJWA. Sources: IOR, J1/1–29; B/40–B/95; P/328/60–64; P/416/77–98; L/AG/34/29/4–22, 185–210, 341–343; TNA, PROB 11/549–1903; NRS, CC16/56, 59, 74, 133; CC3/3/12, 15; CC3/4/32; CC3/5/2, 5–6; CC8/8/84, 90, 105, 110, 112–13, 116, 118–19; 120–36, 138–39, 140–42, 144–46; CC9/7; CC10/5; CC16/4; CC18/4; CC20/7/4, 7; CC21/7/9; SC26/38/1; SC36/48/6–7; SC70/1/3–4, 6–7, 12–14, 17, 22–23; NRS, SC36/48/6; SC70/1/12; CC8/8/125, 132, 141).

associated with Scottish involvement in empire like Lanarkshire, Ayrshire and Dunbartonshire (thirty-eight in total).[52]

While assessments of the eighteenth-century British and Irish Isles acknowledge Dublin's status as a crucial secondary metropole, post-union Edinburgh's role as a functioning political capital has been neglected. Yet the city's prominence emerges clearly through EIC evidence. Although its share of civil service posts was less than that of Dublin's, the city and its Lothian hinterlands still secured 20 per cent of all such offices given to Scots. Burgh of Glasgow families were noticeably underrepresented in comparison.[53] There are major implications in these trends for the conventional emphasis on Glasgow as post-union Scotland's undisputed imperial city.[54] This long-established characterisation only holds true for the Atlantic world. Edinburgh dominated the politics, patronage and finances in Scotland associated with the eastern half of the Empire in the same way as Dublin did in Ireland. The enduring dominance of the national capitals was sustained in part by the new connections to Asia. More generally, the metropolitan provinces engaged with global expansion through a myriad of regional and city economies deploying multiple forms of monetary, social and human capital.

Social factors partly explain variations between countries and regions. The large percentage of unknown family backgrounds in the case of Irish and Welsh appointees limits analysis of the dynamics that linked some localities to the Company more consistently than others. Landed gentry formed a noticeable percentage in the Welsh (23.2 per cent) and Scottish (35.7 per cent) cohorts. There was a lower gentry share in the case of the Irish, which casts into greater relief the confirmed percentages secured by merchant and clerical families. However, the large ratio of unknown Irish social backgrounds (42.1 per cent) makes assessments of the class dynamics at work in that kingdom less robust than evidence from Scotland. Nevertheless, the combined total of burgh elites, clerical, legal and merchant families in both the Scottish and Irish cases was over 20 per cent and is clear evidence that the middling orders could and did access the most lucrative forms of imperial patronage.

The J-series also provides evidence of educational backgrounds. The results in Table 3.2 are constrained by the fact that in over half the Welsh examples no information on training is noted. In the case of the Scots and Irish, the educational history of over half of the civil service entrants can be recovered. England, especially London, was the key, though not singular, site of learning. This is hardly surprising. The directors expected their personnel to have experience of the capital's bureaucratic conventions and accountancy methods for the simple reason these formed the basis of Company practice in Asia.[55] Such expectations ensured that merchant houses in the City acted as finishing schools for those applying for a post. In his 1776 submission to the directors, John Snow from Waterford stressed his training in the Irish-London merchant house of Massey and McKrabie. David Inglis was the son of a loyalist from North Carolina who had returned to Inverness in the 1780s. A key part of his successful petition for a Bombay writership in 1797 involved indicating that the final part of his training took place in London. Banking houses like Coutts and Drummonds offered places to those from more elevated backgrounds such as Charles Stewart, the son of the earl of Blantyre, in the 1760s. This was a logical extension of the economy of credentialism but also shows how educational frameworks extended across national boundaries and blended provincial and metropolitan provision. Banks and businesses like Massey and McKrabie or Messrs Eadie and Laird and David Scott & Company acted as enhancers of human and cultural capital for clients intending to pursue careers overseas.[56] They traded in this form of social resource just as surely as they did in monetary capital and material commodities.

But if the tactics were broadly similar there were some significant differences in the use of education as a means of enhancing human capital. Welsh families relied to a greater extent on provision in English towns like Shrewsbury and Liverpool. By contrast, more Irish and Scots were educated in their own countries up until the point they joined the EIC. The Dublin merchant house of Jonathan Hepburn trained Thomas Bury and Henry Brooke, who became writers in 1749 and 1750 respectively.[57] This pattern of education at the provincial metropole was even more pronounced in the case of Scots. In the 1760s the Rotterdam merchant William Stevenson established a commercial academy in Edinburgh. He trained six individuals who went on to acquire writerships between 1764 and 1770. In the 1790s the Edinburgh-based educationalists William Laidlaw and Allan Masterton between them trained eleven successful applicants, over ten per cent of all Scots appointed to the civil service in that decade.[58] Educational testimonies in the J-series reveal another distinction between the metropolitan provinces. The fiscal-military state's infrastructure in post-union Scotland was considerably smaller than that of post-1690s Ireland.[59] Yet government departments such as the customs and excise operated as educational facilities north of the border in ways that do not seem to have occurred so readily in Dublin. The sons of Seaton of Borrowtouness, Sir Archibald Cockburn of Cockpen, James Fraser of Gorthlick and Robert Gardiner, the son of a London-Scots merchant, received training in the customs establishment at Leith or in the receiver-general's office in Edinburgh.[60] A similar pattern cannot be traced for Welsh or Irish applicants.

Edinburgh-based provision, combined with those educated in the other major burghs of Glasgow, Aberdeen, Dundee and Inverness, meant that

60.1 per cent of Scottish civil servants with a traceable education were trained in Scotland. This compares to 32.7 per cent in the case of Irish individuals and 10.5 per cent for the Welsh. These differences can be explained in part by the accessibility and relatively inexpensive nature of education in Scotland. The result was that more Scots joined the Company's upper echelons after continuing longer in their own country than was the case for either the Irish or the Welsh, an aspect of their personal development that fed into associational tendencies once relocated to Asia.[61] The more pronounced reliance on metropolitan provincial connections should not be viewed as a greater expression of national sentiment among Scots. Scotland was simply better equipped than either Protestant Ireland or Wales with an educational infrastructure capable of generating enhanced human and cultural capital locally as well as in London.

Combining province and metropole: the merchant marine

The civil service represented only one potentially remunerative career path. The same popular images of a hyper-rich 'Orient' that drove enthusiasm for administrative and mercantile posts shaped attitudes to employment in the merchant marine.[62] Much like the civil service, this sector could appear from a metropolitan-provincial perspective as a closed shop, accessible only to those with considerable venture capital. Between the 1750s and 1790s perhaps as few as thirty people at any one time, many related through kinship or marriage, dominated the lucrative world of building and leasing the Company's East Indiamen.[63] Known as the 'shipping interest', this tight-knit group exemplified the London-based gentlemanly capitalist oligarchies that both sustained and manipulated the EIC's monopoly.

Social capital and overlapping financial and familial networks were not the only prerequisites for inclusion in the shipping oligopoly. The construction of East Indiamen required massive reserves of capital and credit. In 1805 John Lennox of Woodhead near Campsie, whose family had been involved in EIC shipping since the 1760s, invested in a new East Indiaman, the *Lord Melville*: the vessel cost £34,226 to build.[64] Expenditure of this magnitude meant that few of the managing agents (known as ship's 'husbands'), or the ex-East Indiamen commanders and London-based financiers who comprised the shipping interest could afford to operate alone. Mutually interlocking credit became a defining feature of the shipping cartels.

Within this framework Scottish, Irish and Welsh participation evolved gradually and through several different avenues. The need to spread risk and costs opened up opportunities to non-London-based investors and made the shipping interest more accessible than its metrocentric location and oligarchic structure might suggest. Strong, vertical micro-networks of trust and familiarity based on local and regional affiliation became a way of partially servicing metropolitan credit requirements. Ships were divided into sixteen or thirty-two shares to accumulate finance from sleeping partners who satisfied themselves with a dividend after each voyage.[65] Taking up shipping shares proved popular with Scottish landed families imbued with a commercial as well as agrarian improvement ethic. Managing these transactions provided the Scottish legal establishment with a role in empire finance that has not been sufficiently recognised. During the 1770s and the 1780s the Edinburgh advocate Thomas Tod, brother of James, commander of the *Rochford* East Indiaman, used his legal business to attract investors. In 1780 he persuaded the sixth marquis of Tweeddale to invest £800. Thomas Graham of Airth did much the same in 1801 when he secured capital for his new vessel, the *Walpole*, from James Sandilands, ninth lord Torphichen. The transaction was expedited by the fact that the vessel's commander was a kinsman and namesake of Torphichen. It was through such seemingly prosaic interchanges that micro-networks centred on kin links morphed into meso-level networks.[66] The effect was to connect kith and kin interests in the metropolitan provinces to one of the most capital-reliant sectors of British gentlemanly capitalism.

Lawyers were not the only agents generating avenues into the shipping interest. As increasing numbers of EIC personnel returned home in the 1760s and 1770s, profits acquired in one area of the corporation were reinvested in another. Robert Lindsay of Leuchars, a Company civil servant who made much of his fortune shipping salt and piece goods in the Bay of Bengal, retired to Edinburgh in the mid-1780s. His experience prompted him to invest £1,200 in the *Lady Jane* East Indiaman in 1804. These trends created a dense web of connections between Edinburgh, London and the Company.[67] Local networks drew the metropolitan provinces into the gentry capitalist economy just as surely as the influence of major financial institutions or state policy. The business activities of Robert Preston of Woodford in Essex and Valleyfield in Perthshire reveal the scale of investment. A former East Indiaman commander, he was part owner or 'husband' of seven vessels in 1783 and 1784 alone. During these years he sold £10,925 in shares to fourteen investors: three were from Scotland while a further two were London-Scots.[68]

Preston's prominence in London shipping circles and the fact that over one-third of his investors came from Scotland is not as incongruous as it might at first seem. His contacts north of the border supplemented his sources of capital, reducing his reliance on metropolitan connections while enhancing his creditworthiness in the City. In return, his Scottish investors gained influence in the metropole and were better able to place sons and associates in marine employment. As economies of monetary, human and social capital intertwined, they facilitated a productive circle of influence in much the same way as shareholding secured civil service patronage. The ways in which credit demand and supply moved beyond London support reassessments of the Empire's financial services sector.[69] Edinburgh did not undermine London's hegemony but neither did it remain marginalised from the gentlemanly capitalist order. The city evolved systems of genteel investment which were organised around the distinctive legal and landed order north of the border and that paralleled on a much smaller scale those of the metropolis. Edinburgh loomed large in Scotland's emerging gentry capitalist economy.

Alongside the percentage of civil servant posts secured by Edinburgh and Lothian families shown in Table 3.2, this culture of provincial investment underlines the need for a major reappraisal of the Scottish capital and legal establishment's engagement with empire. Both are usually written out of analyses in favour of Glasgow's commercial prominence. Yet far from remaining sealed north of the border, Scotland's lawyers begin servicing imperial finance through the marshalling of surpluses derived from landed incomes. Edinburgh acted as a significant imperial sub-metropole in this respect, becoming substantively involved in one of the most profitable aspects of early modern British expansion. This was accomplished through the adaptation of its civic and legal infrastructure rather than as a one-way dependency on London. This development has implications for assessments of when and how regional Britain integrated into empire. These trends began fifty to sixty years before the rise of the industrial and manufacturing cities more usually associated with the increasing influence of the gentlemanly capitalist order in the English and Scottish regions.[70]

The movement of monies from Ireland into EIC shipping does not seem to have matched that of Scotland. Just why the Irish presence, either as investors or owners, should be smaller than that of the Scots is puzzling given the extent to which Ireland's shipping and trade centred upon the metropolis.[71] Irishmen were certainly not excluded from the Company's merchant's fleet: Catholics obtained high rank as merchant marine officers as early as 1712. In that year Captain Edward Arlond, part owner of the *Cambridge* East Indiaman, petitioned to become her commander. The case of Arlond, originally from near Waterford, challenges the argument that the elite levels of British imperialism were closed to Catholics until near the end of the eighteenth century. The Company directors were well aware of his religious allegiances but accepted that the *Cambridge* was Arlond's property and his to do with as he saw fit within reason. They conceded that he could command provided he employed a Church of England clergyman as ship's chaplain rather than a Catholic.[72]

Civil servants and mariners 101

Property rights mattered to the directors, however much they might have preferred to avoid any Catholic presence. Upon stepping down from command in 1716 Arlond's response reveals how the realities of property ownership cut across sectarian regulation aimed at keeping the corporation Protestant. He nominated as his replacement another Irishman, James Tobin from Kilkenny, purser on the *Donegal* East Indiaman since 1707. Tobin is better known for his later role in the Ostend Company and as a prominent figure in a web of émigré Irish commercial networks operating across maritime Western Europe.[73] By basing himself in the Austrian Netherlands Tobin conforms to the model of the Irish entrepreneur driven to the continent in the face of sectarian exclusion from Britain's Empire. Yet Tobin was no marginalised refugee. He had prospered in English Company service since the 1700s and in December 1716 was appointed commander of the *Cambridge*. It was Tobin's later flouting of specie regulations, not his nationality or his religion, that ensured his dismissal from the EIC and subsequent migration to Ostend.[74] The surviving evidence confirms that Tobin did not covert to Protestantism in order to secure his command. When he died in 1732 his will made provision for a substantial donation to the Catholic clergy of Kilkenny.[75] Tobin's example demonstrates how a Catholic Irish network penetrated the heart of the EIC's shipping interest, one of the Empire's most charmed inner circles, at a remarkably early stage of the eighteenth century.

The cases of both Tobin and Arlond raise fundamental questions about the potential for a productive relationship between Catholic Ireland, the English East India Company and British imperialism a century before emancipation. If Catholic Irishmen with sufficient capital were not automatically barred from joining the shipping interest, then the lack of an Irish presence cannot be understood purely in terms of sectarian prohibition. There is a need to rethink assumptions that Irish Catholics wished to access British imperialism but were always blocked from doing so. Exclusion was certainly prevalent, especially in state institutions like the army and navy, and should not be underplayed. However, the case of the EIC points to a more subtle process that shifts the spotlight onto the limited and temporary attractiveness of Britishness rather than simply assuming a marginalised role for Ireland and the Irish. Irish Catholics could and did participate in the Company's expansion; but this does not mean they felt any compunction to accept all or even most aspects of Britain and Britishness. Evidence from Ireland demonstrates the very real limits of the Empire's attractiveness as a cultural and nation-building project. Although Tobin lived in London and retained strong connections with Company directors like Alexander Hume, his will left £4,000 to establish his nephew, James, in a merchant house at Cádiz. The family's future lay in Catholic Europe, not in the British metropolis. Ironically, empire made this realignment to Europe possible. Here was a Catholic Irish kin network testing all commercial avenues and career horizons. Having experimented with enterprise via London for over quarter of a century, the network eschewed British imperialism and relocated to a part of Europe that better reflected its membership's economic, political, social and cultural preferences. While historical analysis has problematised Ireland's Catholics because they do not seem to easily fit models of Britain's emerging empire and nationalism, it seems the response of some Irish Catholics was to marginalise Britishness.

Notwithstanding the examples of Arlond and Tobin, Protestants from Ireland assumed a more prominent role in the shipping interest over time. Albert and Arnold Nesbitt were co-owners of the *Royal Charlotte* in 1771. Meanwhile, Robert Wigram from Wexford served as an East Indiaman surgeon during the 1760s and 1770s; by the 1810s he was a ship's husband with investments in seventeen vessels totalling £88,048.[76] This made him one of the early nineteenth-century shipping sector's most prominent individuals and certainly meant he was one of the most successful metropolitan provincials within the organisation at that time. However, the Nesbitts and Wigram were atypical. Their prominence disguises the fact that Irish personnel and connections never acquired the same density of meso-level networks in the merchant marine as did the Scots.

Scottish participation in the ownership and management of East Indiamen dates from the same period as that of Tobin and Arlond. The key difference lay in the slow but persistent build-up over several generations of durable connections centred upon London-Scots merchants, financial and landed interests in Scotland, and a web of officers in the merchant marine. This crucial development began prior to 1707 and was well established by the 1740s. John Leckie from Kippen, commander of the *Constant Friend* as early as 1701, had taken service in the merchant marine in the later decades the seventeenth century. But a self-sustaining, critical mass of individuals capable of snowballing into meso-networks took time to evolve. Involvement in shipping was a gradual, unspectacular process; by 1722 Andrew Drummond of Charing Cross was part owner of two East Indiamen.[77] Few other kin-interests from metropolitan provincial backgrounds matched the early influence of Alexander and Abraham Hume. Having accrued capital and experience in the Ostend Company, the brothers quickly cemented their influence at East India Company House during the 1730s.[78] While Alexander served as a director, Abraham emerged as a major player in shipping. Their business operations were transnational and transoceanic. Towards the end of his career in 1769, Abraham Hume, in conjunction with his nephew Alexander, completed shipping transactions with the Company totalling £64,000 in one year.

Besides leasing vessels to the Company during the period from the 1730s to the 1750s, the Hume brothers were patrons for a number of Scots who rose to become East Indiamen commanders. These included George Cumming from Edinburgh, Alexander Macleod from Harris (a kinsman by marriage) and Alexander Hume's own son, also called Alexander.[79]

While Irish networking revolved round a limited number of extremely successful individuals like the Nesbitts or Wigrams, a dense lattice of investors, ship husbands and marine patronage connected the Scottish shires, the coastal burghs, Edinburgh, London and the Company. These meso-networks transcended families or localities and proved effective at embedding Scots in the merchant marine. An important aspect of this development lay in the way in which these informal webs were renewed from one generation to the next. Networks are often seen as dependent on a small number of participants with strong vertical ties. Such arrangements could be vulnerable to fracture over time.[80] In the case of Scots in the shipping sector this eventuality was avoided through constant renewal and extension of membership. By the 1760s and 1770s this process of evolution encompassed Mackenzie of Delvine in Edinburgh, metropolis-based Scots such as the Moffat brothers, the Madeira merchant house of Robert Scott & Co., and retired commanders like George Cumming and Charles Foulis. These men acted as patrons to the next generation of clients, so multiplying and entrenching Scottish participation in the merchant marine. The established figures blended their provincial and metropolitan interests in ways that nurtured the early careers of men like Robert Preston, Burnett Abercrombie, Robert Munro, James Dundas and William Fullerton-Elphinstone.[81] The snowball effect generated by such meso-networks took over fifty years to become fully apparent, but the impact by the 1770s was unmistakeable.

East Indiaman officers: backgrounds, careers and networks

The cumulative effect of these developments can be traced in the growing number of Irish, Scots and Welsh merchant marine officers. Prior to the rapid expansion of the presidency armies in the late 1740s and early 1750s, the officer ranks of the East Indiaman fleet constituted the corporation's largest pool of middle-ranking employment. These posts became available on a predictable year-on-year cycle as each new round of voyages commenced. Along with the commander, each vessel retained a purser, a surgeon and assistant surgeon, six mates and around four midshipmen. With a minimum of twenty ships at sea by the 1740s, rising to fifty-one by the 1800s, the number of officers grew from around 280 to over 714 in any one year.[82] The most exhaustive survey of this part of the corporation gives an estimate of 10,184 merchant marine officers between 1690 and 1813. This amount provides the overall context for the Scots, Irish and Welsh figures in Table 3.3.

The totals seem to show metropolitan provincial involvement at the officer level to be marginal at best. However, the very small percentages (shown in round brackets) relate only to confirmable Scottish, Irish and Welsh numbers as set against the overall amount. Within the 10,184 total there are thousands of individuals who are only identifiable by name, their vessel and their dates of service. If only those with a known place of origin are included, a new more specific comparator of 2,044 officers is arrived at for the same period. Set against this revised amount the totals in Table 3.3 take on a different complexion and are illustrated by the percentages shown in square brackets. These suggest just over 20 per cent of all maritime officers with confirmed backgrounds can be identified as Scots: the equivalent Irish and Welsh presence also increases but remains well below what might be expected relative to their overall populations.

Both methods of calculation have their drawbacks. Comparison with the total of 10,184 artificially lowers the metropolitan provincial share as many individuals cannot be assigned a place of origin, especially those serving in the fleet in the first half of the eighteenth century. The lack of biographical details for maritime personnel means that the percentages in round brackets are too conservative. Equally, however, the weightings derived from the 2,044 amount over-inflate the Scottish presence both as an overall ratio and in relation to the Irish and Welsh. As already highlighted with regard to the civil servants, the survival of wills and testaments in Scotland enable the background of more Scots to be securely identified. This disparity is compounded by the fact that the recording of East Indiamen officer origins steadily improved after the 1760s, precisely at the point when metropolitan provincials joined the fleet in greater numbers. The result is a double skewing of the Irish, Scottish and Welsh profiles, first disguising likely numbers for the earlier decades and then producing more robust totals precisely when these groups became more prominent. All that can confidently be stated is that metropolitan provincial involvement in this part of the organisation was almost certainly lower than per capita shares of population. Secondly, while the Scottish total is significantly larger than that of either the Irish or Welsh, all three formed a minority when set against the large numbers serving from 1690 to 1813.

The timing of the slowly increasing provincial profile also matches findings in Table 3.1, with the 1750s to the 1780s showing a clear rise in the volume and ratio of posts secured. This change may be less dramatic than the figures suggest. The better quality of records after the 1750s, combined with the lack of systematic evidence relating to the first half of the

Table 3.3 Scottish, Irish and Welsh merchant marine officers, 1690–1813

Years	1690–1709	1710–29	1730–49	1750–69	1770–89	1790–1813	Totals	10,184	[2,044]
Scots	2	1	11	46	205	163	428	(4.2%)	[20.9%]
Irish	0	4	0	7	57	34	102	(1%)	[4.9%]
Welsh	0	0	0	7	8	24	39	(0.3%)	[1.9%]

(SIWA. Source: Anthony Farrington, *A Biographical Index*, pp. 1–885; IOR, B/40-B/95; P/328/60–64; P/416/77–98; L/AG/34/29/4–22, 185–210, 341–343; TNA, PROB11/549–1903; NRS, CC1/6/56, 59, 74, 133; CC3/3/12, 15; CC3/4/32; CC3/5/2, 5–6; CC8/8/84, 90, 105, 110, 112–13, 116, 118–19, 120–36, 138–39, 140–42, 144–46; CC9/7; CC10/5; CC16/4; CC18/4; CC20/7/4, 7; CC21/7/9; SC26/38/1; SC36/48/6–7; SC70/1/3–4, 6–7, 12–14, 17, 22–23; NRS, SC36/48/6; SC70/1/12; CC8/8/125, 132, 141).

century, might well disguise a more gradual build-up within the merchant marine over many decades. Beyond overall numeric trends, the sociology of these mariners provides another indication of how provincial regions used the metropolis as a stepping stone to Asia. Known origins and career trajectories are summarised in Table 3.4. The high percentages of unknown class backgrounds for all three national groups make firm conclusions difficult. What evidence there is indicates those joining the merchant marine came from lower-status circumstances than those entering the civil service, although the range of middling-sort origins again indicates how empire service offered upward social mobility. There are some important similarities with the patterns in Table 3.2. The same regions that supplied noticeable numbers of civil servants also feature prominently in the distribution of merchant marine personnel. Leinster and Ulster provided over 53 per cent of known Irish individuals while the four counties of the South Wales area were responsible for 41 per cent of all confirmable ships' officers from that part of the United Kingdom. Similarly, the tendency for other districts such as Connacht and north-west Wales to contribute negligible percentages is repeated. Leinster, Ulster and the southern Welsh counties were Ireland and Wales's demographic and economic centres, so substantial returns for these areas are hardly surprising. Yet the high variation in rates of participation illustrates how empire in Asia contributed to existing regional diversity and entrenched unequal economic development.

Scotland offers a clear contrast. There is the same tendency towards the roughly equitable spread of regional representation which characterised the country's contribution to the civil service. However, involvement in the merchant marine exhibits a more pronounced concentration of personnel from the country's east coast, around the Lothians, the Firth of Forth, Fife, the Firth of Tay and the north-east of Scotland. The counties in these districts supplied 70 per cent of East Indiaman officers with traceable backgrounds – 205 individuals. By contrast, maritime personnel from west-central Scotland were far less prevalent, at only 6.5 per cent of those with known origins. As with the civil service, this pattern of heavy east-coast representation challenges assumptions about which areas of Scotland engaged strongly with empire. Evidence from the EIC's merchant marine shows that the country's North Sea littoral, burgh ports and hinterlands contributed significantly to a previously unrecognised branch of sojourning.[83] The well-known integration into the Atlantic of the Clyde ports was matched on the other side of the country by a shift of personnel into Asia via London and the Company's maritime sector.

The central role of human mobility in facilitating movement into the EIC's fleet becomes clear once professional backgrounds are considered. East Indiaman officers were highly skilled mariners with global careers.

Table 3.4 Merchant marine officers: regional, social and educational backgrounds

	Region	Social Origins	Career Background
Irish 102	Leinster = 36 (35.2%) Ulster = 19 (18.6%) Munster = 11 (10.7%) Connacht = 2 (1.9%) Unknown = 34 (33.3%)	Landed gentry = 3 (2.9%) Clergy = 2 (1.9%) Education = 2 (1.9%) Unknown = 95 (93.1%)	RN = 15 (14.8%) West Indies trade = 11 (10.8%) Coasting trade = 8 (7.9%) North America trades = 8 (7.9%) Europe trades = 4 (3.9%) Unknown = 55 (54.4%)
Scots 428	Central = 77 (17.9%) Edinburgh = 50 (11.6%) NE = 45 (10.5%) Lothians = 34 (7.9%) Borders = 32 (7.4%) Highlands = 27 (6.3%) West Central = 20 (4.6%) The North = 5 (1.1%) England/London = 4 (0.9%) Unknown = 134 (31.3%)	Aristocracy/Gentry = 39 (9.1%) Merchant = 21 (4.9%) Clergy = 13 (3%) Misc. = 13 (3%) Legal = 10 (2.3%) Military & Medical = 9 (2.1%) Mariner = 9 (2.1%) Tenant Farmer = 4 (0.9%) Unknown = 310 (72.4%)	Coasting trade = 51 (11.9%) RN = 44 (10.2%) West Indies trade = 42 (9.8%) North Europe & Baltic = 40 (9.3%) North America trades = 24 (5.6%) Iberian & Med. = 14 (3.2%) Unknown = 213 (49.7%)
Welsh 39	South Wales = 16 (41.0%) East Wales = 10 (25.6%) W/N Wales = 2 (5.1%) Unknown = 11 (28.2%)	Landed gentry = 1 (2.5%) Medical = 1 (2.5%) Unknown = 37 (94.8%)	Coasting trade = 6 (15.3%) West Indies trade = 6 (15.3%) RN = 2 (5.1%) Europe trades = 1 (2.5%) Military = 1 (2.5%) Unknown = 23 (58.9%)

(SIWA. Source: Farrington, *A Biographical Index*, pp. 1–885; IOR, B/40–B/95; P/328/60–64; P/416/77–98; L/AG/34/29/4–22, 185–210, 341–343; TNA, PROB 11/549–1903; NRS, CC16/56, 59, 74, 133; CC3/3/12, 15; CC3/4/32; CC3/5/2, 5–6; CC8/8/84, 90, 105, 110, 112–13, 116, 118–19; 120–36, 138–39, 140–42, 144–46; CC9/7; CC10/5; CC16/4; CC18/4; CC20/7/4, 7; CC21/7/9; SC26/38/1; SC36/48/6–7; SC70/1/3–4, 6–7, 12–14, 17, 22–23; NRS, SC36/48/6; SC70/1/12; CC8/8/125, 132, 141).

As Table 3.4 demonstrates, many commenced their professional lives on the British and Irish coasting routes before picking up experience on voyages to Iberia, the Mediterranean and, in the case of Scots in particular, Northern Europe and the Baltic.[84] Long-established maritime and commercial connections into these regions did not compete with the Empire's economy; instead they directly facilitated the transfer from intra-European shipping into oceanic voyaging. Time spent on the transatlantic routes to North America and especially the Caribbean was often matched by time in the Royal Navy. Maritime officers crossed and recrossed the whole span of Britain's oceanic empire as a matter of routine. Few other forms of movement, including those of capital and commodities, were as global in this period as the career cycles of these mariners.

A typical example is Robert Reay from Wexford. After training as an able seaman on the Irish coasting trade in the late 1760s, he served as a ship's mate on voyages to Jamaica and Antigua in the 1770s. His involvement in Britain's transatlantic system of enslavement and its associated trades was followed by a stint in the Royal Navy during the American War of Independence. Five voyages to Asia followed in the 1780s to the 1790s before he took command of the *Dublin* East Indiaman in 1797, the owner of which was another Irishman and former commander, John Clements from Cavan. Jeremiah Dawkins from Llanelli in Carmarthen had a similar career. Early experience on the Iberian routes was followed by time as a midshipman on the *Harcourt* East Indiaman from 1769 to the early 1770s. A switch to the Jamaica trades and time as commander of a Royal Navy vessel ended with three round trips to Asia in the 1780s before Dawkins took command of the *Earl Talbot* from 1791 to 1797. The movement of Scots officers into the fleet is exemplified by the career of James Haliburton, the son of a Dundee merchant. Gravitating initially into the port's long-established Baltic routes, he later became a mate on a vessel bound for the Caribbean in the 1770s. During the 1780s and 1790s six round trips to Asia as a senior mate ended with his appointment as commander of the *Glatton* in 1804.[85]

Numerous professional life cycles such as these account for the patterns in Table 3.4. An obvious effect of the larger Scottish numbers was that more individuals can be confirmed as East Indiaman commanders, a highly lucrative and prestigious post with major opportunities for profit and patronage. In 1803 Thomas Graham, whose brother James Graham of Airth served as a Bengal civil servant, obtained command of the *Windham*. He calculated that once his expenses were accounted for he would make approximately £5,000 on a round trip from Britain to Madras, Bengal and Benkulen. His estimated profits can be contextualised by the fact that his brother's estate in Stirlingshire had an annual rental of £2,277. Some routes held out the prospect of substantial returns if commercial options were properly exploited. As a former free merchant, David Scott of Dunninald was ideally placed to make a realistic assessment of the profitability inherent in the command of an East Indiaman. In 1796 he estimated that a return voyage from Europe to Bombay and China (the most lucrative route) could net the commander £10,000.[86]

Given this potential it is significant that a total of 138 Scots can be identified at commander rank from 1700 to 1813. Over such an extended timeline this may not seem an especially significant amount. However, the bulk of appointments occurred in a more concentrated period: 130 of the 138 served between 1750 and 1813. By comparison twenty Irish and seven Welshmen can be identified as commanders during these years. With metropolitan provincials only appearing in meaningful numbers after the 1750s, the narrower timescale suggests a concentration effect as these men advanced up the ranks and emerged at the top of the merchant marine between the 1770s and the 1790s. Analysis of the Company's business structures has argued that around 28 per cent of identifiable East Indiaman commanders in the 1790s to the 1800s were Scots. This disproportionate presence arose from a similar form of metropolitan-regionalism in the shipping interest to that exhibited by David Scott and Charles Grant in the directorate. A Scot commanded over two-thirds of all voyages by East Indiamen owned or managed by Robert Preston.[87] This pattern of prominence in the upper echelons of the merchant marine mirrors trends in the officer profile of Liverpool slave ships during the 1750s to the 1800s. While Scots provided 14.3 per cent of ordinary crewmen on such vessels they made up 20 per cent of captains.[88]

Although the overrepresentation of Scots at the higher reaches of the eighteenth-century army is well known, their relative prominence at the command level in two of Britain's most important branches of oceanic trade needs to be better delineated and understood. However, metropolitan provincials were not exceptional in developing a networked presence in the Empire's various commercial marines. Families and interests from London and the English regions acted in similar ways. Micro- and meso-level networks can be traced to a number of Devon families who also specialised in intergenerational service on East Indiamen.[89] A reliance on the social capital inherent in networks as means of pursuing gentry capitalism was common to all nationalities and regions of the British and Irish Isles. The difference lay in the way these networks shaped variable patterns of involvement that reflected and reproduced provincial distinctions.

The pooling of venture capital among metropolis- and province-based investors and the accumulation of professional experience on coastal and international shipping routes influenced the personnel profiles of the corporation's vessels. The East Indiaman fleet acted as a melting pot, bringing Irishmen, Scots, Welsh and English together in a common culture of highly technical seafaring, navigational science and the prestige associated with oceanic commerce. In 1783 the Welshman John Lewis took command of the *Valentine* after working his way up the ranks since 1767. His officers included a midshipman from Wales, a fifth and sixth mate from Scotland and Patrick Ivory, a Catholic from County Louth, who acted as ship's surgeon.[90] In bringing together people from across the British and Irish Isles, the Company's marine can be viewed in much the same light as the army and Royal Navy, as a means by which common professional identities and sentiments might be nurtured.[91]

Yet the inculcation of common Britishness through empire did not proceed in a unidirectional manner. As the examples of Castlereagh, Grant, Scott and others demonstrate, national and especially regional influences remained powerful. Metropolitan provincial webs of affiliation produced concentrations of personnel on particular vessels. Patronage extended down the marine officer hierarchy as owners and commanders promoted and protected kinsmen, local and regional associates.[92] This clustering effect is evident in the officer profile of the *Phoenix* in 1790. The commander was a Scot, Alexander Gray, as were the first, third and fourth mates and two midshipmen; the surgeon's mate also originated from north of the border. This meant 50 per cent of the officers were from Scotland, with personnel from the Lothians and the north-east especially prominent. A lower but still substantial ratio (35.7 per cent) of Scots officers appeared on the *Neptune* in 1783 and the *Airly Castle* in 1787.[93]

The same tendency for regional influence to draw personnel together can be seen on vessels with Irish commanders. In 1801 Robert Patterson from Camus in County Tyrone took command of the *Royal Charlotte*; one of the midshipmen was also from Camus, the sixth mate too was from Ulster and yet another midshipman from Kerry.[94] However, with far fewer officers in the upper echelons, this concentration of Welsh and Irish personnel was less likely to occur on a routine basis. These patterns of hybrid local and professional association raise questions about how best to understand the Company as the embodiment of London's gentlemanly capitalist order and as the mechanism by which British colonialism was imposed across Asia. Alongside these formal functions the corporation was also a social framework of lived experience. In ways that mirror the credentialism of Irish and particularly Scottish directors, the merchant marine enabled and modernised local, regional and familial networks. Embedded within the imposing edifice of the shipping interest and its oceangoing East Indiaman fleet lay a surprisingly intimate combination of the local and the global.

Conclusion

When, how and to what extent individuals and networks from Ireland, Wales and Scotland entered the Company's civil service and merchant marine provides one way of understanding 'semi-peripheral' Europe's participation in corporate empire. Through processes of political incorporation and economic integration, the metropolitan provinces were increasingly part of one of Europe's most 'advanced' regions. But the criteria used to define 'advanced' – surplus monetary capital, a highly monetised economy, the replacement of labour with technological innovations, and a structurally integrated rural and urban society geared towards market production – were only partially evident in Scotland, Wales and Ireland.[95] The existence of such internal complexity challenges explanatory models that homogenise Europe's 'advanced' regions in order to explain global trajectories. Ongoing national and intra-provincial difference, just as surely as generic 'advanced' characteristics, shaped capacities to exploit the Company's expansion. This dynamic of integration through difference ensured that the British and Irish Isles's diversity was projected outwards into the Empire. The process manifested itself in different chronologies and trajectories of participation and in the embedding of diverse regional and socio-economic profiles in the civil service and merchant marine. While the Company's trade and dominion in Asia questionably homogenised aspects of British and Irish society, it also sparked complex national, regional and local adjustments.[96] Growing provincial involvement in the British Atlantic contrasts strongly with the marginal presence of Scots, Irish and Welsh in the upper echelons of the Company until as late as the 1740s. The differences in accessibility between the two hemispheres confirm the extent to which the British Empire remained a mosaic of constitutional arrangements, regulatory structures and jurisdictions. These differences in turn shaped variable patterns of participation and the capacity to exploit opportunities.[97]

As an aggressively expansionist global organisation, the Company sparked uneven dynamics across both Asia and the British and Irish Isles. Scots began acquiring a proportionate share of civil service employment by the 1750s, increasing to a situation of substantial overrepresentation in the 1790s and 1800s. Welsh society experienced a diametrically opposite trajectory. In the 1690s individuals from that part of Britain secured posts at a rate equal to the country's share of population and above comparable Irish and Scottish levels of employment. By the 1730s and 1740s this profile had declined and left Wales structurally underrepresented for the rest of the long eighteenth century. Ireland presents a more ambiguous scenario still. Early Catholic involvement in shipping never diversified into a regionally or confessionally broad set of connections with the Company's higher echelons. Established Anglo-Irish interests also took longer than comparable Scottish networks to secure a reasonable share of civil service posts. Despite a substantial commercial infrastructure in London, as well as micro-networks of both Catholics and Protestants active in the fleet by the 1710s and 1720s, neither did Irish interests break into the merchant marine in a substantial way.

The Scottish profile in shipping can be easily overestimated as a consequence of the patronage wielded by large-scale investors like Andrew Moffat and Robert Preston or the presence of at least 130 East Indiaman commanders between c.1750 and c.1810. The development of influence in shipping through monetary investment enabled the deployment of human capital in much the same way as shareholding facilitated civil service patronage. The ability of one metropolitan province to do noticeably better than its counterparts demonstrates the acute sensitivity of societies like Ireland, Scotland and Wales to conditions in London and across the Empire. Far from reacting to obstacles and opportunities in uniform ways, the particular political, religious, regional and local attributes of Irish, Scottish and Welsh society directly shaped patterns of engagement with the Company. Existing differences and local distinctiveness were consolidated in the process and remained active ingredients in the process of exploiting proto-globalisation. Empire in Asia entrenched in new ways Leinster and Ulster's political, economic, social and material dominance of Ireland. In the case of Wales the southern counties predominated. In Scotland, the political capital, Edinburgh, along with the eastern coastal localities did well, a pattern which brings ports like Leith, the Fife burghs, Perth, Dundee, Montrose and Aberdeen more fully into the history of the country's role in the pre-1815 empire.

Ironically, the creation of new differences within and between metropolitan provinces was driven not by a lack of contact with the metropole but by growing and deepening interaction. The successes and the limitations of Irish, Welsh and Scottish involvement in the corporation's commercial and maritime sectors illustrate the sophisticated intersection of human and monetary capital and the underestimated role of this combination in shaping pre-1815 British imperialism in Asia. By working through the metropolis, undercapitalised provincials were able to deploy their social networks and human capital into the English East India Company in the hope of an eventual financial return. At the upper levels of the corporation at least, Scottish society managed this process far more successfully than either Irish or Welsh interests. These deployments of social and human capital challenge ideas about a 'core' Europe that exploited global expansion largely through monetary forms of wealth, technological innovation, and innate 'comparative advantage'. Local diversity and the sophisticated use of social and human wealth were the defining hallmarks of how the conventionally 'poor' provinces of the British and Irish Isles accessed half of world trade and empire. Until the 1740s involvement was focused on the civil service and merchant marine. With the rapid expansion of the Company's military complex in the late 1740s and early 1750s, new avenues of employment became available.

Notes

1 Geoffrey Quiley, 'The East India Company's Patronage of Eighteenth-century Art', in Huw V. Bowen and Nigel Rigby (eds), *The Worlds of the East India Company* (London: Boydell & Brewer, 2004), pp. 183–99; D. Armitage, *The Ideological Origins of the British Empire* (Cambridge: Cambridge University Press, 2000), p. 171.
2 Marshall, *East Indian Fortunes*, pp. 9–27; Bernard S. Cohn, 'Recruitment and Training of British Civil Servants in India, 1600–1860', in Ralph Braibanti (ed.), *Asian Bureaucratic Systems Emergent from the British Imperial Tradition* (Durham, NC: Duke University Press, 1966), pp. 87–140; Bowen, *The Business of Empire*, pp. 84–150; Mentz, *English Gentleman Merchant*, pp. 215–59.
3 P. J. Marshall, 'Economic and Political Expansion: The Case of Oudh', *Modern Asian Studies*, 9 (1975), 465–82; R. Mukherjee, 'Trade and Empire in Awadh, 1765–1804', *Past & Present*, 94 (1982), 88–90; Jon Wilson, *The Domination of Strangers: Modern Government in Eastern India, 1780–1835* (Basingstoke: Palgrave, 2008), pp. 19–74.
4 IOR, J/1/1 to J/1/28. See too, Cohn, 'Recruitment and Training', pp. 102–40.
5 Parker, 'The Directors of the East India Company', vols I and II, passim; Farrington, *Biographical Index*, pp. 1–882. For embarkation rolls of rank and file see IOR, L/MIL/9/85–98. For Company army muster rolls, 1708 to 1813: IOR, L/MIL/10/122–139; MIL/11/109–124; L/MIL/12/117–134.
6 IOR, L/MIL/9/85–98; O/5/26–7, 30–1.
7 Suzanne Rigg, *Men of Spirit and Enterprise: Scots and Orkneymen in the Hudson's Bay Company, 1780–1821* (Edinburgh: John Donald, 2011), p. 174.
8 McGilvary, *East India Patronage*, pp. 113–20; Bowen, 'Asiatic Interactions', pp. 168–92.
9 Cook, 'The Irish Raj', 510; Thomas Bartlett, '"This Famous Island Set in a Virginian Sea"', p. 272.
10 Bowen, *The Business of Empire*, pp. 274–5; Marshall, 'The Caribbean and India', p. 12.
11 Andrew Dewar Gibb, *Scottish Empire* (Glasgow: A. Maclehose, 1937), pp. 3–5, 310–15; C. D. Rice, 'Scottish Enlightenment, American Revolution and Atlantic Reform', in O. D. Edwards and G. Shepperson (eds), *Scotland, Europe and the American Revolution* (Edinburgh: Edinburgh University Student Publications, 1976), pp. 75–6; Riddy, 'Warren Hastings', pp. 47–8; Fry, *The Dundas*

Despotism, p. 112; Devine, *Scotland's Empire*, pp. 251, 269; T. M. Devine, 'The Spoils of Empire', in T. M. Devine (ed.), *Scotland and the Union, 1707–2007* (Edinburgh: Edinburgh University Press, 2008), pp. 104–5; Colley, *Britons*, p. 128.
12 Marshall, *East Indian Fortunes*, pp. 11–13; IOR, L/F/10/1–5; L/F/10/111–113.
13 *A Letter to the Proprietors of East India Stock from John Johnstone, Esq* (London: n.p., 1766), pp. 5–6; HL, Pulteney Papers, Box 3, Calcutta, 23 December 1761.
14 Julian Hoppit, 'Scotland and the Taxing Union, 1707–1815', *The Scottish Historical Review*, 98 (2019), 52.
15 NRS, GD110/987/2; NRS, GD24/1/464 (c), 147; GD24/1/464 (n), 27–8, 33–4; GD248/60/3/28; NLS, MS1336, fos. 143, 205; MS1142, fos. 130, 144–5; MS1336, fos. 171, 174; MS1337, fos. 6, 205, 208, MS1367, fo. 39.
16 NRS, GD18/5218/10, 20, 36, 40, 42, 49; GD24/1/464 (c), 34, 75.
17 Karras, *Sojourners in the Sun*, pp. 1–11; Hancock, *Citizens of the World*, p. 195.
18 Mario Varrichio, 'Introduction: The Other Side of Leaving', in Mario Varrichio (ed.), *Back to Caledonia: Scottish Homecomings from the Seventeenth Century to the Present* (Edinburgh: John Donald, 2012), pp. 1–33; Mark Wyman, 'Emigrants Returning: The Evolution of a Tradition', and Patrick Fitzgerald, '"Come Back, Paddy Reilly": Aspects of Irish Return Migration, 1600–1845', both in Harper (ed.), *Emigrant Homecomings*, pp. 16–31, 32–51; Karras, *Sojourners in the Sun*, pp. 125–9.
19 NRS, GD248/413, p. 63; NRS, GD87/1/34/1–2; NRS, GD1/1155/69/14–15.
20 GCA, Bo. 2, pp. 55–7; NLS, MS1367, fo. 114; NLS, MS3385, pp. 77–9; NLS, MS11020, fos. 2–5; NLS, MS9246, fo. 46; NRS, GD29/2063/3; GD29/2144; GHL, MS5881/5, fo. 15; TCD, MS 3767/1/22.
21 Helenus Scott, *The adventures of a rupee* (London: J. Murray, 1782), pp. 50–62; GCA, Bo. 2: Letter Book of George Bogle: Calcutta, September 1771; KH, Graham Papers, 2nd Series, 51–126, Bundle 57: Calcutta, 21 August 1776: Thomas Graham to George Graham; NRS, GD1/594/1: Edinburgh, 22 March 1796; TCD, MS3767/25; NLI, MS14337: 9 March 1809: William Conwell to John Conwell.
22 HL, Pulteney Papers, Box 7: Broomholm, 18 October 1769; NRS, GD345/1175/2/26x; GD 248/60/3/28; GD248/226/5/38; NRS, GD1/736/5: Fassifern, 10 Feb 1794; NRS, GD1/594/1: Edinburgh, 22 March 1796; NLS, MS1336, fos. 207–8; MS1367, fo. 66; IOR, F128/23/1: Dublin, 14 November 1758; TCD, MS3767/8; TCD, MS3551/2, fos. 96, 108–9.
23 NRS, GD1/1155/69/14; GD18/5218/27–8, 38; NRS, GD110/987/2; NRS, GD38/2/8/125; NLS, MS1336, fos. 143, 171, 188, 205; MS1337, fo.10; NLS, MS1073, fo. 6; MS1074, fo. 122; AUL, MS3346, Box 8: London: 13 February 1765: George Ross to John Ross.
24 NRS, GD1/594/1; GD248/179/1/74; GD248/453/1: 8 August 1783: James Grant to Lewis Grant; NLS, MS6360, pp. 134–6; BC, Box 1: Brodie House, 1 July 1789: James Brodie to James Brodie; TCD, MS 3767/21.

25 E. W. Said, *Orientalism* (London: Penguin, 2003), pp. 58–73; Jürgen Osterhammel, *Unfabling the East: The Enlightenment's Encounter with Asia* (Princeton, NJ: Princeton University Press, 2018), pp. 171, 272–84, 351–8, 448–56.
26 IOR, B/70, p. 364; *Scots Magazine*, 9 (1747), pp. 162–5, 293, 347; NLS, MS1367, fo. 161; GCA, Bo 20/17: London, 18 November 1773.
27 GCA, T-SK11/2/22; NRS, GD110/987/2; GD110/1021/12; NLS, MS11005, fo.21; NLS, MS10920, fos. 145–6.
28 IOR, L/F/10/1–5, 111-113; *A List of the Honourable and United East India Company's civil and military servants on the Bengal establishment, 1785* (Calcutta: n.p. 1785).
29 TCD, MS3551/2, fos. 92–3; GCA, TD219/8/4/Madras, 25 March 1771; P. J. Marshall, 'Masters and Banians in Eighteenth-Century Calcutta', in Blair B. Kling and M. N. Pearson (eds), *The Age of Partnership: Europeans in Asia before Dominion* (Honolulu, HI: University of Hawaii Press, 1979), pp. 191–213; Susan Neild-Basu, 'The Dubashes of Madras', *Modern Asian Studies*, 18 (1984), 4–31.
30 GCA, Bo 12/12: Calcutta, 1 September 1771; Bo 12/2, Calcutta, 5 September 1770; P. Nightingale, *Fortune and Integrity; A Study of Moral Attitudes in the India Diary of George Paterson, 1769–1774* (Oxford: Oxford University Press, 1985), pp. 5–6; IOR, B/76, p. 276; GCA, TD219/8/4; NRS, GD112/74/852/8; NRS, GD137/1134; NLS, MS19298, fos. 7–9; CSAS, Hunter-Blair Papers, Box 1/1/34; NLS, MS1367, fos. 64, 82; MS1256, fos. 174–5.
31 Sanjay Subrahmanyam and C. A. Bayly, 'Portfolio Capitalists and the Political Economy of Early Modern India', *The Indian Economic and Social History Review*, 25 (1988), 401–24; Farhat Hasan, 'Indigenous Cooperation and the Birth of a Colonial City: Calcutta, c.1698–1750', *Modern Asian Studies*, 26 (1992), 71–5.
32 NRS, GD164/1698/5(1–4). See also, GCA, TD219/8/1/23.
33 Bailyn, *Voyagers to the West*, pp. 29–56.
34 PRONI, D654/B1/2A, pp. 14–15.
35 NRS, GD248/227/1/1; NRS, GD51/3/99; NRS, GD29/2063/3; NLS, MS10872, fos. 126–7; NLS, MS19298, fos. 7–9; NLS, MS49, pp. 13–14; MS56, p. 12; MS1073, fo. 6; MS1074, fo. 116; NLS, MS1328, fos. 126, 244; NLS, MS1367, fo. 86; GCA, TD219/10/1.
36 C. A. Bayly, *Indian Society and the Making of the British Empire* (Cambridge: Cambridge University Press, 1988), pp. 7–9, 46–128; Douglas M. Peers, 'State, Power, and Colonialism', in Douglas M. Peers and Nandini Gooptu (eds), *The Oxford History of the British Empire: India and the British Empire* (Oxford: Oxford University Press, 2012), pp. 17–23.
37 IOR, L/MIL/9/85, 89–90; L/MIL/10/131; L/MIL/11/109.
38 IOR, J/1/9 [1775], pp. 243–4.
39 IOR, J/1/4 [1777], [1779]; J/1/11 [1784–1786].
40 IOR, B/85, pp. 257–9, 323; J/1/16, pp. 48–52; J/1/19, pp. 88–91, 191–3; J/1/21, pp. 251–5; J/1/22, pp. 283–5.

41 NRS, GD29/2127; IOR, J/1/1, pp. 197–9; J/1/16, pp. 76–9; J/1/18, pp. 438–9; J/1/22, pp. 113–14; J/1/26, pp. 269–75.
42 IOR, B/41, pp. 99, 110; B/48, pp. 786, 797–8, 822; J/1/13, pp. 207–10; J/1/18, pp. 62–5, 159–63; J/1/19, pp. 127–3; J/1/28, pp. 52–60.
43 Mackillop, 'Accessing Empire', 15; Mackillop, '"A Reticent People?"', pp. 146–8.
44 T. M. Truxes, *Irish-American Trade, 1660–1783* (Cambridge: Cambridge University Press, 2004), pp. 46–50; R. C. Nash, 'Irish Atlantic Trade in the Seventeenth and Eighteenth Centuries', *The William and Mary Quarterly*, 42 (1985), 329–56.
45 IOR, J/1/4 [1761], pp. 238–42; J/1/7 [1768], pp. 42–6; J/1/14 [1793], pp. 182–4; J/1/16 [1796], pp. 104–7.
46 Thomas Bartlett, *The Fall and Rise of the Irish Catholic Nation: The Catholic Question, 1690–1830* (Dublin: Gill & Macmillan, 1992), pp. 82–125.
47 McGilvary, *East India Patronage*, p. 49; Mackillop, 'Accessing Empire', 15.
48 Riddy, 'Warren Hastings', pp. 30–57; McGilvary, *East India Patronage*, pp. 151–2.
49 Michael Fry, *The Dundas Despotism*, pp. 216–23; Devine, *Scotland's Empire*, p. 261; Brown, 'Henry Dundas', pp. 30–6.
50 SIWA. Sources: IOR, J/1/1, pp. 177–80, 356–9; J/1/4, pp. 238–42; J/1/5, pp. 107–10; J/1/6, pp. 23–6, 37–9, 204–7; J/1/7, pp. 42–6; J/1/8, pp. 99–103; J/1/9, pp. 240, 268–9; J/1/10, pp. 193–4; J/1/13, pp. 18–21, 332–5; J/1/15, pp. 6–10; J/1/17, pp. 205–9, 276–9; J/1/18, pp. 28–32, 71–4, 207–14; /1/18, pp. 404–7; J/1/19, pp. 70–4, 222–5, 385–8; J/1/21, pp. 18–20; J/1/23, pp. 17–26; J/1/28, pp. 124–33; B/43, pp. 463–4; B/48, p. 840; B/51, pp. 232, 276; B/58, pp. 259–60; B/78, pp. 183–4, 188–9, 233; B/80, pp. 232, 248; B/81, pp. 163–4; B/84, pp. 172–4; B/86, p. 25; L/AG/34/29/341; IOR, P/416/83 [1748], pp. 20–2; IOR, MSS Eur. F.128/12: Dublin, 1762; CSAS, Boileau Papers, Box 1/1; TCD, MS 3767/1–108; MS 3768/109–133.
51 SIWA: Sources: IOR, J/1/2, pp. 309–13; J/1/4, pp. 165–8; J/1/12, pp. 83–7, 313–19; B/41, pp. 102, 109; B/43, pp. 679–80, 697–8; B/77, p. 188; B/79, pp. 171, 189, 192.
52 SIWA. Sources: IOR, J1/1–29; B/40–B/95; P/328/60–64; P/416/77–98; L/AG/34/29/4–22, 185–210, 341–343; TNA, PROB 11/549–1903; NRS, SC36/48/6; SC70/1/12; CC8/8/125, 132, 141.
53 SIWA. Sources: IOR, J/1/3, pp. 193–7; B/83, p. 385; J/1/13, pp. 354–7; J/1/14, pp. 169–72; J/1/15, pp. 73–6; NRS, GD29/1876, GD29/2063, GD29/2122/4; GD29/2132, 2136.
54 Devine, *Scotland's Empire*, pp. 76–83.
55 Cohn, 'Recruitment and Training', pp. 110–11.
56 IOR, J/1/9 [1776], pp. 199–202; J/1/16 [1797], pp. 353–7; J/1/4 [1761], p. 233; J/1/16 [1796], pp. 148–51; J/1/15 [1794], pp. 188–91.
57 IOR, J/1/5 [1763], pp. 31–6; J/1/6 [1765], pp. 149–51; J/1/16 [1797], pp. 308–11; J/1/1 [1749], pp. 46–8; J/1/1 [1750], pp. 139–42.
58 IOR, J/1/4 [1762], pp. 348–53; J/1/5 [1764], pp. 150–3, 244–7; J/1/6 [1765], pp. 235–9; J/1/7 [1768], pp. 18–24; J/1/8 [1770], pp. 76–9; J/1/13

[1790], pp. 125–9, 153–6, 181–5; J/1/13 [1791], pp. 362–5; J/1/14 [1792], pp. 136–9; J/1/16 [1796], pp. 138–41; J/1/16 [1797], pp. 472–6; J/1/17 [1798], pp. 42–5, 149–52, 163–8; J/1/17 [1799], pp. 283–6; NLS, MS19300, fos. 32, 36.
59 Walsh, 'The Fiscal State in Ireland', 629–56.
60 IOR, J/1/13 [1790], pp. 181–5; J/1/15 [1794], pp. 193–7; J/1/16 [1796], pp. 53–6; NLS, MS10953, fos. 3–5.
61 GCA, Bogle Papers, Bo. 2, pp. 80, 116; Bo 12/3: Calcutta, 25 October 1770; Bo 12/9: Calcutta, 25 February 1771; Bo. 25: Calcutta, 24 February 1771; KH, Graham Papers, 2nd series, Nos. 51–126, Bundle 53: Sackville St., London, 14 May 1797.
62 NRS, GD24/1/464/c/160–1.
63 C. H. Philips, *The East India Company, 1784–1834* (Manchester: Manchester University Press, 1968), pp. 80–4; McGilvary, *Guardian of the East India Company*, p. 33; Bowen, *Business of Empire*, p. 90.
64 Charles Hardy, *A Register of Ships, Employed in the Service of the Honorable the United East India Company* (London: W. Heseltine, 1811); GCA, T-LX3/26/2: London, 30 Dec 1805; NLS, MS10872, fos. 236–7.
65 Jean Sutton, *Lords of the East: The East India Company and Its Ships* (London: Conway Maritime Press, 1981), p. 21; McGilvary, *East India Patronage*, pp. 85–9; GCA, T-LX3/13/24; NLS, MS10872, fo. 224; NLS, MS1170, fos. 30, 79.
66 NLS, MS1170, fos. 30, 33; MS10872, fos. 214–18, 222; MS10921, fo. 106; MS14439, fo. 78; NRS, GD1/736/52; GCA, T-SK 15/11, p. 6; Farrington, *Biographical Index*, p. 693.
67 NLS, Acc 9769/30/5/16; NRS, GD23/6/261: London, 26 December 1785.
68 NRS, GD1/453/Boxes 1–3; GCA, T-LX3/22/3.
69 Porter, '"Gentlemanly Capitalism" and Empire', 265–95; Bowen, *Elites, Enterprise*, pp. 16–21.
70 Webster, 'The Political Economy of Trade Liberalization', 404–19.
71 Cullen, *Irish Trade*, pp. 43–5.
72 IOR, B/41, p. 411; B/52, pp. 189–90; B/54, p. 190; TNA, PROB 11/630, pp. 119–21.
73 L. M. Cullen, 'Apotheosis and Crisis: The Irish Diaspora in the Age of Choiseul', in Connor and Lyons, *Irish Communities*, p. 18.
74 IOR, B/54, pp. 203, 225.
75 TNA, PROB 11/672, pp. 173–4.
76 IOR, B87, p. 409; Bowen, *The Business of Empire*, pp. 274, 284, 293–4; Bailey, 'The Nesbitts of London', pp. 231–49.
77 TNA, PROB 11/486, pp. 116–17; IOR, B/57, p. 174; B/87, p. 381–2.
78 IOR, B/61, p. 440; B/62, pp. 144–5; B/63, p. 158; B/64, pp. 308, 312.
79 IOR, B/64, pp. 158, 356; B/66, pp. 128, 200, 434; B/69, p. 143; B/70, p. 467; B/71, pp. 637–40; B/79, p. 61; B/85, p. 19.
80 Hancock, 'Combining Success and Failure', pp. 24–7.
81 McGilvary, *East India Patronage*, p. 156; Parker, 'The Directors of the East

India Company', vol. I, pp. 114–16; IOR, B/83, pp. 224, 548; B/87, p. 409; B/88, p. 215; B/89, p. 821; NLS, MS1170, fo. 30.
82 Sutton, *The East India Company's Maritime Service*, p. 8.
83 Devine, *Scotland's Empire*, pp. 69–89; T. M. Devine and Phillip Rössner, 'Scotland and the Atlantic Economy, 1600–1800', in MacKenzie and Devine, *Scotland and the British Empire*, pp. 39–49.
84 NRS, GD18/5218/1–2, 12, 33, 35, 38, 42, 52.
85 Farrington, *Biographical Index*, pp. 208, 343, 654; Johnston, *History of the Irish Parliament*, vol. III, p. 425; NLS, MS6360, pp. 91–4.
86 NLS, MS10802, fos. 130–1; MS10872, fos. 26–7, 60–1; Philips, *The East India Company*, pp. 15–16.
87 Bowen, The Business of Empire, p. 273; NRS, GD104/297/2; GD248/179/3/6; NLS, MS10872, fos. 70–75; GCA, T-LX3/22/3.
88 Suzanne Schwarz, 'Scottish Surgeons in the Liverpool Slave Trade in the Late Eighteenth and Early Nineteenth Centuries', in T. M. Devine (ed.), *Recovering Scotland's Slavery Past: The Caribbean Connection* (Edinburgh: Edinburgh University Press, 2015), p. 148; John Cookson, *The British Armed Nation, 1793–1815* (Oxford: Oxford University Press, 1997), pp. 128–9; James Hayes, 'Scottish Officers in the British Army, 1714–1763', *The Scottish Historical Review*, 37 (1958), 24–9.
89 Sutton, *The East India Company's Maritime Service*, pp. xi, 1–16, 77–9, 135–8.
90 Farrington, *Biographical Index*, pp. 127, 204, 413, 473, 760; NLI, MS10242; TNA, PROB 11/1514, pp. 186–9.
91 Stephen Conway, *The British Isles and the War of American Independence* (Oxford: Oxford University Press, 2002), pp. 186–96; Sarah Caputo, 'Scotland, Scottishness, British Integration and the Royal Navy, 1793–1815', *The Scottish Historical Review*, 97 (2018), 94–6.
92 NLS, MS10872, fos. 1–2, 259–60; EUL, Mic M. 920, p. 13; GCA, T-LX3/13/24–25; T-LX3/18/1; T-LX3/22/3.
93 NLS, MS14528, p. 1; Farrington, *Biographical Index*, pp. 87, 101, 117, 192, 447, 518, 699, 700, 750.
94 Farrington, *Biographical Index*, pp. 165, 293, 531, 608.
95 Wallerstein, *Modern World System II*, pp. 179–203; Prasannan Parthasarathi, *Why Europe Grew Rich*, pp. 51–85.
96 Murdoch, *British History*, pp. 8–9; Mackillop, '"Subsidy State" or "Drawback Province"', pp. 179–99.
97 Marshall, 'The Eighteenth-Century British Empire', pp. 181–2.

4

The military: economies of high- and low-value human capital

Armed service constituted the most accessible route for metropolitan provincials hoping to participate in the Asian hemisphere of British imperialism. The use of military manpower as an export economy was a centuries-old characteristic of Irish and Scottish society by the time the Company began the build-up of its armed forces in the 1740s.[1] It is hardly surprising in these circumstances that the corporation's fastest-growing sector of employment attracted soldier-entrepreneurs of varying social, confessional and regional backgrounds. The diversification of Scottish and Irish military migration to the Americas and South Asia occurred rapidly after 1740 and formed a defining feature of both countries' experience of empire and of proto-globalisation.[2]

New global geographies of opportunity aligned with older cultures of service-led mobility. The extent of this overlap resonates with assessments of historic globalisation which stress the interaction of pre-existing conditions with the new dynamics driving wider developments.[3] Proto-globalisation involved the reuse in new ways of older socio-economic structures of power and associated cultural attitudes to soldiering. The intersection of the old and the new ensured that customs of military entrepreneurship that might otherwise have been rendered obsolete and even undesirable within the British and Irish Isles were transferred over oceanic distances and gained a new lease of life in North America and Asia. However, the evolution into niche but global roles altered profoundly the character of military migration in countries like Ireland and Scotland in ways that belie the outward continuities. Exploring how the metropolitan provinces' traditional military economies connected with the EIC offers new interpretations of the geographies, chronologies, dynamics and consequences of proto-globalisation. Attention shifts from economic processes of 'hard globalisation', with their corresponding focus on the metropoles of European finance capital, to the migratory dimensions of 'soft globalisation'.[4] This alternative emphasis connects the metropolitan provinces' use of human capital to reassessments of the variegated nature of early modern imperialism and expansion.

The emergence in Britain's Eastern Empire of new forms of military service is usually associated with the adjustment of South Asia's 'peasant soldiers' to the rise of the EIC.[5] Yet this realignment was equally evident among Britain and Ireland's gentry and reveals how the Company cannibalised existing sociocultural formations in Asia and in Europe.[6] Fully understanding this development demonstrates how finance-poor European regions like Ireland and Scotland used (rank and file) high-volume/low-value and (officers) low-volume/high-value human capital to exploit proto-globalisation.

Changing patterns of military entrepreneurship from an intra-European to a global framework have major implications for debates in Irish, Scottish and British histories. Eighteenth-century Scotland and Ireland came closest to a common experience of British imperialism through their respective contributions to the armed forces.[7] Yet the structural parallels hide key differences that contributed to the countries' divergent trajectories within the British state and empire. Scotland's role is now well known. While interpretations are prone to focus on the scale of involvement, there is no doubting the country's distinctive place within Britain's pre-1815 military complex.[8] Participation encompassed society from top to bottom, the urban and rural sectors and all the regions to a greater or lesser extent.

The consequences arising from Protestant Ireland's commitment to the Empire's military structures are far more ambiguous.[9] While the number of Protestant officers and Catholic rank and file in the British army is a well-established theme within assessments of pre-union Ireland, participation in the corporation's armies is still far from comprehensively understood.[10] Irish manpower was central to the Company's 'European' garrisons for over a hundred years after 1750. This human link means South Asia should loom much larger in early modern Ireland's migration histories than it does currently.[11] Only by fully recovering the salient characteristics of Irish and Scots involvement within the EIC's fiscal-military complex can the scale and effectiveness of metropolitan provincial adjustment to emerging global military markets be properly appreciated.

The metropolitan provinces and corporate militarism

In the early 1700s a career in the EIC's forces was not an appealing prospect. The organisation's ethos remained suspicious of army personnel and the directors made a point of periodically reaffirming that civil servants and not 'military gentlemen' controlled affairs in Asia.[12] Although the status of the officer corps improved from the 1750s onwards as a result of victories over the French, Dutch, Bengali, Awadhi and Mughals, accepting a cadet commission often represented an inability to acquire a more prestigious merchant marine or civil service position.[13] This displacement into the armed forces played a key role in shaping what was by far and away the largest numeric component of Scots, Irish and Welsh in the EIC. Severe competition in the civil sector drove thousands into what amounted to a second-best route to Asia. Relying on social and human capital as a substitute investment strategy carried its own limitations even as it determined the broad lineaments of participation.

The small volume of military appointments, a lack of career progression and preferable conditions of service in Europe, Ireland or the Atlantic Empire constituted the primary factors deterring involvement in the early eighteenth century.[14] Prior to the late 1740s the EIC's forces were numerically insignificant. In 1709 the Bombay garrison consisted of 591 men and six officers: in Bengal in 1723 the military establishment stood at only 461 men and seven officers.[15] Neither was army patronage as regular as its mercantile or merchant marine equivalents. The 1690s to late 1740s witnessed periodic downsizing of garrison numbers in efforts to curb expenditure.[16] In stark contrast to the regularised recruitment of its mercantile and merchant marine personnel, soldiers and officers were sought in ad hoc ways and with no consistent sense of the geo-military needs of the corporate polity in Asia.

These realities meant that the drift of Irish, Scots and Welsh into the Company's armed forces evolved in a stop-start fashion and remained acutely sensitive to changing conditions in Europe and in South Asia. Successive expansions and contractions of British and European militaries between 1688 and 1815 created surplus pools of commissioned personnel willing or forced to consider Asia as a career option.[17] The end of the Spanish War of Succession in 1713 is an underappreciated moment in the gradual realign of employment from European to Asian locations. John Campbell, second duke of Argyll, and John Dalrymple, second earl of Stair, enabled veteran officers to seek alternative options when prospects dried up in the downsized British army of the mid-1710s to 1740.[18] Four Scots officers joined the EIC between 1720 and 1723 citing professional expertise acquired in the earlier European war. Although Richard Temple, first viscount Cobham provided similar support for William Fitzgerald's application in May 1720, Protestant Irish officers were less conspicuous lobbyists at this juncture, at least as recorded in the directors' minutes. This is most likely the result of the army establishment in Ireland offering a more palatable alternative for the placement of clients at home.[19]

If the peace of 1713 initiated a discernible if still insignificant drift of military migrants to Asia, the final phase of the Austrian War of Succession marked a turning point. In a telling example of the ways in which proto-globalisation cannibalised pre-existing economic, social and cultural conditions, a decision was made to target Scottish and Irish manpower. As part of the expedition to the Indian Ocean of Admiral Edward Boscawen, the war office sanctioned the creation of six 'Scotch' and six 'Irish' independent companies. On 11 July 1747 Captain Archibald Grant, son of the laird of Monymusk in Aberdeenshire received notice that: 'the granting such [a] Company to you was on such a condition ... it is expected that they will be composed of R—ls [Rebels] and they [the War Office] declared they will accept of any man fit for service without enquiring into his former life.'[20] Imperial priorities ensured the extension of William Augustus, duke of Cumberland's post-Culloden punitive policy into an official cannon-fodder strategy.[21] Given recent events in Scotland this was hardly surprising. The creation of the Irish companies at the same time illustrates that the kingdom's reputation as a source of manpower was already well understood at the metropole. Ireland shaped the EIC's evolution as an employer of military personnel from the very start. As a result, both metropolitan-provinces engaged with corporate and state militarism in Asia a decade earlier than is usually supposed.

Commanded by a veteran Irish officer, William Muir, each of the six Irish companies consisted of one hundred men and four commissioned personnel. The Scottish units followed the same pattern, generating twenty-five officer posts. Recruitment for the Scottish companies drew heavily from among Jacobite prisoners held at Dumbarton Castle, at Carlisle and across the Highlands, while the majority of the officers hailed from the pro-Hanoverian Campbell and Grant families.[22] As befitted their title, these units were understood to be Scottish in character, with Lieutenant Alexander Campbell noting from Fort St David in 1748 that 'the rest of our Scotch officers, both that came from the North and Argyllshire are in good health'.[23] Given the insignificant volume of military migrants trickling out to Asia over the previous half century, the independent companies represented the step change which connected Ireland and Scotland's pre-existing economies of military emigration to one hemisphere of expansion. India as much as North America provided the precedent for the British army's large-scale use overseas of metropolitan provincial manpower. The Seven Years' War simply deepened pre-existing trends.

These emerging province-to-corporation intersections mirrored the directors' flexible approach to acquiring soldiers more generally. Enlistment strategies in the early to mid-eighteenth century mimicked those of the VOC. The English organisation was only one of many corporate and national employers within a transnational, Europe-wide military market characterised by cosmopolitan 'occupational fraternities' and porous national boundaries.[24] This 'military Europe' facilitated the search for veteran officers with a high human capital value and for large volumes of low-value rank and file. The EIC's militarism evolved as a potent mixture of London gentlemanly capitalism and older economies of military migration associated with mountainous-pastoral regions like the Swiss Cantons, Ireland and Scotland. This military complex interlaced economies of human and finance capital in ways that offered substantial opportunities to Irish and Scottish society. Supposedly 'semi-peripheral' regions which lacked the 'comparative advantages' of areas like England and the Netherlands used this avenue of service to participate fully in proto-globalisation.

From the 1740s to the 1770s the Company received employment requests from demobilised officers from the British armed forces, the Scots-Dutch brigade, Austrian, Prussian, Hanoverian, Portuguese, Brunswick and Modenese armies.[25] Between 1751 and 1755 Scots such as Daniel McAplin and Hugh Mackie from demobilised British regiments, Captain John Murray of the Royal Marines, and Ensign David Urquhart and Lieutenants David Munro, Alexander Cameron and Aeneas Sutherland from reduced Scots-Dutch battalions obtained posts in Bengal and Madras.[26] The range of service backgrounds challenges the conventional emphasis on the exclusively British character of imperial service in this period. On 4 February 1736 the directors appointed Captain Francis Cooke from the French army's Irish regiment of Fitzjames as a Madras ensign.[27] The employment of even one or two Irish Catholic officers during the era of the Penal Laws underlines how the EIC tapped into 'military Europe' from an early date. It is testimony to the severe manpower shortages created by hostile conditions in Asia that professional qualifications were prioritised over official sectarian exclusions.[28]

Developments in South Asia drove this process of transfer from one military market to another. Relations between the Company and regional 'successor states' such as Arcot (Carnatic), Hyderabad, Bengal, Awadh, Mysore and the Marathas deteriorated for a variety of diplomatic, fiscal and economic reasons. Internal South Asian dynamics were compounded by Anglo-French hostilities.[29] As a result, military expansion proceeded apace between the 1750s and mid- to late 1810s. In 1748 the Company's forces in Bengal, Madras and Bombay totalled approximately 3,720 men (not including officers): by c.1778 the number stood at over 60,070, increasing to around 154,500 men by 1805.[30] This extraordinary rate of growth does not include the increasing deployment of royal regiments; by mid-1783 the Madras presidency alone contained twelve British army battalions, a total of 6,767 men and 214 officers.[31] The scale of the Crown's commitment to the South Asian theatre can be grasped by the fact that this force was comparable to the army which surrendered with momentous consequences at Yorktown less than two years earlier.

Intensifying interaction between Irish and Scottish society and this corporate military complex can be clearly seen in the number of tenders to raise men. Between 1750 and 1780 the directors' minutes record a total of sixty-nine proposals for recruiting contracts.[32] A striking feature of these requests is their cosmopolitan nature. Swiss and German officers featured prominently during the first two decades of the EIC's military build-up. The reliance on 'military Europe' remained a feature of the corporation's non-sepoy regiments until the early nineteenth century.[33] While the Company's institutional character remained resolutely English, its human resources now drew from across South Asia and swathes of Western Europe.

The high profile of German-speaking military entrepreneurs in the 1750s mirrored the enthusiasm of service gentry from the provinces of Britain and Ireland: eleven of the sixty-nine offers to recruit between 1750 and 1780 (16 per cent) involved Irish officers or Irish manpower. The example of Robert Brooke, who enlisted substantial numbers in Ireland in the late 1770s and early 1780s, has been analysed as part of a major reassessment of the pre-union kingdom's interaction with the Eastern Empire.[34] Yet he was simply one of many. Building upon the precedent established in 1747, a number of applications occurred during the Seven Years' War and the subsequent war against the North American colonies. These included the tender in September 1757 of Captain James Speirs to levy men in Ulster and that of Robert Snow in Waterford, who offered to enlist one hundred recruits in 1758. The kingdom's elites also participated: in March 1760 Stratford Eyre, the Governor of Galway offered to enlist 1,000 men.[35]

These developments reflected local sensitivities to global trends. Conditions in each hemisphere influenced the other, determining the precise timing and volume of movement into the military complex. The presence of Scotland's gentry within the British army in North America occurred simultaneously with increasing involvement in corporate militarism in Asia.[36] Proposals from Scots officers surpassed even the Irish rate, constituting eighteen out of the sixty-nine applications (26 per cent) between 1750 and 1780.[37] The disproportionate percentage is partly explained by the serial solicitations of Major Allan Maclean of Torloisk. A former Jacobite and Scots-Dutch officer, he, like the Irish veteran, Grainger Muir, fought in North America during the Seven Years' War. His refusal to take no for an answer was less typical; between 1768 and 1775 he made five offers to raise men in Scotland. Between 1750 and 1780 there were two proposals relating specifically to Wales: John Evans's petition of 20 October 1758 and Captain William Skinner of the Royal Welch Fusiliers' application of 6 August 1760 to enrol 300 men.[38] The rapid engagement with military developments in Asia ensured that 45 per cent of all recruitment tenders during the early crucial phase of the EIC's expansion listed in the directors' minutes originated from the metropolitan provinces.

This intersection of provincial and metropolitan interests shaped perceptions of Britain and Ireland's internal character in subtle but powerful ways. The Company directors approached the problem of domestic recruiting by envisaging England, Wales, Ireland and Scotland as distinct units. Theirs was a noticeably disaggregated vision of the British-Irish monarchy. The tendency to compartmentalise the older polities is explained in part by the directorate's metrocentric priorities. Excessive recruitment within the metropolis itself threatened to compound labour shortages, increase wages and undermine relations with other civic and economic interests.[39] Protecting the capital's economy drove a deliberate focus on the metropolitan provinces as the most cost effective source of manpower. Those contracted to find men were instructed to operate at more than one hundred, fifty or twenty miles from London. They were given clear incentives to do so by the establishment of a rate of nine guineas for an individual enrolled in the provinces and eight guineas for a man enlisted in the city.[40]

This hierarchy of military labour reveals how regional economies of human capital evolved across the British and Irish Isles. These activities linked the domestic provinces to the metropolis in new ways while emphasising the distinctive status and functions of both. This compartmentalising generated a form of corporate Britishness configured differently from the better understood 'national' British identity that emerged at the same time. The Eastern Empire shaped multiple forms of Britain rather than one overriding type. As the Company's military evolved from its English and corporate origins into a multilayered structure, it replenished its constant losses through diverse recruitment strategies in Europe and in Asia. London finance was combined with South Asian tax revenues on a huge scale. The resultant fiscal power enabled the presidency armies to employ tens of thousands of sepoys at any one time while developing a recruitment economy of high- and low-value human capital in officers and men from the provinces of the British and Irish Isles.[41]

Ireland increasingly loomed large in this complex fiscal-military structure. Given the kingdom's substantial population this was hardly surprising. A key reason for the country's importance lay in the Company's capacity to secure men from the majority Catholic population from the earliest build-up of its European regiments. Yet the question of recruitment further irritated the constitutional tensions between the Protestant Irish nation and the English East India Company.[42] Dublin Castle's anxieties centred on the confessional backgrounds of recruits: on 16 January 1760 the directors received a complaint regarding the activities of Lieutenant Robert Fraser. Six months earlier on 13 June 1759 Fraser received permission at Leadenhall Street to raise 'Protestants' on the island. The authorities in Ireland noted that they had detained and questioned fifty of Fraser's men in Dublin as they prepared to embark for London. It turned out that thirty recruits were Catholics and the remainder Protestants.[43] While expressing dissatisfaction that enlistment had commenced without the lord lieutenant's permission, the real anxiety was that 60 per cent of the men came from religious backgrounds subject to exclusion from public and military life.

Ultimately, however, the pressures exerted by the Company's global operations overrode the concerns of Protestant Ireland. The directors were aware by 1770 that recruitment in the monarchy's other possessions of Hanover and North America was impermissible. These developments simply increased Ireland's importance. After experimenting with private contractors like Robert Brooke in the 1770s and 1780s, recruitment depots were established in Ireland and in Scotland. The Company's presence in both countries reflected their relative importance to the military complex. By 1813 there were depots in Belfast, Enniskillen, Dublin, Carlow and Limerick. Meanwhile, Scotland had two: in Edinburgh and Glasgow.[44]

Beyond the reputation for lethal rates of mortality which Asia shared with the Caribbean, it is not clear why enlistment in the Company's armies was so unattractive in Wales. The booming urban economies in the English regions that ringed Wales in the north, east and south may have provided sufficient labour opportunities to soak up any workforce surpluses from the relatively small population. The reluctance of large numbers in Scotland, a society otherwise strongly associated with military migration, to soldier in Asia was doubtless shaped by similar concerns over death rates and chances of return.[45] Low Scottish enlistment rates were also driven by positive alternatives rather than just negative assessments. In a striking example of how provincial populations of all social classes understood which parts of the Empire worked best for their own priorities, North America emerged as the favoured destination among ordinary Scots soldiers. Grants of land ownership to enlisted men, NCOs and officers in 1763 and 1783 created substantial upward social mobility among those from poor backgrounds and regions.[46] Set against an empire of land, liberty and security of property across the Atlantic, the prospect of serving in Asia held little attraction for many ordinary Scots, Welsh or Irish.

Additional influences, peculiar to Scotland, further impaired corporate enlistment. Faced with limited demographic reserves and slow population growth, the country's elite monitored the pool of labour more tightly than in any other part of the British and Irish Isles. Emigration was opposed by propertied classes across Ireland, Scotland, Wales and England. But only in Scotland did an effective ban come into force before the outbreak of war in North America in 1775. Henry Dundas attempted unsuccessfully to have an official prohibition implemented again in 1785.[47] These efforts are testimony to how population was viewed as a vital but limited resource. Men were a cash crop and guarded accordingly. There was a clear understanding among landlords in Scotland that manpower traded at variable rates of value across the Empire's different military institutions. The recruiting for rank method used by the British army when raising new regiments meant local recruits became an alternative means of acquiring prestigious royal commissions.[48] This method involved the use of high-volume/low-value human capital rather than the deployment of conventional monetary resources. A key consequence of this approach was that it shaped the belief in Scotland that manpower was a currency best reserved for state service.

These attitudes worked against Company recruitment of rank and file north of the border. On 17 April 1764 the Convention of Royal Burghs secured the removal of the Scots-Dutch brigade's right to seek men while citing problems caused by ongoing EIC enlistments.[49] Opposition in the towns was matched by attempts in the countryside to discourage entry into the corporation's military. In January 1773 Sir James Grant of Grant, the owner of a large Highland estate, learnt that one of his senior tenants, the half pay captain John Grant of Pitkerrald, had begun recruiting for the EIC. Already facing the loss of tenantry through emigration to North America, Grant ordered his factor to protect and dissuade local men from joining, noting that 'when he [Captain Grant] came here, I told him I would not hear of his taking any of our people, either in Urquhart or Strathspey'. After two local men enlisted, Captain Grant came under pressure to give up his claims and both men were subsequently released, enabling the factor to write to Sir James that 'the present bustle is necessary and it has endeared you greatly to your tenants'.[50] Legal and tenurial leverage blunted the development in Scotland of an open labour market in manpower of the sort emerging in Ireland from the 1740s to the 1770s.

Scottish landlords retained for longer than their English, Irish or Welsh counterparts the view that their tenantry were a valuable source of low-value/high-volume human capital. The sense of themselves as 'lords of men' is yet another example of the blending of older traditions of landed power with new financial and proto-global dynamics.[51] This was a distinctively Scottish variant of gentry capitalism. Shielding local populations for state rather than corporate service had little to do with empathy for the tenantry. It was an astute calculation of the variable value of manpower across the Empire's different military structures and geographic theatres. The increasing divergence between Ireland and Scotland and Wales in the recruitment of rank and file points to how metropolitan provincial gentry and ordinary people reacted to colonialism and proto-globalisation on their own terms. Responses were determined by the particular political, economic, social and cultural conditions in each country. The result was highly variably patterns of participation in the EIC military by the component parts of the British

128   *Human capital and empire*

and Irish Isles that in turn reproduced existing distinctions and generated new internal divergences.

Economies of high- and low-value manpower

One of the most attractive aspects of the EIC for those contemplating a career in Asia lay in the fact that commissions could be acquired through the expenditure of social capital via patronage rather than the use of monetary resources. In contrast to the British army there was no substantial upfront financial outlay for a commission.[52] Equipment and travel expenses however could be considerable. Upon his appointment to the Madras army in 1775 as a senior staff officer, Lieutenant Colonel James Stuart of Torrance in Lanarkshire borrowed £5,000 from the London-Scots financier, George Wilson and the director, Sir James Cockburn.[53] Career investment was also important for those at the lower end of the military hierarchy. Lachlan Mackintosh from Inverness-shire, a lieutenant in Bombay, received £100 in 1713 to augment his assets.[54] Career and material progression were certainly easier if finance was available to enhance liquidity. However, for undercapitalised British and Irish families, military migration to Asia enabled the most cost-effective use of human and social capital to access genteel employment without paying for the privilege. This approach facilitated the retention of a greater share of venture finance for use overseas.

Opportunities were initially limited. Officer appointments noted in the directors' minutes during the last decade of the seventeenth and first half of the eighteenth centuries are outlined in Table 4.1. The figures do not represent the sum of all commissioned posts. Local promotions by governors at the presidency settlements were not usually subject to scrutiny in London and so the numbers are illustrative rather than definitive.[55] Officers like Captain John Lloyd from Cardigan, who commanded a company of European soldiers in Calcutta in 1741, or Ensign Borthwick from Forfar who died in Bombay in July 1744, do not show up in the directors' minutes and so are not included.[56] Allowing for the limitations of the evidence, what Table 4.1 does illustrate is the tentative nature of metropolitan provincial participation in the Company's garrisons during first half of the eighteenth

Table 4.1 Military officers, 1690–1749

Total	Scots	Irish	Welsh
1690–1719 = 56	4 (7.1%)	1 (1.7%)	0
1720–1749 = 60	10 (16.6%)	2 (3.3%)	0

(Source: IOR, B/40–B/70).

century. However, by the 1720s and 1730s Scots began to acquire a per capita share of posts slightly above the country's weight of population.

The Company archive begins to offer much more detailed evidence from the 1750s onwards, both in relation to officers and enlisted men. Appendix 4.1 is drawn from sample lists of personnel embarked on East Indiamen and destined for the European-manned regiments of the Bengal, Bombay and Madras armies. It shows, too, the provincial share of commissioned cadets from the 1750s to the early 1760s, from the mid-1770s to the early 1780s and for NCOs and private men in sample years between the 1750s and the 1810s. Although prone to annual fluctuation, the Scots, Irish and Welsh profiles exhibit sharply contrasting characteristics from the earliest decades of territorial expansion. These patterns represent the specific ways the metropolitan provinces connected with the Company's armed forces and how each society differed markedly from the other in the nature of these connections.

The clearest contrast with Table 4.1 is the much greater presence of Irish personnel at all levels, as enlisted men, as NCOs and for the 1750s to the 1780s as commissioned officers. This growing input was part of a more general diversification of the Empire's manpower.[57] EIC reliance on Irish rank and file grew from around 12 per cent in the 1750s to 23–25 per cent by the 1780s and 1790s. By the 1810s it touched 58 per cent – a considerably greater proportion than the country's share of the British and Irish Isles' population. There was a noticeable profile too among NCOs, with 40 per cent from Ireland as early as the 1770s: this remained the case in the 1810s. Irishmen made a vital contribution to the key, intermediate roles of sergeant and corporal during the first three generations of EIC expansion in India. They formed the single largest per capita nationality in that echelon of the European military.[58] The embarkation samples in Appendix 4.1 are weighted towards the earlier decades of the 1750s to the 1780s and are less comprehensive for the 1790s to the 1810s, when Ireland's contribution became more pronounced. Allowing for this underrepresentation would point to a robust projection of $c.11,000–13,000$ Irishmen in Company regiments from the 1750s to the 1810s. To this total needs to be added those in the British army sent to Asia during the same period. Irish enlistment in the regular forces was considerable, often running at around 33–40 per cent of all recruits by the 1790s and 1800s.[59] If taken together, these ratios make an informed case for a conservative estimate of between 16,000 and 18,000 Irish rank and file in Asia from the 1750s to the early 1810s. The appendix evidence for rates of participation prior to the 1820s is unambiguous. It confirms that the Eastern Empire's dependency on Irish manpower was substantial, evident across all ranks, and stretched from the 1750s up to the 1810s, before continuing into the better-known era of the

Company's dependency on Irish manpower from the 1820s to the 1850s.[60] Ireland contributed a central human element of the Company's military power for over a century.

The incidence of recruits from the other two metropolitan provinces offers a stark comparison. The underrepresentation of the Welsh evident in the civil service and merchant marine was replicated in the military, although set against the country's relatively small share of population the percentage are reasonable in per capita terms.[61] Averaging the samples from Appendix 4.1 indicates that approximately 900–1,000 Welsh enlisted as ordinary soldiers and NCOs in the Company army between 1753 and 1813. The country with the most substantial underrepresentation among the rank and file compared to its demographic weight was Scotland. The build-up of Scots in the civil service and merchant marine found no parallel in the enlistment of rank and file. The clear trend was for a progressive decline towards an ever-smaller percentage share. Despite their well-known prominence in the British military, Scots were conspicuously absent from the EIC's ordinary European soldiery. These sharp variations point to the importance of the provincial societies' pre-existing characteristics in shaping interaction with the Empire's major institutions. Using the same averaging of samples that provide the indicative Irish and Welsh totals suggests a probable Scottish figure of around 2,500 rank and file. However, the weighting towards the earlier decades of the 1750s and 1760s, when Scottish recruits formed a larger proportion, means care must be taken not to inflate the likely total. In the 1800s the Scots' share of enlisted personnel dropped to a statistical irrelevance, below even that of Wales on a per capita basis. The caveat to the near absence of Scots is at the level of NCOs, which held up well until dipping in the 1810s to a ratio roughly equivalent to the country's population profile.

In contrast to their near absence in the European units, substantial clusters of soldiers from Scotland did arrive in Asia through the deployment of six Highland Regiments between 1760 and 1788 and the reconstituted Scots-Brigade (94th Regiment) in 1794.[62] Establishing the number of Scots in these units is problematic. Earlier formations such as the 89th Highland Regiment sent to India in 1760 and the 78th (later 72nd) and the 73rd (later 71st) Highland Regiments committed to the Mysore-Maratha conflicts in 1778 and 1781 respectively, were composed mainly of Scottish recruits. Other units, such as the 2nd battalion of the 42nd Black Watch (renumbered in 1786 as the 73rd Highland Regiment) and the 74th and 75th Highland Regiments raised in 1787 contained men from across the United Kingdom and Ireland.[63] If these variations in composition are set alongside the average manpower in battalions and regiments, it is realistic to suggest a further 3,000 or so Scottish rank and file in the regular units. Together

The military

Table 4.2 Scots, Irish and Welsh military officers in Asia, 1690–1813[64]

Years	1690–1709	1710–1729	1730–1749	1750–1769	1770–1789	1790–1813	Total
Total	26	52	41	654	–	5,352	–
Scots	2	8	30 #	225	560	1,245* [22.9%]	2,070
Irish	0	1	28 #	175	376	677* [12.5%]	1,256
Welsh	0	0	2	27	29	133 [2.4%]	191

(SIWA. Sources: IOR, B/40–B/95; L/MIL/9/85, 107–127; L/MIL/10/131; L/MIL/11/109; P/328/60–64; P/416/77–98; L/AG/34/29/4–22, 185–210, 341–343; TNA, PROB 11/549–1903; *The East India Kalendar ... 1791 to 1800* (London: J. Debrett, 1791–1800); V. C. P. Hodson, *List of the Officers of the Army of Bengal, 1754–1834*, I–IV (London: Longman, Orme, Brown & Co., 1927); Dodwell & Miles *Alphabetical List of the Officers of the Indian Army* (London: Longman, Orme, Brown & Co., 1838); Duncan Campbell, *Records of Clan Campbell in the Military Service of the Honourable East India Company, 1600–1858* (London: Longman's, Green and Co., 1925); Bernard Burke, *A Genealogical and Heraldic History of the Landed Gentry of Ireland* (London: Harrisons & Sons, 1912)).

with projected numbers in the Company's European regiments and recruits spread throughout other British army battalions, a realistic estimate places a minimum of around 5,500 to a more generous figure in the region of 6,500 Scots soldiers in Asia between 1753 and 1813.

Very different social, economic and regional dynamics shaped the contours of participation in the officer corps. The figures in Table 4.2 provide a comparative analysis of the Irish, Scots and Welsh within the commissioned ranks of the East India Company and, less exhaustively, British units in Asia during the first phases of conquest. In common with quantitative summaries of the corporation's other sectors, establishing definitive numbers is challenging. The figures in the 'total' row in Table 4.2 are compiled from cadetships or higher commissions noted in the directors' minutes. However, the recording process was far from comprehensive. Only after 1789, with the survival of cadet applications, do the percentages become robust and reliable.

Some trends are immediately identifiable, the most obvious being the magnitude of commission-level employment after 1750. The total of 1,256 Irish officers represents just those clearly traced to Ireland or an Irish father, a method also used in relation to their Scottish and Welsh peers. With only twenty-nine individuals confirmed up to 1749, the vast majority of these Irish men served between 1750 and 1813. One way of appreciating such numbers is to note that approximately 1,000 Protestant Irish became British army officers from 1700 to 1760; the Company appointed 671 between 1790 and 1813 alone.[65] At an average of twenty-nine per annum, the flow eastwards in these years equated to the officer corps of a battalion each year for nearly a quarter of a century. Although subject to peaks and troughs, some years involved especially large numbers; seventy-four Irishmen obtained cadet posts in 1803, well in excess of the total required to staff a regiment of two battalions.[66]

Even these figures do not capture the full volume of employment. Surviving embarkation lists from 1763 to 1775 and 1781 to 1789 do not include the nationality of commissioned personnel. These gaps mean an indeterminate number of Welsh, Irish and Scots officers cannot be traced for the years involved.[67] Another cohort largely missing from Table 4.2 are officers in British regiments sent to the East Indies. Irish Protestants provided a consistently high ratio of the commissioned ranks in regular units across the whole empire. They comprised 166 of the 429 officers of the British army at Halifax in Nova Scotia in 1757. Similarly, Irishmen constituted ninety of the 161 officers listed in five British battalions stationed in south India in the 1780s.[68] These individuals are not included in Table 4.2. If both branches of military service – corporate and state – are combined, it is likely that approximately 1,400 Irish officers served in the eastern half of the Empire between 1753 and 1813. This volume of elite and middling employment means Asia needs to be considered alongside better-known destinations such as France and Spain as one of the most significant branches of Irish military-gentry migration during the entire early modern era.

Assessing these patterns is complicated by the fact that an overwhelming majority of Company commissions went to scions of Protestant gentry, clerical (both established and dissenting) and mercantile families.[69] With only 5–6 per cent of the total British and Irish Isles' population, Irish Protestants secured around 12.5 per cent of all Company cadetships from 1790 to 1813. This represents the largest per capita share achieved by any metropolitan provincial group. However, these trends need to be set against the country's overall population. As the war in North America from 1775 to 1783 soaked up officers, Ireland's elite Catholic families found it easier to obtain corporate commissions. This they managed to do thirteen years before it was possible to obtain equivalent rank in the British army.[70] On 5 November 1781 the Irish cadet John Nelley joined the Bengal artillery, rising to the rank of lieutenant colonel before returning home in 1813 with over £10,000. His will confirms his Catholic faith while his career reveals the EIC's military to be more permeable than that of the British state.[71] The reality, however minor and intermittent, of Catholic involvement in the officer corps shifts the demographic benchmark against which the overall Irish share of commissions needs to be calculated. The country's large population means that Irish society as a whole was heavily underrepresented in the military elite and began experiencing a relative decline between the 1770s and the 1810s. The age of union actually marked a loss of percentage share for Irish Protestant families, from a high of 20 per cent in the 1760s to the 1780s to just over half that amount by the 1810s. The trajectory of domestic state formation did not parallel trends in imperial employment, a crucial disjuncture which challenges assumptions about the capacity of empire to generate Britishness on a consistent or coherent basis.

The distribution of Welsh and Scottish personnel mirrors trends in the civil service and merchant marine, while contrasting sharply with the marginal contribution of both societies in terms of rank and file. There were consistently more officers from Wales on a per capita basis than there were enlisted men. In the 1760s Welshmen made up around 4 per cent of commissioned personnel, a rate at or even slightly above the country's demographic profile.[72] By the 1790s and 1800s, however, the Welsh share of cadets had dropped to around 2.4 per cent, although this was still a higher ratio than the country's small contribution of rank-and-file recruits.

If Irish society supplied a considerable number of officers and a disproportionate amount of enlisted men, Scotland developed a radically different mode of involvement. Contributions of low-value/high-volume human capital in the form of ordinary soldiers were consistently minimal and on a downward trajectory. Meanwhile the placement of high-value/low-volume human capital in the shape of officers increased and was persistently well above the country's share of population. Rising from 6.5 per cent of cadets (and 20 per cent of officers) in the 1750s to 20 per cent of cadets by the 1770s and early 1780s, the Scottish profile climbed to an average of 23 per cent in the period from the 1790s to the 1810s. This was almost twice the rate relative to the country's demography. The over numbers in Table 4.2 show that at least 2,070 Scots held commissioned rank in Asia between 1690 and 1813. With only forty individuals identified between 1690 and 1749, the vast majority arrived during a more compressed time period: 2,030 men served between 1750 and 1813 – an average of thirty-two per annum. This is the equivalent of more than the officer cadre of a battalion every year for nearly two-thirds of a century, a figure that underlines the fact that Scotland contributed the greatest number of military officers of any of the metropolitan provinces. As in the case of Ireland, there are fundamental implications arising from such figures. The scale of employment means that Asia must be seen alongside other destinations like Ulster, the Netherlands, Scandinavia and North America as central to early modern Scotland's military history.

Yet even these numbers do not capture the overall Scots total. Only 53 per cent of officers can be identified for one of the six Highland Regiments (the 73rd) deployed in India between 1760 and 1790. A limited number of commission-level individuals in these and other British army units are also recorded in wills and testaments at Bombay, Calcutta and Madras.[73] However, the discounting of name-based evidence and the lack of biographical data relating to the regular army officers mean that an indeterminate number cannot be included in the 2,070 total. The census of line regiments in southern India which revealed ninety Irish officers provides an indication of how many additional individuals cannot be securely identified. None of the units surveyed were linked to Scotland but they still contained twenty Scottish officers.[74] The figures in Table 4.2 and the indeterminate number of commissioned Scots in British regiments in India point to a conservative total of around 2,150 Scottish officers in Asia between 1753 and 1813. Elite military employment on this scale underlines the need to insert Asia more consistently into the country's post-union history. Patterns of overrepresentation in the regular armed forces are well understood.[75] Adding in the EIC dimension reveals the true extent of Scotland's contribution to the Empire's military institutions. Corporate service in Asia and state service in North America rapidly globalised the country's traditional economies of military migration and entrepreneurship.

Appendix 4.1 and the figures in Table 4.2 provide the first systematic enumeration and comparison of metropolitan-provincial army officers in one half of the pre-1815 empire. They show each metropolitan province developed a quite distinct set of interactions with the EIC's forces. Officers constituted higher-value human capital compared to soldiers and NCOs due to their enhanced capacity to turn employment into cultural capital and its financial equivalent. Viewed in this way the figures show that Irish society evolved a diverse export economy of officers and manpower in the 1750s to the early 1780s before developing an increasing reliance on the mass export of ordinary recruits. Meanwhile, Welsh society contributed next to no high-volume/low-value manpower and an increasingly smaller per capita number of officers.

Scotland's trajectory was diametrically opposite to that of Ireland. The concentration of enlisted men in the Highland Regiments risks inflating Scottish rank-and-file numbers beyond what their overall presence in the Company warrants.[76] A clear social and professional divide defined Scottish participation. Recruits destined for the Company's own units fell away to a statistical irrelevance by the 1800s while the share of officers climbed to between one-fifth and one-quarter of all appointments. Scottish society's interaction with the corporation's armies developed as an economy of minimal amounts of low-value/high-volume human capital and the commitment of substantial reserves of the high-value/low-volume equivalent. These patterns shaped the remunerative potential of each country's economy of military migration.

Regional and social characteristics facilitate an evaluation of the nature and consequences of proto-globalised military entrepreneurship. These are summarised in Table 4.3. The figures show important similarities and differences with Tables 3.2, 3.4 and 5.5. The same regions of Ireland and Wales that dominated access to the civil and maritime elite – Leinster, Ulster and the Principality's south and east counties – also provided the largest share of officers. It is, however, noticeable that Connacht and north-west Wales secured a greater ratio of military posts than of elite civilian personnel. As with other, less economically advantaged parts of Europe, military service provided a less capital-intensive route toward material security and social advancement.

The sociology of Scottish officers mirrors key characteristics of the country's contribution to the civil and maritime sectors. Edinburgh and its Lothian hinterlands did well in terms of overall share relative to population. However, it is the central-eastern and northern regions that again stand out: the north-east and the Highlands supplied 634 individuals, equivalent to 36 per cent of all confirmed Scots military officers in Asia. Combining this evidence with known patterns of participation in the British army underlines the extent to which the Highland military economy adapted and globalised from the 1740s.[77] However, an emphasis on regional patterns alone risks disguising sharp variations across and between localities. The number of officers from the city of Dublin (excluding the county) totalled 133; County Cork supplied 75, a comparatively large share of the Irish officers with known origins. Fife and Inverness were prominent in a Scottish context, providing 131 and 153 respectively.[78] Indeed Inverness-shire exported more officers per capita than any other metropolitan provincial county – equivalent to the commissioned cadre of three regiments.

While information on geographic origins is reasonably robust, social and educational details are partial at best, making it difficult to arrive at firm conclusions about these aspects of the officer elite. Little can be said about schooling other than a slightly greater likelihood, if compared with the civil servants, for education to occur in the cadet's country of origin rather than in England. While 38.5 per cent and 60.1 per cent of Irish and Scottish civil servants with known educational backgrounds were trained at home, these ratios rise to 45.1 per cent and 66.6 per cent respectively for officers. The British army, militia and 'fencible' regiments provided training for prospective cadets. Having campaigned with the Louth militia against the French at Bantry Bay, Ensign John George Bellingham wrote to his father on 13 April 1799 confirming his appointment to Madras, adding, 'the directors have seemed very well pleased to get me as an officer with the advantage from my service in the Militia of a military knowledge which the young boys who go out are so totally ignorant of...'. Experience in the Breadalbane Fencibles

Table 4.3 Military officers: regional, social and educational backgrounds

Nationality	Region	Social Origins	Education
Irish 1,256	Leinster = 344 (27.3%) Ulster = 281 (22.3%) Munster = 197 (15.6%) Connacht = 59 (4.6%) Asia = 28 (2.2%) UK = 16 (1.2%) N. America = 3 (0.2%) Europe = 1 (0.07%) Saint Helena = 1 (0.07%) Unknown = 326 (25.9%)	Gentry & Aristocracy = 180 (14.3%) Clergy/Legal/Medical = 118 (9.3%) Military & RN = 51 (4%) EIC = 36 (2.8%) Merch/Manuf. = 26 (2.0%) Artisan = 12 (0.9%) Government = 12 (0.9%) Labourer = 8 (0.6%) Financial services = 7 (0.5%) Municipal = 6 (0.4%) Tenant Farmer = 4 (0.3%) Unknown = 796 (63.3%)	Dublin (inc. TCD) = 28 (2.2%) England = 24 (1.9%) Militia/Yeomanry = 20 (1.5%) Ireland = 19 (1.5%) British Army = 14 (1.1%) Cork = 4 (0.3%) RN = 3 (0.2%) French Army = 1 (0.07%) Unknown = 1,143 (91%)
Scots 2,070	Highlands = 354 (17.1%) Central = 305 (14.7%) NE = 280 (13.5%) Edinburgh = 211 (10.1%) West Central = 188 (9%) Borders = 187 (9%) Lothians = 110 (5.3%) Asia = 38 (1.8%) England = 36 (1.7%) The North = 21 (1%) Atlantic Empire = 14 (0.6%) Europe = 4 (0.1%) Unknown = 322 (15.5%)	Gentry & Aristocracy = 395 (19%) Clergy/Legal/Medical = 272 (13.1%) Tenant Farmer = 166 (8.0%) Merch/Mar/Manuf. = 158 (7.6%) Military & RN = 100 (4.8%) EIC = 56 (2.7%) Artisan = 50 (2.4%) Government = 46 (2.2%) Municipal = 41 (1.9%) Education = 34 (1.6%) Financial services = 18 (0.8%) Labourer = 11 (0.5%) Caribbean = 10 (0.4%) Misc. = 8 (0.3%) Unknown = 705 (34.0%)	Scotland = 82 (3.9%) British Army = 42 (2%) Edinburgh (inc. Uni) = 27 (1.3%) Aberdeen = 24 (1.1%) England = 20 (0.9%) Glasgow = 14 (0.6%) St Andrews = 8 (0.3%) Militia/Fencibles = 6 (0.2%) Scots-Dutch = 5 (0.2%) RN = 4 (0.1%) Unknown = 1,838 (88.7%)

Welsh	South Wales = 97 (50.7%)	Gentry & Aristocracy = 16 (8.3%)	England = 14 (7.3%)
191	East Wales = 37 (19.3%)	Clergy = 12 (6.2%)	British Army = 3 (1.5%)
	W/North Wales = 25 (13%)	Medical & legal = 8 (4.1%)	Militia = 1 (0.5%)
	England = 7 (3.6%)	EIC = 4 (2%)	Scotland = 1 (0.5%)
	Asia = 1 (0.52%)	Misc. = 10 (5.2%)	Clerical = 1 (0.5%)
	Unknown = 24 (12.5%)	Unknown = 141 (73.8%)	Unknown = 171 (89.5%)

(SIWA. *Sources*: IOR, L/MIL/9/85, 107–127; L/MIL/10/131; L/MIL/11/109; B/40–B/95; P/328/60–64; P/416/77–98; L/AG/34/29/4–22, 185–210, 341–343; TNA, PROB 11/549–1903; *The East India Kalendar … 1791 to 1800* (London: J. Debrett, 1791–1800); V. C. P. Hodson, *List of the Officers of the Army of Bengal, 1754–1834*, I-IV (London: Longman, Orme, Brown & Co., 1927); Duncan Campbell, *Records of Clan Campbell in the Military Service of the Honourable East India Company, 1600–1858* (London: Longman's, Green and Co., 1925), pp. 1–274).

from 1793 to 1795 underpinned the successful application for a Bengal army cadetship by Duncan Macpherson, son of the minister of Laggan in Inverness-shire.[79] Home defence establishments expanded disproportionately in Ireland and Scotland in the 1790s and 1800s and acted as professional nurseries for those seeking military employment in Asia.

Information on socio-religious backgrounds is similarly fragmentary. The piecemeal participation of Ireland's Catholics, already evident in the persons of Francis Cooke in 1736 and John Nelley in 1781, continued but in a limited fashion. Three scions of a prominent Catholic merchant from Cork city, John Fagan, obtained cadetships in Bengal between 1797 and 1804.[80] But cadet applications do not indicate a more general movement of Catholic families into the Company's officer corps. The failure to systematically engage Ireland's majority community represented a seminal failure of British political leadership. It was also an indication of how the Company's *ancien régime* character generated patronage links which worked to consolidate the existing landed, mercantile and clerical order in the metropolitan provinces.

Landed families, including the aristocracy but more especially the middling and lower gentry, sent hundreds of their sons into the presidency armies. This social group secured the largest known share of officer posts in all three countries. Clerical, legal and medical families, however, were well represented. Alexander Fullerton, the son of an Episcopalian minister from Haddington, joined the Madras garrison as early as 1709; Richard and Thomas Macan, sons of an Armagh lawyer, became officers in Bengal in 1772 and 1784; and Nathan Powell, whose father was a doctor in Brecon, took a commission in the Bombay army in 1799.[81] These examples form part of a significant pattern of social mobility through imperial service. Material and social expectations explain why gentry and middling families across Wales, Ireland and Scotland supplied the Bengal, Madras and Bombay armies with nearly 40 per cent of their officers by the 1790s. The conquest nature of empire in Asia acted as a major conduit for upward social mobility among families with material ambitions but little or no formal political rights. In providing genteel, 'honourable' forms of occupation and a realistic chance for advancement, Company employment eased potential frustration and alienation at the restricted pre-1829 and -1832 franchises.

One aspect of the officers' origins outlined in Table 4.3 points to an important contrast between the three metropolitan provinces. Tenant farmers in the Scottish Lowlands and tacksmen in the Highlands secured commissions for their sons at a much higher rate than their counterparts in Wales or Ireland. John Jones, the son of a farmer from Llanbeulan in Anglesey and Bernard Ryan, whose father farmed in Newbridge, Kildare, did become cadets; but these examples are atypical for Ireland and Wales in terms of officers with identified social origins.[82] By contrast, the scions of tenant farmers formed the third largest social grouping within Company officers from Scotland, comprising one in eight of all those with traceable backgrounds.

There are major implications in these trends for assessments of Scotland's post-union political culture. Often seen as narrow, complacent and corrupt, especially when set against the vibrant patriot politics evident in England and Ireland, Scottish patronage could in fact be responsive and, within obvious limits, inclusive in a regional and social sense.[83] The country's notoriously unrepresentative electoral system still managed to deliver substantial opportunities to social groups not usually assumed to be part of the old propertied, political or imperial elite. These outcomes reflect the influence of directors at Leadenhall Street and the heavy reliance on Company patronage exhibited by the third duke of Argyll and Henry Dundas.[84] The findings in Table 4.3 also confirm how empire in Asia formed a central element of the sophisticated response of Highland tacksmen to rent increases, estate 'improvements' and commercial change.[85] The MacAlisters in Snizort, Macleods in Glenelg and Macphersons in Laggan and Kingussie proved adept at securing multiple cadetships to consolidate their material and social status.[86] The combined effect of local initiative, the patronage strategies of the political managers and the directors' brokering of human capital ensured that corporate employment trickled down the social hierarchy and across all of Scotland's localities. This intersection of regional, metropolitan and global factors shaped the emergence of variable patterns of high- and low-value human capital recruitment which in turn defined the overall characteristics of provincial involvement in the corporate military.

From human to monetary capital: predatory military entrepreneurism in Asia

The profit motive drove soldiers as surely as it did merchants or mariners. The expectation of prize money and looting on a scale that was simply not possible elsewhere in the Empire constituted a key attraction of Company service. As Major William Baillie of Dunain in Inverness-shire noted from Madras in 1775: 'India now promises better for the military than it had done some time past the more mischief the better for us.'[87]

The older traditions of service in Europe offered the prospect of material security, social advancement and the occasional acquisition of substantial wealth. Asia promised similar but also different prospects. India contained huge populations, sophisticated rural and urban economies and a scale of wealth few if any early modern theatres of war could match. These realities explain why the Company's military elite exhibited a predatory, asset-stripping imperialism, which more closely resembled the sixteenth-century Spanish assaults on the Aztec and Incan Empires than eighteenth-century Britain's representation of itself as an empire of liberty, property and trade.[88] The military commanders during the early phases of territorial expansion – men like Robert Clive, Eyre Coote and Hector Munro – were the nearest British figures to Spanish conquistadors. The conduct of corporate and British forces during the second Anglo-Mysore War exemplified the drive for primitive capital accumulation through looting and depredation. Rumours of atrocities against civilians were overshadowed in the public imagination in Britain and Ireland by the fall of places like Bednore in February 1783 and the alleged capture of £1.2 to £1.9 million.[89] Such events happened thousands of miles away from Ireland, Scotland or Wales in locations only vaguely understood: but they were far from distant in an imaginative sense. In a revealing example of the close attention paid to the possible gains of predatory imperialism, John Cochrane of Rochsoles wrote in September 1799 to his son, James in Madras. He informed him that the newspapers in Scotland were replete with news of the imminent fall of Seringapatnam, the capital of Mysore. There was widespread speculation that the prize money alone would amount to between £3 million and £30 million.[90] Such sums were wild exaggerations. But if never on the scale suggested by such ill-informed gossip, the asset stripping of South Asian society was still extremely profitable. On 9 March 1799 the Madras presidency published details confirming that the Seringapatnam prize money amounted to £1,295,483. It also listed the military units entitled to receive a share: of the ten European regiments in the 44,000-strong force that invaded Mysore, four (the 73rd, 74th and 75th Highland Regiments and the reconstituted Scots Brigade) contained substantial numbers of Scots officers and residual pockets of Scottish rank and file.[91] The injection of imperial wealth that the fall of Mysore's capital delivered to Scottish military personnel means the event should be seen in the same light as state compensation schemes like the Equivalent in 1707, the buying out of heritable jurisdictions in 1752, payouts to North American loyalists in the 1780s, and the much larger windfall given to owners of enslaved people in the 1830s.[92] These episodic but substantial injections of public and imperial wealth are an underappreciated feature of Scottish society's successful primitive capital accumulation over the course of 130 years after union.

While the magnetic appeal of 'Oriental' wealth proved persistent, the reality was that substantial prize money did not materialise for many officers or men. Just as the civil servants and marine officers struggled with issues of credit, career progression and wealth acquisition, so the corporation's military personnel often found Asia did not answer expectations.[93] Securing profits or even a steady livelihood occurred in a number of ways and produced dramatically different results based on social standing, rank, Asia- and London-based networks and, up to a point, luck. In 1783 Major General James Stuart from Lanarkshire replaced Sir Eyre Coote, the scion of an Anglo-Irish family from Limerick, as commander of the Madras army. In their different ways both officers reveal the scale of potential profits available to those at the top of the military complex. Many of his contemporaries believed that Coote accrued £100,000 during the Bengal and Madras phases of his career.[94] Most fortunes made in Asia were susceptible to overexaggeration as part of the commonly held belief that the 'Orient' was a place of limitless and easily acquired wealth. Whatever the precise nature of Coote's profits, there is no doubting the scale of his fortune. In September 1763, after his first return home from Bengal, he purchased five estates across Kildare, Queen's, King's, West Meath and Roscommon in addition to property in Hertfordshire and Wiltshire. His will twenty years later left a major bequest of £1,000 per annum to his wife and similarly substantial gifts to various associates.[95]

Stuart was less successful as either a commander or a military entrepreneur. Yet while his brother's estate in one of the most 'improved' districts of Scotland rented at £610 per annum, James's salary as commander at Madras was £3,200 in addition to £2,500 in pay and disbursements he received as colonel of a garrison regiment at Tanjore.[96] These high-ranking officers were not of course typical; for every successful senior figure there were many more who died before they arrived in Asia or succumbed quickly to disease and the climate before making any fortune at all. Roderick Forbes from Aberdeenshire, an officer at Bombay, died in 1760 with £20; Robert Parkinson from Ireland deceased in Madras in 1774 with £40; and Thomas Morgan from Glamorgan, left £100 in his Calcutta-registered will of 1792.[97]

Outcomes for rank and file are far less easy to judge. The question of how much these men could accrue is of particular relevance in the case of Ireland given the substantial numbers moving to Asia. Thousands of Irishmen, hundreds of Scots and the majority of the limited number of Welsh either died on the journey or while in service. Few ever returned.[98] One of the many powerful silences within the Company's archive is the lack of wills from tens of thousands of soldiers and sailors. The absence does not denote a lack of property, simply that most trusted to verbal agreements with regimental friends or shipmates and left their pay, prize money and belongings to comrades or to South Asian women and the children produced by such relationships.[99] What evidence does exist demonstrates that enlisted men could accrue considerable sums through pay, 'batta' (field pay), prize dues and the proceeds of lending to officers for use in commercial ventures. When private

John MacKenzie of the 73rd Highland Regiment died at Seringapatnam in June 1801, he left £400 to his sister in Assynt in Sutherland. The remittance can be contextualised by the fact that in the 1790s the landed rental for MacKenzie's home parish was £1,000.[100] NCOs like Sergeant John Hoare from Cork and Corporal James MacBain from Inverness-shire also sent sums back to their families, augmenting household incomes and solvency in ways that have left little or no permanent legacy or memory but were doubtless significant at the time.[101]

The lack of evidence for the bulk of enlisted men and the corresponding prominence of unrepresentative examples like Coote and Stuart impairs assessments of how well soldiering for the Company could generate monetary returns. One means of providing an overview of profits is a survey of wills and testaments.[102] Even this method has its limitations. Most Europeans dying in Asia, regardless of rank, did not leave a will, so the problem of typicality remains. Yet these records constitute one of the best sources for reconstructing the scale, nature and transfer of profits from military and imperial service. The findings in Table 4.4 are compiled from 4,157 wills lodged at Madras and Bombay from 1753 to 1813, at Calcutta from 1780 to 1803 and for a further two sample years (1805 and 1810).

The patterns of capital accumulation in Table 4.4 reveal how an economy of high-value human capital transformed social standing, rank and reputation into monetary fortunes. Even a small number of officers could accrue large sums. Only 6 per cent of Scots, 4.9 per cent of Irish and 1.5 per cent of Welsh commissioned personnel listed in Table 4.2 left a will recording the value of their property. Yet the combined capital of this small ratio was greater than £1 million. The larger number of Scots is reflected in the incidence of wills and in a greater total in two of the three presidencies. The figures for Irish officers are impressive on a per capita basis and exhibit a definite pattern of overrepresentation among those with fortunes greater than £10,000: eleven officers from Ireland achieved this milestone and they formed 75 per cent of metropolitan provincials with proceeds in excess of £50,000 or £100,000 recorded in testaments. This preponderance towards a smaller clique securing substantial fortunes explains why the Irish total of £577,999 is larger than that of Scots (£511,031) despite having fewer officers in service. Viewed as an exercise in the realisation of human capital, the patterns in Table 4.4 illustrate the highly effective use of corporate militarism by Ireland's Protestant gentry and middling orders. While this community's role in Ireland's domestic history tends to dominate assessments, their profile in Asia was disproportionate until the 1780s and involved the acquisition of some of the largest military fortunes of the pre-1815 era. A select number proved adroit at transforming their high-value human capital into profits. The wealth, success and resultant political influence of the

Table 4.4 Military profits: Bengal, Bombay, Madras wills, 1753–1813

Fortune [Bengal]	£0–£99	£100–£999	£1,000–£9,999	£10,000–£49,999	£50,000–£99,999	>£100,000	Total
Irish	0	10	8	2	2	0	£181,173
Scots	1	13	17	4	1	0	£214,492
Welsh	0	0	0	0	0	0	0

Fortune [Bombay]	£0–£99	£100–£999	£1,000–£9,999	£10,000–£49,999	£50,000–£99,999	>£100,000	Total
Irish	2	5	3	2	0	0	£46,173
Scots	3	11	16	0	0	0	£67,251
Welsh	0	0	0	0	0	0	0

Fortune [Madras]	£0–£99	£100–£999	£1,000–£9,999	£10,000–£49,999	£50,000–£99,999	>£100,000	Total
Irish	2	15	11	4	0	1	£350,653
Scots	4	19	29	7	0	0	£229,288
Welsh	0	2	1	0	0	0	£2,000

(SIWA. Sources: IOR, P/328/60–64; P/416/77–98; L/AG/34/29/4–22, 185–210, 341–343).

Wellesleys may have been exceptional but they were part of a wider pattern of niche Irish engagement with new globalised forms of military service.

Yet concentrating on the overall totals alone risks neglecting the distinctive configurations in Table 4.4. Major James Kilpatrick from Cavan campaigned with Robert Clive up until his death in 1759, amassing in the process the colossal sum of £207,336. This single will amounts to 35.8 per cent of the overall Irish total. Kilpatrick personifies the socially narrow and regionally focused nature of Ireland's involvement in the military elite. The next two largest Irish military fortunes recorded in testaments were those of Lieutenant Colonel Jacob Camac, one of four brothers of Huguenot descent from Lurgan in the Company armies, who died in 1785 worth £56,600, and Major James Crawford, who died in 1787 with £55,100.[103] Not only were these men and Kilpatrick all from Ulster but their combined profits amounted to 55 per cent of the Irish total in Table 4.4. By contrast, the top three Scottish fortunes – those of Major Samuel Kilpatrick from Campbeltown (£71,684), Major Alexander Grant from Forres (£28,000) and Major General Hay MacDowell from Wigton (£27,700) – amounted to only 25 per cent of Scottish military profits.[104]

High-value Irish human capital in the armed forces created a small number of spectacular fortunes that consolidated the existing configuration of regional and social power. The equivalent Scottish economy produced a broader diffusion of profits. The pattern in Table 4.4 shows that thirty-three Irish officers acquired more than £1,000 compared to seventy-four Scots. The difference points to how military profits secured by Scots officers were dispersed across a wider range of social and regional backgrounds. The larger numbers outlined in Table 4.2 fed through into a greater number of the senior-ranking personnel who were best placed to accrue loot, prize money, contracts and field-officer salaries. The profile of metropolitan provincials traced to the higher echelons of the Company's three armies and British units serving in India is outlined in Table 4.5. What it illustrates is the transfer to Asia through military migration of high-value human capital and its subsequent enhancement by means of promotion. This hierarchy of human wealth shaped the capacity of Irish, Scottish and Welsh society to extract and accumulate monetary profits through service in the armed forces.

If testaments registered in India, in London and in Edinburgh are aligned with evidence from private papers and the directors' minutes, which record remitted bills of exchange, an informed assessment of military profiteering is possible. The first confirmable summary of material returns arising from the investment in Asia of metropolitan provincial high-value human capital is charted in Table 4.6.

The same pattern of a small number of high-ranking Irish individuals acquiring large fortunes is confirmed by the addition of Generals Coote

Table 4.5 Irish, Scots and Welsh senior officers, Asia, 1747–1813

Major	<1750	1750–1769	1770–1789	1790–1809	1810–1813	Total
Irish	1	8	22	66	21	115
Scots	0	14	43	126	12	195
Welsh	0	1	2	3	1	7
Lt.-Colonel						
Irish	0	4	16	49	8	77
Scots	0	9	26	86	8	129
Welsh	0	0	2	3	1	6
Colonel						
Irish	0	2	7	15	11	35
Scots	0	0	13	30	6	49
Welsh	0	0	1	1	0	2
Maj.- & Lt-General						
Irish	0	0	0	12	9	21
Scots	0	0	4	21	16	41
Welsh	0	0	0	3	0	3

(SIWA. Sources: IOR, L/MIL/9/85, 107–127; L/MIL/10/131; L/MIL/11/109; P/328/60–64; P/416/77–98; L/AG/34/29/4–22, 185–210, 341–343; TNA, PROB 11/549–1903; *The East India Kalendar ... 1791 to 1800*; Hodson, *List of the Officers of the Army of Bengal, 1754–1834*, I–IV; Dodwell & Miles, *Alphabetical List of the Officers of the Indian Army*; Campbell, *Records of Clan Campbell*).

and John Carnac alongside James Kilpatrick. From a confirmed number of 1,256 officers in Asia before 1813, it is possible to trace a total of over £1 million secured by only fifty individuals. This represents the best per capita return on military migration realised by any metropolitan provincial group and is the equivalent today in real price terms to £129.5 million.[105] As with all officers, wealth was acquired through a combination of salary earnings, military contracts for gunpowder, salt, clothing, bullocks, prize money, bills of credit from local rulers like the Nawab of the Carnatic and private commercial ventures.[106] The regional origins of these Irish military nabobs match the findings in Table 4.3. Individuals from Protestant-dominated counties and provinces, especially Ulster, acquired the bulk of the profits, although officers from Connacht were slightly more conspicuous among those with fortunes greater that £1,000 than their general share of military posts would suggest.

At almost £1.8 million – equivalent in today's real price terms to £215.3 million – the confirmed proceeds made by Scottish officers were even more substantial. This was the product of a greater volume of commissioned individuals rather than the exceptionally high return on

Table 4.6 Irish, Scots and Welsh military profiteering

Irish	£1,000–£9,999	£10,000–£19,999	£20,000–£49,999	£50,000–£99,999	>£100,000	Total
Ulster =16	29	8	7	3	3	50
Leinster = 12	£101,811	£113,678	£194,250	£191,700	£474,336	£1,075,775
Munster = 9						
Connacht = 5						
Unknown = 8						

Scots	£1,000–£9,999	£10,000–£19,999	£20,000–£49,999	£50,000–£99,999	>£100,000	Total
Highlands = 49	99	19	18	6	3	145
Central = 19	£343,306	£274,804	£394,913	£354,008	£421,615	£1,788,646
NE = 17						
Edinburgh = 12						
W. Central = 12						
Borders = 10						
Lothians = 3						
Unknown = 22						

Welsh	£1,000–£9,000	£10,000–£19,999	£20,000–£49,000	£50,000–£99,999	>£100,000	Total
W/North =1	1	0	0	0	0	£2,000

(SIWA. Sources: IOR, B/40–B/95; P/328/60–64; P/416/77–98; L/AG/34/29/4–22, 185–210, 341–343; MSS Eur F.128/12; DCM, 3/70/1–4; TNA, PROB 11/549–1903; NRS, CC1/6/81; CC8/1/113; CC8/4/2–3; CC8/8/118, 120–123, 125–128, 129–132, 134–136, 138–140, 142, 145–6; CC8/11/4–5; CC9/7/69; CC10/5/12; CC20/5/12; SC26/38/1; SC36/48/7; SC70/1/6, 12, 14, 17, 22).

human capital exhibited by a small number of personnel from Ireland. A more significant characteristic than the overall sum secured by Scots was the fact that these profits accrued to a broader range of regional and social groups. There was a thicker layer of military nabobs from Scotland acquiring fortunes between £10,000 and £50,000. Officers from the Highlands were conspicuous in terms of those securing substantial material returns, although the central and north-eastern counties also did well. These patterns underline the human capital economy's acute sensitivity to regional differences while also revealing the aggressive involvement of almost all of Scotland's localities in this form of colonial exploitation. More generally, the acquisition of such a substantial amount by just 145 individuals reinforces the example of the senior Irish officers and confirms the profitability of an investment strategy that blended high-value human capital with high-risk/high-return forms of global migration.

Conclusion

Irish and Scottish society traditionally relied on military service to export their human capital. Interaction with the EIC's armed forces demonstrates that this dependency continued through the eighteenth and into the early nineteenth centuries. The adaptation in cultures of militarism could be highly profitable. Lacking the monetary reserves to participate extensively in the capital-reliant aspects of early modern expansion, the metropolitan provinces mobilised one of their most realisable forms of available wealth. This form of political economy has major implications for how human mobility should be understood in this period. Migration is often assessed as a manifestation of, and reaction to, the separate deployment and influence of monetary capital. Yet it also needs to be evaluated as an alternative mode of global investment. Ireland and Scotland were not alone in this use of people. These military migrations occurred at the same time as 'peasant soldiers' in India adjusted to the new influence of the English East India Company.[107] That such a comparison can be realistically drawn underlines how the second half of the eighteenth century inaugurated a final phase of proto-globalisation that connected widely separated parts of the world in more sustained ways. The results involved confluences and connections that generated new regional, provincial and national distinctions both in Asia and in Britain and Ireland.

The different trajectories of Irish and Scottish society in this context reveal how traditional, manpower-exporting economies exploited the pressures facing nation states and sovereignty-wielding corporations as they sought to manage processes of expansion and empire.[108] Materially poor societies did not wait passively to be subjected to the new global forces. Pre-existing human, social and political resources enabled modes of participation that surmounted the lack of other competitive advantages. The realignment of Ireland and Scotland's older economies of manpower is an example of proto-globalisation's cannibalising and reuse of existing conditions rather than simply removing them completely.[109] The economies of human capital that evolved in response to the Company's need for European manpower show this process in action at the imperial metropole. At the very same time as the corporation tapped into traditional recruitment markets for sepoy manpower, it exploited and entrenched sociocultural distinctions across the British and Irish Isles.

Both Ireland and Scotland developed economies of high-value/low-volume human capital in the form of commissioned officers. This facilitated involvement in overseas forms of gentry capitalism. The profitability of this approach relied heavily upon primitive capital accumulation through the asset stripping of large parts of post-Mughal India and the diversion of the Company's public revenues into private hands.[110] The scale of the resultant military fortunes can now be better appreciated and incorporated into assessments of how empire reshaped the metropolitan provinces. Yet participation took significantly different forms and produced equally different consequences. Irish society evolved a niche export economy of large numbers of low-value/high-volume soldiers and an extremely successful but socially and regionally restricted stream of high-value/low-volume officers. The returns were substantial but weighted heavily towards certain regions and social interests. There are parallels to be drawn here with debates in Scottish history over whether the slavery related profits of tobacco and sugar spread widely through the post-union economy or remained largely within an enclave centred on Glasgow and the Clyde.[111] Whether this was the case in Scotland with Asia-derived profits will be considered under the theme of returning influences. The configuration of Irish military profiteering in India, however, did result in an enclave of imperial wealth among nabobs who originated largely from the Protestant propertied classes in Ulster, Leinster and to a lesser extent, Munster.

These trends point to comparisons with the post-Culloden Highlands' supply of large numbers of officers and enlisted men to the British army.[112] A similarly configured movement of high- and low-value manpower occurred in Ireland and was likewise directed into state service. It is measure of Ireland's centrality to the Empire's demographic requirements that the EIC also relied on the kingdom for thousands of its ordinary 'European' recruits. Yet the departure of these men did not produce substantial material returns for the sending society. The drain of social and human wealth which this represented was not lost on those who, like the prominent United Irishman and leading protagonist in the 1798 rising, Wolfe Toone, opposed constitutional subordination to Britain and its corporate subsidiary, the East India Company.[113]

Scottish landed elites, meanwhile, guarded their much more limited reserves of manpower for investment in state service. One result was that connections with the Company evolved along radically different social lines to that of Ireland. The movement east of military Scots consisted of surprisingly small amounts of high-volume/low-value manpower, a lot of which congregated in British army regiments, and substantial inputs of high-value/low-volume human capital. This configuration produced some of the largest per capita financial returns of any form of early modern Scottish migration.[114] In sharp contrast, and in parallel with other sectors of the corporation, the telling aspect of Welsh evidence is a pattern of limited involvement overseas.

The salient characteristic of metropolitan provincial interaction with the Company's military complex was diversity and difference. Yet the consequences of this involvement extended well beyond the implications for Ireland, Wales and Scotland's trajectories within the British and Irish Isles. Armed service became the primary route into a corporation at the cutting edge of trends in metropolitan and colonial state formation as well as monetary, commodity and population flows which shaped processes of proto-globalisation. Despite apparently lacking the finance capital to participate in these crucial aspects of Europe's expansion, Ireland and Scotland both made disproportionate contributions in very different ways to the Company's aggressively expansionist military complex. Understanding how they achieved this facilitates a more decentred appreciation of early modern global expansion and of the diverse, pluralist tactics that enabled it. The adaptability of these supposedly 'underdeveloped' and 'undercapitalised' regions demonstrates the value of Irish and Scottish evidence to wider histories of proto-globalisation and British imperialism.

Notes

1 Ditchburn, *Scotland and Europe*, pp. 218–32; Steve Murdoch, 'Introduction', in Steve Murdoch (ed.), *Scotland and the Thirty Years' War* (Leiden: Brill, 2001), pp. 14–20; Harman Murtagh, 'Irish Soldiers Abroad, 1600–1800', in T. Bartlett and K. Jeffery (eds), *A Military History of Ireland* (Cambridge: Cambridge University Press, 1996), pp. 294–9; Stephen Conway, 'The Scots Brigade in the Eighteenth Century', *Northern Scotland*, 1 (2010), 30–41.
2 Stephen Brumwell, 'The Scottish Military Experience in North America, 1756–1783', in Edward M. Speirs, Jeremy A. Crang and Matthew J. Strickland (eds), *A Military History of Scotland* (Edinburgh: Edinburgh University Press, 2012), pp. 383–401; McGrath, *Ireland and Empire*, pp. 145–66; Wayne E. Lee, 'Subjects, Clients, Allies, or Mercenaries? The British Use of Irish and Amerindian Military Power, 1500–1800', in Bowen, Mancke and Reid (eds), *Britain's Ocean Empire*, pp. 179–217.
3 Hopkins, 'Introduction: Globalisation – An Agenda for Historians', pp. 3, 7; Bayly, *The Making of the Modern World*, pp. 28–47.
4 Jan de Vries, 'The Limits of Globalisation in the Early Modern World', *Economic History Review*, 63 (2010), 711–14.
5 Dirk Kolff, *Naukar, Rajput and Sepoy: The Ethnohistory of the Military Labour Market in Hindustan, 1450–1850* (Cambridge: Cambridge University Press, 1990), pp. 170–81; Seema Alavi, *The Sepoys and the Company: Tradition and Transition in Northern India, 1770–1830* (New Delhi: Oxford University Press, 1998), pp. 11–94; Bayly, '"Archaic" and "Modern" Globalisation in the Eurasian and African Arena', p. 66.
6 Hopkins, 'The History of Globalisation', p. 24.
7 Stephen Brumwell, *Redcoats: The British Soldier and Wars in the Americas, 1755–1763* (Cambridge: Cambridge University Press, 2002), pp. 266–89;

Colley, *Britons*, p. 126; Laurence Brockliss, 'The Professions and National Identity', in Laurence Brockliss and David Eastwood (eds), *A Union of Multiple Identities: The British Isles, 1750–1850* (Manchester: Manchester University Press, 1997), p. 9.
8 Cookson, *The British Armed Nation*, pp. 126–7; A. Mackillop, *'More Fruitful than the Soil': Army, Empire and the Scottish Highlands, 1715–1815* (East Linton: Tuckwell, 2000), passim.
9 Barnard, *A New Anatomy of Ireland*, p. 178; Alvin Jackson, *The Two Unions*, pp. 196–9.
10 Bayly, *Imperial Meridian*, pp. 86–7; Cookson, *The British Armed Nation*, pp. 153–81; Peter Karsten, 'Irish Soldiers in the British Army, 1792–1922: Suborned or Subordinate?', *Journal of Social History*, 17 (1983), 31–64; Lee, 'Subjects, Clients, Allies, or Mercenaries?', pp. 179–217.
11 Cadell, 'Irish Soldiers in India', pp. 75–6; Peter Bailey, 'Irish Men in the East India Company Army', *Irish Family History*, 17 (2001), 84–92.
12 Stern, *The Company State*, p. 64; G. J. Bryant, 'The East India Company and Its Army, 1600–1778' (PhD dissertation, King's College, 1975), pp. 43–7; HL, ST57/30, p. 112; HL, PO1032; IOR, B/75, p. 79; NRS, GD51/3/305.
13 NRS, GD24/1/464/n/41, 45; GD24/1/484/57, 60, 145; GCA, T-SK11/2/16, 19, 22; NLS, MS1337, fos. 6, 204–5; MS1367, fo. 41; NLS, MS19298, fos. 28–31; MS14828, fo. 23; CSAS, Hunter-Blair Papers, Box 1/4: Calcutta, 20 October 1770; PRONI, D572/19/64.
14 IOR, B/66, p. 408; B/67, p. 57.
15 Bryant, 'The East India Company and Its Army', pp. 44–7; IOR, L/MIL/12/117/ Part 1, fos. 6–8; L/MIL/10/130; B/58, p. 214.
16 IOR, B/51, p. 418; B/52, p. 145; B/56, p. 358; B/57, p. 466; B/59, p. 161; B/64, p. 329; B/70, pp. 634–644.
17 Conway, 'The Scots Brigade', 36–7. NLS, MS1367, fo. 117; NRS, GD132/768/8: 31 December 1783; NRS, GD23/1/312/15; NLS, MS49, p. 73; MS50, fo. 43; MS52, p. 37.
18 HL, Loudon (Scottish) Papers, Box 6: LO7569; LO1120; LO/9964; Victoria Henshaw, *Scotland and the British Army, 1700–1750: Defending the Union* (London: Bloomsbury, 2014), pp. 97–8.
19 IOR, B/56, pp. 14, 20, 87, 347; B/57, pp. 216, 436; McGrath, *Ireland and Empire*, p. 118.
20 NRS, GD248/49/1/17; NRS, GD345/1173/1/21–22x; GD345/1175/2/26x-28X; GD345/1195, London, 11 July 1747.
21 *The Scots Magazine*, 9 (1747), pp. 243, 350–1, 402.
22 NRS, GD248/413/1, pp. 3–4; NRS, GD345/1195, 'Accompt of Men Enlisted for HM's service in Captain Grant's Independent Company'; GCA, T-SK/11/2/42.
23 NRS, GD87/1/34/2: Ft. St. David, 12 October 1748.
24 Stephen Conway, *Britain, Ireland and Continental Europe in the Eighteenth Century* (Oxford: Oxford University Press, 2011), pp. 267–82; R. van Gelder, *Het Oost-Indisch avantuur: Duitsers in dienst can de VOC, 1600–1800* (Nijmegen: Sun, 1997), passim.

The military

25 IOR, B/69, p. 313; B/71, pp. 234, 454–5; B/72, pp. 77, 500; B/73, p. 202; B/75, pp. 121, 127, 217, 238, 264, 355, 431; B/76, p. 134; B/78, p. 305; B/81, p. 324; B/83, pp. 431, 438, 474; B/85, p. 257; B/95, p. 435.
26 IOR, B71/p. 448–9; B/72, pp. 127, 529; B/73, pp. 294, 339.
27 IOR, B/63, pp. 549, 569; Bernard Burke, *A Genealogical and Heraldic History of the Landed Gentry of Ireland* (London: Harrisons & Sons, 1912), p. 214.
28 Cadell, 'Irish Soldiers in India', p. 76; Bartlett, 'The Irish Soldier in India', p. 14.
29 Mukherjee, 'Trade and Empire in Awadh', 85–102; P. J. Marshall, 'Early British Imperialism in India', *Past & Present*, 106 (1985), 164–8; Bayly, *Indian Society and the Making of the British Empire*, pp. 30–48; Peers, 'State, Power, and Colonialism', pp. 23–5.
30 IOR, H/84, pp. 203, 685; NLS, MS1062, fos. 95–115; Bryant, 'East India Company Army', pp. 47–216; Lawson, *The East India Company*, pp. 132–3.
31 TNA, WO17/1738.
32 IOR, B/71–B/95.
33 IOR, B/71, pp. 454–5; B/74, pp. 211–12, 464; NLS, MS1060, fo. 158; H. V. Bowen, 'The East India Company and Military Recruitment in Britain, 1763–1771', *Bulletin of the Institute of Historical Research*, 59 (1986), 78–89.
34 Crosbie, *Irish Imperial Networks*, pp. 75–81.
35 IOR, B/74, p. 489; B/75, pp. 117, 125, 374; B/78, pp. 336, 341; B/80, pp. 128, 172; B/85, p. 415; B/93, p. 217; B/95, p. 252.
36 Brumwell, *Redcoats*, pp. 87, 318–19; Matthew P. Dziennik, *The Fatal Land: War, Empire, and the Highland Soldier in British America* (New Haven, CT: Yale University Press, 2015), pp. 6–7.
37 IOR B/75, pp. 121, 671; B/79, p. 166; B/82, p. 296; B/83, p. 485; B/84, p. 222; B/85, pp. 79, 174, 335; B/87, pp. 68, 103, 139; B/89, pp. 282, 483; B/90, p. 211; B/91, p. 436; B/92, p. 484; B/93, p. 93.
38 IOR, B/75, p. 151; B/76, p. 134.
39 Wrigley, 'A Simple Model of London's Importance', 44–70; Bowen, 'The East India Company and Military Recruitment', 80–7.
40 IOR, B/93, pp. 217, 304; B/95, pp. 245, 253; NLS, MS11041, fos. 41–42.
41 Alavi, *The Sepoy and the Company*, pp. 11–94; Channa Wickremesekera, *'Best Black Troops in the World': British Perceptions and the Making of the Sepoy, 1746–1805* (New Delhi: Manohar, 2002), pp. 1–31, 76–129.
42 Martyn J. Powell, *Britain and Ireland in the Eighteenth-Century Crisis of Empire* (Basingstoke: Palgrave Macmillan, 2003), pp. 89, 113, 136–8; James Kelly, *Prelude to Union: Anglo-Irish Politics in the 1780s* (Cork: Cork University Press, 1992), pp. 90–1.
43 IOR, B/75, pp. 374, 587.
44 IOR, B/86, pp. 192, 291; Bowen, 'The East India Company and Military Recruitment', 78–89; Crosbie, *Irish Imperial Networks*, pp. 75–81; *The East-India Register & Directory for 1813* (London: W. H. Allen, 1813), p. lvii.
45 D. Arnold, 'India's Place in the Tropical World, 1770–1930', *Journal of Imperial and Commonwealth History*, 26 (1998), 6–11; Mark Harrison,

Medicine in an Age of Commerce and Empire: Britain and Its Tropical Colonies (Oxford: Oxford University Press, 2010), pp. 15–21, 35–6, 207–8, NRS, GD44/43/205/34–5.

46 Mackillop, 'More Fruitful than the Soil', pp. 183–9; Matthew P. Dziennik, 'Through an Imperial Prism: Land, Liberty, and Highland Loyalism in the War of American Independence', *Journal of British Studies*, 50 (2011), 332–58.

47 R. A. Houston, 'The Demographic Regime', in T. M. Devine and Rosalind Mitchison (eds), *People and Society in Scotland, 1760–1830, vol. 1* (Edinburgh: John Donald, 1988), pp. 12–13; Fry, *The Dundas Despotism*, pp. 65–7.

48 NRS, GD248/226/5/41: 15 December 1775; GD248/227/2/57: Grantown, 25 April 1778; GD 46/17/11: Letter, 24 December 1798; Mackillop, *'More fruitful than the soil'*, pp. 130–67.

49 James David Marwick (ed.), *Extracts from the Records of the Convention of the Royal Burghs of Scotland, 1759–79* (Edinburgh: H. & J. Pillans & Wilson, 1868), pp. 154–5; Conway, 'The Scots Brigade', 30–41.

50 NRS, GD248/226/2/84, 86, 88, 99. See too, IOR, B/85, pp. 290–1.

51 Bayly, *The Birth of the Modern World*, p. 59.

52 Marshall, *East Indian Fortunes*, pp. 16–18; Marshall, 'British Society in India', 98; G. Bryant, 'Officers of the East India Company's Army in the Days of Clive and Hastings', *The Journal of Imperial and Commonwealth History*, 6 (1978), 203–4; NRS, GD51/4/43; NLS, MS11041, fo. 7; HL, Pulteney Papers, Box 5: Douglas, 22 January 1767.

53 NLS, MS8434, pp. 4–7; MS8437, fo. 5; MS8250, fo. 20; MS8252, fos. 1–4; MS8207, fo. 15e; MS8220, fo. 691; NRS, RH4/121/6, pp. 104, 118.

54 IOR, B/49, p. 452; B/52, p. 325; B/54, p. 42; B/55, p. 323; Julian James Cotton, *List of Inscriptions on Tombs or Monuments in Madras*, vols. I–III (Madras: Government Press, 1905), vol. III, p. 17; GCA, TD219/10/152; NRS, GD1/398/54.

55 IOR, B/62, p. 15; NRS, GD22/2/145/2; I. B. Watson, 'Fortifications and the "Idea" of Force in Early English East India Company Relations with India', *Past & Present*, 88 (1980), 80–6.

56 TNA, PROB 11/755, pp. 78–9; IOR, P/416/81 [1744], p. 17.

57 Matthew P. Dziennik, 'The Fiscal-Military State and Labour in the British Atlantic World', in Aaron Graham and Patrick Walsh (eds), *The British Fiscal-Military States, 1660–c.1783* (Abingdon: Routledge, 2016), pp. 159–77; Bartlett, 'The Irish Soldier in India', pp. 13–18; Crosbie, *Irish Imperial Networks*, pp. 68–75; Jackson, *The Two Unions*, pp. 207–12.

58 IOR, L/MIL/11/109: 'Roll of the Hon. Company's Troops on the Coast of Coromandel, 1762.'

59 Cookson, *The British Armed Nation*, pp. 126–9.

60 Karsten, 'Irish Soldiers in the British Army', 31–64; Cullen, 'The Irish Diaspora', pp. 140–1; T. Bartlett and K. Jeffery, 'An Irish Military Tradition', in Bartlett and Jeffery, *A Military History of Ireland*, pp. 7, 12.

61 A. Mackillop, '"A Reticent People?"'.

62 Bryant, 'Scots in India', 24; IOR, L/AG/34/29/201, pp. 63–64; L/AG/34/29/205, pp. 66–7.
63 TNA, WO 120/5: Royal Hospital, Chelsea, Regimental Registers of Pensioners: Returns for 72nd and 73rd Highland Regiments; IOR, H/85, p. 1; NRS, GD51/4/16; NLS, MS1060, fos. 131–3.
64 #: Includes the two groups of twenty-five officers appointed to the Scots and Irish Independent companies in 1747. *: 17 of the 1,245 Scots and 6 of the 677 Irish officers listed for 1790 to 1813 were in the British Army and are subtracted from the percentage share of Company personnel.
65 Barnard, *A New Anatomy*, p. 178; IOR, L/MIL/9/107–110.
66 IOR, L/MIL/9/113/1–3/1–502; L/MIL/9/114/1–377.
67 Embarkation lists from 1764 to 1775 do not include officers: IOR, L/MIL/9/87–88. For lists of cadet appointments between 1775 and 1791 that do not include nationality, see IOR, L/MIL/9/256–59.
68 HL, LO1345(5); LO1384(2); LO3936(1); LO2533(4); LO4011(1); LO1683(1); LO4012(1); LO1391; LO4068 (2); LO2529 (1 & 5); NRS, GD305/1/162/260.
69 IOR, L/MIL/9/108/2/24; MIL/9/110/2/183, 301, 334; L/MIL/9/111/34, 261; L/MIL/9/113/1–4/432; L/MIL/9/114/, 173, 180, 241; L/MIL/9/126/140.
70 Thomas Bartlett, 'The Origins and Progress of the Catholic Question in Ireland, 1690–1800', in T. P. Power and Kevin Whelan (eds), *Endurance and Emergence: Catholics in Ireland in the Eighteenth Century* (Blackrock: Irish Academic Press, 1990), pp. 13–15.
71 Hodson, *Officers of the Army of Bengal*, vol. III, pp. 379–80; TNA, PROB 11/1778, pp. 135–7.
72 SIWA. Sources: IOR, L/MIL/9/85, 89–90; 107–126; P/328/62 [1763], pp. 9–10; P/416/78, pp. 119–23; L/AG/34/29/6 [1786], 34; L/AG/34/29/7 [1792], 4; TNA, PROB 11/11/697, pp. 308–9; PROB 11/755, pp. 78–9; Hodson, *Officers of the Army of Bengal*, I–IV, passim; Bowen, 'Asiatic Interactions', pp. 171–2.
73 SIWA. Sources: IOR, LAG/34/29/187, pp. 128–30; L/AG/34/29/193, pp. 865–7; L/AG/34/29/194, pp. 221–2, 224–5, 255–6; L/AG/34/29/197, pp. 233–5; L/AG/34/29/198, p. 43; L/AG/34/29/341, p. 47; NRS, Registers of Sasines, Inverness (284); NLS, MS8326, fos. 135–138; MS8330, fo. 87.
74 NRS, GD305/1/162/260.
75 Cookson, *The British Armed Nation*, pp. 126–8; Mackillop, 'Military Scotland', pp. 16–20; Caputo, 'Scotland, Scottishness, British Integration and the Royal Navy', 85–118.
76 Peter Harrington, 'The Scottish Soldier in Art', in Speirs, Grang and Strickland, *A Military History of Scotland*, pp. 690–4; Mackillop, 'Military Scotland', p. 23.
77 Mackillop, 'Military Scotland', pp. 13–31; Dziennik, *The Fatal Land*, pp. 220–8.
78 SIWA. Sources: IOR, L/MIL/9/85, 107–126; L/MIL/10/131; L/MIL/11/109; P/328/60–64; P/416/77–98; L/AG/34/29/4–22, 185–210, 341–343; MSS Eur. F128/23/1–8; MSS Eur. F291/119/21; CSAS, Boileau Papers, Box 1/1; TNA,

PROB 11/549–1903; NRS, CC8/8/129, p. 1258; CC/8/146, pp. 449–52; CC8/8/130, pp. 550–1, pp. 645–6; SC70/1/12, pp. 421–35; NRS, Registers of Sasines, Fife (1771) (9525); Midlothian (2250); Kinross (226, 241, 250, 287); Inverness (284) (930); Argyll (1616) (1619)' NRS, GD29/2063/6; NRS, GD80/904/1: Cawnpore, 21 July 1783; NRS, GD164/1698/1–6; GD164/1699/1–2; GD164/1700/1–4; GD164/1709/1–11; NRS, GD128/1/1/22; GD128/1/3: 29 May 1775; GD128/1/4/1: 24 February, 1784; GD248/51/3/28, 51; GD248/52/1/2, 45, 69–70; GD248/227/1/32; GD248/227/2/77; Hodson, *List of the Officers of the Army of Bengal*, I–IV; Burke, *A Genealogical and Heraldic History of the Landed Gentry of Ireland*, passim.

79 IOR, L/MIL/9/108/3; L/MIL/9/109/1/88; TCD, MS11414/10, 16; Hodson, *Officers of the Army of Bengal*, vol. III, pp. 194–5; NRS, GD112/52/601/13.

80 IOR, L/MIL/9/109/1/75; L/MIL/9/108/3/112; L/MIL/9/114/360.

81 TNA, PROB 11/596, pp. 309–10; IOR, B/57, p. 377; B/58, p. 237; L/MIL/10/131; Hodson, *Officers of the Army of Bengal*, III, pp. 107–8.

82 IOR, L/MIL/9/108/1; L/MIL/9/125/77.

83 Shaw, *The Political History of Eighteenth-Century Scotland*, p. 32; Johnston, *History of the Irish Parliament*, vol. II, p. 382; Cullen, 'Scotland & Ireland, 1600–1800', pp. 231–43.

84 IOR, L/MIL/9/111/236; L/MIL/9/126/138. For tenant farmers' sons receiving commissions, see SIWA. Sources: L/MIL/9/108/3; L/MIL/9/114/205; L/MIL/9/116/1–3/193; L/MIL/9/124/162.

85 Mackillop, 'More fruitful than the soil', pp. 130–67; David Taylor, *The Wild Black Region: Badenoch, 1750–1800* (Edinburgh: John Donald, 2016), pp. 178–209.

86 SIWA. Sources: IOR, L/MIL/9/85, pp. 226–9; L/MIL/9/108/3; L/MIL/9/113/115; L/MIL/9/116/1–3/280, 283, 352; L/MIL/10/131; L/AG/34/29/5/41; L/AG/34/29/195, p. 110; NRS, GD80/904/1: Cawnpore, 21 July 1783; GD80/913/2: Vellore, 27 August 1801; GD80/904/2; GD80/914/11; NRS, GD44/23/33/2: Ruthven, 17 September 1776; Hodson, *Officers of the Army of Bengal*, vol. III, pp. 179, 191–3; NRS, Register of Sasines, Argyll (10) (1619) (1674); Perth (2641–45) (3054–55).

87 NRS, GD128/1/3: Madras, 1 July 1775; NLS, MS1256, fos. 171–2; GCA, TD219/5/83: London, 31 March 1787; Hodson, *Officers of the Army of Bengal*, vol, I, p. 426.

88 Marshall, *The Making and Unmaking of Empires*, pp. 230–7; Bayly, 'The British Military-Fiscal State and Indigenous Resistance', pp. 324–5; GCA, TD219/8/4: Madras, 11 September 1771; TD219/8/5: Madras, 27 February 1772; GCA, Bogle Papers, Bo. 20/14: Glasgow, 24 Feb 1773; Armitage, *The Ideological Origins of the British Empire*, pp. 170–98; Margot C. Finn, 'Material Turns in British History: I. Loot', *Transactions of the Royal Historical Society*, 28 (2018), 5–32.

89 NLS, MS13775, pp. 14, 32, 41–7; *A Vindication of the Conduct of the English Forces, Employed in the Late War, under the Command of Brigadier General Mathews against Nabob Tippoo Sultaun* (London: J. Walter, 1787), pp. 22–7.

The military 155

90 NRS, GD1/594/1: Edinburgh 23 September 1799; Kinross House Papers, 2nd Series, No. 51-126, Bundle 57: Calcutta, 21 April 1799: Thomas Graham to George Graham.
91 IOR, L/MIL/5/159, pp. 121-2, 181-207, 191, 200-9.
92 Watt, *The Price of Scotland*, pp. 224-37; John W. Cairns, *Law, Lawyers, and Humanism: Selected Essays on the History of Scots Law, Volume I* (Edinburgh: Edinburgh University Press, 2015), pp. 128-9; Maya Jasanoff, 'The Other Side of Revolution: Loyalists in the British Empire', *The William and Mary Quarterly*, 65 (2008), 215-16; Nicholas Draper, 'Scotland and Colonial Slave Ownership: The Evidence of the Slave Compensation Records', in Devine, *Recovering Scotland's Slavery Past*, pp. 171-82.
93 NLS, MS1336, fo. 257; MS1337, fos. 34, 40.
94 Tillman W. Nechtman, *Nabobs: Empire and Identity in Eighteenth-Century Britain* (Cambridge: Cambridge University Press, 2010), pp. 11-15, 88-95; NLS, MS8252, fos. 173-176; IOR, B/79, pp. 85-6, 135; B/80, p. 242; B/81, p. 82; B/82, p. 98.
95 PRAI, Register of Deeds, Vol. 223, pp. 144-7 [147708]; IOR, L/AG/34/29/180, pp. 196-211.
96 NLS, MS8220, fo. 69; MS8257, fo. 45; MS8330, fo. 1; NLS, MS3971, fos. 92-5; R. Callahan, *The East India Company and Army Reform 1783-1798* (Cambridge, MA: Harvard University Press, 1972), p. 134.
97 IOR, P/416/90, pp. 21-2; P/328/63 [1774], pp. 88-9; L/MIL/9/90, p. 173; L/AG/34/29/7 [1792], 45; Hodson, *List of the Officers of the Army of Bengal*, vol. III, pp. 330-1.
98 NRS, GD128/1/1/1: 'Return of soldiers formerly in HM 89th Regt., 1778'.
99 See IOR, P/328/60 [1757], pp. 126-7; P/328/61 [1761], pp. 36, 61-2, 87, 159; L/AG/34/29/5. No. 2-86; L/AG/34/29/342, 7 December 1798-13 Dec 1802, pp. 1-5, 9-10, 31.
100 IOR, L/AG/34/29/201, pp. 270-272; https://stataccscot.edina.ac.uk/static/statacc/dist/viewer/osa-vol9-Parish_record_for_Golspie_in_the_county_of_Sutherland_in_volume_9_of_account_1/.
101 For Irish, Scots and Welsh NCOs see, IOR, P/328/63 [1769], p. 99; P/328/64 [1779], p. 12; LAG/34/29/191, p. 77; L/AG/34/29/193, pp. 1040-2; NRS, CC/8/8/136, pp. 226-7; GD1/768/10: Dinapore, 8 January 1772.
102 IOR, P/328/60-64; P/416/77-98; L/AG/34/29/4-22, 185-210, 341-3.
103 PRAI, Registry of Deeds, Vol. 337, p. 19 [No. 224482]; IOR, L/AG/34/29/6 [1787], 32; IOR, L/AG/34/29/5 [1785], 86; Hodson, *List of the Officers of the Army of Bengal*, vol. I, pp. 277, 409.
104 IOR, L/AG/34/29/202, pp. 58-62; L/AG/34/29/210, pp. 34-9; L/AG/34/29/4 [1781], pp. 135-43; Hodson, *List of the Officers of the Army of Bengal*, vol. II, pp. 594-5.
105 Both the Irish and Scottish estimates are taken from the MeasuringWorth.com calculator with a 1790 base year using the conservative 'real price' total. See: www.measuringworth.com/calculators/ppoweruk/.
106 IOR, L/AG/34/29/200, p. 115; L/AG/34/29/7 [1792], 47; MSS Eur. F.128/14/1;

PRONI, D2432/1/4: Arrah, 16 January 1770; TCD, MS3767/22, 40–41; NRS, GD29/2063/3; GD29/2067/17; GD305/1/162/190; NRS, GD51/3/14/2, 10; NLS, MS1256, fos. 171–2.
107 Kolff, *Naukar, Rajput and Sepoy*, pp. 27–8; Alavi, *The Sepoy and the Company*, pp. 56–94; Rickramishran, 'The Best Black Troops', pp. 96–105.
108 Dziennik, 'The Fiscal-Military State', pp. 159–77.
109 Bayly, *Birth of the Modern World*, pp. 44–5.
110 William Dalrymple, *The Anarchy: The Relentless Rise of the East India Company* (London: Bloomsbury, 2019), pp. xxii-xxxiii, 106–35, 259–305.
111 T. M. Devine, 'The Colonial Trades and Industrial Investment in Scotland, c.1700–1815', *Economic History Review*, 29 (1976), 1–13; Bruce Lenman, *An Economic History of Modern Scotland 1660–1976* (London: B. T. Batsford, 1977), p. 91; T. M. Devine, 'Industrialisation', in T. M. Devine, C. H. Lee and G. C. Peden (eds), *The Transformation of Scotland: The Economy since 1700* (Edinburgh: Edinburgh University Press, 2005), p. 43; T. M. Devine, 'The Golden Age of Tobacco', in T. M Devine and Gordon Jackson (eds), *Glasgow, Volume I: Beginnings to 1830* (Manchester: Manchester University Press, 1995), p. 367.
112 Richards, 'Scotland and the Uses of the Atlantic Empire', pp. 67–114; Mackillop, 'More Fruitful than the Soil', pp. 41–76.
113 Wolfe Toone, *An address to the people of Ireland, on the present important crisis* (Belfast: n.p., 1796), pp. 19, 33–4.
114 Andrew Mackillop, '"As Hewers of Wood and Drawers of Water": Scotland as an Emigrant Nation, c.1600–c.1800', in Angela McCarthy and John M. MacKenzie (eds), *Global Migrations: The Scottish Diaspora since 1600* (Edinburgh: Edinburgh University Press, 2016), pp. 36–7.

5

Circuits of human and cultural capital: medicine and the knowledge economy in Asia

Reassessments of medical-related sojourning across Britain's pre-1815 Empire can draw upon important reconceptualisations of the nature of colonial knowledge generated in the early modern period.[1] Older interpretations that stressed the diffusion of home-grown scientific ideas and medical practices outwards from Europe into overseas territories have been challenged by an awareness of the dynamic role of so-called peripheries in the construction of hybrid forms of colonial learning.[2] The process involved mutually influencing exchanges between local experts and Western personnel as each encountered the other in situations of inquiry, reaction, negotiation, coercion and material and intellectual appropriation. This dialogue was rarely if ever equal. Cross-fertilisation occurred but did so in ways increasingly shaped by the realities of colonial power. Empire mobilised its intellectual resources as surely as its venture capital and its armed forces. The privileges of colonial influence facilitated the observation of environments, the gathering and reordering of specimens, pharmaceuticals, chemicals and their medical or commercial applications. This 'information' could then be transformed into socially and cultural acceptable forms of useful 'knowledge'. Such repackaging meant resources acquired at the geographic frontiers of expansion and empire became intellectual and cultural assets that were transferred back to metropolitan centres of learning.[3] The completion of this geographic and cultural relocation occurred through the codification and publication of observations, findings, and new specimens in line with epistemological and taxonomic norms. The new 'knowledge' was then taught as European science and learning at the universities. These transformations ensured that material resources and the intellectual achievements of non-European societies became metropolitan cultural capital and scholarship. This colonial knowledge economy buttressed the professional standing of individuals and the institutional prestige of learned societies and universities.[4]

The example of Scots in the EIC's medical employment fits closely into this dynamic of knowledge creation through human mobility, colonialism and intellectual appropriation. Historians of medicine and science acknowledge the ubiquity of Scots and Scottish-trained personnel in the global world of eighteenth-century British medicine.[5] This awareness of substantial Scottish involvement enables a greater appreciation of the multicentred nature of metropolitan and provincial engagement with colonial medicine, its associated sciences, institutions and publications. One effect of empire was to decentre and recentre enlightenments even as the process privileged Europe. Yet Scottish prominence in overseas medicine poses questions about the balance of local, national, metropolitan and global influences in the evolution of cosmopolitan and provincial enlightenments.[6] Explanations of the large number of Scottish medical practitioners in this period rely on a 'national enlightenment' or an 'emigration-led' approach. The first interpretation holds that medical men represented the extension abroad of the advanced training offered by the country's university colleges between c.1720 and c.1820.[7] Drawing on Newtonianism from England and medical practice from Paris and the Netherlands, Scottish society generated a distinctively configured 'medical enlightenment' which radiated outwards into the Empire through the export of surplus surgeons and physicians.[8]

The alternative, migratory perspective adopts a socio-economic and human emphasis. In this perspective medical professionals emerge as exemplars of a culture of mobility that encompassed aristocrats, gentry, merchants and tenantry across the Lowlands and Highlands.[9] Bringing these approaches together enables an exploration of how two of the great influences on post-union Scottish society – enlightenment and migration – intertwined and reshaped each other. Imbued with elevated levels of embodied cultural capital in the form of literacy, numeracy, appropriate professional rhetoric and applied skills, physicians and surgeons constitute a prime example of high-value human capital.[10] Framed in this way, medical migration represented one of early modern Scotland's most successful non-monetary forms of export economy.

Ireland is far less associated with colonial medicine prior to the 1830s, with the emphasis still largely on developments in domestic institutions and practices, although the role of Irish surgeons in the knowledge and race discourses surrounding transatlantic slavery is now increasingly understood.[11] By the 1830s and 1840s the number of Irish surgeons in EIC service began to increase as a result of enhanced educational provision within Ireland as well as the introduction of competitive entrance exams.[12] These trends formed part of an intensifying engagement with Asia by various institutions and social interests in mid-nineteenth-century Ireland.[13] If Scots doctors seemed to represent the transfer into the Empire of a provincial medical enlightenment, the timing and pattern of Irish medical mobility reflects the deleterious effects of the Penal Laws and the eventual lessening of these barriers during the early to mid-nineteenth century.

An especially useful rationale for a comparison between Irish and Scottish medical men in the EIC is that both groups were endowed with similar levels of embodied cultural capital through their shared experience of professional training in London and in Edinburgh.[14] The significance of meso-networks in determining access to imperial employment can be better assessed in the context of this relatively level playing field. The career networks used by EIC surgeons also enable a better understanding of economies of human and social capital emanating from the metropolitan provinces. The means by which high-value human capital could be exported globally and circulate back into Ireland and Scotland is a prominent example of the mutually constitutive relationship between migration and enlightenment.[15] Besides raising questions about the nature of provincial enlightenments, the development of long-distance professional mobility and medical knowledge economies underscore how the metropolitan provinces accessed proto-globalisation using human and social as well as monetary resources.

Creating human and cultural capital: training and professional mobility

In 1813 the Madras government sponsored the publication of *Materia Medica of Hindoostan*, a major new compendium of medical knowledge produced by the presidency's superintending surgeon, Whitelaw Ainslie.[16] The work exemplified the imposing of European taxonomies upon South Asian botanical and pharmaceutical materials and the appropriation of local knowledge and treatments derived from sacred learning and accumulated practice.[17] Beyond what it reveals about the hybrid nature of colonial medicine, the *Materia Medica* marked a personal triumph for its author. Born in Berwickshire, the son of an estate factor, Ainslie was one of many knowledge specialists from across Europe using publication to enhance their material and professional standing. The Scot dedicated his work to the French missionary-botanist Johan Peter Rottler. In doing so he demonstrated his own intellectual gentility while locating himself in a dynamic transnational European community of learning. Ainslie noted his mentor's 'kind liberal aid' and, in a revealing phrase, his 'scientific celebrity'. By paying respect to his intellectual patron the author advertised and added to his own cultural capital. This he did by projecting an image of assiduous service to the Company, a command over South Asian languages, self-improvement, systematic observation and cutting-edge experimentation.

Historians of colonial knowledge have highlighted this tendency towards 'scientific celebrity' and stressed how medical specialists across the Empire promoted themselves as leading practitioners of a wave of new theories, empirical methods and diagnostic discoveries.[18] Innovative forms of information and learning became emblematic of the 'progressive' nature of European learning. Immersed in novel environmental situations, surrounded by exotic plants, sacred texts and ancient forms of learning, colonial practitioners exemplified Europe's supposed superiority in medical research, experimentation, diagnosis and the useful collation and publication of findings.

Much like their military counterparts, the increasing professional and social prestige associated with the Company's medical personnel by the 1800s developed over a protracted period. While health provision on board the Company's vessels had been regularised well before the 1690s, conditions at the presidency settlements were less impressive.[19] Recruitment remained haphazard compared with the requirements demanded of civil servants and merchant marine officers. In January 1724 the directors agreed that two surgeons should be stationed at Madras at any one time. Yet it would take until 1763 before medical establishments were instituted as a distinct branch of the presidency governments.[20] This infrastructure continued to expand, first in the mid-1780s when medical and military rank became linked to attract a higher calibre of practitioner, and again in the 1790s when the relationship between regimental provision and central hospitals underwent major rationalisation.[21]

Attitudes in the early 1700s among the EIC's elite in London and its senior civil servants overseas did little to encourage well-qualified individuals to consider a medical career in Asia.[22] Social snobbery ensured medical provision was viewed as an ancillary occupation, often best combined with other activities. In November 1717 the directors appointed a Scot, Lieutenant Andrew Douglas, to Bombay for his military skills but added 'he being also a good surgeon and useful on that account'.[23] The lack of appreciation for professional specialisation and the incidental status afforded medical personnel was both a career problem and an employment opportunity.

Explanations of when and how metropolitan provincials from Ireland, Scotland and Wales entered this branch of the EIC focus almost exclusively on Scots. Their high profile tends to be linked uncritically to the diffusion model of enlightenment. The advanced nature of training in Scotland and the disproportionate number of Scottish ship's surgeons by the 1730s become simple cause and effect.[24] The reality is more ambiguous and challenges notions of a discrete, nationally defined Scottish medical enlightenment leading directly to high levels of surgeons within the corporation. The problem in the early to mid-eighteenth century lay in establishing credibility with a London-centred organisation. Provincials needed to surmount a perceived lack of cultural capital. Supposed deficiencies ranged from a lack of appropriate professional rhetoric to insufficient experience in the use of relevant medicines. John Drummond of Quarrell made this point to Sir John Clerk of Penicuik in 1729 regarding the latter's nephew and his attempts to secure an East Indiaman surgeon's post.

> As our young men generally come up very green and half bred I advise all to learn the English method of making up medicines, and something of their smartness and language, which I find your nephew much in want of and consequently not so ready for his examination at Surgeon's Hall, which must afford him a certificate of qualification into a man of war or an India ship.[25]

This is a radically different state of affairs to the stereotype of the well-trained Scots surgeon. Rather than a simple dissemination of high-value provincial human capital directly into the Empire, medical careers involved phases of step mobility, intermediate and multiple sites of learning and the gradual accumulation of cultural capital. This process of enhancement occurred by crossing and recrossing geographical locations. As with so many other aspects of involvement in the EIC, there was an understanding that space and distance could augment human capital. This was the case for medical men as much as merchants and military officers.

In this context London acted as a stepping stone which facilitated professional sojourning. By offering opportunities to accrue culturally privileged forms of learning, the metropole needs to be factored more effectively into assessments of the nature, boundaries and chronology of Scotland's medical enlightenment as well as educational trends in Ireland. Greater attention to the city's role does not diminish the provincial factors shaping the intersection between migration and enlightenment. The social networks that enabled the metropolitan phase often relied on expatriates and reinforced patterns of association based on local identities.[26] Equally, while there is no doubting the dynamism of educational provision in Scotland, the development of a knowledge economy centred on high-value human capital did not happen in isolation.[27] The European centres of learning, accessible education in Scotland, credentialism in London and transhemispheric sojourning all combined to create a highly distinctive interaction between migration and enlightenment.

Even as Edinburgh's reputation in medicine blossomed and training provision at the other university colleges in Scotland and in Dublin expanded in a parallel fashion, surgeons seeking EIC posts still sought training in London. This was the case throughout the long eighteenth century but often occurred in individualised, difficult-to-trace ways. John Ferguson from Ayr spent 1731 in the city acquiring additional skills and contacts before embarking as an East Indiaman surgeon. Different examples reveal that pathways into and out of London varied and that the city's role as an enhancer of provincial human capital was widely appreciated. George Skene, brother of a prominent Aberdeen physician, attended lectures at St George's Hospital before another London-based Scots doctor recommended in November 1769 that he take a surgeon's mate position on the *Bridgewater*.[28] In this instance it was micro-networks of association based on Aberdeen connections in the metropole which shaped professional trajectories. Ferguson and Skene were part of a fluid pattern of province–metropole–empire human and intellectual transfers.

The same intermediate training and educational mobility characterised the careers of Irish surgeons. Although remembered primarily for his self-serving narrative of the 'Black Hole of Calcutta' incident of 20 to 21 June 1756, the Dublin-born John Zephaniah Holwell's training involved an apprenticeship at Southwark and lectures at Guy's Hospital. This provided him with the qualifications to become a ship's surgeon in 1732. He rose to become the principal doctor at Calcutta by 1746, acquire a fortune of £30,937 and a reputation as a prolific if controversial writer on subjects ranging from medical research to the Company's administration of Bengal.[29]

Holwell's journey was a geographic, intellectual and social one. He constitutes a revealing example of the repackaging of colonial knowledge to generate 'scientific celebrity'. His move from Dublin to London, then to the Company's maritime and Bengal medical establishments enabled the acquisition of skills, experience, information and reputation. These facilitated the image of a learned polymath possessed of knowledge conducive to the public good. This acquired cultural capital ensured his election as a Fellow of the Royal Society, an accolade that further advertised his status as a member of the respectable service-gentry.[30] His career cycle could stand for the hundreds of individuals from the metropolitan provinces who used London and an EIC career to first enhance and then cash in their cultural capital.

Beginning a medical career in the Company involved passing an exam at the Surgeon's Hall in London. This produced a certificate that the directors required as part of any application to become an East Indiaman surgeon or surgeon's mate – the usual starting point for a subsequent appointment at the presidency establishments in Asia.[31] These processes constituted a form of educational credentialism. In this variant there was greater emphasis on professional qualifications than was the case with the underwriting of human capital by shareholders and directors outlined in Chapters 2 and 3. Acquiring the capacity to pass this test happened in a number of different

Table 5.1 Educational backgrounds, EIC surgeons, 1764–1800

Bengal	Madras	Bombay
Total = 418	Total = 324	Total = 193
Corp. of Surgeons = 135	Corp. of Surgeons = 125	Corp. of Surgeons = 65
Edinburgh = 22	Edinburgh = 12	Edinburgh = 13
Aberdeen = 11	Aberdeen = 11	Aberdeen = 8
Glasgow = 1	Glasgow = 1	Glasgow = 0
St Andrews = 4	St Andrews = 1	St Andrews = 3
TCD = 0	TCD = 0	TCD = 0

(Source: D. G. Crawford, *Roll of the Indian Medical Service*, pp. 638–41).

ways. Attendance (if rarely completion of an MD) at Edinburgh or another Scottish university college formed a foundation which was supplemented by a finishing experience in London in the same manner as Holwell, Ferguson and Skene. Another method involved qualifying through London's premier medical institution, the Corporation of Surgeons (after 1800, the Royal College of Surgeons). This was the preferred route into Company service in 1809 used by Anthony Conwell, cousin of William Conwell from Ballymilligan in County Londonderry, himself an EIC assistant surgeon already serving in Bengal.[32]

The findings in Table 5.1 confirm that a large majority of surgeons at the Bengal, Madras and Bombay establishments after 1764 arrived without a formal university or corporate qualification: only 9.3 per cent of Company surgeons acquired an MD in this period. Charles Allen from Coleraine, stationed in Bengal in the later 1780s, was unusual in that he acquired his full degree at Glasgow prior to arrival in Asia.[33] Regional variation characterised the medical sector just as it did in the civil service and officer corps. Edinburgh and Aberdeen stand out in terms of the small minority of Scots personnel with the full qualification: 12 per cent of medical graduates from Marischal College Aberdeen between 1700 and 1799 ended up in Asia. Meanwhile Glasgow's low profile might well be linked to the city's extensive commercial and migratory connections with Britain's Atlantic Empire.[34] Even the Royal Corporation of Surgeons in London trained only around one-third of medics heading to Asia in an era when institutionalised provision became more firmly established in the main ports and settlements.

The most common method of acquiring the basic cultural capital for entry into Company employment involved informal, short-term educational sessions with London-based surgeons or apothecaries, supplemented by certified attendance at lectures by eminent practitioners at the main teaching hospitals. In the early 1770s Kenneth Murchison from Ross-shire used a similar route to that of Howell a generation earlier. As had been the case with Skene, strong micro-networks forged around kin links marked the early stage of Murchison's career. His patron was Colin Mackenzie MD, an individual typical of the many Scots operating in the capital's large medical market.[35] On 27 November 1771, two days prior to Murchison's examination for an East Indiaman surgeoncy, Mackenzie certified to the College of Surgeons that his client had attended six of his lectures and would attend a further four on *materia medica* at Guy's Hospital.[36] The blending of local association, formal credentialism and clientage in such actions underscores the flexible ways social capital enabled the mobilisation of its human equivalent. These webs of professional patronage underline how the metropole did not subsume older affiliations, and in fact often amplified them. This dynamic ensured that local forms of association often marked out the early phases of what would become global careers. Understanding this social aspect provides an additional dimension to Europe's medical enlightenment beyond interpretations which stress its philosophical and cosmopolitan character.

The variety of these examples drives home the point that careers in colonial medicine in this period did not have a defined programme of training. Formal instruction was often combined with periods of working as a ship's surgeon or at one of the settlements in Asia. Learning and migration combined in ways that decentre and blur the working nature, geographies, spaces and boundaries of national or colonial medical enlightenments. On 6 January 1725 the Scot George Ramsay petitioned to be made a surgeon at Madras. His experience reveals the interplay of provincial, metropolitan and sojourning for the purposes of training that characterised the early careers of these medical men. His education began in Scotland and continued in London with certificates from 'several eminent physicians'. Ramsay then completed an East Indiaman voyage to improve his understanding of the diseases and treatments peculiar to the geographies and environments in which he would operate.[37] This marine phase underpinned his successful application to the directors.

Multi-step career pathways characterised the professional lives of some of the most prominent metropolitan provincials in the corporation's service. Dr Robert Coult from Inveresk acquired his early experience on an East Indiaman voyage of 1709. This enabled him on 12 October 1712 to write to the directors stressing his skills as a physician and surgeon as well as his detailed knowledge of the diseases common in Asia.[38] Coult's appointment to Bengal on a salary of £36 per annum initiated a lucrative career: he returned home to Scotland in the early 1730s with £17,324. His intellectual reputation was secured through correspondence between the 1710s and the 1720s on South Asian smallpox inoculation practices with Charles Mead, one of London's most prominent medical intellectuals and a member of the Royal Society.[39] While Coult's experience can be envisaged as a cycle of departure and return, a key step in the acquisition of embodied cultural capital came not in Scotland or even in London but on the oceans between Europe and Asia.

Transhemispheric movement for the purposes of professional development remained a pronounced feature of the EIC's medical world throughout the long eighteenth century. Medical specialists embody the role of migration as a means of capital accumulation. Terence Gahagan from Ireland, an assistant surgeon on the Madras establishment, asked in October 1776 to be allowed to return to Britain to complete his qualifications. Acquiring additional cultural capital involved interactive phases of mobility and education. Upon completing his training, Gahagan again set out to Asia a year later as a newly promoted surgeon. He would eventually become the head of the Madras medical establishment in the early 1800s.[40] These phases of different professional geographies mirror the training of the EIC merchant marine officers. In the case of James Johnson from County Londonderry, country practice, additional experience with a London apothecary and a qualification from Surgeon's Hall by 1798 was followed by a career in the Royal Navy. The same production of colonial knowledge evident with Whitelaw Ainslie followed. Observation and experimentation while stationed with the Bay of Bengal squadron shaped his highly regarded work of 1815, *The Influence of Tropical Climates*.[41] As service-related mobility gave access to new information, opportunities for experimentation and the use of exotic medicinal materials, it generated enhanced human, intellectual and cultural capital. Enlightenment and migration blended in ways that point towards their status as two sides of the same coin rather than discrete phenomena.

The long-term significance of unofficial educational pathways and social networks is exemplified in the person of Ninian Ballantyne. In 1742 to 1743 the Scot served as surgeon on the *Hardwick* East Indiaman. Company employment continued through the 1750s when he completed a number of Europe–Asia voyages. His career trajectory reveals how networked human capital accumulated experience, reputation and trust in ways that generated new reserves of social capital. Ballantyne built his status as an apothecary in London in the 1760s and early 1770s upon his earlier experience as an EIC ship's surgeon.[42] The enhancement overseas of cultural capital secured his occupational standing in the metropole and facilitated the sponsorship of the next generation into the same cycle of professional mobility. His metropolitan reputation enabled him to provide bonds of security at Leadenhall Street for five other Scots. Among those who benefited from his credentialism were the Madras writer Duncan Munro and fellow Scots surgeons John Ferguson and Archibald Sands. The now London-based

Ballantyne also acted as an executor for Scots in Asia, including the surgeons James Campbell and William Clark from Ayr.[43] An apothecary was not an especially prestigious occupation: yet Ballantyne's network stretched across hemispheric distances and illustrates the powerful connective capacity of human and social capital. His professional life cycle demonstrates how socially constructed forms of wealth proved in some ways a more readily deployable and realisable form of investment than standard monetary assets.

Although this province–metropolis–Asia mobility remained a constant characteristic of the corporation's medical world, the geographies of training and the enhancement of cultural capital evolved over the eighteenth and early nineteenth centuries. Edinburgh demonstrates these changing trends. The city developed as a British-Irish medical metropole partly through serving transnational and imperial needs. Between 1775 and 1800 the university graduated no fewer than 800 MDs: 237 were Irish; 217 were English and 179 Scots. By the mid-1790s, medical students from Ireland were estimated to bring £20,000 into the city annually and overall estimates of the value to Scotland of its medical knowledge economy over the eighteenth century have been put at £840,000.[44] The Scottish capital's educational economy reveals how provincial civic institutions successfully attuned themselves to serving expansion. Indeed, the provision of technocratic training alongside contributions in settler colonists and military manpower became defining features of the metropolitan provincial contribution to empire.[45] The city's reputation was such that on 10 April 1799 the EIC directors agreed to recognise diplomas issued by its Royal College of Surgeons as equivalent to that of the corporation of surgeons in London.[46] In a reversal of the usual complaints emanating from Scotland concerning breaches of the Union, England's medical institutions objected to the recognition of provincial qualifications as early as the late 1740s.[47] However, imperial needs superseded metropolitan chauvinism and the decision stood. When David Boyd, the son of a tenant farmer from Carridan in Linlithgow, applied for a surgeon's post in 1813 his London patron noted: 'He has a diploma from the College of Surgeons at Edinburgh which renders an examination before the College of Surgeons here, unnecessary.'[48] The diploma from Glasgow's Corporation of Physicians and Surgeons received similar Company recognition in 1820.[49] Imperial priorities did much to generate a genuinely 'British' medical world of interconnecting metropolitan and provincial institutions.

Once extant applications for surgeon posts begin from 1805, educational backgrounds can be traced with considerable accuracy. The figures in Table 5.4 show the appointment of 146 Scots, Irish and Welsh individuals between 1805 and 1813: only four held MDs; a further six had experience as surgeons or as a surgeon's mate in the Company's merchant marine. Meanwhile, sixteen had acquired the Edinburgh diploma, making that qualification the most important educational attainment among metropolitan provincials joining the medical corps.[50] The figures correspond to the patterns of minimal formal training evident in Table 5.1 but also confirm Edinburgh's status as a key production centre of specialists in colonial and tropical medicine.

While the role of Scottish institutions in British medicine in this period is well known, military, naval and imperial expansion also helped to reposition Trinity College Dublin and the Royal College of Surgeons of Ireland. In 1804 the Scots-born president of the latter organisation, George Renny, recommended curricular and examination reforms to expedite the supply of army and navy surgeons.[51] Innovations such as these ensured Irish and Scottish medical institutions morphed from provincial guilds of learning to imperial service providers.

Appointment patterns

Along with the Royal Navy and British army, the EIC was by far the largest employer of medical expertise in the British Empire throughout the eighteenth and early nineteenth centuries. The totals in Table 5.1 demonstrate that between 1764 and 1800 the corporation employed 935 surgeons in its presidency medical departments. By 1800 the Bengal, Madras and Bombay governments between them retained 337 physicians, surgeons and assistant surgeons at any one time. The fact that the most informed estimate for the total number of surgeons and physicians in Scotland in 1778 is 256 underlines the scale of the Company's medical infrastructure. *The Dublin Directory* of the same year noted that the city, the second largest in the British and Irish Isles, contained forty-five registered physicians and fifty-two surgeons.[52] Yet even the substantial numbers in Table 5.1 do not fully convey the scale of the Company's medical employment. While many of those stationed in the main settlements in South Asia previously served on East Indiamen, the 935 total excludes many surgeons who only served in the merchant marine.[53]

Although overall numbers can be sketched with some confidence, surviving source material complicates attempts to extrapolate origins and social backgrounds, exactly the sort of information that is necessary if the intersection between mobility, empire and provincial medical enlightenment is to be understood. This problem is addressed in Table 5.2 by using two sets of sources to track the growth in surgeon numbers and to provide an evaluation of what percentage-share Scots, Irish and Welsh medics secured.

Table 5.2 Metropolitan provincial surgeons: directorate minutes and Probate Court of Canterbury wills, 1690–1800

Years	1690–1709		1710–1729		1730–1749		1750–1769		1770–1779		1780–1799
Source	BSer	PCC	BSer	PCC	BSer	PCC	BSer	PCC	BSer	PCC	PCC
Total	8	20	48	14	110	30	220	55	152	24	60
Scots	0	2 (10%)	8	3 (21%)	12	8 (26%)	20	13 (23%)	16	6 (25%)	12 (20%)
Irish	0	0	1	0	1	1 (3%)	2	1 (1%)	2	3 (12%)	5 (8%)
Welsh	0	0	0	0	0	0	1	0	0	0	2 (3%)

(SIWA. Sources: IOR, B40–B/95; TNA, PROB 11/401–1321).

Circuits of human and cultural capital 169

The 'BSer' column under each time sample refers to the directors' minutes, which were surveyed from 1690 to 1780. Although never comprehensive, the records routinely noted requests from ship's surgeons for the proceeds of their private trade.[54] Appointments to positions at the presidency settlements were listed far less consistently and, when they do appear, only names are recorded alongside occasional references to previous experience.[55] So while useful as a conservative indication of overall surgeon numbers, the directors' minutes are of limited value in tracking origins and social backgrounds.

Cross-referencing the 538 surgeons noted in the B Series from 1690 to 1780 with the 203 wills of EIC medics identified in the Probate Court of Canterbury (PCC) from 1690 to 1799 partially addresses problems of identification. This method makes possible a robust projection of the Scottish, Irish and Welsh profile in the medical sector. By their very nature, last wills and testaments usually named family and associates from the deceased's place of origin. On 29 December 1703 Matthew Colvill, surgeon on *The Duchess* East Indiaman left his property to his sister and sole executor Elizabeth Colvill, 'spinster of Edinburgh'. This information confirms Colvill's Scottishness. The case of Pitcairn Buchanan, surgeon on the *Nassau* in June 1772 and Thomas Hamilton, a surgeon in Calcutta from 1768, underline the rich qualitative data in wills and the pitfalls of relying on surname evidence as proof of origin. Assessments of Scottish involvement in the Company's medical sector assume both Buchanan and Hamilton were Scots based on their admittedly Scottish-sounding surnames. Yet their testaments confirm they were in fact from the parishes of Donacavey and Termonamongan in County Tyrone.[56]

The trends outlined in Table 5.3 confirm and expand the findings in Table 5.2. Drawing on surgeon applications, presidency censuses and wills registered at Calcutta, Madras, Bombay and London (including a limited number of British army and RN surgeons in Asia), it outlines the growth of metropolitan provincial involvement in the Company's medical services. The Scottish total is considerably less than existing estimates of 320 surgeons between 1720 and 1780 and the even greater number of 132 proposed for Bengal alone between 1776 and 1785.[57] The discrepancy arises from the fact that only those clearly identified as Scots, Irish and Welsh are included in Table 5.3. The results represent an undoubtedly conservative but verifiable assessment. Allowing for the untraceable origins of several hundred ship and presidency surgeons from 1690 to 1813, and the lack of systematic recording of British army and Royal Navy personnel in Asia, there were at least 400–20 Scots, 80–90 Irish and about 30 Welsh employed as medics in Asia between 1690 and 1813.

The volume of employment can be put into perspective if set against the total of 170 university-trained Scots medics estimated to have migrated

Table 5.3 Irish, Scots and Welsh medical personnel in Asia, 1690–1813

Years	1690–1709	1710–1729	1730–1749	1750–1769	1770–1789	1790–1813	Total
Scots	8	11	25	58	99	174	375
Irish	0	1	2	11	16	16	46
Welsh	0	0	0	4	4	12	20

(SIWA. Sources: IOR, B40–B/95; L/MIL/9/358–365; L/MIL/10/131; P/328/60–64; P/416/77–98; L/AG/34/29/4–22, 185–210, 341–343; TNA, PROB 11/401–1321; Farrington, *A Biographical Index*, passim; Crawford, *Roll of the Indian Medical Service*, pp. 638–641; Dodwell and Miles, *Alphabetical List of the Medical Officers of the Indian Army* (London: Longman, Orme, Brown, 1839)).

to North America from 1700 to 1799.[58] In the realms of Scottish medical sojourning at least, Asia loomed larger than North America, although not the Caribbean, where overall numbers have yet to be calculated. The totals in Table 5.3 confirm there was a discernible Scots profile as early as the 1690s and 1700s.[59] By the 1720s and 1730s this increased to one-fifth to one-quarter of wills registered by Company surgeons, a percentage which Table 5.2 demonstrates never fell below 20 per cent for the rest of the century and more usually stood closer to one quarter. Set against Scotland's population, these figures mean that there were nearly twice as many Scots medics in the Company from the 1720s onwards as might reasonably be expected.

Once detailed records for assistant surgeon appointments become available from 1805, these trends are confirmed. As Table 5.4 reveals, the Scottish share of posts regularly stood at 40 per cent to 50 per cent in the 1800s and 1810s, and even briefly touched nearly 60 per cent in 1811. At around four times the country's share of population, this disproportionate acquisition of patronage represents the statistical manifestation of a high-value human capital economy in action. In no other part of the Empire, except perhaps in Tobago and in the Hudson's Bay Company, did Scots form such a noticeable presence within the formal structures of power.[60]

The Irish and Welsh figures cast into stark relief the prominence of Scots. Irish society was noticeably underrepresented in this part of the Company's operations given the kingdom's population and Dublin's substantial medical provision. The incidence of Irish surgeons did climb during the 1750s to the 1770s to around 12 per cent, before slipping back to the approximate level of 3 per cent shown in Table 5.4. This declining share mirrors trends in the military officer corps after 1780 and is a characteristic of Ireland's interaction with Asia in this period that has not been sufficiently

Table 5.4 East India Company assistant surgeon appointments, 1805–1813

Years	Total	Scots	Irish	Welsh
1805	42	5 (11.9%)	1 (2.3%)	1 (2.3%)
1806	52	14 (26.9%)	2 (3.8%)	1 (1.9%)
1807	42	12 (28.5%)	1 (2.3%)	0
1808	41	22 (53.6%)	1 (2.4%)	2 (4.8%)
1809	31	16 (51.6%)	1 (3.2%)	0
1810	27	12 (44.4%)	0	0
1811	27	16 (59.2%)	1 (3.7%)	1 (3.7%)
1812–13	60	30 (50%)	2 (3.3%)	5 (8.3%)
Total	322	127 (39.4%)	9 (2.7%)	10 (3.1%)

(SIWA. Source: IOR, L/MIL/9/358–365).

recognised or explained. Its occurrence in the professional and technocratic areas of employment is another illustration of the Empire's inconsistent and unstable links to Irish society. The last quarter of the eighteenth and early decades of the nineteenth centuries are usually associated with increasing Irish participation in imperialism. Yet evidence from the Asian hemisphere shows the dynamics of integration were never linear, inevitable or even predictable. The acquisition of high-value corporate patronage stagnated and indeed went into relative decline just as Ireland obtained full access to the Atlantic Empire in 1780. This development also ran counter to claims that accepting union with Great Britain would expand Irish access to imperial opportunities.[61]

The Welsh ratio of appointments presents a more complex trajectory. As in all other sectors of the Company, a pattern of under-presentation is evident, although this was prone to fluctuation in the medical sector. Acquiring 2–3 per cent of medical posts equated to around a half to three-quarters of the volume of offices which might be expected relative to Wales's demographic position within the United Kingdom. The figures for Welsh surgeons can be viewed as another way of confirming the underdeveloped Irish presence among the medical elite.

The differences shown in Tables 5.2 to 5.4 were not simply the result of greater Scottish access to medical education. Given the number of students from Ireland known to have attended Scottish universities, the Irish percentages are surprisingly small. Training and opportunities in London were broadly accessible to all metropolitan provincials, or at least those who professed Protestantism. Part of the answer to these divergent profiles lies in the fact that the Dublin medical institutions focused on surgery in ways that directed the flow of personnel towards the regular forces. It has been estimated that about 33 per cent of all British army surgeons by the early 1800s were Irish or trained in Ireland.[62] This pattern of specialisation demonstrates how educational and civic institutions in the metropolitan provinces developed distinctive and niche responses to imperialism. The result was a clustering effect of Scots surgeons in the Company and Irish medical men in the army. Patterns of professional and geographic mobility reflected the strategic decisions made by provincial institutions.

The high profile of Scots in Company medicine also arose from the convoluted patterns of patronage and education that characterised early career trajectories. The influence exercised by Scottish brokers of human capital in London and the greater number of directors with connections north of the border also explain the contrasts in Table 5.4. Yet viewing participation only in terms of bilateral province–metropole links risks underestimating the importance of mutually reinforcing dynamics across the Company's different sectors. Success in one part of the organisation generated access in another. The increasing number of Scots in the shipping interest, in particular the 130 individuals appointed as East Indiaman commanders between the 1750s and the 1810s, enabled early-career medics to obtain a vital foothold in the organisation. Ninian Ballantyne's tenure as a ship's surgeon on the *Royal Duke* from 1752 to 1753 is a good example of this intra-corporate patronage. The vessel typifies the overlapping Scottish interconnections emerging within the merchant marine. The two charter parties were Scots, the London merchants, William Black and Abraham Hume. The commander was a Scot, George Cumming; the first mate, Alexander Macleod hailed from the Isle of Harris, while nepotism secured the fourth mate's berth for Alexander Hume, the co-owner's cousin.[63] With Scots making up one-third of the *Royal Duke*'s officers, this was more than just a micro-network. The geographic spread of Scots reveal how beneath its outwardly metropolitan and 'gentlemanly capitalist' character the Company hosted open-ended meso-networks forged by metropolitan provincials. The use of social capital as a bridging mechanism for its human and cultural equivalents enabled the placement of clients across the EIC's various professional sectors, in this case from shipping into medicine.

The same pattern characterised the officers of the *Asia* East Indiaman. In 1768 her commander was Robert Preston from Culross in Fife, later to be another high-profile figure in the shipping interest.[64] Alongside one of the midshipmen, Charles Mitchell, both the surgeon and the surgeon's mate were Scots: Andrew Duncan, also from Fife, and James Kerr from Beith in Ayrshire.[65] Similar sponsorship of Scots medics occurred on the *Phoenix*, *Ocean* and *Lord Nelson* from the 1780s to the 1800s while a Scot commanded these vessels.[66] If looked at in isolation these instances of patronage can seem prosaic, but they help to explain the major differences outlined in Tables 5.3 and 5.4. These dynamics show that the location and nature of eighteenth-century Scotland's prominent contribution to medicine needs to be rethought. It developed in its universities, obviously, but also on vessels and in locations thousands of miles from Scotland. Mobility also became self-sustaining. Given the importance of voyage experience in securing a permanent promotion to one of the presidency establishments, an initial appointment as a ship's surgeon or surgeon's mate was invaluable. The ability to cascade patronage down and across the corporation's employment hierarchies was a crucial advantage arising from greater Scottish involvement in shipping. The influx of Scots surgeons into the presidency governments developed from a confluence of factors rather than as an uncomplicated extension of the medical enlightenment north of the border.

The quality of the Company's extant archive and the details available in wills and testaments make it possible to recover some of the local and social characteristics of these personnel. The results are shown in Table 5.5 and demonstrate that Ireland and Wales shared a clear tendency for uneven regional contributions: Ulster and South Wales supplied 41 per cent and 50 per cent respectively of each country's known total. Medicine was one of the few areas where the north of Ireland made a greater traceable contribution than Leinster, the province with the most significant profile in the civil service and in the military elite. As with trends in other sectors of the organisation, these patterns reveal how the Empire's gravitational pull worked differently across the different countries. In Scotland the tendency was towards broadly even distribution, although the north-east and central districts between them supplied almost one Scottish surgeon in three. This corresponds to the noticeable profile of Aberdeen's university colleges in Table 5.1 and reinforces the argument that the country's North Sea-facing regions exploited step migration to London and Asia as an alternative to large-scale involvement in the Atlantic Empire.[67]

Information on the social origins of surgeons is far less comprehensive compared to that for civil servants. It is at its most complete for the larger known number of Scots. The extant evidence confirms that provincial gentry saw colonial medicine as a respectable option for younger sons.[68] Yet the combined share of posts acquired by families from maritime, mercantile, clerical, medical and legal backgrounds outnumbered that of the landed classes. Two examples serve to illustrate the social mobility made possible by a career in EIC medicine. Patrick Ivory came from a non-landed Catholic family in County Louth: after serving for twenty years in Bengal he returned to Britain in 1800 with a fortune of £15,914. He lived in Bedford Square, London, counted the Catholic peer Arthur Plunkett, eighth earl of Fingal among his acquaintances and left in his will sufficient money to purchase for his family a farm at the place of his birth near Drogheda.[69]

The case of Kenneth Murchison, the son of tacksman from Lochalsh is a Scottish equivalent. His medical sojourn as a regimental surgeon in the Bengal army from 1771 to 1784 enabled him to accumulate a fortune of £29,038. Upon his return he purchased and improved the estate of Tarradale in Ross-shire, lent £9,400 to other Scottish landed gentry and maintained a townhouse in Cromarty.[70] It is important that these and the other instances of material success through imperial medical service are not treated as routine. These men were unusually successful. However, the rise of individuals from the lower ranks of middling society indicates how the inclination to exploit colonialism in Asia extended well beyond the aristocratic, military, financial and commercial elites. Through organisations like the EIC the Empire reached deep into Britain and Ireland's social hierarchy, prompting engagement and commitment by a range of familial, regional and religious interests.

Table 5.5 East India Company surgeons: regional and social backgrounds

Scottish Region	Scottish Soc. Origins	Irish Region	Irish Soc. Origins	Welsh Region	Welsh Soc. Origins
NE = 65	Gentry = 46	Ulster = 19	Gentry = 3	S. Wales = 10	Tenant Farmer = 1
W. Central = 57	Clergy = 29	Leinster = 11	Merch. = 1	E. Wales = 4	Unknown = 19
Central = 53	Mar/Merch/Manf = 21	Munster = 5	Mariner =1	W./N. Wales = 3	
Edin./Loth'n = 46	Misc. = 19	Connacht = 1	Legal = 1	Unknown = 3	
Borders = 38	Medical = 19	Unknown = 10	Unknown = 40		
Highlands = 36	Legal = 13				
North = 1	Tenant Farmer = 15				
England = 1	Unknown = 208				
Unknown = 78					

(SIWA. Sources: IOR, L/MIL/9/358–365; L/MIL/10/131; P/328/60–64; P/416/77–98; L/AG/34/29/4–22, 185–210, 341–343; TNA, PROB 11/401–1321; Farrington, *A Biographical Index*, passim).

Career cycles and returns

The considerable material gains accrued by Ivory and Murchison were only one outcome in a wider knowledge economy that connected Asia and Europe. Once assigned to an East Indiaman or appointed to a Company settlement, surgeons and physicians encountered a wide variety of challenges and opportunities not evident in Britain or Ireland. In common with other medical specialists across the Empire, they gained access to a broad spectrum of diseases, diagnostic opportunities, potential new remedies and a steady supply of cadavers. Asia's environmental and climatic conditions killed large numbers of Europeans on a routine basis and provided ample opportunities to develop skills in anatomy, pathology and epidemiology.[71] The ability to exercise medical sovereignty over the bodies of patients obviously did not match conditions in the slave colonies of the Atlantic, where experimenting on human beings treated as chattel property drove major developments in European knowledge, including in Scotland.[72] The Company too traded in enslaved people, shipping them from the southern and eastern African coasts, particularly Madagascar, to India and South-East Asia.[73] In 1736 the Scot, David Drummond, surgeon on the *Harrington* East Indiaman, took medical charge of 164 enslaved people. He received a rate of two shillings and sixpence per individual to ensure their arrival in Bombay in a state of health that would maximise their sale value. Another Scot, Walter Wemyss, surgeon on the *Prince William*, received the same rate for ten enslaved persons in 1742. Drummond and Wemyss's medical authority over these individuals would have paralleled that of a plantation surgeon in the Caribbean. Advances in metropolitan provincial medical science through the exploitation of trafficked human beings were not restricted to the Atlantic world.

Medical practices in Asia drew upon and in turn reinforced evolving ideas of race and colour in Europe. This Eastern influence warns against assumptions that Atlantic slavery constituted the only factor shaping a heightened awareness of racial demarcations or that empire may have mattered less than established, scriptural-based European conceptualisations of race.[74] In a treatise of 1786 on the treatment of 300 Madras army troops published in the prestigious Edinburgh periodical the *Medical Commentaries*, the Scots surgeon William Dick highlighted the ability to autopsy large numbers of deceased soldiers. The mutually influencing relationship between colonial medicine and hierarchies of colour were evident when he noted that the bodies of 'black men' (it is unclear if he was referring to enslaved Africans or South Asian sepoys) showed the same symptoms which killed Europeans. The expectation that pathologies might be different depending on skin colour motivated Dick's initial thinking. His labelling of patients revealed similar assumptions and hierarchies. While he carefully recorded the individual surnames of European soldiers, Dick talked only in general terms of 'a number' of 'black' cases.[75] The nature and circumstances of his experiments and their publication in Edinburgh show how coercive access to human bodies under the aegis of colonial authority contributed directly to the content, timing and the discursive place of race in Scotland's medical enlightenment. The Asian branch of the country's knowledge economy benefited directly from various forms of slavery and colonial control.

The Company's European workforce never faced the racial brutalities experienced by enslaved peoples on vessels like the *Prince William* or *Harrington*. Nevertheless, ordinary soldiers and sailors found themselves in situations that left them beholden to their employer's medical experts in ways that differed radically from conditions in Britain or Ireland. The regime of authority utilised in 1786 by William Dick also enabled Maxwell Thompson, surgeon of the 4th European battalion in the Madras army, to dissect cadavers of enlisted men and discuss findings in the presence of senior colleagues. Thomas Clark, surgeon in the British army's 19th regiment, noted in his publication of 1801, *Observations on the Nature and Cures of Fevers*, that his time in Colombo, Ceylon (Sri Lanka), had involved him keeping exact case notes from the dissection of soldiers who deceased under his care. A regular supply of cases and a climate of employer-sanctioned medical control aided systematic observation and experimentation which lent greater intellectual weight to diagnostic methods and published conclusions.[76]

Highly experimental treatments could be trialled on personnel with little or no recourse to alternative health provision.[77] Alexander Stuart from Aberdeenshire, surgeon on the East Indiaman *Europe* from 1704 to 1707, exhibited the polymath outlook expected of learned gentlemen of the time. His activities included metrological observations off Bombay while treating the crew for dysentery with a range of highly invasive experiments. Assiduously recorded in medical notes, such observations and findings gave Company surgeons a tangible intellectual resource with which to accumulate cultural capital.[78] The transhemispheric voyages undertaken by the Company's ships were much longer than any other routine form of commercial sailing. East Indiamen became concentrated sites of disease, infection, diagnoses and treatments. Typical in this respect is the experience of James Bryce. He sailed on 15 April 1792 as surgeon on the *Busbridge*, commanded by a fellow countryman, Thomas Robertson from Edinburgh.[79] If the pattern of merchant marine patronage was routine, conditions on board were not. In a celebrated publication based on his observations and treatments, Bryce noted how the long voyage offered him unique insights that were far more transformative than his education in Edinburgh, London, Bombay, Madras or Bengal.[80]

The intellectual, scientific and medical advances signposted by the likes of Bryce were understood to have immense practical value beyond saving life. The chemical properties of treatments, plant extracts and minerals could have a number of applied uses in textile processing and dyeing. The emphasis on applied knowledge meant that medicine and its related specialisms became highly commercialised, a development which explains why surgeons could often make substantial fortunes. By the 1790s the widespread perception existed that a ship surgeon's post offered trading and fee opportunities worth £700 per annum.[81] Alexander Maconochie's appointment as a surgeon in Bombay occurred in 1788. By the mid-1790s the Scot had diversified his activities and operated more as an entrepreneur than a medical professional. His career reveals the intersection between medicine, applied botany, natural resource exploitation and the commercialisation of such knowledge in the name of scientific patriotism. In 1795 he supervised the construction of large sawmills at Beypur on the Malabar coast in order to improve timber supplies to the Bombay Marine. This was a capital-intensive project, with the presidency council advancing no less than £10,000. The next logical step was ship construction, although in 1805 the court of directors refused his proposals for the building of large warships. Maconochie's experience shows how malleable occupational and professional boundaries remained within the Company's early nineteenth-century colonial state. His ownership of the *Duncan*, at 300 tons one of the largest country trading ships operating out of Bombay, enabled him to advance his personal interest while still technically a public servant on the medical establishment. His senior colleague, Helenus Scott, derived profits from a land development scheme on Salsette Island at Bombay which involved 'resettling' 300 local people.[82]

The acquisition of monetary capital by Maconochie, Scott, Holwell and Ivory went hand in hand with the cultivation of its intellectual and cultural equivalents. The accumulation in Asia of such assets and their realisation and impact back in Scotland and Ireland is an understudied phenomenon. Yet the commercial aspects of information gathering and knowledge transfer directly shaped the tone, timing and focus of medical science in Britain and Ireland. Company, army and navy surgeons serving in the eastern half of the Empire passed innovative forms of medical intelligence back to patrons in Europe. These backflows did not initiate the advanced state of medical knowledge in places like Scotland, but they did form a vital stage in the appropriation of local materials and practice and their reconfiguration into culturally European forms of learning.[83] The value of viewing this phenomenon through a Scottish or Irish lens is that the effects of the knowledge economy can be clearly traced in societies only beginning sustained interactions with Asia after about 1700. These were not abstract, purely intellectual flows of information. Such returns show how medical sojourners realised their cultural capital. The cashing in of intellectual wealth happened in a number of different ways and encompassed individuals, institutions and even whole cities.

Discourses of professional gentility ensured that medical men across the Empire advertised their obligations to scientific celebrities, just as Ainslie did with Rottler. In 1773 Dr James Kerr, a former pupil of William Cullen, professor of medicine at Edinburgh University, sent back from Calcutta plant specimens, wood samples and *coria mimora* (japonica) drawings as well as seeds for the college's museum and garden. This routine process of exchange produced subtle intellectual and social consequences. The gift enabled Kerr to correspond as something more than just a conscientious former pupil. As his professional relationship shifted from dependent to confidant and collaborator, Kerr noted how 'you first taught me to study nature' while adding that further information on insects, dyes and vitriol would have numerous practical applications back in Britain. Cullen in turn enhanced his own, Kerr's and the university's reputation by ensuring the resultant botanical experiments received fulsome coverage in the *Medical Commentaries*.[84]

By enabling the maximum positive professional effect, publication involved more than just the dissemination of information. Formative mentor relationships could be publicised and the quality of education in the metropolitan provinces cast in a virtuous, productive and patriotic light. Civic Edinburgh proved adroit at this process. In the preface of his *Observations*, Thomas Clark thanked his old teacher, Benjamin Bell, described as 'surgeon in Edinburgh'. Burnishing reputations in this way benefited all concerned. William Dick thanked his old teacher, Andrew Duncan at the start of his tract. As the editor of the *Medical Commentaries*, the well-respected Duncan aligned himself with the prestige associated with exotic medical intelligence while assisting a former pupil's accumulation of cultural capital. This is exactly what Cullen did for William Kerr. The 'scientific celebrity' associated with surgeons who served overseas became the means of reinforcing Scottish civic society's reputation in medical science. The third volume of *Medical Commentaries* was dedicated to the East India Company surgeon, William Fullerton of Carstairs, whose exploits and career were taken to be both exotic and enlightening.[85] This use of overseas connections for the purposes of domestic profile had the effect of rendering a previously distant and 'othered' empire in Asia more familiar, intimate and mundane.

The acquisition of cultural and social prestige extended beyond micro-networks of medical associates to include civic and professional infrastructures more broadly. Educational strategies developed during the second half of the eighteenth century enabled university colleges to bask in the aura of innovation associated with overseas medicine. Former students in Asia and those who had returned to Europe supplemented the intellectual capital and material resources of their alma mater by providing valuable information relating to that part of the world. If occurring on a less systematic scale than in Scotland, this crucial process was evident in Ireland. In 1788 Trinity College Dublin received from the Company army officer, Captain Richard Long from Tipperary, a language manual designed to impart everyday phrases and the basics of grammar in Persian and Hindi. The simple, comparative format and 'users-guide' tone demonstrate how teaching cultures were aligning towards an overtly imperial curriculum which would prepare Trinity students considering a career in Asia. As with linguistics, so with medicine. In 1805 another Irish military officer gave the college a copy of the Khulāsat-al-Hikma or 'Epitome of Medicine' by Hakim Hamid of Dībāfoūr.[86] The use of human mobility to ensure the next generation of students acquired practical knowledge of Asia again demonstrates the close relationship between migration, enlightenment and empire. These appropriations of intellectual capital enabled the development of applied as opposed to theologically derived Orientalism. Indeed, Ireland's premier educational institution began recalibrating its curriculum and content towards serving imperial agendas in Asia fifty to sixty years before the better-known reforms of the 1840s and 1850s.[87]

The absorption of colonial and 'Orientalist' knowledge in Dublin formed part of a Europe-wide bureaucratisation and institutionalisation of medical facts, anatomical research and botanical resources. This did not happen simply through the compilation and dissemination of printed information. Professional migration shaped the timing and content of the incorporation process. The volume of Scots and Scots-educated personnel in Company service means the productive intersection of human mobility and enlightenment was more comprehensive in Scotland than in the other metropolitan provinces. Marischal College Aberdeen evolved what amounted to an institutional strategy to nurture human and intellectual links with the knowledge economy in Asia. The policy of aligning educational content to imperial service partly explains the high percentage of the college's students active in the Eastern hemisphere.[88] As early as 1756 the Royal Navy surgeon, David Ramsay Kerr, who served in Admiral Boscawen's expedition in 1747, was awarded an MD from Marischal on the basis of his work on fevers prevalent among the fleet's crews. Kerr in return presented his thinking to a society of medical men in Aberdeen, enabling the city's educational authorities to claim access to the latest evidence and diagnostic trends.[89]

Flows and counter-flows of specialised information as well as cultural and intellectual capital could serve institutions as well as individuals, with university colleges drawing from the sojourner just as surely as the other way around. This relationship complicates conceptions of a pre-existing, nationally demarcated Scottish medical world that produced a large surplus of surgeons fit for imperial service.[90] The dynamic also operated the other way around, with returning overseas specialists enhancing the intellectual capital and cultural prestige of the Scottish universities. Empire, sojourning and economies of knowledge meant that Marischal's reputation and its finances were supplemented through its human links to the other side of the world. The college authorities understood this and made the Asia connection work for the institution's status and its reserves of intellectual capital. The policy is evident in the awarding of MDs. On 28 July 1788 William Gilles, described as 'in a great line on the Bengal establishment and [so] no certificate required', was granted a degree. The Royal College of Physicians in Edinburgh followed suit a year later and made Gilles a fellow. The geographic and cultural dynamics of expertise are the diametric opposite to the poorly trained Scots surgeons noted by John Drummond in 1729. Experience overseas now generated prestige in Scotland rather than the other way around. Between 1790 and 1805 Marischal awarded a further twenty MDs to prominent Company surgeons. This was mutually beneficial credentialism. Professional standing and status in Asia now bestowed high-value cultural capital and reputation on both individuals and on institutions. Through these very public acts of association the Aberdeen college projected its standing as a modern, leading centre of medical expertise.[91] Professional mobility and imperial service were not just a manifestation of a fully formed provincial medical enlightenment. Migration contributed directly to the public character and perpetuation of advanced knowledge at the seats of learning.

Processes that worked for a university college in Aberdeen could shape developments in whole cities. Reciprocal links between Edinburgh's educational elite and sojourning students across the Empire enhanced and projected the Scottish capital's standing as a metropole of learning in a number of ways.[92] The scale and diversity of its civic economies of knowledge challenge assessments of Asia's marginal place within the eighteenth-century city's intellectual climate. Interest in the East Indies is judged to be little more than a series of 'idiosyncratic and disassociated' personal preferences rather than an institutional priority pursued by the university and the Royal Society of Edinburgh.[93] This assessment underestimates the extent to which the Eastern half of the Empire increasingly occupied the attention of the city's literati. In 1781 Hugh Blair informed John Macpherson of the Bengal Council, that '[Alexander] Carlyle and Dr [William] Robertson are both well and often among us all when we meet, your health is drunk, and much conversation carried on about all that you are to do in India.'[94]

Scholarly inquiry extended beyond conjectural and stadial philosophy into more practical activities. In 1797 William Moodie, the chair of Oriental languages, asked James Cochrane from Lanarkshire, a Company civil servant in Madras and a former student, to liaise with other acquaintances in Asia in order to acquire Persian manuscripts. Moodie had already requested that the rest of the Edinburgh professoriate write to their friends, associates and former students across India to help supplement his research and teaching materials. As a result, he acquired a major intellectual resource that augmented his class sizes, fees and educational standing.[95] Edinburgh's civic economy of professional mobility, knowledge accumulation and repatriation encompassed medicine, applied botany, philosophy, linguistics and political economy. This knowledge economy generated transhemispheric networks that criss-crossed the entirety of Britain's Empire by the 1770s and cemented the city's reputation as a medical metropole of global standing.

The working out of these connections are evident in the content of Edinburgh's premier medical periodical. The first twenty years of *Medical Commentaries* from 1773 to 1793 show a considerable and consistent flow of information, theories and practice back into Scotland by means of surgeons active across the Empire. The total from the British Caribbean amounted to sixty-four cases: those from Asia numbered thirty-six.[96] While the slave colonies of the Atlantic world clearly loomed larger in the intellectual horizons of Edinburgh's medical community, the Eastern Empire was already a major source of information and inspiration. The positive effects on perceptions of the city are revealed by developments in 1792. When the Scottish surgeon at Madras, William Roxburgh, sent to London a large consignment of bark with potential medicinal and economic applications, the directors distributed the samples for testing. The material was sent to the Royal College of Physicians in London and in Edinburgh.[97] The choice of institutions is a telling indication of the Scottish capital's co-equal status in medicine with the metropole. The directors' decision seven years later to accept the Edinburgh diploma as proof of professional competence represented the culmination and public acknowledgement of the city's well established and highly successful professional migration and knowledge economy.

Conclusion

The reciprocal influences between human mobility, empire and economies of knowledge have significant implications for the Scottish character of Scotland's medical enlightenment, and to a lesser extent that of Ireland prior to the 1820s. With Irish personnel only a marginal presence in the medical sector before 1815, the capacity of the Eastern Empire to shape knowledge appropriation trends in that kingdom was marginal beyond the general influence exerted by 'Orientalist' discourse. However, the basic model of sojourning and sending back colonial information was already underway by the 1780s and evident in the collecting strategies and curriculum of institutions like Trinity College Dublin. As in politics and economics, Asia was reshaping Irish society decades before the Union in 1800.[98]

The much larger number of Scottish personnel meant the impact was more substantial and sustained in Scotland. Far from springing up organically within its own educational and related civic institutions, the country's leading position in British medicine by about 1800 was partially contingent upon a host of migratory and imperial connections. Overseas influence is a well-established part of explanations for the surge in medical expertise in post-1707 Scotland. Advances in anatomical and epidemiological learning always drew on innovations in Europe, especially from the great medical schools at Leiden and at Paris.[99] Far less well appreciated is the fact that after the 1760s Asia became a major source of knowledge flowing back into the country's university colleges. At the centre of this exchange lay the capacity for individuals overseas to develop their cultural capital in the form of professional experience and reputation before realising its value through completion of the sojourning cycle. Knowledge constituted another form of capital that could be mobilised, accumulated and realised. Its impact could be significant precisely because provincial societies lacked diverse and deep-rooted reserves of monetary wealth.[100] The benefits extended beyond individuals. Institutions like Aberdeen's Marischal College, Edinburgh University and the college of physicians in Edinburgh and Glasgow used the final stage of the knowledge economy cycle to reinforce intellectual capital and institutional prestige through association with Company medics.

Exploring these circuits and knowledge economies involves rethinking how Scotland's cultures of enlightenment shaped and were reshaped by interactions with empire.[101] Growing human and intellectual links with Asia increasingly influenced the content and the timing of medical-scientific innovation. The transfer out and back again of human and cultural forms of capital highlights the extent to which Scotland's later medical enlightenment had a definite if underappreciated Eastern Empire dimension. Sojourning by medical men was not simply an extension of a fully matured or pristine Scottish enlightenment. In its medical manifestations at least, the country's intellectual and scientific climate was a profoundly hybrid phenomenon influenced by province–metropole links in Europe and by global human mobility. Empire influences certainly did not create

Scotland's noticeable profile in British science and medicine. Mobility over transhemispheric distances did, however, enhance pre-existing high-value human capital and helped to generate a powerful provincial knowledge economy that sustained, perpetuated and globalised the country's medical enlightenment between about 1750 and 1820. Enlightenment and migration became deeply interconnected and mutually constitutive. The development of medical expertise north of the border was shaped by a global geography of learning that encompassed places like Aberdeen, Edinburgh, London, the Company's oceanic shipping routes, Madras, Bombay, Calcutta and China. These spaces of learning and their crossings and recrossings did not make enlightenment in Scotland any less distinctive or significant: but they did make it something more than a self-contained 'national' Scottish phenomenon. As with so many other areas of post-union Scottish society, from a commitment to stadial progress, the prestige of its seats of higher learning, or ideals of patriotic 'improvement', the country's undoubted achievements in medicine contained a powerful imperial and global thread.

Notes

1 C. A. Bayly, *Empire and Information: Intelligence Gathering and Social Communication in India, 1780–1870* (Cambridge: Cambridge University Press, 1999), pp. 267–8; Drayton, *Nature's Government*, pp. 65–118; Harrison, *Medicine in an Age of Commerce*, pp. 5–6, 31; Sanjay Subrahmanyam, *Europe's India: Words, People, Empire, 1500–1800* (Cambridge, MA: Harvard University Press, 2017), pp. 189–207.
2 Mark Harrison, 'Networks of Knowledge: Science and Medicine in Early Colonial India, c.1750–1820', in Peers and Gooptu, *The Oxford History of the British Empire: India and the British Empire*, pp. 192–5; Osterhammel, *Unfabling the East*, pp. 205–9.
3 Richard Drayton, 'Empire and Knowledge', in Marshall, *The Oxford History of the British Empire, Vol. II*, pp. 231–52; Kapil Raj, *Relocating Modern Science: Circulation and the Construction of Scientific Knowledge in South Asia and Europe* (New Delhi: Permanent Black, 2006), pp. 7–16, 107–14; Kapil Raj, 'Colonial Encounters and the Forging of New Knowledge and National Identities: Great Britain and India, 1760–1850', in Roy Macleod (ed.), 'Nature and Empire: Science and the Colonial Enterprise', *Osiris*, second series, 15 (2000), 119–13.
4 Arnold, 'India's Place in the Tropical World', 6–11; Hamilton, *Scotland, the Caribbean and the Atlantic World*, p. 116; Kapil Raj, 'Mapping Knowledge Go-Betweens in Calcutta, 1770–1820', in Simon Schaffer, Lissa Roberts, Kapil Raj and James Delbourgo (eds), *The Brokered World: Go-Between and Global Intelligence, 1770–1820* (Sagamore Beach, MA: Science History Publications, 2009), pp. 105–9.

5 D. G. Crawford, *A History of the Indian Medical Service, 1600–1913*, vols. I–II (London: Thacker, 1914), vol. I, pp. 134–97; D. G. Crawford, *Roll of the Indian Medical Service, 1615–1930* (London: Thacker, 1930), p. 649; Marika Vicziany, 'Imperialism, Botany and Statistics in Early Nineteenth-Century India: The Surveys of Francis Buchanan (1762–1829)', *Modern Asian Studies*, 20 (1986), 630–1, 648–9; Raj, *Relocating Modern Science*, pp. 170–1; Harrison, *Medicine in an Age of Commerce*, pp. 172–3.

6 John Robertson, 'The Scottish Contribution to the Enlightenment', in Paul Wood (ed.), *The Scottish Enlightenment: Essays in Reinterpretation* (Rochester, NY: Rochester University Press, 2000), p. 41; Roger L. Emerson, *Essays on David Hume, Medical Men and the Scottish Enlightenment* (Farnham: Ashgate, 2009), pp. 227–37; Charles W. J. Withers, *Placing the Enlightenment, Thinking Geographically about the Age of Reason* (Chicago: University of Chicago Press, 2007), pp. 25–43; Robert Cairns Craig, 'An Empire of Intellect', in MacKenzie and Devine, *Scotland and the British Empire*, pp. 85–9; Janet Starkey, *The Scottish Enlightenment Abroad: The Russells of Braidshaw in Aleppo and on the Coast of Coromandel* (Leiden: Brill, 2018), pp. 6–12, 36.

7 Mark Harrison, 'Tropical Medicine in Nineteenth-Century India', *The British Journal for the History of Science*, 25 (1992), 301; Helen M. Dingwall, *A History of Scottish Medicine* (Edinburgh: Edinburgh University Press, 2003), pp. 119–20.

8 Roger L. Emerson, 'Science and the Origins and Concerns of the Scottish Enlightenment', *History of Science*, 26 (1988), 342–6; Paul Wood, 'The Scientific Revolution in Scotland', in Roy Porter and Mikuláš Teich (eds), *The Scientific Revolution in National Context* (Cambridge: Cambridge University Press, 1992), pp. 263–87; Richard Sher, 'Science and Medicine in the Scottish Enlightenment: The Lessons of Book History', in Wood, *The Scottish Enlightenment: Essays in Reinterpretation*, p. 107; Paul Wood and Charles W. J. Withers, 'Introduction: Science, Medicine and the Scottish Enlightenment: An Historiographical Overview', in Paul Wood and Charles W. J. Withers (eds), *Science and Medicine in the Scottish Enlightenment* (East Linton: Tuckwell Press, 2002), pp. 1–9; Guenter B. Risse, *New Medical Challenges during the Scottish Enlightenment* (New York: Rodopi B.V., 2005), pp. 5–13; Sarah Irving-Stonebraker, 'Disease and Civilization: A Scottish Atlantic Network of Physicians in the Enlightenment', *Britain and the World*, 10 (2017), 197–216.

9 John Hill Burton, *The Scots Abroad*, vols. I–II (Edinburgh: William Blackwood, 1864), vol. II, pp. 112–20; Peter Ross, *The Scots in America* (New York: Raeburn, 1896), pp. 197–203; Gibb, *Scottish Empire*, p. 190; Mackenzie, *The Scots in South Africa*, pp. 216–23.

10 R. H. Girwood, 'The Influence of Scotland on North American Medicine', in Derek A. Dow (ed.), *The Influence of Scottish Medicine* (Carnforth: Parthenon, 1988), pp. 33–42; Hamilton, *Scotland, the Caribbean and the Atlantic World*, pp. 112–39.

11 James Kelly, 'The Emergence of Scientific and Institutional Medical Practice in Ireland, 1650–1800', in Greta Jones and Elizabeth Malcolm (eds), *Medicine, Disease and the State in Ireland, 1650–1940* (Cork: Cork University Press, 1999), pp. 21–35; Jennifer McLaren, 'An Irish Surgeon in Barbados and Demerara: Vexation, Misery and Opportunity', in D. S. Roberts and J. J. Wright (eds), *Ireland's Imperial Connections, 1775–1947* (Cambridge: Cambridge University Press, 2019), pp. 252–3.

12 Kevin Lougheed, 'National Education and Empire: Ireland and the Geography of the National Education System', in David Dickson, Justyna Pyz and Christopher Shepard (eds), *Irish Classrooms and British Empire: Imperial Contexts in the Origins of Modern Education* (Dublin: Four Courts, 2012), pp. 5–13; Karly Kehoe, 'Accessing Empire: Irish Surgeons and the Royal Navy, 1840–1880', *Social History of Medicine*, 26 (2013), 204–24; Crosbie, *Irish Imperial Networks*, pp. 171–2.

13 Cook, 'The Irish Raj', 507–29; Bayly, 'Ireland, India and the Empire', 390; Crosbie, *Irish Imperial Networks*, pp. 169–93.

14 TCD, MS3767/95; P. Foggatt, 'The Irish Connection', in Dow, *The Influence of Scottish Medicine*, pp. 65–8.

15 Starkey, *The Scottish Enlightenment Abroad*, pp. 21–2; Cairns Craig, 'Empire of Intellect', pp. 87–8.

16 Whitelaw Ainslie, *Materia Medica of Hindoostan and Artisan's and Agriculturalist's Nomenclature* (Madras: n.p., 1813), passim.

17 Bayly, *Empire and Knowledge*, pp. 264–75.

18 Harrison, *Medicine in an Age of Commerce*, pp. 89–91, 105, 148; For the example of Gilbert Pasley from Dumfriesshire, chief surgeon at Madras in the 1780s, see NRS, GD246/41/1: Masulipatnam, 24 June 1777; NLS, MS8252, fos. 23–7.

19 IOR, B/43, p. 207; B/49, pp. 12, 733; B/52, pp. 164–5, 562; IOR, P/1/1/PT2, fos. 234, 268, 286; P/1/1/PT3, fo. 347; Harrison, *Medicine in an Age of Commerce*, pp. 21–3.

20 IOR, B/58, pp. 219, 227; H/78, pp. 53–5; Crawford, *A History of the Indian Medical Service*, vol. I, p. 197.

21 NRS, GD51/3/3/106: 8 October 1799; GD51/3/164.

22 Harrison, *Medicine in an Age of Commerce*, p. 16; Charles Maclean, *To the British Inhabitants of India* (Calcutta: n.p., 1798), p. 3.

23 IOR, P/1/1/PT1, fo. 286; B/54, p. 496.

24 Devine, *Scotland's Empire*, p. 263; McGilvary, *East India Patronage*, p. 63; Bayly, *Empire and Information*, pp. 267–8.

25 NRS, GD18/5368.

26 Harrison, *Medicine in an age of Commerce*, pp. 69–70.

27 Starkey, *The Scottish Enlightenment Abroad*, pp. 25–33.

28 McGilvary, *East India Patronage*, p. 116; AUL, Skene Papers, MS38/45: London, 13 November 1769: George Skene to David Skene.

29 D. L. Prior, 'Holwell, John Zephaniah (1711–1798)', *Oxford Dictionary of National Biography*: www.oxforddnb.com/view/article/13622; J. M. Holzman,

The Nabobs in England: A Study of the Returned Anglo-Indian, 1760–1785 (New York: P.P., 1926), p. 10.
30 J. Z. Holwell, *Important facts regarding the East-India Company's affairs in Bengal, from the year 1752 to 1760* (London: T. Becket & P. A. De Hondt, 1764); J. Z. Holwell, *An account of the manner of inoculating for the small pox in the East Indies* (London: T. Becket & P. A. de Hondt, 1767); J. Z. Holwell, *A review of the original principles, religious and moral, of the ancient Bramins* (London: T. Vernor, 1779).
31 IOR, B/56, p. 464; B/58, p. 219; B/67, p. 416; B/91, p. 425; NLS, MS1074, fos. 130, 132. P. J. Anderson (ed.), *Records of the Marischal College and University of Aberdeen*, vol. II (Aberdeen: Aberdeen University Press, 1898), p. 119.
32 NLI, MS14337, Camp near Saulnah: 9 March 1809: William Eugene Conwell to John Conwell Esq.
33 IOR, L/AG/34/29/7 [1791], 21; W. Innes Addison (ed.), *A Roll of the Graduates of the University of Glasgow from 31 December 1727 to 31 December 1897* (Glasgow: James Maclehose & Co., 1898), p. 14.
34 R. B. Sheridan, 'The Role of the Scots in the Economy and Society of the West Indies', in V. Rubin and A. Tuden (eds), *Comparative Perspectives on Slavery in New World Plantation Societies* (New York: New York Academy of Sciences, 1977), pp. 96–8; Hamilton, *Scotland, the Caribbean and the Atlantic World*, pp. 112–39; Emerson, *Essays on David Hume, Medical Men*, pp. 184–8.
35 Anita Guerrini, 'Scots in London Medicine in the Early Eighteenth Century', in Nenadic, *Scots in London*, pp. 165–85; NLS, MS1055, fo. 12; NRS, GD113/5/365A/6.
36 EUL, MS2263/3/1–3; NRS, GD51/4/3.
37 IOR, B/58, p. 219; B/60, p. 167; L/MIL/9/365, pp. 162–5; Farrington, *Biographical Index*, pp. 602, 648.
38 IOR, B/52, p. 184; B/61, pp. 368, 393, 395; B/64, p. 79; TNA, PROB 11/788, pp. 145–6; NRS, GD24/3/296/1; RS27/133, fo. 384; RS27/135, fos. 165–6; George Frederick Russell Colt, *History & genealogy of the Colts of that Ilk and Gartsherrie, and of the English & American Branches of that Family* (Madison, WI: n.p., 1887), pp. 153–4.
39 Rajesh Kochhar, 'Smallpox in the Modern Scientific and Colonial Contexts, 1721–1840', *Journal of Biosciences*, 36 (2011), 761–8.
40 IOR, P/328/63 [1774], pp. 71–2; IOR, B/83, p. 558; B/86, p. 288; Crawford, *A History of the Indian Medical Service*, vol. II, p. 59.
41 IOR, B/61, p. 157; B/92, pp. 349, 355; B/93, p. 49; Harrison, *Medicine in an Age of Commerce*, pp. 89–91.
42 IOR, B/67, p. 310; B/71, p. 637; *A Summary View of the Rise, Constitution, and present state of the Charitable Foundation of King Charles the Second commonly called the Scots Corporation in London* (London: W. Strahan, 1761), p. 13.
43 IOR, B/76, p. 271; B/78, p. 343; B/80, p. 248; B/87, p. 451; B/89, p. 532; P/328/62: Madras Wills [1763], p. 8; TNA, PROB 11/1001, pp. 152–5; PROB 11/1002, p. 311.

44 Charles A. Cameron, *History of the Royal College of Surgeons in Ireland* (Dublin: Fannin, 1886), pp. 333–43; Emerson, *Essays on David Hume, Medical Men*, p. 181; Christopher Shepard, 'Cramming, Instrumentality and the Education of Irish Imperial Elites', in Dickson, Pyz and Shepard, *Irish Classrooms*, pp. 178–9.
45 Dziennik, 'The Fiscal-Military State', pp. 159–77; Mackillop, '"Subsidy State" or "Drawback Province"?', pp. 179–99.
46 NLS, MS1074, fo. 18.
47 *An address to the College of Physicians, and to the Universities of Oxford and Cambridge; occasion'd by the late swarms of Scotch and Leyden physicians, &c* (London: M. Copper, 1747), pp. 1–30.
48 IOR, L/MIL/9/365, pp. 14–17.
49 RRCPG, GB250 70/3: 14 July 1820.
50 IOR, L/MIL/9/358–365.
51 Charles A. Cameron, *History of the Royal College of Surgeons in Ireland* (Dublin: Fannin, 1886), pp. 104, 318.
52 *The East India Kalendar; or, Asiatic Register for Bengal, Madras, Bombay, Fort Marlborough, China, and St. Helena. For the Year 1800* (London: J. Debrett, 1800), pp. 50–5, 129–31, 165; *Wilson's Dublin directory, for the year 1778* (Dublin: W. Wilson, 1778), p. 90; Harrison, *Medicine in an Age of Commerce and Empire*, p. 80; Raj, *Relocating Modern Science*, p. 17.
53 Farrington, *Biographical Index*, passim.
54 Huw V. Bowen, 'Privilege and Profit: Commanders of East Indiamen as Private Traders, Entrepreneurs and Smugglers, 1760–1813', *International Journal of Maritime History*, 19 (2007), 43–88.
55 IOR, B/49, p. 319; B/51, p. 718; B/58, p. 20; B/62, p. 68; B/65, p. 247; B/70, p. 191; B/75, p. 650.
56 McGilvary, *East India Patronage*, p. 211; TNA, PROB 11/487, pp. 100–1; PROB 11/995, p. 292; IOR, L/AG/34/29/6 [1788], 26.
57 McGilvary, *East India Patronage*, pp. 209–32; Riddy, 'Warren Hastings', p. 42.
58 Devine, *Scotland's Empire*, p. 98; Emerson, *Essays on David Hume, Medical Men*, pp. 220–4.
59 Crawford, *A History of the Indian Medical Service*, vol. I, p. 59; Mackillop, 'Locality, Nation and Empire', p. 61.
60 Hamilton, *Scotland, the Caribbean and the Atlantic World*, p. 43; Rigg, *Men of Spirit and Enterprise*, pp. 174–5.
61 Thomas Bartlett, 'An Union for Empire': the Anglo-Irish Union as an Imperial Project', in M. Brown, P. M. Geoghan and J. Kelly (eds), *The Irish Act of Union, 1800: Bicentenial Essays* (Dublin: Four Courts, 2001), pp. 50–7.
62 Shepard, 'Cramming, Instrumentality', pp. 178–9; McLaren, 'An Irish Surgeon in Barbados and Demerara', pp. 252–3.
63 IOR, B/71, pp. 637, 640.
64 IOR, B/83, p. 548; B/86, p. 277; McGilvary, *East India Patronage*, pp. 157–8.
65 IOR, B/83, p. 636; B/84, p. 349; B/87, p. 277; L/AG/34/29/4/37; *Answers for James Ker of Crummock, surgeon in the service of the East India Company*

(Edinburgh: n.p., 1768); Farrington, *Biographical Index*, p. 548; Thomas Thomson (ed.), *A Biographical Dictionary of Eminent Scotsmen* (Glasgow, Edinburgh and London: Blackie, 1855), vol. II, p. 170.
66 Farrington, *Biographical Index*, pp. 8, 110, 189, 322, 479, 511, 592, 608, 636, 798.
67 Mackillop, 'Dundee, London and the Empire in Asia', pp. 160–85.
68 Campbell, *Records of Clan Campbell*, pp. 131, 172, 175; Hodson, *List of the Officers of the Army of Bengal*, vol. IV, pp. 420–1; TNA, PROB 11/740, p. 20; PROB 11/1405: pp. 63–4; NRS, CC8/8/135, pp. 91–2; IOR, L/MIL/9/359, pp. 50–3; L/MIL/9/361, pp. 153–6; L/MIL/9/365, pp. 92–6; L/AG/34/29/17/42; L/MIL/10/131; DCA, Wedderburn of Pearsie, Box 7/26/8: 21 March 1791; Box 7/25/1: Dundee, 31 December 1767; Box 7/25/16: Pearsie, 31 Jan 1779.
69 NLI, MS10242; TNA, PROB 11/1514, pp. 186–91; Farrington, *Biographical Index*, p. 413.
70 Eric Grant and Alistair Mutch, 'Indian Wealth and Agricultural Improvement in Northern Scotland', *Journal of Scottish Studies*, 35 (2015), 25–44; EUL, MS2263/1–10; NRS, Register of Sasines, Ross (100) (320) (324); Midlothian (6777); Farrington, *Biographical Index*, p. 568.
71 Harrison, *Medicine in an Age of Commerce*, pp. 104–6.
72 Richard B. Sheridan, *Doctors and Slaves: A Medical and Demographic History of Slavery in the British West Indies, 1680–1834* (Cambridge: Cambridge University Press, 1985), passim; Sowande Mustakeem, '"I Never Have Such a Sickly Ship Before": Diet, Disease, and Mortality in 18th-Century Atlantic Slaving Voyages', *Journal of African American History*, 93 (2008), 474–96; Hamilton, *Scotland, the Caribbean and the Atlantic World*, pp. 122–4.
73 Richard B. Allen, 'Satisfying the "Want for Labouring People": European Slave Trading in the Indian Ocean, 1500–1850', *Journal of World History*, 21 (2010), 45–73; Richard B. Allen, 'Ending the History of Silence: Reconstructing European Slave Trading in the Indian Ocean', *Dossiê O Tráfico De Escravos Africanos: Novos Horizontes*, 23 (2017), 296–9.
74 *Medical and Philosophical Commentaries. By a Society in Edinburgh* (London: J. Murray, 1774), pp. 367–79; Silvia Sebastiani (translated by Jeremy Carden), *The Scottish Enlightenment: Race, Gender, and the Limits of Progress* (New York: Palgrave Macmillan, 2013), pp. 11–13.
75 *Medical Commentaries for the year 1785* (London: J. Murray, 1786), 'Observations on Dropsies prevailing among the Troops in the East Indies', pp. 207–29. For Dick's career see: CSAS, MacPherson Papers, Microfilm 9/T1-3; Farrington, *Biographical Index*, p. 215; NRS, Register of Sasines, Perth (4578–9) (5424) (5571) (5475) (6027) (6971); TNA, PROB 11/1639, pp. 180–2.
76 GUL, MS GEN 1476A/1238; NRS, GD29/2067/29: Calcutta. 23 August 1794; Thomas Clark, *Observations on the Nature and Cure of Fevers, and of the Diseases of the West and East Indies and of America* (Edinburgh: n.p., 1801), preface.
77 Harrison, *Medicine in an Age of Commerce*, pp. 8–12, 52, 104.

78 GUL, MS50. T.2.8: 'Medical Observations of Alexander Stuart', pp. 94–6, 123–8, 134, 145–6, 150; Anita Guerrani, 'A Scotsman on the Make: The Career of Alexander Stuart', in Paul Wood (ed.), *The Scottish Enlightenment: Essays in Reinterpretation* (Rochester, NY: University of Rochester, 2000), pp. 157–76.
79 NRS, SC70/1/27/429; Hardy, *A Register of Ships*, pp. 71, 96, 133, 150, 200.
80 James Bryce, *An Account of the Yellow Fever, with a successful method of cure* (Edinburgh: W. Creech, 1796), pp. 6–7; John Clark, *Observations on the diseases in long voyages to hot countries, and particularly on those which prevail in the East Indies* (London: G. Nicol & D. Wilson, 1773), viii; Harrison, *Medicine in an Age of Commerce*, p. 153.
81 NRS, RH4/121/1, pp. 91–2.
82 IOR, L/MIL/12/87/17 IOR, L/MIL/9/90, pp. 195–6; Anne Bulley, *The Bombay Country Ships, 1790–1833* (Abingdon: Routledge, 2000), p. 135; GD51/3/3/58: Bombay, 9 Jan 1794; TNA, PROB 11/1661: pp. 58–9.
83 Hamilton, *Scotland, the Caribbean and the Atlantic World*, pp. 127–35; C. Jones, 'Collectors of Natural Knowledge: The Edinburgh Medical Society and the Associational Culture of Scotland and the North Atlantic World in the 18th Century', *Journal of the Royal College of Physicians, Edinburgh*, 48 (2018), 160–2; IOR, MSS Eur. E276, Letter Book of Claud Russell, vol. III, Madras, 6 February 1777.
84 GUL, MS Cullen/141: Calcutta, 29 September 1773.
85 *Medical and Philosophical Commentaries*, vol. III (London: J. Murray, 1784).
86 TCD, MS1612: Persian and Hindustani Dictionary; MS1576: Khulāsat-al-Hikma or Epitome of Medicine by Hakim Hamid of Dībāfoūr.
87 Shepard, 'Cramming, Instrumentality', and David Dickson, '1857 and 1908: Two Moments in the Transformation of Irish Universities', in *Irish Classrooms and British Empire*, pp. 175–7, 187–90.
88 Emerson, *Essays on David Hume, Medical Men*, pp. 184–8.
89 Anderson (ed.), *Records of the Marischal College*, vol. II, p. 118.
90 Devine, *Scotland's Empire*, p. 233.
91 Anderson, *Records of the Marischal College*, vol. II, pp. 138–41; *Medical and Philosophical Commentaries*, vol. IV (1776), p. 470; vol. V (1777), p. 111.
92 Warren McDougall, 'Charles Elliot's Medical Publications and the International Book Trade', in Wood and Withers, *Science and Medicine*, pp. 215–33.
93 Beatrice Teissier, 'Asia in Eighteenth-Century Edinburgh Institutions: Seen or Unseen?', *Proceedings of the Societies of Antiquaries of Scotland*, 134 (2004), 500, 527.
94 IOR, MSS Eur. F291/83/1: Edinburgh, 28 November 1781; MSS Eur. F291/83/2: Edinburgh, 1 August 1785.
95 NRS, GD1/594/1: Edinburgh, 3 May, 23 May 1797.
96 Schwarz, 'Scottish Surgeons in the Liverpool Slave Trade', pp. 148–59; *Medical and Philosophical Commentaries*, vols I–VI (1773–1779); *Medical Commentaries*, vols VII–X; I–VIII (1780–1793).
97 *Medical Commentaries for the Year 1792*, VII (Edinburgh: Peter Hill, 1793), pp. 547–8.

98 Barry Crosbie, 'Ireland, Colonial Science and the Geographic Construction of British Rule in India, c.1820–1870', *Historical Journal*, 52 (2009), 965–6.
99 Dingwall, *A History of Scottish Medicine*, pp. 84–7; Matthew H. Kaufman, *Medical Teaching in Edinburgh during the Eighteenth and Nineteenth Centuries* (Edinburgh: RCSE, 2003), p. 5; Mackillop, '"As Hewers of Wood"', pp. 29–30.
100 Bayly, *Empire and Information*, p. 5.
101 Alexander Broadie, *The Scottish Enlightenment* (Edinburgh: Birlinn, 2001), pp. 58–9; Kevin Whelan, 'Ireland, Scotland and Britain in the Long Eighteenth Century', in Brotherstone, Clark and Whelan, *These Fissured Isles*, pp. 51–6.

6

The free traders: connecting economies of human and monetary capital

The growing importance of private traders is an established feature of debates on the Company and its expansion. British, Irish and other European nationals, known as 'free merchants' and 'free mariners', operated outside the corporation and pursued a range of mercantile, shipping and financial activities.[1] This 'country trade' was vast in extent and seminal in its consequences. It stretched from the Gulf and Red Sea to both coasts of South Asia, South-East Asia and the coast of China. Eventually it reached Britain's new colonies in Australia.[2] Active from the 1660s up until the termination of the corporation's India and China monopolies, this subset of the EIC's wider world has been the subject of a number of interpretations.

One perspective stresses an ambiguous dynamic of competition and complementarity. Private merchants and mariners undermined the Company's economic performance by exploiting inter-Asia trades more effectively while diverting civil servants away from their official responsibilities.[3] Yet the positive consequences, for the EIC at least, have also been acknowledged. Free traders helped embed the organisation into local financial, economic and political systems by accessing additional sources of South Asian capital and developing an extended web of commercial exchanges. This deepening interdependency facilitated the EIC's political power in South, South-East and East Asia.[4] So it was that free merchant and free mariner commerce both made and unmade the Company.

The nature and consequences of these intersections between corporate and private trading form part of a wider reconsideration of free merchants and mariners and their contribution to the development of global commerce. There is a greater awareness of the transhemispheric links created by private European commercial networks across and beyond Asia and the role these played in supplementing the nascent capacities of the early colonial state.[5] Their increasing oceanic reach was impressive. Capital, commodities and profits linked major entrepôts like Calcutta, Madras, Bombay, Batavia and Canton to London, a development that involved the transfer of the 'gentlemanly capitalist' order into one entire hemisphere of world trade.⁶ This blending of official corporate economy and private commerce aligns with debates over the significance of the Asia trades in the final phases of proto-globalisation between about 1760 and 1820.⁷

Much like the medical sector, the incidence of Scottish personnel appearing as free merchants and mariners after *c.*1760 has attracted some historical commentary.⁸ Yet explanations have not moved much beyond the matter of numbers and observing the reliance on kin-based business practices in the larger agency houses controlled by Scottish partners.⁹ The use of familial and kin mechanisms as 'trust-inducing connections' within British and Irish commercial co-partnerships in this period remains an understudied topic. Such arrangements not only point to the significance of social capital in processes of global expansion, they shaped the nature of the colonial state. These forms of co-partner organisation constituted a logical response to the lack of developed legal or financial services in Company India and fit a pattern of kinship-based 'trading diasporas' across early modern Asia.¹⁰ In this respect the free traders exemplify the importance now attached to the 'familial proto-state' within explanations of British colonialism. This formulation emphasises how kin and kith groups worked beneath and through the formal structures of corporate and state power. In doing so they shaped the timing and character of early British imperialism in Asia.¹¹

These reassessments frame an analysis of metropolitan provincial involvement in the free merchant and mariner sectors and give wider significance to what their example reveals. While some basic understanding exists in relation to Scottish involvement in this sector, overall trends in participation remain largely unknown. Even less is known about Irish free traders. The web of connections which facilitated the EIC careers and private enterprise of Laurence Sulivan and William Hickey have received illuminating attention and reveal the transhemispheric reach of Irish networks.¹² Some analysis has been developed for a limited number of Welsh businesses and the developing links between the Asian and Welsh economies.¹³ However, much like their Irish counterparts, the timing and means by which micro- and meso-networks from this part of Britain established themselves in the informal colonial economy remain elusive.

Free merchants and mariners: patterns of participation

The appointment of free merchants and mariners was intended to augment the demographic, economic and financial potential of the Company's settlements. It was hoped private trading would increase customs revenue, diversify commercial services and create a supplementary class of entrepreneurs willing to lend to the presidency governments. The result was the

Table 6.1 Official free merchants and mariners, 1690–1780

Decade	Total Appointments	Scots	Irish	Welsh
1690–1699	28	0	0	0
1700–1709	38	0	0	0
1710–1719	56	2 (3.5%)	0	0
1720–1729	22	4 (18.1%)	1 (4.5%)	1 (4.5%)
1730–1739	36	12 (33.3%)	1 (2.7%)	0
1740–1749	57	7 (12.2%)	0	0
1750–1759	92	24 (26.0%)	3 (3.2%)	0
1760–1769	398	43 (10.8%)	5 (1.2%)	1 (0.25%)
1770–1779	102	22 (21.5%)	1 (0.9%)	0
Total	829	114 (13.7%)	12 (1.4%)	2 (0.24%)

(SIWA. Sources: IOR, H/78, pp. 49–51; B40–B/95).

implementation by the directors of a licensing system which in return for a £1,000 bond of security granted permission to trade in Asia, although not back to European markets or in the wider Atlantic world.[14] The imposition of the same method of credentialism used for the covenanted civil servants indicates the growing importance of the country trade. The framework established in 1716 determined the pattern of official appointments in London for the rest of the century. The reality, however, was that efforts at regulatory oversight did little to prevent those with no formal permission becoming involved in the private sector.

The free merchant and mariner licences recorded in the court of directors' minutes from 1690 to 1780 are listed in Table 6.1. The figures give an indication of when and in what quantities metropolitan provincials received permission to participate in the country trade. These totals do not include the substantial annual drift out to Asia of persons without permission. This feature of the official record explains why the quantities in Table 6.1 diverge so dramatically from pre-existing estimates of 211 Scottish free merchants cited for the period between 1776 and 1785.[15] What the numbers do reveal is how effectively or otherwise provincial networks of credentialism in the metropole secured official licences. What is also clear is that the emergence of metropolitan provincials in this sector was a protracted process.

As with other areas of the Company's activities, the nature of the surviving archive underestimates the number of Irish, Scots and Welsh appointments. Unless supplemented with details of those supplying bonds of surety, it is invariably name evidence alone which survives in the directors' minutes.[16] As already noted, this is not a robust method for confirming place of origin. The existence of the Scots Corporation of London enables many of those providing credentialism in the form of bonds to be identified

The free traders 195

as brokers of human capital. This enables the Scottish numbers to be more securely, although never comprehensively, ascertained. Unfortunately evidence does not exist in the same way for Irish or Welsh patrons and so the figures for these nationalities are artificially lowered. Yet even allowing for the gaps in the record, the overall patterns are clear from a relatively early point in the eighteenth century. As official permissions rose after the 1720s, Scots averaged almost 20 per cent of all those licensed by the directors. In line with other areas of the corporation, this ratio was above Scotland's share of Britain and Ireland's population. Welsh and Irish rates are noticeably lower, although care is needed with this assessment given the difficulty in identifying individuals from these societies.[17] The figures in Table 6.1 are important in one other respect. They confirm a pattern of displacement into the less competitive areas of employment when viewed in conjunction with trends elsewhere in the civil service and merchant fleet.

This clustering in less prestigious and less sought-after activities is much easier to track once the censuses of non-Company employees become available from the late 1770s.[18] The annual audits listed those in the main settlements that did not hold a civil service, medical or military office. The nature of the documentation reflected the corporation's conception of Britain and Ireland as a composite set of kingdoms or polities and explains why people were listed as 'English', 'Scots', 'Irish' and 'Welsh'. This method of recording means that the identification of metropolitan provincials is straightforward, although the ability to self-identify meant that those like the Dublin-born portrait painter, Thomas Hickey, could and did list themselves as 'English'.[19] This corporate Britishness reflected the EIC's *ancien régime* understanding of nation and society even as it constructed a new colonial regime in India. The corporation focused on professional hierarchies, licensed privileges and the national demarcations of its heterogeneous European workforce just as surely as it did on racial and ethnic distinctions among the South Asians increasingly subjected to its authority.[20]

The census of privately employed Europeans at Madras and Calcutta enumerated in Table 6.2 gives an exact picture of the Irish, Scots and Welsh distribution within the free trader community at two of the Empire's most significant port cities. The figures confirm the marked differences in profile between the provincial groups already evident from the patterns in Table 6.1. Unfortunately, no similar registration procedure occurred in Bombay prior to 1815, and so it is not possible to reconstruct the presence of these groups in the western presidency with the same certainty. A published list from 1800 shows a total of 270 private merchants, mariners, lawyers, clerks and retailers residing in Bombay.[21] An unknown number would have been metropolitan provincials.

Table 6.2 Irish, Scots and Welsh free merchants and mariners, Calcutta and Madras, 1778–1812

Presidency	Year	Total	Irish	Scots	Welsh
Calcutta	1804	882	63 (7.1%)	178 (20.1%)	6 (0.6%)
	1812	636	52 (8.1%)	146 (22.9%)	6 (0.9%)
Madras	1778	145	14 (9.6%)	35 (24.1%)	2 (1.3%)
	1789	202	35 (17.3%)	49 (24.2%)	3 (1.4%)
	1800	271	27 (9.9%)	58 (21.4%)	3 (1.1%)
	1810	139	14 (10%)	41 (29.4%)	2 (1.4%)

(Source: IOR, O/5/26: 'List of Private Trade Europeans resident Calcutta and in the several districts, 13 November, 1804.'; O/5/27, 'General List of Europeans not in H.M.'s or the Honourable Company's Service for the Year 1812.'; O/5/30, fos. 7–15, 130–134; fos. 198–206, 210–13).

These patterns are summarised in Table 6.3 by combining known applications for free merchant and mariner licences, ten census samples, and information from wills and testaments lodged at Bombay, Calcutta and Madras. The same trajectory of increasing Irish, Scots and Welsh involvement evident in other parts of the workforce was replicated in the private trading sector. The verifiable totals in Table 6.3 support existing assessments of at least 300–400 private trading Scots in Bengal over the course of the later eighteenth and early nineteenth centuries. Although not connected directly to the economy in Scotland in the same manner as the Caribbean or North America trades, the build-up of numbers from the 1740s meant Asia hosted one of the largest concentrations of Scots mercantile personnel beyond Europe in this period.[22]

There is a consistency to the percentages in Tables 6.1 to 6.3 which broadly match the distribution of provincials in other areas of the Company. Scottish overrepresentation compared to the other two national groups was sizeable, evident in both main settlements and consistent over a number of decades. It found its mirror opposite in the lack of a proportionate Welsh presence. Meanwhile, Irish underrepresentation relative to population was

Table 6.3 Scots, Irish and Welsh free merchants and mariners, 1690–1813

Years	1690–1709	1710–1729	1730–1749	1750–1769	1770–1789	1790–1813	Total
Scots	0	6	26	85	228	290	635
Irish	0	1	5	10	86	113	215
Welsh	0	0	0	2	7	15	24

(SIWA. Sources: IOR, B/40–B/95; IOR, O/5/26–27, 30–31: P/328/60–64; P/416/77–98; L/AG/34/29/4–22, 185–210, 341–343; TNA, PROB 11/549–1903; *The East India Kalendar, 1791 to 1800* (London: J. Debrett, 1791–1800)).

also a feature of the free merchant and mariner community. These trends again underline the acute sensitivity of provincial societies to the distinctive character and timing of the Company's expansion and empire. The result was another layer of intra-provincial divergence, with Scots establishing a far more numerous and prominent role within the private trader sector compared to the Irish or Welsh.

Free traders were a socially, financially and economically heterogeneous group. They created ventures that spanned small artisanal and retail outlets, legal and clerical services, medium-sized wholesale businesses, indigo plantations and shipping operations, to agency houses with transhemispheric reach.[23] Although Scots were noticeably more prominent in overall numbers and percentage share, the occupational profiles did share some key similarities as well as some important differences with the other metropolitan provinces. These are outlined in Table 6.4, which shows the range of activities undertaken by those enumerated in Tables 6.2 and 6.3.

Merchants and mariners made up a substantial part of the overall Scottish presence, a configuration shared in common with the small numbers of Welsh. These two activities were less prominent in the case of the Irish. Some of the free merchants and mariners were among the most influential private businessmen in the entire Empire. A report in 1799 on the clandestine use of British capital on Danish vessels operating out of Batavia noted that the Calcutta-based Scottish agency house of Ferguson, Fairlie & Co., the Scottish co-partnership of Forbes & Co. in Bombay and one other business had stockpiled cargoes requiring 50,000 tons of shipping. The magnitude of these ventures can be contextualised by the fact that in 1787 the entire registered shipping of Scottish ports amounted to 133,046 tons. The total capital value of cargoes sent from London in 1802 by David Scott of Dunninald's East India agency house amounted to £260,000.[24] The functioning of the merchant houses in Asia exemplifies the deployment of human and social capital to build reputation, trust and credit in order to generate the accumulation of monetary capital. This exchange in the forms of capital was one of the defining characteristics and functions of the private trading sector.

While the scale of Ferguson, Fairlie & Co. and Scott & Co.'s operations was unusual, they were only one of a number of such companies. Thomas Parry and Joseph Price, two Welsh free traders, were major ship owners whose careers have received attention from historians of Wales.[25] Irish merchants operated in the same manner. Robert Gregory from Galway's career in Bengal culminated with his election as a director in the 1770s, while Peter Brodkin developed a web of financial and business activities in the Madras to China trades between 1775 and the 1790s. All exemplify the commercial reach of the free merchants and the methods used to trade in

Table 6.4 Private traders: occupational profiles

Irish	Scots	Welsh
215	635	24
Free merchant = 52 (24.1%)	Free merchant = 197 (31%)	Free merchant = 6 (25%)
Free mariner = 25 (11.6%)	Free mariner = 121 (19%)	Free mariner = 5 (20.8%)
Indigo = 25 (11.6%)	Indigo = 54 (8.5%)	Indigo = 3 (12.5%)
Artisan = 19 (8.8%)	Artisan = 110 (17.3%)	Artisan = 3 (12.5%)
Retail = 27 (12.5%)	Retail = 69 (10.8%)	Retail = 2 (9%)
Admin./legal = 60 (27.9%)	Admin./legal = 77 (12.1%)	Admin./legal = 5 (20.8%)
Unknown = 7 (3.2%)	Medical/Unknown = 7 (1.1%)	

(SIWA: Source: IOR, B/40–B/70; O/5/26–27, 30–31: P/328/60–64; P/416/77–98; L/AG/34/29/4–22, 185–210, 341–343; TNA, PROB 11/549-1903; *The East India Kalendar, 1791 to 1800* (London: J. Debrett, 1791–1800)).

multiple forms of wealth: human, social, cultural and monetary.[26] Given the potential profit capacity of the larger partnerships such as Ferguson, Fairlie & Co. and Brodkin & Co., it is significant that there were more Scots in this layer of the private trade sector.

High-profile examples of success are easy to highlight but should not detract from the general characteristics of metropolitan provincial involvement. Tavern owners and shopkeepers retailing European-style food, wine, books, clothing and equipment, or artisans with tailoring, furniture or jewellery workshops formed an important numeric presence even if their financial resources were insignificant when set against those of the major merchants. This less-prestigious sector remains understudied but attracted people from a range of social backgrounds and was often characterised by small, kin-based partnerships. It included men like David Jones from Wales who arrived in Calcutta in 1794 and established a sugar distilling business, Alexander Stuart, a ladies' hairdresser from Scotland who arrived in Madras in 1787, and Henry Lamy from Ireland who set up shop at Trichinopoly (Tiruchirappalli) in 1785, the year after his brother William became a merchant in Ganjam.[27]

Noticeably more Scots congregated in this retail-artisan layer of activity. By contrast, a feature of the Irish and Welsh profile is the higher percentages in clerical, administrative and legal services when compared with Scots. Not enough is known about how Britain and Ireland's different legal jurisdictions influenced engagement with expansion and empire.[28] Because legal culture in Ireland and Wales was derived from English common law, those completing their training did so at the Inns of Court in London. This education made them familiar in the principles, procedures and terminologies used in the Company's mayor courts. The overlap meant that Welsh and Irish individuals were ideally placed to act as attorneys, advocates, registrars and court clerks, acting in effect as legal adjuncts to the official civil service. Four of the eighteen individuals listed as legal personnel in the 1800 Madras census were Irish: Benjamin Sulivan, the presidency's attorney general, and the advocates, Disney, MacMahon and Walters.[29]

Knowledge of English law assisted the careers of a coterie of Anglo-Irishmen at the top of the colonial legal establishments. Sir George Shee, MP for Knocktopher, held an attorney's post in the Bengal court of exchequer in the 1780s, while Sir William Dunkin from Antrim benefited from Lord George McCartney's regional associationalism and the patronage of Henry Dundas. In 1791 he obtained a judicial post at the supreme court of Bengal and in turn supported his son in law and fellow Antrim man and attorney, Francis MacNaghtan.[30] The most spectacular example of the drift to India of Irish Protestants with a background in English law was Stephen Popham, MP for Castlebar before bankruptcy forced him to

Madras in 1778. As court receiver he made substantial commissions on the high turnover of legal business. He dabbled in town planning and refitting decommissioned East Indiamen for voyages to South-East Asia and China. When he died in Madras in 1795 his will listed assets worth £434,000 – the single largest confirmed fortune made by any metropolitan provincial in this period. Popham sought to repay his debts to Irish aristocrats while leaving tens of thousands of pounds to family and relatives in Cork and his children in England and North America.[31] The scale of his fortune was certainly not typical, but it points to why Irish, Scots, Welsh and English alike were attracted to private commercial, financial or professional ventures in Asia.

Popham's estate shared one characteristic in common with many other fortunes in this period. Much of it existed only on paper, in the form of unrealised bonds of credit and speculative investments in plantations and maritime commerce. Lacking the formal status and creditworthiness of the civil servants could leave private traders vulnerable to the unstable nature of capital accumulation which characterised the early phases of British colonialism in Asia.[32] These challenging realities helped to define the business networks and associative strategies not just of free merchants, mariners and professionals like Popham but of all those sojourning under the Company's protection.

Networks and the transformation of human to monetary capital

Fairlie, Gregory, Parry and the far less successful Stuart and Lamy, were part of an increasingly intrusive European commercial and colonial presence in the East Indies. How metropolitan provincials functioned in this context casts important light on the activities required to turn human capital into monetary wealth. The fact that surviving correspondence generated by European sojourners reveals a world of incessant networking provides a telling indication of how this vital transformation occurred. Streams of letters, accounts, bills of credit, wills and remittances generated global webs of epistolary, financial, professional and kin-based bonds of mutual trust and obligation.[33] This oceanic community of correspondence connected Bengal, Madras, Bombay, Benkulen and Canton, and stretched back via sites of transition at the Cape of Good Hope and Saint Helena to London and the rest of Britain and Ireland. Micro- and meso-networks formed, flourished, declined and reformed constantly. While recovering the shape and function of such networks is useful, they were ultimately only a means to an end. The underlying purpose was to create and consolidate professional and commercial avenues of opportunity and financial advancement before facilitating completion of the sojourning cycle.

In a febrile climate of interdependence and competition sojourners worked together in new ways. Free traders often formed the pivotal link in these arrangements. The career of George Graham, a Bengal-based free mariner at the centre of a kin-based micro-network with three other brothers in Asia from the 1750s to the early 1800s, typifies this connective function. The eclectic, experimental and transnational nature of their networking illustrates what was required to operate successfully in the East Indies. George and his brothers branched out as a hybrid kin co-operative into a range of contacts with military officers, civil servants and merchants based at the metropoles of the Asia trades in Europe such as London, Lorient and Lisbon. George contracted with fellow Scots, the free merchant and later civil servant William Berrie and Colonel Hugh Grant to supply 200 bullocks for Grant's regiment stationed on the Awadh frontier. Compared to the scale of his other activities the resulting profits of £440 were marginal.[34] What the example reveals is the associative tendencies that often underpinned business between Europeans and the enabling role played by free traders in such profiteering. In the case of the Grahams the result was a sprawling transhemispheric meso-network which encompassed strong, vertical family and regional-based bonds of trust and mutual obligation but that also branched out horizontally into extensive but less permanent connections (Table 6.5 and Appendix 6.1).[35]

Business practices had to be flexible and open ended. A crucial way in which private traders helped the transformation of human capital into material profits was though organising contacts with Asian merchants and financiers, both on their own behalf and as agents for Company employees. Europeans could not operate in India, South-East Asia or China without establishing such working relations.[36] Transactions often involved obtaining loans either from other Company officials or trusted Asian merchants and financiers which were lent in turn to other local businessmen and artisans. Designed to exploit the high interest rates which characterised India's money markets, credit brokering operated on a vast scale. Archibald Cockburn, the son of a baron of the Scottish exchequer, used the embodied human capital inherent in the office of a Company civil servant to turn socially constructed ideas of wealth into monetary surpluses. As a revenue official in Mysore he borrowed from South Asian merchants on preferential conditions which he then lent to other local businesses at a higher rate of interest. When combined with his official salary, the result by 1802 was an annual income of £5,000 per annum. This was a mere eight years after his arrival in India.[37] The ability to overlap official and private credit inevitably favoured the covenanted civil servants. Viewed in this way, the substantially greater number of these posts secured by Scots compared to the Irish or Welsh amounted to a major competitive human-capital advantage, one which was amplified by the presence of greater numbers of free traders from Scotland. The different patterns of engagement with the Company's various sectors outlined in Chapters 3 to 5 left Scottish society far better placed to benefit from the political, economic and social conditions in Asia which enabled the transformation of one variety of capital into another.

Interaction with local expertise partly determined the productivity of these forms of enterprise, especially prior to the consolidation in the later eighteenth century of British-owned financial services in Asia.[38] John Maxwell Stone, a relative of the archbishop of Armagh with family connections to Ireland, was a Madras civil servant from 1755 until his death in 1786. Despite acting as secretary for the presidency council, he spent much of his time dealing in diamonds, coral and bills of exchange. Many of these ventures were on behalf of a senior colleague, Josias Du Pre, a governor of Madras who returned to England and married a sister of the Bengal civil servant, James Alexander from County Londonderry. These connections meant that corporate and kin associations overlapped with Ulster-aligned interests and shaped Stone's dealings with South Asian entrepreneurs. In 1775 to 1776 he completed transactions on six separate accounts for diamonds and coral destined for Du Pre totalling £7,558: five were with local merchants, 'Jontee Soobayah', 'Jafferboy', 'Nellacutauker', 'Sunkeryporam Chitty' and 'Lucmadaos Commerjee'.[39]

Senior civil servants and private traders alike relied on these types of local commercial contact. Despite having returned home some years earlier, James Alexander was forced to leave behind considerable capital, a problem common to many successful sojourners. In order to keep his assets productive he authorised a range of ventures during the early 1770s, the largest of which was a contract for £25,951 of Bihar opium managed by 'Mur Ashruff'.[40] Stone's fleeting interactions did not make 'Soobayah' or the other local merchants part of his network in the way that reliance on Ashruff's management of a large capital stock placed him at the outer limits of Alexander's meso-network.

One of the key pressures bringing Company employees into association with private traders was the change in regulations which previously allowed officials to undertake commerce on their own account. The corrupt use of public monies, the awarding of large-scale salt, shipping, opium and military contracts on terms that inflated private gain at the expense of public probity badly damaged the Company's reputation.[41] The Regulating Act and the legislation passed by the Pitt ministry in 1784 were designed to restrict the private concerns of civil servants and military officials. The way was cleared for free merchants and mariners to redeploy the salaries, profits and credit of the corporation's officially employed elite as working capital for their commercial purposes.[42] The arrangement was mutually beneficial.

It meant civil servants and military officers knew their accumulated wealth was earning a return while undercapitalised free traders gained access to reserves of venture finance not so readily available in societies like Ireland, Scotland and Wales. In this way India's public revenues were redirected into private European commerce. The resultant activities could be extremely lucrative. Claud Alexander, a civil servant from Renfrewshire, complained in July 1783 that giving up his salt contracts, for which he had invested £4,981, coupled to the loss of commission fees on loans and commodity brokering on behalf of other Company employees reduced his annual profits from around £12,000 to £4,000.[43]

Siphoning off public revenue for the purpose of private commerce, either through lending to the presidency treasuries or winning major contracts was a consistent feature of the highly unstable economic regimes created by the Company's early raj. Prior to being forced like Claud Alexander to give up his business portfolio in 1784, Robert Lindsay, the son of the fifth earl of Balcarres, combined his official duties with a range of entrepreneurial projects. As revenue collector at Sylhet he had preferential access to a secure stream of public income with which to collateralise his personal credit and trade. He shipped piece goods from Calcutta to Dacca, controlled a manufactory producing 10,000 tons of lime per annum, and in 1783 secured a government contract to ship rice to Madras. Progress on the rice contract was expedited by a £10,000 advance from the presidency government to facilitate a ship-building programme. The extent of his own textile and foodstuff shipping operations can be grasped from the fact that by 1785 Lindsay owned a fleet of fourteen vessels, one of which included the oceangoing 600-ton *Caledonia*. Unable after 1784 to conduct such commerce openly, Lindsay used trusted free merchants and medical associates. He relied on the Scots surgeon Robert Hunter as his permanent contact in Dacca and a free merchant Mr Bruce acted as a front for his activities. This type of networking involved sustained, strong vertical links based on mutual trust and reciprocal interest.

The advantageous conditions created by the Company's growing political, financial and economic power enabled social and human capital to combine in highly productive ways. Micro- and meso-networks constituted substantial if intangible commercial assets. They could mobilise and project a person or a commercial partnership's reputation for honesty, trustworthiness and competence in ways that enhanced human capital.[44] As in other areas of Company expansion, the key to success lay in combining and exchanging these social assets for monetary gains. The capacity to manage this transformation consistently and successfully brought wealth and power for many, although certainly not all. James Alexander used the free mariner Captain Thomas Powney to ship large quantities of Bengal rice into Madras. In 1763 the Ulsterman's possession of the rice contract for the Madras army was worth £12,767. Thomas Parry from Montgomery developed his Madras free merchant house without the advantage of the cultural and human capital invested in a senior civil servant like Alexander. His route to wealth initially involved offering civil servants and other Europeans credit facilities at 12.5 per cent interest, a borrowing rate simply not possible in Europe. By 1800 profits stood at £4,000 per annum, which enabled diversification into shipping and presidency government contracts. In July 1806 Parry & Co. won an order to supply belts and accoutrements to the Madras army worth £9,600.[45]

The diversity of business strategies points to the importance of free traders in the quasi-public–private partnerships that enabled the accumulation of monetary capital. Whatever the specific commercial activity, all these connections aimed at the same basic objective. The common use of micro- or extended meso-networks, and the blending of social and financial credit was designed to turn a sojourner's human capital into its financial equivalent. Scots, Irish and Welsh individuals were no different from their English, French, Dutch or other European counterparts in this respect. But similarity of tactics does not mean micro- and meso-level networks were all alike. Profiteering was common to all, but regardless of their size, location and function, networks were intrinsically social constructs. They evolved particular configurations which relied on intangible assets such as reputation and verifiable personal attributes like education, competence and family status. Pre-existing social and cultural standing derived from a sojourner's place of origin assumed a new importance in the context of the extreme distances and high-risk, high-return character of the Asia trades. Distance amplified the problem of ensuring trust and effective, secure commercial activity. Dependence to a greater or lesser extent on human and social capital in these circumstances often meant relying on links shaped by kinship, locality, region and even perceptions of Irishness, Welshness and Scottishness. Reusing kinship or co-operating with individuals from the same place of origin was underpinned by the knowledge that poor performance or an abuse of trust in Asia would become known and create problems for families at home.[46] These dynamics explain why the transhemispheric nature of business in the Eastern Empire ironically encouraged local, regional and, less consistently, national patterns of affiliation. The 'clannishness' associated with Scots in the Empire, for example, can be read in this context as less a matter of national chauvinism and more a manifestation of the fact that conditions in Asia made glocalism an act of economic rationalism.[47] The operating realities of a proto-global empire meant there was a surprising amount of dependency on assumptions about an individual's human and social capital.

Networks and identities: European, national and familial

While the private traders' role in linking South Asian merchants and Company officials to commodities and markets shaped the expansion of the country trade, the sociocultural environment in which these exchanges were situated remains underexplored. Networking was not just about making money. Intimate micro-bonds of familiarity and sociability made daily life manageable in the face of extreme conditions. Arthur Cole and Archibald Seton of Touch, a Bengal civil servant stationed in Delhi in the early 1800s, exhibited forms of acute cultural disorientation, isolation and homesickness that were probably common to most, although certainly not all, Europeans.[48] The high-risk/high-return sojourn to Asia left many fearing for their health and lives. The climate and environment threatened a sudden death, messy in a bodily, legal, financial and familial sense. Over and above the cultural, religious and social 'otherness' of Asia was the pervasive awareness of demographic insignificance. However powerful the English East India Company became, its employees and those licensed by it always retained a nagging awareness of the severe population imbalance between themselves and local people.[49] Unsurprisingly, sojourners developed a range of coping and acculturating strategies. Not the least of these was the attempt to recreate Europe in Asia. The social, cultural, artistic and recreational norms of the larger settlements as well as the food, drink, fashions and publications associated with the latest trends in Europe became markers of 'white', 'Christian' and 'European' identity.[50]

These conditions necessitated the constant development and redevelopment of micro- and meso-networks that could bind together dispersed populations exposed to high death rates and constant turnover. An awareness of their dependency, however limited, on South Asians shaped the ways in which Europeans of all nationalities conceived of themselves. Monetary gifts authorised by last wills and testaments show that relations between Irish and Scots officials and their 'dubashes' and 'banyans' could be cordial. Whether these were magnanimous gestures or a device calculated to secure post-mortem reputations is less significant than the fact that the number of testaments leaving such bequests constituted a small percentage of the total.[51] Formulaic acts of generosity should not disguise the growing social distancing and discrimination that characterised European attitudes, Scots, Irish and Welsh included, towards Asians and their societies. Cultural and increasingly racial stereotypes absorbed at home were reinforced overseas in ways that heightened a sense of common European-ness while 'othering' Asians, often in highly prejudicial ways.[52] The language of 'colour' was always evident in an era supposedly less concerned with ideas of racial superiority when compared to attitudes after the early 1800s.[53] The use by Scots, Irish and Welsh sojourners of such rhetoric demonstrates how they internalised and redeployed European notions of difference. The terminology of John Maxwell Stone in 1771 shows the negative tone around 'colour' becoming embedded in everyday thinking. Stone noted that a deceased associate's business involved 'money lent out to black people', by which he meant 'Kachur Varmiah' and 'Abarah Khan', both major creditors of the Nawab of Arcot.[54] His comments at once capture the pragmatic need for commercial association with South Asians and the simultaneous heightened awareness of 'white' identity. In adopting such attitudes Scots, Irish and Welsh buttressed their own national, British and corporate identities, but also developed a more explicit sense of cosmopolitan, transnational European-ness.

Despite the argument that empire created new forms of Britishness, the nature of expansion in Asia challenges assumptions that one identity was privileged by involvement overseas. Co-operation among different European nationals generated expansive but ephemeral business links.[55] Cultural, social, financial and professional contacts blossomed at various levels. The legacy of the Company's use of 'military Europe', for example, produced an enduring Swiss and German-speaking presence in the presidency armies into the early 1800s. The cosmopolitan demography of the main settlements is captured in the 1810 Madras census of private residents. It showed that the forty-one Scots comprising the second most significant British and Irish nationality were still outnumbered by forty-two Danish-Norwegians. If the Company remained resolutely 'English' in its official structures, its human resources and associational cultures support the characterisation of imperial Britain as an innately European society.[56]

There was one reason more than any other which drew British and Irish individuals and networks into close commercial and professional contact with other European nationals. One of the greatest ironies of sojourning under the auspices of the English East India Company was that while human capital was highly mobile, accumulations of finance capital were not. The problem of remitting fortunes back to Europe was a persistent complaint and a constant source of anxiety. High-ranking civil servants like John Graham, senior military officers like Sir John Cumming of Altyre and Sir Archibald Campbell of Inverneill and medical men like Dr John Fleming, all complained about the obstacles to safely realising their profits. As John Maxwell Stone noted in 1771, 'it is indeed a general complaint that people know not how to get their money home'.[57] The issue brought into sharp relief the ambiguous relationship between the Company's public interests and the private concerns of its employees. Severe restrictions were placed on the number of bills of exchange which could be lodged with the treasuries in Calcutta, Bombay, Madras, Benkulen and Canton for repayment in

London. The purpose was to ensure that presidency governments balanced their accounts. In Madras in 1771 the amount was only £35,000–50,000 per annum, with preferential rates of access and exchange given to civil servants.[58] While these arrangements were eminently sensible from the viewpoint of the corporation as a government, they constituted a frustrating choke point in the final stage of the sojourning cycle. The result was that British and Irish civil servants, officers and free merchants and mariners alike sought alternative arrangements with European East India companies and private merchant houses in order to bypass official restraints on remittance.[59] Examples of the vital European dimension to the return phase of the British and Irish sojourning cycle in Asia are shown in Table 6.5.

All British and Irish personnel used these trans-European connections. In the mid-1770s John Maxwell Stone, despite his Protestant background, relied on a merchant house with diasporic Irish connections, Messrs Sulivan and De Souza at Manila, to transfer £17,800 in bills to Canton for his

Table 6.5 Transnational remittance networks

Date	Remitting individual	Free merchant	European channel	Total
1775	John Maxwell Stone (Anglo-Irish)	–	Law de Lauriston (French)	£1,160
1775	John Maxwell Stone (for Josias De Pre)	–	Messrs Sulivan & De Souza (Manila & Canton)	£17,800
1776	Edward Monkton (Irish)	George Smith (Scot)	Swedish EIC	£15,588
1775	George Graham (Scot)	Robert Mayne (Scot)	Mayne & Co. (Libson)	£8,250
1775	John, George, Thomas Graham (Scots)	Messrs Le Ray de Chaumont & Gourade		£10,000
1775	George & Robert Graham (Scots)	David Killican	Lorient	£11,125
1780	Alexander Pringle (Scot)	–	VOC	£2,235
1786	George Graham (Scot)	Mayne & Co.	David Brown & De Connich & Co. (Copenhagen)	£26,805
1799	Thomas Graham (Scot)	Messrs Edwards & Temple (London)	Mayne & Co. (Lisbon)	£11,466

(Source: TCD, MS3551/2, fos. 60, 63–4, 120–2; NRS, GD29/2058/4, 6a; GD29/2075/5; GD29/2061/5; GD2066/1; GD29/2146: Calcutta, 8 April 1799; NRS, GD246/30/2/4).

patron in England.[60] By connecting senior Company officials with private traders Stone enabled the boundaries of the British, Spanish and Chinese empires to be blurred and traversed so that a major segment of Du Pre's fortune could be successfully transferred. Scots utilised the same financial strategies but relied to a larger extent on northern European channels through links to the Danish, Swedish and Dutch companies.

The patterns in Table 6.5 point to how the metropolitan provinces' historic alignments within Europe's internal economy shaped global networks servicing the return of colonial capital from Asia. One example of this tendency is the interaction between Scottish free traders and the Swedish and Danish companies, in which a number of Scots served throughout the eighteenth and early nineteenth centuries.[61] In 1776 George Smith from Fordyce in Banffshire, a Bombay-based free merchant, deployed contacts in Gothenburg created during the earlier North Sea phase of his career. The Scot arranged for the Swedish Company to use the capital of Edward Monckton, a Bengal official and scion of an Anglo-Irish aristocratic family, to transfer to Europe via Canton £15,588 worth of cargo.[62] The alignment of these remittance channels represent the transplantation of older Northern Europe connections into Asia's dynamic economies.

The pragmatic but ephemeral nature of these links should not detract from their importance. Irish, Scots or Welsh individuals quickly adopted whatever connections were appropriate for the conditions they faced. Irish Protestants like Stone used Spanish conduits but also developed credit and remittance transactions with French merchant houses. A key reason for the success of the Graham meso-network lay in combining the different functions of civil servants and free merchants and mariners to facilitate intra-corporate and transnational channels of remittance (Table 6.5 and Appendix 6.1). The Grahams' social capital functioned as a complex series of trust connections and financial transactions. Strong vertical bonds of kinship operated with intra-European and new Asia-based contacts to move large volumes of human, social and monetary capital over oceanic distances. The proto-global connections generated by these activities were noticeably hybrid in character, combining provincial, regional, national and transnational bonds in new ways.

Similar dynamics helped forge new levels of association that constituted a corporate form of Britishness, unique to the regulatory frameworks and social world created by the English East India Company. Sojourners arriving in Asia sought the acquaintance and patronage of senior merchants, financiers, administrators or military officers, regardless of nationality. This was only logical: material and career progress were the ultimate aims of human mobility in the East Indies, not the transplantation of local or provincial Irish, Scottish and Welsh loyalties. Commercial and financial tactics adapted accordingly and influenced the protean nature of associational identities. When he arrived in Calcutta, George Bogle had letters of introduction to no fewer than seventeen individuals. While Scots formed an important minority of these potential friends, they were not the most immediately effective. In his early letters back to Scotland Bogle singled out a non-Scot, Henry Higginson, for the value of his friendship. Similarly, Thomas Graham believed that much of his early career benefited from the patronage of his English superior, Nathaniel Middleton. A key positive influence for Arthur Cole upon taking up his civil servant post in Madras was the professional and personal friendship of Sir John Craddock, an English military officer with strong connections to the Wellesley circle. As commander in chief of the Madras army Craddock was expected to offer such protection to new arrivals from genteel or aristocratic backgrounds. A common way of building the trust and familiarity that convinced senior patrons to endorse the human capital of their clients was to invite them to become members of their extended households.[63] This form of 'familial proto-state' combined older ideas of kinship, protection and personal loyalty with official status and colonial power. It was a key operating characteristic of the Company's early raj.[64] Such arrangements were a practical recognition of the potential for transforming human capital into professional standing, career advancement and, hopefully, material gain.

These types of connections emerged organically over the span of a person's time in Asia. They usually evolved as stronger vertical micro-networks compared to the transient European contacts that characterised the remittance phase of the sojourning cycle. This more defined layer of association was supplemented by other influences. The British and Irish populations of the main Company settlements were exposed to new languages and conceptions of corporate as well as national Britishness. Debates over the jurisdiction of the supreme court of Bengal in the 1770s and 1780s generated a public discourse that envisaged the Company's employees and those licensed by it as a transplanted community with the same legal and political privileges as those in Britain and Ireland. The growth in identification with Britishness can be traced in the censuses of Madras and Calcutta from the 1770s to the early 1800s. In response to the question of their nationality, a number of free traders (although always a minority) began self-labelling as 'Britons'.[65] The broadening of identities sparked by residence in Asia can also be glimpsed in the wide circle of friends and associates who entrusted their letters to Robert Lindsay when he departed Calcutta for Britain in 1789. Ongoing attempts to secure his family's estates in Fife ensured that Lindsay remained strongly focused on priorities in Scotland: yet of the forty-five letters he carried back only nine were from Scots to other Scots, the rest reflected the extent of his English and Irish acquaintances in India and in London.[66]

If the example of the Irish, Scots and Welsh show the emergence of new European modes of business and British self-identification, they also point to the ongoing importance of the provincial and the local. The persistence and renewal of Scottish, Irish and Welsh national identities occurred in a number of ways. The practice by which established figures offered new arrivals the use of their households until they found their own accommodation has already been highlighted in the case of Cole and Craddock. While essentially a practical exercise, this social convention cocooned sojourners in domestic situations that perpetuated links to their place of origin in Britain and Ireland.[67] The tendency to invite individuals from the same backgrounds to join households was a pronounced sociological feature of the Company's settlements.[68] When Peter Boileau, son of a Dublin merchant, arrived Madras in 1764 it was a fellow Irish Huguenot, Brigadier-General John Caillaud, who offered him his residence. When Arthur Cole disembarked at Calcutta his equivalent hosting network took the form of an invitation to stay with Francis MacNaghtan, a fellow Ulsterman and son-in-law of yet another Irishman, the Bengal court justice, Sir William Dunkin (Appendix 6.2).[69]

The small number of Welsh in Asia makes recovering similar examples for that group more challenging. However, the published comments of the free mariner Joseph Price, who described himself as a 'Taffy', show that ideas of transnational Welshness retained some currency in Asia.[70] With much greater numbers joining the civil service, army and medical corps, the capacity to sustain 'Scottish' households was substantial. When George Ross from Aberdeenshire took up his writer's post in Benkulen in 1767, it was another Scot, the senior council member Robert Nairne from Perthshire, 'who nearly acts in some measure the part of a father to me'.[71] The explicit allusion to quasi-paternal support resonates with the emphasis placed on the familial proto-state as a key determinant shaping the tenor and tone of Company expansion in this period.[72] In Ross's case it also demonstrates that ideas of imagined family went beyond immediate kin links to encompass imagined regional and national affinities. The example of Stair Dalrymple, who disembarked at Calcutta as a Company writer in 1752, confirms that wider loyalties, beyond family or locality, could drive such hybrid familial-commercial patronage. In a letter home to his family in North Berwick, he noted:

> Upon my arrival here, Mr John Brown, a Scottish gentleman of distinguished veracity and honour, sent me an invitation to come and stay at his house until I got lodgings, without the least knowledge of me, or without recommendation of any sort, but only from a knowledge of my friends in Scotland.[73]

These trends explain why ongoing association with individuals from their regional and national place of origin form such a pronounced feature of the meso-networks developed by the Graham brothers and Arthur Cole (Appendices 6.1 and 6.2). The Graham network shows the innately interactive, overlapping nature of European, British, Scottish, local and familial dimensions. George, John and Thomas became acquainted with some of the most powerful EIC families in London and Asia. George remitted home via Canton over £7,200 in 1774 through the influence of an English supercargo, Charles Crommellin. The Grahams dealt in diamonds with Richard Barwell and William Lushington, scions of two of London's premier merchant-financier dynasties.[74] The pragmatic needs of imperial commerce tempered any counterproductive tendency towards either familial or Scottish exclusivity. The network was open ended, integrative and maximised a wide range of commercial opportunity. Yet a strong local and regionally Scottish foundation still predominated over these less central British connections. The network's key European node at Lisbon relied upon the fact that the Grahams were first cousins of Sir William Mayne who controlled the powerful Lisbon- and London-based merchant house of Mayne & Co. It was often kinship and not Scottish or British nationality that enabled oceanic trading associations.

The Indian account books of George Graham between 1772 and 1775 confirm that kinship and Scottish links remained fundamental during his time in Asia. These years constituted the zenith of George's commercial activities, with a turnover of £97,200 from a variety of ventures including voyages to the Red Sea and army contracts. Of the nineteen separate accounts that made up his portfolio in these years, twelve were with kinsmen or other Scots. This balance between transnational, British and Scottish contacts suggests that the Graham network can be best envisaged as a series of layered associations, with strong, vertical micro-networks branching out into expansive, horizontal connections.

These transposed forms of Irish, Welsh or Scottishness need to be considered alongside the corporate, British, European and 'white' identities which each sojourner adopted in combinations and degrees unique to their own backgrounds and experience. The high-risk environment of Asia shaped the creation of households of familiarity, social intimacy and familial trust. Such strategies did not denote underdeveloped business methods. They represented the reworking of older bonds of kinship and imagined kinship as a logical response to Asia's 'otherness' and its unique trading geographies and environments. This explains why kin-based trust networks formed such a pronounced feature of the Company's professional, administrative, military and commercial world before c.1820. Some of the largest and smallest commercial operations active under the aegis of the Company relied on such links to function effectively. The role of family-based co-partnership has been noted in relation to major agency houses such as Scott & Co. and

Ferguson, Fairlie and Co. But these organisations were not exceptional. The emphasis on the capital-intensive character of British and Irish trade in Asia can be deceptive. Kinship helped drive the country trade, with all its implications for the character and timing of colonial expansion, as surely as the corporate sovereignty of the Company. Parry & Co. and the family outfit of Binny & Co., whose co-partners originated from Montrose, used kinship over four decades to perpetuate capital accumulation and transfer. The same principle was used by the Irish free merchant, Peter Brodkin: when he expanded his operations in 1784 it was his nephew, Nicholas Connolly Hussey, who joined him. The Scot Thomas Umpherston commenced Ceylon trading in 1784 and was joined by his brother, James, five years later.[75]

These arrangements were commonplace rather than exceptional. They were designed to deal with the problem of conducting trade and financial operations over transhemispheric distances, extended timescales and with limited international legal frameworks, credit facilities, shipping and insurance arrangements. The central place of kinship in a globalised sojourning economy where social and human capital remained vital currencies is captured in the reaction of the Stirling of Keir family in 1735 to the news that a younger brother of the free merchant, Archibald Stirling would join him in Asia as a military cadet:

> Two brothers in the same place would be a mutual advantage to one another because in case of an accident the one would be on the spot to take care the effects of the other were not embezelled [sic] as it commonly happens in those distant countries; this would be an indispensable way to raise both their credits.[76]

Conclusion

A better understanding of metropolitan provincials in the country trade enables a more developed sense of how and when Ireland, Scotland and Wales accessed the pre-1815 British Empire's different commercial branches. Far more so than the corporation's monopoly control of international commerce between Asia and Europe, the country trades represented the nearest equivalent in the Eastern Empire to the deregulated conditions that characterised the British Atlantic.[77] Recovering the outlines of involvement in this area provides an indication of whether patterns of metropolitan provincial prominence in areas like transatlantic provisioning, linen, tobacco or slavery found parallels in Asia.[78]

The figures in Tables 6.1 to 6.4 confirm that participation developed very different trajectories across the two hemispheres. Sustained Scottish,

Irish and Welsh engagement with Atlantic world commerce and settlement dated to the seventeenth century. By contrast, neither the Welsh nor the Irish developed a substantial presence in the private trades in Asia, although there was a tendency to cluster around the administrative and legal service sectors. This low profile was part of a wider pattern which had fundamental medium- and longer-term consequences for Irish society and its relations with the United Kingdom and the Empire. In attempting to explain the development of long eighteenth-century Ireland, historians have drawn helpful comparisons with Scotland and its place within expansion and imperialism. There is now a much better understanding of the significance for Britain's longer-term development arising from substantial Scottish commercial and migratory involvement in the Atlantic.[79] By contrast, Britain's ability to limit Irish access to territories and related branches of trade up to and beyond 1780 formed a source of constitutional irritation rather than a means of integration. By the time the kingdom entered into union with Great Britain in 1800, the partially dismembered Western Empire was experiencing major realignments in key economies such as the slave trade and plantation production. These changes served to blunt Ireland's competitive advantages in geography and provisioning at precisely the moment imperial trade was held up as offering the sort of major economic opportunities that had transformed Scotland.[80] Constraint in the Atlantic, already evident by 1780 and becoming more so after 1800, made what happened in Asia all the more important. Proportionate participation in a dynamic area of new imperial growth could have helped offset problems elsewhere. Instead, the underdevelopment of Irish commercial networks in Asia represented a fundamental problem for the new British and Irish union and its capacity to deliver diverse and sustainable avenues of opportunity through empire. Scottish involvement was larger than that of the Irish or Welsh by a considerable margin. By congregating in disproportionate numbers in the free merchant and mariner sectors, Scottish sojourners were able to maximise connections between the official and private economies and play a substantial role in the vitally important remittance trade.

Beyond the implications for assessments of Scotland, Ireland and Wales's place in the Empire, analysis of the country trade points to how finance-poor societies accessed one of the most capital-reliant wings of European expansion. Through these commercial actors, British and Irish society developed diverse monetary and non-monetary investment strategies to fully exploit proto-globalisation in Asia. Recapturing the patterns of association between free traders and the EIC's personnel demonstrates how the corporation's formal economy and its complex governmental and financial systems were more accessible than its outward monopoly character might suggest. Integrating the profits derived from officials with private trade ventures was a key tactic for the likes of James Alexander, Robert Lindsay, the Parrys and the Graham brothers, to less well-known merchants such as Peter Brodkin. Traversing and blurring the official and private worlds of the Company between Asia and Europe meant free traders were at the forefront of the meso-networks that played such a central, connective function in the evolving global economy.

A defining feature of these integrative activities was the intermixing of global and local influences, a dualistic aspect of empire that historians associate with the early modern phase of proto-globalisation.[81] The networking strategies of the Coles or Grahams are case studies of this historicised 'glocalism' in action. Their associative behaviours reveal the complex, polycentric modes of entry into the world economy by parts of Britain and Ireland that had little sustained contact with Asia prior to the eighteenth century. At the heart of these meso-networks lay impressive reserves of human and social capital that belie the reputation of countries like Scotland and Ireland for impoverishment. They also epitomise the difficult-to-trace processes of converting human capital into its monetary form. The pronounced dependency on socially constituted forms of wealth which characterised the commercial world of the country traders underscores the vital role of the 'familial proto-state' in the operation of co-partnerships like Parry and Co. of Madras and Forbes & Co. of Bombay. By the early 1800s these were among some of the Empire's largest and most aggressive private merchant houses.[82] As with so many other features of the Company's world in London and Asia, the old mixed with the new and the familial and the local bled into the imperial and the global.

The fact that Scots formed a substantially larger presence in this private trader economy compared to the other metropolitan provincials was significant beyond simply the matter of numbers. Free merchants and mariners like George Graham were vital in enabling the return phase of the sojourning cycle. In redeploying wealth from one hemisphere to another, this group's importance belies their relatively small numbers and lack of official status. As in the formal employment sectors of the Company, Scots were represented much more prominently compared to Welsh or Irish interests. The consequences of this competitive advantage can be traced in the volume and transformative influence of returning imperial profits.

Notes

1 IOR, B/48, p. 723; B/41, pp. 98, 471; B/43, p. 225; B/47, p. 76; B/53, p. 206; B/57, p. 146; B/61, p. 456.

2 Marshall, *East Indian Fortunes*, pp. 3–24, 48–56; P. J. Marshall, 'Private British Trade in the Indian Ocean before 1800', in A. Das Gupta and M. N. Pearson (eds), *India and the Indian Ocean, 1500–1800* (Calcutta: Oxford University Press, 1987), pp. 276–97; W. E. Cheong, *Mandarins & Merchants, Jardine Matheson & Co., A China Agency of the Early Nineteenth Century* (London: Curzon, 1979), p. 10; Margaret Steven, *Merchant Campbell 1769–1846: A Study in Colonial Trade* (Melbourne: Oxford University Press, 1965), passim.
3 Holden Furber, *John Company at Work: A Study of European Expansion in India in the Late Eighteenth Century* (New York: Octagon, 1970), pp. 161–5; Furber, *Rival Empires of Trade*, p. 185.
4 S. B. Singh, *European Agency Houses in Bengal* (Calcutta: Firma K. L. Mukhopadhyay, 1966), p. 37; Marshall, 'Economic and Political Expansion: The Case of Oudh', 468; Ian Bruce Watson, *Foundation for Empire: English Private Trade in India, 1659–1760* (New Delhi: Vikas, 1980), pp. 7, 16–17, 79–80, 359–60; Bowen, *The Business of Empire*, pp. 89–90; Webster, *The Twilight of the East India Company*, pp. 10–11.
5 Bayly, *Indian Society*, pp. 45–64; Tomlinson, 'From Campsie to Kedgeree', 769–91.
6 Mentz, *English Gentleman Merchant*, pp. 13–14; Tomlinson, 'From Campsie to Kedgeree', 769–86.
7 Bayly, 'The First Age of Global Imperialism', 28–33; Tony Ballantyne, 'Empire, Knowledge and Culture: From Proto-Globalisation to Modern Globalisation', in Hopkins, *Globalisation in World History*, p. 116; Riello, *Cotton*, pp. 89–92.
8 Singh, *European Agency Houses*, p. 10; Tomlinson, 'From Campsie to Kedgeree', 770.
9 Riddy, 'Warren Hastings', p. 42; George McGilvary, 'Scottish Agency Houses in South East Asia, c.1760–1813', in Devine and McCarthy, *The Scottish Experience in Asia*, pp. 75–96.
10 Kenneth Pomeranz and Steven Topik, *The World that Trade Created: Society, Culture and the World Economy, 1400 to the Present* (London and New York: Routledge, 2018), pp. 8–13.
11 Veevers, '"Inhabitants of the Universe"', pp. 101–3; Finn, 'Anglo-Indian Lives', 49–65; Finn, 'Family Formations', pp. 100–17; Tomlinson, 'From Campsie to Kedgeree', 769–85; Stephen Foster, *A Private Empire* (Millers Point, NSW: Murdoch Books, 2010) pp. 10–21; Rothschild, *The Inner Lives of Empires*, pp. 1–58.
12 Crosbie, *Irish Imperial Networks*, pp. 44–51; Bailey, *Irish London*, pp. 124–5, 143–56.
13 Mackillop, 'A Reticent People?', p. 156; Bowen, 'Asiatic Interactions', pp. 171–3.
14 IOR, B/47, pp. 73, 76; B/48, p. 723; B/51, p. 236; B/54, pp. 132, 229; B/67, p. 350.
15 Riddy, 'Warren Hastings', p. 42; McGilvary, *East India Patronage*, p. 232.
16 IOR, B/40, pp. 279, 247; B/41, pp. 98, 101, 11, 260; B/43 pp. 188, 217, 226; B/47, p. 60; B/52, pp. 207, 324.

17 NLS, MS1367, fos. 64, 118; Conway, *Britain, Ireland and Continental Europe*, pp. 93–107.
18 IOR, O/5/26–27: European Inhabitants, Bengal, 1793–1812; O/5/30–31: European Inhabitants, Madras, 1702–1838.
19 IOR, O/5/30, fos. 130–4.
20 Sramek, 'Rethinking Britishness', 822–43.
21 *The East India Kalendar; or, Asiatic register for 1800* (London: J. Debrett, 1800), pp. 169–74.
22 George McGilvary, 'The Return of the Scottish Nabob', in Varricchio, *Back to Caledonia*, pp. 91–2.
23 Marshall, 'Private British Trade', pp. 276–97; P. J. Marshall, 'Private British Investment in Eighteenth Century Bengal', in P. Tuck (ed.), *The East India Company, IV: Trade, Finance and Power* (London: Routledge, 1998), pp. 127–41; Tomlinson, 'From Campsie to Kedgeree', 769–88.
24 NLS, GD 51/3/3/85: 15 February 1799; HL, Stowe Collection, ST34, pp. 4–5; GCA, T-LX3/12/17; T-LX3/16/2: London 15 October 1802.
25 IOR, O/5/30, fos. 7–15, 210–213; O/5/26, 'List of Private Trade Europeans resident Calcutta and in the several districts, 13 November 1804.'; B/71, pp. 520, 565; B/75, p. 648; L/AG/34/29/199, pp. 158–9; L/AG/34/29/10 [1797], 16; TNA, PROB 11/1276, pp. 260–1; Bowen, 'Asiatic Interactions', pp. 156–73.
26 IOR, B/75, p. 538; O/5/30, fos. 77–88, 'Register of Europeans who are not in the Service of the Honourable East India Company, Madras, 1795'; LAG/34/29/188, p. 57.
27 IOR, O/5/26, 'List of Private Trade Europeans resident in Calcutta … 13 November 1804'; O/5/30, pp. 7–15; NLS, MS6360, p. 18.
28 Bailey, *Irish London*, pp. 54–121; B. H. Macpherson, 'Scots Law in the Colonies', *Juridical Review* (1995), pt. 1, 191–207.
29 IOR, O/5/30, fos. 130–4.
30 Bailey, *Irish London*, pp. 144–6; Johnston (ed.), *History of the Irish Parliament*, vol. IV, p. 266; *The East India Kalendar; For the Year 1793* (London: J. Debrett, 1793), p. 57; TCD, MS3767/13.
31 Johnston, *History of the Irish Parliament*, vol. IV, pp. 106–7; IOR, O/5/30, fos. 210–13; L/AG/34/29/197, pp. 160–72.
32 GCA, Bogle Papers, Bo. 12/2: 5 September 1770; Bo 12/3: Calcutta, 25 October 1770; Bo 12/8: 4 February 1771; GCA, T-SK/11/2/29; NLS, MS1256, fos. 174–5; MS1367, fo. 64.
33 Furber, *Rival Empires of Trade*, pp. 299–305; Theon Wilkinson, *Two Monsoons* (London: Duckworth, 1976), pp. 2–16; Marshall, 'British Society in India', 89–105; Kate Teltscher, 'Writing Home and Crossing Cultures: George Bogle in Bengal and Tibet, 1770–1775', in Wilson, *A New Imperial History*, pp. 281–96.
34 IOR, L/MIL/9/85 [1754], pp. 64–5; B/84, pp. 331, 343; B/82, p. 303; Hodson, *List of the Officers of the Army of Bengal*, vol. II, p. 314; NRS, GD29/2057/7, 13–14; GD29/2069/1.
35 NLS, MS1367, fo. 64, MS1091, fos. 169, 212–213; NRS, GD29/2057/2; GD1/594/1.

36 Marshall, *Bengal: The British Bridgehead*, pp. 86–7, 105–11; Marshall, 'Masters and Banians', pp. 191–213; Neild-Basu, 'The Dubashes of Madras', 4–31; NRS, GD248/413/1, 'Journal of Lt. John Grant', p. 38.
37 GCA, Bogle Papers, Bo 12/2: Calcutta, 5 September 1770; IOR, J/1/15, pp. 193–7; NRS, GD1/594/1: Edinburgh, 17 August 1802.
38 Shubhra Chakrabarti, 'Collaboration and Resistance: Bengal Merchants and the English East India Company, 1757–1833', *Studies in History*, 10 (1994), 105–29.
39 TCD, MS3551, fo. 12, No. 23; fo. 23–26: No. 39; MS3551/2, fo. 57, No. 73; PRONI, D/2432/1/2: 'An Account of debts due me at Ft St George as per Mr Russell's Accounts.'
40 PRONI, D2432/1/7: Mootejiul, 24 November 1771; D/2432/5/4/2, 'State of James Alexander's concerns in India'.
41 Nechtman, *Nabobs*, pp. 81–91
42 NLS, MS3385, fos. 77–9; Marshall, *East Indian Fortunes*, pp. 23–4.
43 NRS, GD393/6/1, fos. 1, 99–102, 113–114; GD1/594/1: Edinburgh, 6 March 1797.
44 NRS, GD392/6/1, fos. 99–102; NLS, ACC 9769/30/4/74.
45 Hilton Brown, *Parrys of Madras: A Story of British Enterprise in India* (Madras: Parry & Co., 1954), pp. 8–28; PRONI, D/2432/1/2, Madras, 7 November 1763.
46 IOR, J/1/8, pp. 357–60; B/87, pp. 354–5; NLS, Acc 9769/30/4/375; Acc 9769/30/5/1; AUL, MS3346, Gordon Castle, 29 December 1769: James Ross to Miss Ross of Arnage; No date, 1770: Miss Ross to Forbes of Waterton.
47 Price, *Some Observations and Remarks*, pp. 113–17.
48 GCA, Bogle Papers, Bo. 2: Letter Book of George Bogle of Calcutta, p. 137; NRS, GD1/594/1: Edinburgh, 22 March 1796; NRS, GD128/1/2/1: Seringapatam, 10 January 1783; GD288/322: Madras, 1808; NLS, MS19208, fos. 95–9; TCD, MS3551, fos. 2, 10, 11; TCD, MS3767/1/16, 27.
49 GCA, Bo. 2: Letter Book of George Bogle of Calcutta, 1770–1771, p. 103; NRS, GD248/413/1, 'Journal of Lt. John Grant', pp. 39–42; GD1/768/10: 26 March 1768.
50 P. J. Marshall, 'The Whites of British India, 1780–1830: A Failed Colonial Society?', *International History Review*, 12 (1990), 26–8; Marshall, 'British Society in India', 101–2; GCA, Bogle Papers, Bo 25: Calcutta, 25 December 1770; NRS, GD393/6/1, fo. 1; NRS, GD22/2/145/2: 3 July 1768.
51 IOR, P/328/61 [1759], pp. 43–7; L/AG/34/29/187 [1785], pp. 21–2; [1786] pp. 128–30; L/AG/34/29/188, pp. 92–5; L/AG/34/29/195, p. 634; L/AG/34/29/206, pp. 45–8.
52 NRS, RH4/136/1/84-V2; NLS, MS360, p. 182.
53 L. Poliakov, 'Racism from the Enlightenment to the Age of Imperialism', in R. Ross (ed.), *Racism and Colonialism: Essays on Ideology and Social Structure* (The Hague: M. Nijhoff, 1982), pp. 55–64.
54 TCD, MS3551, fos. 12, 92–3.
55 Douglas Hamilton, 'Brothers in Arms: Crossing Imperial Boundaries in the Eighteenth-Century Dutch West Indies', in Stephanie Barczewski and Martin

Farr (eds), *The MacKenzie Moment and Imperial History: Essays in Honour of Professor John MacKenzie* (Cham: Palgrave Macmillan, 2019), pp. 287–309; Mentz, *English Gentleman Merchant*, p. 242.
56 IOR, O/5/30, fos. 198–219; L/AG/34/29/201, p. 261; TNA, WO17/1738: 'Present State of HM Troops under the Command of Major General James Stuart, 1 Sept. 1783'; NLS, MS13775, p. 2; Conway, *Britain, Ireland and Continental Europe*, pp. 237–8.
57 NRS, GD29/2056/6; GD29/2067/3a; RH 4/121/7, pp. 49, 125; NLS, MS1256, fo. 190; TCD, MS3551, fos. 2, 8–9.
58 TCD, MS3551, fos. 11–12; MS3551/2, fos. 84–5; NRS, GD46/17/4, fo. 210.
59 Ole Feldbæk, *India Trade under the Danish Flag, 1772–1808: European Enterprise and Anglo-Indian Remittance and Trade* (Odense: Studentlitteratur, 1969), pp. 30–45, 121, 255.
60 TCD, MS3552/2, fo. 60, No. 77; fo. 60–3; fo. 99, No. 150–1.
61 C. Konickx, *The First and Second Charter of the Swedish East India Company, 1731–1766* (Kortrijk: Van Ghemmert, 1980), pp. 30–6; Mackillop, 'Accessing Empire', 17–18; L. Müller, 'Scottish and Irish Entrepreneurs in Eighteenth-Century Sweden', pp. 149–63; IOR, MSS Eur/Photo Eur 109, p. 63.
62 IOR, B/81, p. 199; L/AG/34/29/341 [1790], pp. 18–26; J/1/4, pp. 157–60; B/77, pp. 188, 278; TCD, MS3551/2, fos. 120–121, No. 182.
63 GCA, Bo 12/2: Calcutta, 5 Sept. 1770, George Bogle to Robert Bogle; Bo 12/14: Calcutta, 1 Feb. 1773: George Bogle to Robert Bogle; NRS, GD 29/2136: Patna, 27 August 1775; TCD, MS3767/37, 41.
64 Finn, 'Family Formations', pp. 100–17.
65 *A Letter to the R.H. Lord North on the East India Bill now Depending in Parliament* (London: n.p., 1772), pp. 16–17; IOR, H/121, pp. 203–4.
66 NLS, Acc 9769/30/5/3.
67 Mackillop, 'Europeans, Britons and Scots', pp. 19–47; CSAS, Hunter-Blair Papers, Box 1/33; NLS, MS6360, p. 144.
68 NLS, MS1256, fo. 143; MS8252, fo. 157; MS19298, fos. 114–17; NRS, GD393/6/1, fos. 113–14, 119–27; GD1/594/1: Edinburgh, 3 May 1799; GD46/1/10/122; GD128/1/1/122; GD128/1/4/1; GD29/2057/7; GD288/322; 12 October 1805; PRONI, D/2432/1/3; GCA, TD219/8/4; T-SK/11/2/70.
69 IOR, B/75, pp. 185, 193; B/80, p. 232; B/81, pp. 163–4; J/1/5, pp. 107–10; CSAS, Boileau Papers, Box 1/1; TCD, MS3767/13; NLS MS6360, pp. 79, 83.
70 Joseph Price, *The Saddle put on the Right Horse: or, an Enquiry into the Reason why certain Persons have been denominated Nabobs, with Arrangement of those Gentlemen into their proper Classes or Real, Spurious, Reputed, or Mushroom Nabobs* (London: J. Stockdale, 1783), pp. 88–9.
71 AUL, Ross of Arnage Papers, Box 8: Fort Marlborough, 8 March 1767, 5 January 1769.
72 Finn, "Family Formations", pp. 100–17.
73 NRS, GD110/1021/3, 5–6, 8, 13. NLS, MS1367, fo. 82; GHL, MS5881/5, fos. 52–60, 63–8.
74 NRS, GD29/2058/1–32.

75 Brown, *Parrys of Madras*, pp. 41, 49; Anon, *The House of Binny* (Madras: Associated Printers, 1969), pp. 17–27; IOR, O/5/30, fos. 13–17, 77–88.
76 GCA, T-SK 11/2/18: London, 12 December 1735.
77 Devine and Rössner, 'Scotland and the Atlantic Economy', pp. 30–53.
78 Bowen, *Elites, Enterprise*, pp. 12–21; Devine, *Scotland's Empire*, pp. xxv–xxviii,
79 Cullen, 'Scotland & Ireland, 1600–1800', pp. 237–39.
80 Bartlett, 'Ireland, Empire and Union', pp. 87–8; Jackson, *The Two Unions*, p. 85, Bayly, *Imperial Meridian*, pp. 86–9; Evans, 'Wales, Munster and the English South West', pp. 56–8.
81 Bayly, '"Archaic" and "Modern" Globalisation in the Eurasian and African Arena', pp. 62–5; F. A. Nussbaum, 'Introduction', p. 10.
82 Rothschild, *The Inner Lives of Empires*, pp. 1–58; Finn, 'Family Formations', pp. 100–17.

7

Returns:
realising the human capital economy

The extent, visibility and consequences of empire returning to Britain and Ireland have become high-profile and intensely debated themes within British imperial studies.[1] Disagreements between 'maximalist' and 'minimalist' positions encompass a range of theoretical and methodological differences. In broad terms these divide into assessments of political, financial and economic impacts or an emphasis on less obvious but no less powerful influences on society and culture.[2] The claim that British and Irish society owe something of their intrinsic nature to imperialism, particularly in the areas of gender, essentialised ideas of nation and the politics of race and 'difference', elicits a range of sceptical responses. These include doubts over definitions and claims of an ahistorical lack of sensitivity to change over time, to measured assessments of the Empire's indirect role rather than its consistent transformative capacity.[3]

Such debates have led to an interest in the 'unconscious', 'everyday', 'taken for granted' and 'treacherous silences', which disguise the constitutive role of empire in metropolitan society. In this understanding, empire became so pervasive and accepted that it was simply 'there', so mundane and prosaic that it lay hidden in plain sight. Consequently, its domestic influence did not attract sustained observation but nevertheless continually shaped society and culture in direct and indirect ways.[4] If some of the debates on such questions have been combative, there is also common ground. It is significant that factors like region, religion and above all class are understood to have produced major variations in the Empire's influence on the ground.[5] There is also an acceptance that historical specifics must inform conclusions about imperialism's presence 'at home'. Meanwhile, 'minimalists' admit that the Empire did shape conditions throughout metropolitan Britain and Ireland in ways that did not always register directly on public consciousness.[6] The basis of the limited consensus lies in attempting to understand interactions in a holistic way, isolating neither 'imperial' factors nor the 'domestic' contexts that absorbed and reshaped returning empire influences even while being changed by them.

These significant themes frame any attempt to assess the pre-1815 Eastern Empire's impact upon the metropolitan provinces. Equally, however, the example of Ireland, Scotland and Wales offers new and distinctive light on such broader questions. They provide routes into exploring how such returns might look different in the materially less developed regions of the British and Irish Isles. These were, after all, societies deploying different forms of human capital through economies of migration which resulted in financial returns appearing in localities often far removed from the formal centres of imperial power. This mode of wealth exchange has not been sufficiently integrated into debates over the way empire may or may not have transformed places like Scotland, Ireland and Wales.

It is noteworthy that even those scholars sceptical of imperialism's capacity to change the British and Irish Isles accept Scotland may well have been different.[7] Indeed, there is something approaching a consensus around the role of empire in reshaping Scotland in the century or so after union. This judgement is based largely on an understandable focus on the scale and consequences of mass migration, service in the armed forces and the transformative effects of transatlantic slavery and its associated trades. Some work does exist on the possible scale and influence in Scotland of fortunes made in Asia but these remain piecemeal and grounded in a series of case studies.[8] What these explorations have demonstrated is that connections with the East Indies, if not as powerfully felt as the influence of the Atlantic world, were becoming increasingly pervasive from the 1760s onwards.[9] In contrast to this social economic emphasis, there has not been a consistent effort made to trace the Eastern Empire's less obvious sociocultural presence 'at home'.[10]

The 'maximalist' and 'minimalist' debate has, if anything, engaged even less consistently with the case of Ireland. The pre-1815 empire's internal presence is associated with the country's increasingly dynamic constitutional politics and the shaping of the British-Irish union. Detailed studies have demonstrated that the Atlantic provisioning and linen trades played a significant role in redrawing aspects of the rural and urban order, particularly in Munster and Ulster.[11] However, as with Scotland, the extent to which pre-1815 Ireland can cast new light on more general questions regarding the Empire's transformative capacity at the 'core' has yet to be fully explored.

Given the contours of these debates, charting the return of people and capital from Asia into the metropolitan provinces offers a number of fresh perspectives.[12] One is the fact that these societies participated in empire through distinctive chronological trajectories. English society's exposure to Asia, while certainly transformative over time, was gradual and had been ongoing for at least a hundred years before the metropolitan provinces began to experience the sustained effects of the Eastern connection. The compressed timescale means returning influences can be traced in Ireland, Scotland and Wales in more obvious ways and the cultural strategies used to absorb and 'domesticate' these impacts clearly understood. This approach enables a comparative Scottish, Irish and Welsh study to contribute to one of the key methodological controversies over the Empire's effect on metropolitan culture: were overseas influences present 'at home' in important, even fundamental ways, but culturally packaged to suggest otherwise?

Exploring return to Britain and Ireland of people and wealth from Asia is also a case study in the realisation and utilisation of the profits of human capital. In their different and distinctive ways, the metropolitan provinces enable human-to-monetary profits and their influence on politics, economy, society and culture to be assessed. The theme of return offers a historicised example of the full cycle of human capital – from mobilisation to realisation – that underlines the value of the metropolitan provinces in better understanding the pre-1815 empire.

Returning empire and metropolitan provincial politics

One area where it is possible to track people and profits arriving back in British and Irish society is in the realm of politics. Parliamentary elections, the use of patronage to manage pre-reformed propertied electorates and the tone of public life were sensitive barometers of the presence of personnel, money and power from the Eastern Empire. One obvious indicator of a growing intersection between electoral affairs and the EIC took the form of individuals with links to the corporation acquiring parliamentary seats. The first example of this trend in Scotland occurred in 1716 when William Steuart of Weyland, MP for the Inverness Burghs (Fortrose, Inverness, Nairn and Forres) became a director.[13] The legacies of this early metropole–region link seem to have been minimal. The arrival of John Drummond of Quarrell onto the directorate in 1722 and his time as MP for the Perthshire Burghs (Cupar, Dundee, Forfar, Perth and St Andrews) from 1727 was a different matter. His activities marked a more sustained intrusion of the Company's influence into Scotland and of Scots into the Company. People understood this at the time. In 1734 the councillors of Cupar in Fife recorded their appreciation of 'your generous inclinations to your countrymen, especially to doe [for] any one in whom any of your Burrows are nearly concerned'.[14]

By comparison with the relatively early if tentative appearance of EIC connections in Scottish parliamentary politics, Irish and Welsh electoral affairs remained largely untouched. In the case of Ireland this reflected the centrality of the country's parliament, which generated its own alignments and priorities. Patronage brokers willing to service Irish, Welsh or Scottish applications for Company posts also remained too few or intermittent to generate a sustained impact. From the 1750s, however, the factional politics of East India Company House developed a heightened presence in the provinces. The construction of East Indian electoral influence in the House of Commons and in its constituencies increased substantially as part of the infighting that broke out among directors and shareholders in the 1750s and 1760s.[15]

This metropole–province pressure began to impinge on elections in Wales when in November 1759 Robert Clive's father, Richard, was installed in the Montgomery boroughs, a position he held until his death in 1771. Clive also moved against his primary opponent, Laurence Sulivan, by intervening in Irish county politics. He bought Ballykeltie and nine neighbouring townlands in County Clare along with thirty-seven other townlands running south of the Shannon for a total of £30,315. He consolidated the property, renamed it Plassey and immediately engaged in contests against interests aligned with Sulivan.[16] This transfer of proprietary court factionalism into parliamentary seats occurred too in Scotland. The leverage exerted by the Johnstone of Westerhall faction at Leadenhall Street and in certain districts of Scotland corresponds closely to the gentry capitalism identified in relation to Yorkshire families active in the slavery based trades of the British Caribbean.[17] In both cases the resultant networks combined local and regional kinship links with the use of imperial profits and transnational finance.[18] Over and above considerable voting power among the shareholders and his role in the anti-Clive alliance with Laurence Sulivan, John Johnstone constructed a parliamentary profile among the notoriously small Scottish shire electorate. The arrival of Company influence in the Irish and Scottish counties is easy to trace because these areas had been largely free of such connections only to be suddenly immersed in nabob politics after about 1760. This abrupt trajectory explains why studying the dynamics of returning empire beyond London offers fresh perspectives and wider lessons.

Johnstone and his associates embedded themselves and their influence using the standard tactics associated with successful Company personnel contemplating a seat in the British parliament. It began with ensuring John became associated with gentility, respectability and traditions of landholding and public office. This blurred his association with 'Oriental' otherness and replaced it with conventional, respectable and traditional attributes. These repackaging tactics are vitally important in understanding why returning imperial personnel and profits could be at once both prominent and yet increasingly invisible. Johnstone's rebranding is typical to a greater or lesser extent of how senior civil servants, army officers and prominent free merchants completed the sojourning cycle. With its connotations of stability, virtue and the foundation of legitimate political and social power, land was a key commodity in the removal of unwanted imperial connotations.[19] These sociocultural transformations chime with the maximalists' insistence that the effacing of empire profits and influence and their reconfiguration into the local, normative and the mundane was a quite deliberate reintegration strategy.[20] Johnstone's purchase of two estates in the Borders, two in Stirlingshire and two in Clackmannan followed in the wake of the decision in 1768 to contest the constituency of Cromarty. The acquisition of Balconie near the Cromarty Firth bestowed the status afforded to those owning land while facilitating the splitting of feudal superiorities to create new voters. This distinctive system of proprietary electioneering in Scotland was identical to the splitting of Company stock by shareholder groups contesting director elections. Armed with these additional voters, John Johnstone's older brother, William Johnstone-Pulteney, won and held the seat until 1774.[21]

EIC factionalism spilled over into other Scottish seats. George Dempster, the MP for the Perth burghs, supported the Johnstone interest and as a result found himself in the 1768 election facing an opponent sponsored by Clive, the Edinburgh advocate, Robert Mackintosh. The language, rhetoric and impact on perceptions of public probity surrounding the Perth burgh elections are an excellent illustration of how empire in Asia began to influence not just individual families but provincial political culture more widely. In a general election in Scotland marred by unprecedented levels of corruption, the Mackintosh–Dempster dispute attracted more attention than most. The press published accusations of bribery which nurtured a widespread fear that the country's supposedly independent minded electorate were susceptible to culturally alien forms of wealth from the 'Orient'.[22] The controversies surrounding the Perth election were a local but high-profile manifestation of a much wider climate of anxiety, suspicion and hostility towards 'nabobs', their finances and political practices. Unlike John Johnstone, neither Dempster nor Mackintosh were 'nabobs' in the strict sense of the word. However, their contest seemed to herald a new prominence in Scotland of a form of politics derived directly from the empire in Asia.

Clive's attempts to build power at the metropole through use of provincial politics were not unique. Similar examples occurred to a greater or lesser extent across England, Wales and Ireland. A review of Irish, Scottish and Welsh members of the Dublin and Westminster parliaments from 1690 to 1790 demonstrates that each society experienced different levels of involvement in public life by those returning from the East Indies. The constituencies held by an individual who had spent time in Asia or by officials linked to the India Board of Control are summarised in Table 7.1.

Table 7.1 The Eastern Empire in metropolitan provincial politics

Country	Total No. of MPs	Individuals with Links to Empire in Asia	Total Seats	Seats Held by Returnees/Officials
Ireland (1695–1800)	2,271	31 (1.3%)	298	23 (7.7%)
Scotland (1754–1790)	224	20 (8.9%)	45	15 (33.3%)
Wales (1754–1790)	92	1 (1%)	24	1 (4.1%)

(Source: E. M. Johnstone (ed.), *History of the Irish Parliament, 1695–1800*, vols. II–VI (Belfast: Ulster Historical Foundation, 2002); www.historyofparliamentonline.org/research/members/members-1754-1790)

The most obvious conclusion is that returnees or those with governmental experience of Asia formed a small minority of the entire cohort of metropolitan provincial MPs. But beneath this general picture were substantial variations. Scottish society was much more connected to the Company at the political level. Nearly 10 per cent of all Scottish MPs in the second half of the eighteenth century (admittedly a smaller sample than that of Ireland) were either returnees or involved in oversight of the corporation in London. This profile contrasted with the backgrounds of representatives from Welsh constituencies and those sitting in the Irish parliament. The impact on the share of seats is even more pronounced: the vast majority in Ireland and Wales did not experience an MP with links Asia. In Scotland, one-third of all constituencies were at some point between the elections in 1754 and 1790 held by an MP linked directly to the Eastern Empire. This is a far higher percentage than any other part of the British and Irish Isles.

These national frameworks contain diverse regional patterns. James Alexander completed two sojourns to South Asia and capped his material success with the purchase of five estates across Donegal, Londonderry, Tyrone, Armagh and Antrim. Social endorsement followed with his ennoblement as the first earl of Caledon in June 1790.[23] This marked the culmination of a long period of political influence. Alexander was county MP for Londonderry from 1775 until 1790. More so than any other part of Ireland, Ulster's county interests connected to the Company in ways that shaped regional politics. This partly reflected the intergenerational influence of nabob fortunes such as those of Robert Cowan, which in the 1740s facilitated the rise to landed prominence of the Stewart family of Lord Castlereagh. In addition, Lord McCartney's time as governor of Madras and Alexander's own enduring contact with associates in Bengal helped cement the intersection of Ulster gentry with the Company's politics and patronage. In 1799, for example, Robert Brooke wrote from Calcutta thanking Caledon for introductions to a fellow Irishman, Mr Nesbitt, and asking for a recommendation to the Governor-General Richard Wellesley, second Lord Mornington, 'who is our countryman'.[24] This mundane example highlights one of the most important ways returning individuals influenced their own localities. Knowledge of the Company and its operations in Asia acquired by one generation of sojourners enabled a fresh wave of human capital investment.[25] The completion of one cycle of departure and return enabled the next cycle to begin.

Welsh society did not experience the self-sustaining mass of region–corporate links that characterised trends in Ulster from the 1770s to the 1810s, although political contests such as that by the returned Bengal merchant William Paxton in Carmarthen in the 1802 election did involve vast sums and much controversy. A cluster of former EIC personnel with estates and interests in Radnor also developed patronage links to the Company.[26] But in Scotland these connective dynamics occurred on a scale unmatched by any other metropolitan province and indeed most regions of England. The reasons why the Asia half of the Empire intersected with politics north of the border to such a degree demonstrate how global trends produced fresh diversity in the metropole just as surely as in colonial societies.

Post-union Scottish electoral culture has suffered from comparisons with its English, Welsh and Irish counterparts based on assumptions about levels of electoral representation. By this measure Scottish society was indeed the most *ancien régime* of the metropolitan provinces, with most of its middling propertied and social classes lacking voting rights.[27] The reality, however, was more complicated and points to the manner in which imperial impacts often played out in indirect and hard-to-trace ways. Precisely because the electorate in Scotland was so restricted, patronage had an amplified impact. It was impossible to meaningfully influence the 3,500 voters in Antrim or even the 700 or so electors in Anglesey through the dispersal of a limited number of civil service posts or cadetships. But with only sixteen voters in Clackmannan in the 1780s or even seventy-four in the large Highland county of Ross, the dispersal of even a handful of imperial offices could, and did, make a difference.[28] The quirk that fewer voters produced a logical imperative to direct favours towards seemingly underrepresented localities explains why so many Scottish constituencies were targeted by returnees seeking the status and legal protections of public office. The result in Scotland was a concentration of nabob MPs that did not occur elsewhere in the British and Irish Isles. In the British parliament of 1784 to 1790 there were eighty-two MPs with 'East India' interests, either as nabobs, directors, major shareholders or participants in the shipping interest: eighteen of them (21 per cent) were Scots. This prominence translated into thirteen of Scotland's forty-five seats (28.8 per cent) coming under the control of individuals connected to the Eastern Empire (the other five sat for English constituencies). The counties of

Aberdeen and Nairn were won by the returned civil servants David Carnegie and Alexander Brodie. The retired East Indiaman commander Burnett Abercrombie secured Clackmannan while Sir Archibald Campbell, the governor of Madras, held the Stirling burghs.[29] If this level of nabob success had been replicated in England, Wales and Ireland it would have produced respective totals of 140, seven, and eighty-five 'East India' MPs and transformed the composition of both the British and Irish parliaments.

These developments tie directly to debates among maximalists and minimalists over the Empire's capacity to reshape British and Irish society. Assessing the extent and nature of such impacts tends to rely on high-profile individuals at the expense of the often convoluted and gradual processes which produced uneven and obscured patterns of influence. The analysis of John Drummond's political legacy is a case in point. His effect on electoral culture in Scotland during the 1720s and 1730s was doubtless considerable, but it is still prone to overexaggeration. The long-term legacy of his and his associates' distribution of East Indian patronage, it has been argued, was to induce in Scotland a form of 'political sleep'.[30] However, the figures in Table 7.1 warn against suggestions that empire could have such a dramatic impact. The capacity to override local conditions or Jacobite opposition to governments in London, especially before 1746, was limited.

Yet scepticism over the extent and timing of the Asia connection must allow for the often subtle ways returning empire manifested itself. Within the overall Scottish pattern in Table 7.1 lay pockets of concentrated and sustained links to the Company. The tenure of John Drummond and George Dempster as MPs for the Perth burghs meant that between 1700 and 1800 the constituency was held for a total of thirty-nine years by men with experience and status at the highest levels of the corporation. Prolonged occupation of the Inverness-shire burghs seat from 1768 until 1802 by Sir Hector Munro of Novar, the most prominent Scottish military nabob, was part of a wider pattern of returnees becoming active in Highland politics. Inverness-shire was controlled by the Bengal civil servant and director Charles Grant from 1802 to 1818, while his son (who was born in India) sat for the county's burghs after 1811. The MP for Ross-shire in 1780 was John Mackenzie, Lord Macleod, who represented the constituency while campaigning with his Highland regiment in southern India. He was replaced in 1784 by Francis Humberston-Mackenzie, earl of Seaforth, who although not a nabob did have direct links to the corporation's predatory military complex. His brother, the previous earl, Thomas Frederick, acquired £38,700 as a commander in India before dying there and bequeathing his fortune and title to his brother. Seaforth held the seat until 1790 and again in the mid-1790s.[31]

Viewing these examples in isolation could be read as evidence of the narrow, nepotistic and socially exclusive nature of Scottish electoral culture. Yet such patterns also meant that counties like Inverness, Ross or the Inverness and Perth burghs became strongly networked into Company politics, often for several decades and multiple electoral cycles at a time. The consequences could be profound and can be traced in the substantial share of employment secured by the Central and Highland regions outlined in Tables 3.2, 3.4, 4.3 and 5.5. Large swathes of the Highlands were as likely to be connected into the politics of the Eastern as opposed to the Atlantic Empire for much of the period between c.1780 and c.1820.

To the patchwork pattern of political interaction between metropole and locality can be added the question of whether Company patronage determined the attitudes and actions of voters and their families. There is now a greater appreciation of the sophisticated languages and performative discourses that surrounded the exchange of patronage in the long eighteenth century. The act was cloaked in ideals of honour, independency and mutual obligation among gentlemen. If a purely transactional tone was deployed, if voters were ignored and uncritical loyalty demanded from those who received favour, then patrons could and did lose control. The example most cited in a Scottish context is the way David Scott of Dunninald, while at the height of his influence at East India Company House, still lost the confidence of his Angus electors in the mid-1790s.[32]

There were clearly limits to what imperial patronage could achieve in terms of controlling electorates.[33] Equally, however, access to a constantly replenished pool of offices inevitably inflected the tone of politics and contributed to the government's ability to influence electorates during the age of reform and radical politics in the 1780s to 1832. For all the carefully couched language of honour, independency and mutual friendship, it is clear the Scottish manager Henry Dundas expected loyalty both from his appointees in India and aligned MPs in Scotland. This more transactional understanding of the obligations inherent in patronage was captured in comments by George Hay, seventh marquis of Tweeddale, in 1795. Hay was a retired East Indiaman commander who inherited a major Scottish title. Having applied for a military position in India for his nephew, the high-ranking peer understood the implications. He noted:

> Dundas has no view but to attach the member whosoever he is in such a manner to him personally that in the event of [a] change of ministry by commanding a number of votes, he must make himself of such consequence that he must be an object to any. He had adopted this plan in many counties and burghs in Scotland which is undoubtedly good policy for himself.[34]

India patronage was central to this objective. During the 1790 election Donald Macleod of Geanies had opposed the administration's candidate in Ross-shire. By subsequently supporting the placement of Donald's son,

Hugh, in military employment in Bengal, Dundas was able to move a politically important Whig to a position of neutrality.[35] These unspoken transactions facilitated the manager's control of forty-two out of forty-five Scottish seats by 1797. His patronage strategies also reflected and advanced his reactionary stance on constitutional matters. One of the most striking characteristics of Dundas's hegemony in Scotland, especially in the 1790s, was his carefully controlled containment of political reform and radicalism. Typical in this respect is the support shown for the Reverend Robertson of Ratho's request for a Company surgeon's post for his son. It was noted how 'the Glergyman is a most respectable man and has been particularly active in bringing his parishioners into proper sentiments on political subjects which makes it difficult for me to refuse this application'.[36]

Through such actions Dundas ensured that Company employment, in combination with other sources of patronage, acted as an antidote to radicalism. Displacement into empire provided a safety valve for aspiring middling social order families who, if frustrated in their professional and material circumstances at home, might have turned towards a sustained challenge to the constitutional and political order. The deep set of interconnections between Scottish society and imperial institutions like the Company, when compared to the less pervasive presence of similar links in Ireland, have rightly been identified as a contributory factor in the countries' divergent political trajectories in the 1780s and 1790s.[37] Dundas controlled fewer civil servant and military officer appointments than the lord lieutenant of Ireland, who, during the height of Dublin Castle's bribing of Irish MPs to accept the terms of union in 1799, was given seven cadetships in one year.[38] But intermittent and reactive use in Ireland of such offices did not have the same sustained effect as the dense web of links between Scottish county and burgh electorates, managers like Dundas, and London-based directors. Ultimately, the intersection of Scottish and Irish politics with the pre-1815 empire in Asia produced sharply different patterns of impact. One profound medium-term result was a growing divergence in attitudes to the effectiveness and attractiveness of representative or patronage-based forms of enfranchisement and public life.

The proceeds of human capital:
Asia-made wealth and the metropolitan provinces

Gauging the wider effects of returning empire beyond the political world requires understanding the extent and nature of material profits made from sojourning. Existing estimates of the 'drain' of wealth from Asia in this period vary widely, with the lower or higher end of the spectrum determined partly by time frame and method of calculation.[39] Given the potential impact of returning capital on globally transformative phenomena such as the industrial revolution, evidence from the metropolitan provinces has a wider significance. Only in relation to Scotland has there been an effort to quantify possible amounts. An estimate of £34 million has been advanced as a sum possibly made available for domestic reinvestment between 1720 and 1780. The calculations used to arrive at this amount involve a mechanistic scaling-up of varying levels of accumulated profits rather than an amount derived from archival examples.[40] If such a sum did indeed enter the economy and society it would immediately place Asia alongside the Atlantic as one of the most fundamental influences acting on early modern Scotland. The same conclusion would hold for proportionate amounts in Ireland and Wales.

Establishing a clear sense of capital accumulation faces considerable problems of sources and methods. Heavy mortality rates, loss of records and the geographically disparate and protracted nature of the remittance process make establishing definitive numbers impossible. Scaling up from examples is also insufficient. The data compiled from SIWA presented here contains no projections, only specific sums mentioned in private and business correspondence, bills of exchange, financial accounts and wills and testaments. The resulting compilation is far from definitive and inflates the Scottish total relative to the other two societies for reasons already highlighted. These limitations aside, the survey captures the accumulated capital of 445 Irish, Scots and Welsh sojourners with fortunes of £1,000 or more (less than 10 per cent of the total number of sojourners identified on SIWA). It enables a partial but robust reconstruction of the scale and effectiveness of sojourning as a form of human capital investment and offers insights, applicable beyond the metropolitan provinces, into the multiple modes of enrichment made possible through early modern globalisation. The results are summarised in Table 7.2.

One way of placing these amounts in perspective is to note that in 1796 the combined lending stock of Scotland's two national banks, the Bank of Scotland and the Royal Bank of Scotland, was increased to £2 million.[41] By this measure there can be no doubt about the extent to which the Asia link enriched Scots and Scotland. If the overall scale of wealth accumulation was impressive, the differing rates of acquisition between the metropolitan provincial groups are less surprising. Private fortunes in excess of £5.5 million and £2.1 million can be linked to 347 Scottish and ninety-two Irish sojourners respectively. Uneven acquisition of civil service, medical, maritime and military offices explain the variations in levels of secured wealth.

Table 7.2 The proceeds of human capital: metropolitan provincial fortunes, c.1730–c.1820

	£1,000–£9,999	£10,000–£19,999	£20,000–£49,999	£50,000–£99,999	>£100,000	Total
Irish (SIWA Total)						
1,796	53 £182,906	16 £233,428	14 £465,273	4 £248,377	5 £1,042,502	92 (5.1%) £2,172,486
Scots (SIWA Total)	£1,000–£9,999	£10,000–£19,999	£20,000–£49,999	£50,000–£99,999	>£100,000	Total
4,013	234 £824,304	44 £612,012	43 £1,173,783	18 £1,210,215	8 £1,747,207	347 (8.6%) £5,567,521
Welsh (SIWA Total)	£1,000–£9,000	£10,000–£19,999	£20,000–£49,999	£50,000–£99,999	>£100,000	Total
320	5 £19,775	0 –	0 –	0 –	2 £200,000	7(2.1%) £219,775

(SIWA. Sources: IOR, B/40–B/95; P/328/60–64; P/416/77–98; L/AG/34/29/4–22, 185–210, 341–343; MSS Eur F.128/12; DCM, 3/70/1–4; TNA, PROB 11/549–1903; NRS, CC1/6/81; CC8/1/113; CC8/4/2–3; CC8/8/118, 120–123, 125–128, 129–132, 134–136, 138–140, 142, 145–6; CC8/11/4–5; CC9/7/69; CC10/5/12; CC20/5/12; SC26/38/1; SC70/1/6, 12, 14, 17, 22; Registers of Sasines, Aberdeen-Wigton [Abridgements], 1781–1813; PRAI, Register of Deeds, Vols. 115–17, 170, 213, 223, 272, 275, 294–5, 351–2, 465–6, 555–6).

Considerably more Scots served in the upper echelons of the corporation and as surgeons or as private merchants. This left them better placed to covert human capital into material profit. Assessments of Scottish fortunes benefit from additional information in wills registered at the sheriff and commissary courts. By contrast, the Welsh and Irish evidence base is less comprehensive and so the verifiable totals for these societies are certainly less than the actual sums realised.

Yet even allowing for the positive and negative differentials produced by surviving sources, these figures demonstrate that the migration of human capital into Asia generated its monetary equivalent for Irish and particularly Scottish sojourners on a previously unappreciated scale. Moreover, these amounts relate to only 5.1 per cent and 8.6 per cent of traced Irish and Scots civil servants, medical men, private traders and military and merchant marine officers. The totals in Table 7.2 represent the bare minimum secured through this mode of high-risk/high-return migration. By the standards of transatlantic human mobility, movement to Asia occurred on a small scale. But it produced major accumulations of monetary capital. The scale of these fortunes means that the Eastern Empire needs to be incorporated into the metropolitan provinces' long eighteenth-century histories and given comparable attention alongside the established emphasis on the Atlantic world.

The patterns in Table 7.2 also highlight important distinctions in distribution between large, middling and smaller fortunes. With so few personnel in any part of the Company, Welsh society experienced a reduced level of benefit, although the figures undoubtedly fail to capture the full extent of profits. The large fortune of the second-generation Welshman, Elihu Yale, inflates the otherwise negligible verifiable returns for Wales.[42] There is a better balance in the case of the Irish and Scots, but also significant divergences. Although the average amount obtained by Irish personnel (£23,613) was larger than that secured by Scots (£16,130), the distribution pattern was noticeably top heavy. An exclusive set of five nabobs (William and Alexander Popham, James Alexander, Sir Eyre Coote and Major James Kilpatrick) between them held 48 per cent of the imperial wealth traced to individuals from Ireland. By contrast, Scots dominated the small to middle range of capital accumulation, a characteristic which meant profits were dispersed more evenly throughout a larger number of sojourners. The pyramid of imperial wealth was configured differently and produced varying impacts in Ireland and Scotland.

An effective way of evaluating these profits to is assess them in the specific economic and social contexts into which they returned. This method works on the principle that comprehending a large global phenomenon, in this case the transfer of colonial surpluses from Asia to Europe, can be best understood in local terms. One useful indicator is rentals, an aspect of

Table 7.3 Asia-derived wealth relative to landed rents

Estate (Country)	Owner	Rental [Year]	Asia-Made Wealth
Caledon (Ireland)	James Alexander	£1,955 [1799]	£134,471 [1775]
Seaforth (Scotland)	Francis H. Mackenzie	£6,038 [1787]	£38,700 [1787]
Coul (Scotland)	Col. Alexander Mackenzie	£807 [1797]	£7,213 [1784]
Whytebank (Scotland)	Alexander Pringle	£168 [1778]	£1,356 [1778]*
Woodhead & Antermony (Scotland)	Captain John Lennox	£1,952 [1809]	£3,976 [1805]*
Inverneil (Scotland)	Sir Archibald Campbell	£1,773 [1785]	£3,797 [1785]*

(Source: PRONI, D/2433/A/4/1/1, p. 1; NRS, GD46/17/4, pp. 74–75; NRS, GD1/1149/20/7; NRS, GD1/1149/27/4; GD246/30/2/3; NRS, RH4/121/1, pp. 9–13l; GCA, T-LX5/1, 'Rental of Antermony & Woodhead, 1809'; T-LX 3/33.
* Denotes annual as opposed to total income derived from Asia in the same year as the rental).

society directly affecting the bulk of the population. In predominantly rural countries like Ireland, Scotland and Wales, landed income was a key indicator of economic capacity and latent capital value. Rentals provide an excellent baseline against which returning imperial fortunes can be assessed for scale and for their potential socio-economic impact. The figures in Table 7.3 sample a number of properties in Scotland and the large Caledon estate in Ireland against known Asia-derived profits secured by their owners.

The examples demonstrate the extent to which Empire wealth substantially augmented the capital reserves of elites from what were still relatively poor, rural societies. From the early 1780s until his death in 1815, Francis Humberston Mackenzie, earl of Seaforth, represented one of Scotland's most powerful aristocratic families. In a measure of the willingness of socially prestigious but materially straitened regional nobility to engage with high-risk/high-return mobility, his two predecessors died either on their way to India or while campaigning there.[43] These losses in high-value human capital were compensated for with large financial gains which transformed the family's short- and medium-term ability to manage indebtedness and hold off insolvency. The Seaforth family controlled vast acreage in Ross-shire and the Western Isles. Their rentals were impressive by Scottish standards and yet were reduced to a secondary income stream when set against the large fortune of £38,700 acquired through predatory military service in India.

Caledon was James Alexander's trophy estate; yet its annual rental formed a marginal percentage of his capital assets. What is most telling about the sample is that even medium/small fortunes such as that of Colonel Alexander Mackenzie of Coul, a neighbour of Seaforth's, was many times larger than the annual rent of his medium-sized property. If £2.1 million or £5.5 million seem insignificant when set against earlier estimates of Asia profits running into tens of millions, the confirmed amounts take on a new consequence when compared against typical landed incomes in the metropolitan provinces. Caledon and Seaforth's imperial wealth might not have seemed especially impressive when placed in the affluent context of London and the Home Counties. But the status of such profits and their capacity to reshape society looked very different indeed if viewed from the Highlands or Armagh.

Domesticating empire: land and credit

Land purchases ensured that the practical, socio-economic effects derived from the Asia link were more substantial, sustained and widespread when compared with the world of pre-reform politics. Land was the foundation of society and formed the economic and cultural bedrock around which the lives of most of the population revolved. With their smaller urban base, less developed manufacturing, finance or service sectors, the rural order loomed large in the metropolitan provinces. Besides providing a practical way of assessing returning imperial personnel and profits, the acquisition of an estate represented a fundamental material and symbolic moment in the completion of the two dynamics at the heart of this book: the sojourning cycle and the conversion of human capital into its monetary counterpart. Land and its possession were vital ingredients in the sociocultural politics and performance of return. As both a material and symbolic resource, landed acreage was also important in the still only partially understood process of domesticating empire and rendering it 'mundane' and 'everyday'.[44] It played the same deflecting, reshaping role as holding honourable public office. The excessive desire for a landed estate exhibited by many nabobs, what one commentator in the Scottish borders in 1774 described as their 'earth greed', was testimony to an appreciation of the de-Orientalising properties of landholding. Ownership enabled the realisation and enjoyment of imperial profits while simultaneously removing or downplaying obvious signs of the 'Asiatick' nature of a returnee's new wealth and status.[45]

The fortunes recorded in Table 7.1 explain why an increasing number of properties began to fall into the hands of returnees. The phenomenon began slowly in the 1730s and 1740s, with one of Scotland's earliest nabobs,

James MacRae purchasing in Ayrshire. Meanwhile, similar developments occurred in Ulster through the fortune of Robert Cowan.[46] Acquisitions increased steeply between the 1760s and the 1820s and continued at a slower rate through to the 1840s with the acquisition of large properties like the Isle of Lewis by the opium dealer, James Matheson.[47] In the case of Scotland, Asia's impact on landed society was of longer duration than some of the other colonial trades such as tobacco. The relationship between imperial proceeds and the estate sector has received some attention in a Scottish context but less scrutiny in relation to Ireland or Wales. One estimate puts the number of properties acquired in Scotland with Asia-made wealth at 208, although the method used to arrive at this total is not clear. The most accurate survey has the additional merit of drawing important comparisons between Scotland, Ireland, Wales and England on the question of domestic imperial influence. This assessment cites a much smaller number. Total purchases by nabobs (but excluding senior military and naval commanders who served in Asia) between 1700 and 1850 across the UK and Ireland is listed at 229, with forty-four properties identified in Scotland, ten in Ireland and eighteen for Wales.[48] The major difference between the two existing Scottish estimates underscores the methodological pitfalls in reaching a robust conclusion. Establishing figures for Ireland and Scotland is aided by the existence of centrally compiled land registers – the Irish Register of Deeds and the Scottish Sasines – although only the latter enable empire-related searches, and only after 1781 in an accessible way. No equivalent record type exists for Wales, which is why it is difficult to recapture ownership trends in that part of Britain.

The incidence and distribution of estates bought with profits from Asia between c.1740 and c.1820, or already held by those who had a career in the Eastern Empire in the same period are shown in Maps 7.1, 7.2 and 7.3. It is possible to confirm 347 estates in Scotland, sixty-eight in Ireland and twenty-one in Wales. The verifiable number of Irish and Scottish properties are much larger than any previous estimate.[49] The disparity is explained partly by the nature of the sources. The post-1781 Scottish sasines enable empire wealth to be traced far more easily compared with Irish land deeds, a feature which serves to inflate the difference between the two societies. The Irish total is undoubtedly larger than sixty-eight. Yet the clear disparity in numbers is another manifestation of the differing rates of involvement in the Company's higher echelons.

With nearly 350 properties now firmly identified, it is clear that a structural and geographically widespread intersection between imperialism in Asia and landed society developed in Scotland. It is possible to compare the rate of land acquisition by eastern returnees against estate purchases by merchants involved in the slave-related trades in tobacco and sugar. The most comprehensive survey has identified 145 estates in west-central and central Scotland held by Glasgow colonial merchants, with 124 of these concentrated in the counties of Lanark, the Barony of Glasgow, Renfrew and Dunbarton.[50] Appendix 7.1 demonstrates that capital derived from Asia secured sixty estates in this region. Even in the part of Scotland most closely associated with the Atlantic world, the Eastern Empire loomed large. The overall scale of estate purchases and their dispersal across Scotland is striking and more than matches the known impact of Atlantic-derived wealth in the landed sector. This pattern means that the debate over whether tobacco- and sugar-related profits tended to enclave in limited sectors of the economy or in certain regions does not apply with fortunes from Asia. Appendix 7.1 and Map 7.2 confirms nabob landholding spread throughout Scotland when compared to the more concentrated pattern of investment preferred by Glasgow merchants.[51] Yet within the overall pattern of dispersal there was a discernible concentration in the eastern borders, the Lothians and the east-central counties.

Returnees were prompted by an amalgam of motives. These included, but were not limited to, social aspiration, sentimental attachment to their place of origin and cold economic calculus. All these elements were present in the negotiations that occurred in 1775 and 1776 between Colonel Hugh Grant of the Bengal army, a scion of the Grants of Lochletter, and Sir James Grant of Grant. News of Hugh's return with a £72,000 military fortune produced speculation that a much-needed windfall might circulate through the territories of the Grant kindreds. The prospect was all the more urgent given the recent loss of tenants through migration to North America, unstable rents and restricted local credit. But there also existed a fear that sudden injections of liquidity would raise prices, wages and upset the land market.[52] These conflicting social reactions were transient but important. They provided pressing reasons for returnees to deploy their wealth in ways that remained sensitive to local sentiment and conditions. More immediately, as expectations rose among those considering a sale of their land, so too did the asking price. This clash of expectations often soured relations between resident and returning kinsmen. The East Indiaman commander Alexander Macleod's purchase of the Isle of Harris in 1779 from Norman Macleod of Dunvegan exposed deep cultural anxieties around the impact of new imperial wealth and the erosion of long-established social hierarchies.[53] The same problems afflicted the Grants. In an example of how transhemispheric mobility did little to remove familial and local identities, Hugh initially sought to purchase Urquhart, where his family had held leases from the Grants for well over a century. The asking price of £60,000 proved too high and instead the estates of Moy and Kintessack in Moray were exchanged for £18,000.[54]

The method Colonel Grant used to assess the potential of his prospective properties gives a revealing insight into the dynamics that linked localities in Inverness-shire and Moray to money markets in London and in India. Grant insisted that the asking price be calculated as a multiple of the annual rental. He reasoned that if his prospective landed income did not equate to 3.5 per cent of the sale price then investing in the public funds would take priority over any purchase. This balancing act between the social prestige of estate revenue and higher returns from City investments ensured that the metropole's financial sector and provincial land markets were deeply intertwined rather than one simply dependent on the other. One profound effect of wealth returning from Asia was to deepen this pre-existing interconnection. The lack of credit in London in 1778 due to the war in North America resulted in Scottish landowners struggling to access loans to service their debts. This commercial intelligence persuaded Thomas Graham, even while he was still in Bengal, to offer a lower price for Cleish and Burleigh in Kinross knowing the owner had little option. Graham's advantageous deployment of surplus capital raises questions about the globalised nature of land markets, the extended boundaries of Scotland's landed society and the interplay of investment decisions in Asia and in finance-'poor' regions of Europe. Problems with remittance could and did leave considerable amounts of notional capital stranded in the East Indies. While often a cause for profound anxiety, this routine problem was also treated as an opportunity. Interest rates in India were much higher than in Europe, allowing sojourners to continue to accrue rentier profits for years after returning home. Forced to leave considerable sums in Calcutta, James Alexander deployed these funds into country trading ventures even as he purchased estates in Ireland. In 1813 Colonel George Constable of Liff in Angus declined to buy an estate in Fife because his £10,000 in Calcutta earned a 6 per cent return. The best he could hope for in Scotland from rentals was 5 per cent.[55] This seamless combining of local and imperial horizons was entirely routine and underlines that arrivals back home were never a single moment but a protracted process which always remained cloaked in global influences. Under these complex circumstances it is hardly surprising that the Eastern Empire shaped the metropolitan provinces in uneven and usually oblique ways.

The familial, local, national and supranational dimensions shaping Grant's, Graham's and Alexander's investment decisions could stand for most of the purchases represented in Maps 7.1 to 7.3 and Appendix 7.1. Property exchanges on this scale involved imperial capital reshaping rural society while itself undergoing a crucial conversion into domestic property, improved landscapes, and socially and culturally legitimated power. This absorbing and transforming process meant returning empire could and did have major socio-economic effects but in ways that left little apparent evidence of the original imperial link. The complex reconfiguring of overseas wealth formed the backdrop to some major property transfers among the landed classes in Ireland and in Scotland. Conspicuous acquisition was an undoubted characteristic of the top rank Irish returnees. When Sir Eyre Coote purchased Mountrath, Mountmellick, Ballycowan, Bracklone and Acreboy in 1763 they contained 227 townlands spread across Queen's, King's, Roscommon and West Meath.[56] There were similar examples of large-scale transfers in Scotland: on 20 September 1777 the former Madras free merchant George Patterson took possession of Longforgan in the Carse of Gowrie for a price of £40,000. In 1808, Basil Cochrane, a returned Madras civil servant, bought the entire barony of Auchterarder for £93,441. Both events involved the displacement of established families in ways that seemed to confirm fears over the socially destabilising effects of empire wealth.[57]

Yet the dramatic intrusion of global capital into areas like Mountrath or Auchterarder was only one possible way money from overseas influenced conditions on the ground. Imperial fortunes did not always have consistent or obvious impacts: they both changed and left unchanged the existing social order. One noticeable trend in Ireland was the rise of new regional dynasties such as the Caledons and Castlereaghs, although service in India also preserved and augmented the status of older families. The Wellesleys of Dangan in Meath and Eyre Coote's retrieval of the patrimony of the Cootes of Mountrath are the most dramatic examples of this preservation effect.[58] The retrenchment dynamic operated with even more force in Scotland, playing a major role in the renewal and resurgence of a number of regionally significant aristocratic families such as the Tweeddales of Yester and Lindsays of Balcarres. It is clear from Tables 3.2 and 4.3 that landed gentry or their sons featured prominently among those Scots joining the civil and military branches. Resultant profits helped stave off debt foreclosure and facilitated resilience in the face of mounting improvement costs, tenant migration and the growing hegemony of the great aristocratic families. These were the practical dividends of the risky option of journeying to Asia. Captain Archibald Fergusson of Dunfallandie in Perthshire could have been speaking for hundreds of his fellow sojourners when he wrote home from Bengal to his mother in 1780, noting how he hoped to 'return with a fortune to retrieve if possible the old remains of Dunfallandie [and] to see my native country with a fortune at least sufficient to pay off what debts I and my family owe in Scotland'. James Taylor from Rockbrooke in County Dublin, a lieutenant in the Madras army, similarly sought to manage from India his father's heavily mortgaged property.[59]

For many, perhaps even a majority, the gamble did not work. Death or financial failure in Asia brought foreclosure in Wales, Ireland or Scotland. But for others expansion and imperialism in Asia altered possibilities at home in complex and profound ways. The legacy for the Scottish Highlands arising from disproportionate numbers in the Company's officer corps or in Highland Regiments is a case in point. By the mid-1780s the two premier landed families in Ross-shire – Lord Seaforth and John Mackenzie, Lord Macleod – had resurrected their propertied, political and social power through either personal or immediate family involvement in Asia. These service aristocracies would go on to dominate that part of Scotland for a further half century. Much of the west Highlands experienced a similar dynamic as befitted a region which sent so many officers east. Through the 1770s to the 1800s the Macdonalds of Kinlochmoidart used a global strategy which encompassed Jamaican plantation income and military earnings from Ceylon to reacquire their forfeited estate and then improve it.[60] Asia could reappear in the British and Irish Isles in highly concentrated clusters, often at their most obvious in localities hundreds of miles from London. On the Isle of Skye, Norman Macleod of Dunvegan staved off bankruptcy and refurbished Dunvegan Castle through a short but highly successful military sojourn in the southern Indian theatre. By the early 1780s individuals with Asia-made fortunes owned half of Skye, the entirety of the Isles of Harris and Lewis and St Kilda.[61] Such developments are significant in one other respect. These were ancient, well-established families. Their use of imperial service to endure at a time of major structural change in the regional and national economies meant that there was little outward sign of change at the top of the social order. As a result, the injection of overseas wealth often happened through reassuringly familiar landlord channels and in ways that left impacts underestimated, disguised and more easily forgotten.

Another reason why the presence of the Asia link can be overlooked is that returns were often on a small, intimate scale. Many of the land purchases summarised in Appendix 7.1 and Map 7.2 were barely more than extended feus or one or two acres in extent. This was especially the case with returnees choosing to live near a provincial urban centre, which many sojourners preferred over the heavy costs of residence in London.[62] Colonel John Crow bought the suburban villa of Amelia Bank and its associated parkland on the outskirts of Dundee, while Major William Greene secured the small estate of Lota just to the east of Cork.[63] Maps 7.1 and 7.2 show this pattern clearly; the towns of Ayr, Saltcoats and Irvine, Stirling, Perth, Dundee and Inverness, and Cork in Ireland were ringed with small estates acquired by returnees. Given the pattern of concentration in Ayrshire it is unsurprising that John Galt should depict a nabob in the 1822 novel, *The*

Provost, his at once scathing and humorous treatment of rampant political and commercial ambition.[64] These lesser nabobs did not have the resources to practice the 'earth greed' of a James Alexander, Eyre Coote or John Johnstone. Yet their everyday influence and the immediate effects of their spending power would have been significant, if now largely lost to history. As provincial gentry capitalists they took Asia-derived wealth far from London and created clusters of high localised empire impacts.

There is one last dimension of the nexus between land and returning overseas capital that requires consideration. Because contemporary commentators fixated on the scale of estate acquisition by nabobs, historians attempting to evaluate the possible impact of the Asia connection have concentrated on landed purchases as the key indicator. But imperial wealth could enter provincial societies in multiple ways and through less dramatic channels. One of the least investigated of these is the combining of land and overseas profits by offering credit secured on estate collateral. Large-scale speculation on EIC shares by the London financier Sir George Colebrooke extended into Ireland through his use of such funds to purchase the Tully estate in Longford, Castlemore and Costello in Mayo and Boyle in Roscommon. These were essentially mortgage ventures rather than investments with the intention of developing the estates. Land in Ireland in this instance acted as collateral for debts of over £100,000 owed to a circle of City financiers.[65]

Lending on land in Scotland evolved in a different mode, with returnees and those still in Asia advancing credit against acreage. The sasine register offers a unique window into the nationwide scale and importance of this augmenting of credit and liquidity. A survey of 125,982 printed sasine abridgements from 1781 until 1813 is summarised in Appendix 7.1. It reveals that over £1.6 million accrued in Asia was lent out across Scotland in these years. This major injection of global capital has not been previously recognised and needs to be factored into explanations for the intensifying pace of economic development, agrarian improvement and growing capital self-sufficiency in Scotland. In 1790 alone, £111,273 was lent out across the country in this way. Given that the total lending stock of the average provincial bank in this period was approximately £50,000, this sum means the Eastern Empire contributed the lending capacity of two extra banks in just one year. This was at a time when the number of such institutions in Scotland amounted to no more than twenty-five.[66] The overall amount of £1.6 million also stands direct comparison with the total lending stock of the two major national banks.

The effect of these substantial injections of liquidity was more than just financial. Lending was designed to enhance the social prestige of the lender by divesting their wealth of the taint of 'Oriental' riches. A typical example was the joint loan on 27 May 1791 by Lieutenant-Colonel Patrick Ross of the Madras army and the Bombay civil servant David Carnegie of £6,000 to Sir William Maxwell of Calderwood. Maxwell represented an established Lanarkshire family but had mortgaged his barony to Archibald Menzies of Culdares. Empire credit was used to immediately repay Menzies while the two Company officials, with ample external resources, waited repayment until 1799.[67] Everyone gained from the arrangement. Menzies was repaid, Maxwell's hereditary barony remained safe and Ross and Carnegie's reputations as honourable and genteel men were confirmed in the social circles they sought to move in. They also earned a rentier income on the repayment interest, a flow of culturally prestigious wealth derived from landed sources which raises fundamental questions about the physical boundaries and social character of Scotland's restricted propertied order. The connecting of land and finance through credit rather than purchase was a central feature of provincial gentry capitalism and blurred the financial and social boundaries between landed and imperial service gentry. In such prosaic ways did imperial wealth seep back into society. The circuitous, hard-to-trace nature of these transactions was deliberate. They served to obscure the presence and influence of empire behind the apparent continuity, stability and respectability of Scotland's old landed order. The process occurred on a huge scale, encompassing 40 per cent of all Scottish parishes between 1781 and 1813 alone. There is no better example of the capacity of the human-to-monetary capital cycle to deliver substantial liquidity and broadly dispersed credit into a previously undercapitalised society.

Disguising empire: 'improvement'

Estate acquisition, the protection of existing landed holdings and the widespread use of overseas wealth as credit ensured that empire returned home in direct and indirect ways. Some manifestations were obvious, but others far less so. Personnel returning from Asia understood the anxiety caused by the large, culturally alien and chaotic empire they helped create and expand. Before the British constructed discourses of societal stagnation, racial inferiority and ideas of civilising mission to legitimise their position in South Asia, the Eastern Empire was the source of anxiety and angst as much as pride. It was cloaked in a reputation of corrupt conquest and unsustainable profiteering derived from plunder and asset stripping or questionable commercial practices based on unstable, transient financial derivatives and luxuries.[68] A key challenge for those arriving back was to make productive use of their imperial wealth in ways that deflected from or even disguised its origins. These pressures resulted in a cultural politics of return that deliberately attempted to efface the presence of personnel and profits from Asia. Three tactics for achieving this aim, entering public life, becoming part of the landed order and buttressing local liquidity, have already been considered. A fourth method focused on estate, infrastructural and industrial improvements, as well as conspicuous civic philanthropy. All served as a means of countering and negating the negative connotations associated with the Eastern Empire.

Given the scale of estate purchasing it is hardly surprising that agrarian development became a primary means of transforming both capital and the returned sojourner into virtuous agents of patriotic improvement. Once he acquired Longforgan, George Patterson commenced a sustained and multifaceted development programme that transformed the estate and the lives of its tenants. If atypical in its scale and comprehensiveness, the ploughing of colonial wealth into domestic improvement was a standard activity employed by the majority of landowners shown on Maps 7.1 to 7.3. All over Scotland, Wales and Ireland, empire disappeared into new elegant country houses, genteel parklands, enclosed fields and improved local economies and amenities. James Alexander at Caledon, the East Indiaman commander Robert Haldane at Airthrey and Gleneagles, Robert Lindsay at Leuchars and Sir Hector Munro at Novar initiated large-scale ditching, field enclosure and tree planting projects which generated employment but also raised rentals and transformed local landscapes and economy.[69] The commercial nature of these policies warn against assumptions that nabob fortunes were deployed largely in cosmetic and consumption orientated activities.[70] In specific localities, if not nationally, Asia fortunes transformed communities. In the 1780s Captain Alexander Macleod began establishing new fishing settlements on the east coast of his Harris estate. This set the template for a sixty-year pattern of population eviction and resettlement that ultimately involved thousands of people and entirely reorientated local society.[71]

Eastern profits did, however, play a less important role in the textile and manufacturing sectors compared to Atlantic-generated wealth. Nevertheless, its presence beyond the landed sector was much larger than previously thought. In Ireland a number of manufacturing ventures relied on capital from Asia. In the 1780s the EIC officer and recruiting agent Robert Brooke developed cotton and linen weaving on his estate of Prosperous in County Kildare. As part of his improvement policies he lobbied for and received a controversial parliamentary loan of £40,000, an act of perceived political favouritism which contributed to severe crowd disturbances in Dublin in 1783.[72] James Alexander, as a Trustee on the Irish linen board, did much the same in Caledon. The Bengal army officer, Captain Richard Long, purchased the estate of Ardmayle in Tipperary in 1787 and constructed a substantial woollen mill complex by 1804.[73] The military nabob Turner Camac conveyed lands in Wicklow to the Hibernian Mining Company while another returnee, the EIC civil servant William Digges La Touche, subscribed £2,000 to the Grand Canal Company. Camac's portfolio is evidence that Asia wealth did circulate in the wider Irish economy beyond mortgage speculation, estate purchases and improvement.[74]

The accessible nature of sasine records after 1781 mean that more consistent evidence of empire capital at work in the manufacturing and urban economies can be traced in Scotland. Appendix 7.2 summarises twenty-three industrial, textile and commercial ventures in which such profits were invested. Compared to the 128 businesses in receipt of Atlantic-made monies, the deployment of Eastern fortunes in this sector appears to have been much more limited. However, some of these projects were large and extremely capital intensive. Claud Alexander's profits established the planned village of Catrine and enabled the construction of the Catrine Mills in the 1780s, one of the largest and earliest cotton ventures in Scotland.[75] Moreover, while Atlantic-derived wealth tended to circulate narrowly within the west-central economy focused on Glasgow and hinterlands, Asia fortunes spread across different regions. Neither does the list of twenty-three businesses include those which relied on the EIC's vast purchasing power. The corporation was a key customer for two of eighteenth-century Scotland's most important iron manufactories. By 1773 the Carron works began a regular supply of heavy ordinance for the merchant fleet and the military while the Cramond complex of Messrs Cadel and Edington, valued in 1791 at £30,000, sent much of its output to markets in India.[76] One final piece of evidence provides another indication of how the Asia link influenced the commercial and manufacturing economy. Appendix 7.1 shows that west-central Scotland attracted the greatest share of Asia-derived credit. If not invested directly into business and manufacturing, the injection of over £400,000 (the equivalent of the lending stock of eight provincial banking companies) could only have helped general conditions of liquidity and investor confidence in one of the most economically dynamic and significant regions of the country.[77]

Although land purchases and a major augmentation of mortgage credit formed the primary use of returned fortunes, such wealth was evident throughout the economy and society. Philanthropy acted as a virtuous and moral gloss on money acquired through the exercise of colonial power and by often highly coercive means. Aligning profits with economic and civic improvement was important enough for sojourners to begin the process while they were still in Asia. In 1789 Governor-General Lord Cornwallis sponsored a subscription for the British Fisheries Society which intended building a series of planned villages in the west Highlands. A number of the sojourning elite in Bengal subscribed, producing an eventual sum of £4,400 which was remitted back to London by Ferguson, Fairlie and Co. Although the Society did draw support from Irish, Welsh and English individuals, it is striking that eighty of the 138 donations were from Scots.[78] In this way money generated in India percolated into domestic development schemes like Ullapool or Stein in Skye, the latter constructed in the 1790s on land feued from Norman Macleod of Dunvegan, who had just returned from Asia.

Urban and civic improvement offered returnees another context in which to disperse parts of their wealth to aid their reintegration and reputation. Sir Hector Munro helped rebuild the Tolbooth of Nairn in the 1760s and that of Inverness in 1791, two of the most important towns in his parliamentary constituency. The returned Bombay free merchant John Forbes not only acquired a number of estates in Strathdon, visible as a cluster on Map 7.2, but contributed £10,000 of the original £13,135 required to begin work in 1819 on Aberdeen's new asylum.[79] An even more telling example is the global character of subscriptions in the early to mid-1800s for the new northern infirmary in Inverness. While the largest overseas amount was raised among Scots active in the slave-economy of the Caribbean, free merchants, EIC administrators, marine and military officers and enlisted men in two Highland Regiments stationed in India raised the substantial sum of £985.[80]

Support for education provided another means of representing returnees as virtuous and patriotic members of society and their wealth as conducive to the public good. The free merchant, George Smith left a bequest that enabled the establishment in the early 1790s of an academy in his home town of Fordyce.[81] Just as the university colleges benefited from intellectual capital acquired in Asia, so they received endowments and gifts to support part of their activities. In his will Sir John Macpherson, the interim governor-general who served between Warren Hastings and Cornwallis, remembered his alma mater, King's College in Aberdeen. He left bursaries for a number of studentships, including one which would support Gaelic-speakers. In the case of Patrick Ivory, a successful Company surgeon, imperial wealth facilitated the development of educational provision in Ireland's new Catholic college at Maynooth. His will of 1809 reveals how colonial profits seeped into Catholic communities in Ireland. Besides buying a small portion of land for his own family, he left £1,000 (Irish) for the education of two boys from his extended kin.[82]

Ivory also left donations for the refurbishment of Tullyallan and Mooretown chapels, fees for saying Mass and for poor relief to be applied on a strictly ecumenical basis. This focus on augmenting educational and charitable provision, often in the sojourner's place of origin, was a common practice. Such actions were aimed at securing a respectable postmortem reputation. But as with land acquisition and improvement, the practical effect involved the absorption of empire money into the existing civic, religious and educational fabric in ways that left little trace of its origins, as indeed was the intention. Appendix 7.3 lists a number of parishes in Ireland and Scotland that benefited from the redirecting of overseas profits into local learning and health provision. The Statistical Account of Scotland often lists the annual relief fund raised in parishes along with the number of people it maintained. These figures provide an indication of the local significance of what could otherwise appear to be very small sums. In the case of John Moore, a free merchant who died in Madras in 1753, his donation of £1,600 to the parish of Morebattle in Roxburghshire was sufficiently transformative to be published in the statistical account over forty years later. Even small amounts, such as the £5 given to the parish of Petty by the ex-governor of Madras, William Fraser, in 1715, constituted a major injection of cash: seventy-seven years later the original donation was still equivalent to the entire amount raised in the parish for the purposes of poor relief.[83]

The trickling down of wealth meant that empire influence, however indirect, percolated into localities and homes far removed from those parts of Britain and Ireland usually associated with imperialism in Asia. This process would not have registered in the consciousness of the vast majority of the population. Yet in some localities the influence of the Asia connection could be profound and impossible to ignore. The burgh of Elgin is not a town usually linked with a major role in empire. However, the wealth of two returnees was responsible for the creation of major public buildings that completely transformed the townscape. In the 1810s and early 1820s Major General Andrew Anderson of the Bombay army and Dr Alexander Grey each left their home town over £10,000. By the 1830s these fortunes had resulted in the creation of a state-of-the-art hospital which dominated the burgh skyline and a dedicated educational and poor relief institute sitting opposite the ruined medieval cathedral.[84] In the conspicuous transformation of its civic infrastructure and built environment, Elgin was as imperial a burgh as Glasgow. Both towns were reshaped in very similar ways by the very different hemispheres of Britain's global Empire.

Two last examples, one from the Lowlands and one from the Western Isles, reveal how overseas wealth embedded itself at 'home' in ways that projected local continuity and the calculated absence of empire. George Patterson's acquisition of the Castle Huntly estate seemed to typify the destabilising, threatening nature of 'Oriental' wealth. Like all nabobs, Patterson's improvements were part revenue enhancement and part cultural repackaging. The strategy worked. His estate was painted in the early 1800s by the famous landscape artist Alexander Nasmyth. The painting encapsulates the cultural completion of the high-value human capital cycle. It projects a romanticised, rural idyll, an 'improved' landscape inhabited by contented rustics but with the traditional castle projecting an historic stability and ancient authenticity.[85] While the entire landscape was testimony to the capacity of imperial capital to transform conditions on the ground, the Empire itself was literally embedded in the earth and domesticated out of existence.

Precisely the same cultural dynamics occurred at the other end of Scotland. Captain Macleod of Harris's management of his return involved projecting both a modern, patriotic and improving ethos alongside public demonstrations that his new wealth and power were simply an extension of the old social order. The first dimension he achieved through his implementation of new forms of tenure and his promotion of the fishing industry. The construction of a new pier, salt and fish processing buildings and boat-serving facilities beside his new estate house at Rodel proclaimed his commitment to agrarian and maritime improvement. Expenditure on the ancient church of St Clements, burial place of the Macleod chiefs and their senior clan gentry, a scion of which Captain Macleod was, balanced the modernising aspect of his return and reintegration.[86] This was a conscious effort to make him and his imperial wealth seem less threatening or 'other', to hide the overseas connection in plain sight. The transformative effect of empire profits was plainly evident through estate and tenurial change, and yet at exactly the same moment became part of a historically legitimated continuity led by the representative of an ancient, local family. This crucial balancing act was caught perfectly by William Daniell in his 1815 print, 'Rowadill in Harris', an image of the modern and the old, of change and of continuity, and with empire nowhere to be seen.[87] The effacement of global empire through the recrafting of localities as diverse as Harris, Castle Huntly, Elgin or Irish estates like Caledon was quite deliberate and remarkably successful.

Conclusion

The ways in which the EIC's personnel, commerce, wealth and ideas returned to the provinces of the British and Irish Isles speak closely to debates over the reshaping of metropolitan society by its own imperialism.[88] By moving the geography of return away from the wealthy and developed urban and cultural hinterlands of the metropolis, the character and visibility of the Empire's impact takes on a different though no less subtle and complex light. The means by which Irish, Scottish and Welsh society connected to Asia inevitably shaped the dynamics of arrival back in localities and regions. At one level interaction with the eastern hemisphere occurred through the consumption of commodities. To this well-known connection is now added the cycle of human capital. At the heart of this interaction lay the nexus between the human and social variants of wealth which enabled sojourning mobility and primitive capital accumulation. Individuals and their wider networks moved out and, if successful, both the person and their new monetary wealth returned. All sojourners from Europe, regardless of their social or national background, entered this economy of converting one form of capital into another. However, because patterns of participation were so different for each of the metropolitan provinces, the returning influences also varied. With many more sojourners inside the high-value human capital cycle, Scottish society realised greater proceeds. This was true in a human as well as a monetary sense. The only dedicated club outside London for elite returnees from Asia was created in Scotland in 1787 and had over 130 members by the 1810s. As civil servants, military officers and surgeons arrived back, they joined what amounted to a clearinghouse for the mobilisation of social networks and the investing of the next cycle of human capital.[89]

There is now clear evidence that sojourning in Asia could produce substantial primitive capital accumulation. Fewer than one hundred elite Irish returnees secured over £1.2 million. The greater outward movement in the case of Scotland produced even greater profits, with 347 individuals commanding financial resources worth over twice the total stock held by the two national banks. These are just the sums that can be traced and relate to only a small percentage of those known to have sojourned to Asia in this period. Both the Irish and Scottish totals are conservative but confirmable. More so than the other two metropolitan provinces, Scotland experienced considerable injections of Asia-made wealth across its different regions, rural order and civic infrastructure. Although these processes happened all over Britain and Ireland, the difference in the metropolitan provinces was that the returns loomed larger in societies with less diverse economies or reserves of monetary wealth. Precisely because the impact became so noticeable, Scottish society was at the forefront of economic tactics and social strategies designed to maximise the potential of empire wealth while minimising its cultural imprint. In the political world, imperial patronage became an antidote to pressure for electoral or constitutional reform.[90] In turn, land and 'improvements' became an antidote to empire. While landed estates could be sites of uncertainty over returning imperial influences, the scale of purchases in Scotland point to the pervasive belief that the domestication of empire was possible by absorption into a virtuous and improving rural order.[91] An important lesson to be drawn from how empire arrived back in Ireland and Scotland is that the multilayered nature of such returns is revealed in stark clarity. Improved rural landscapes and new civic buildings soaked up profits, transforming society while disguising, normalising and naturalising empire and its domestic presence in the process.

The homecoming of imperial personnel and their wealth to any locality inevitably induced change. However, it is also clear that returnees understood the imperative to manage the process so that the impact left little or no lasting impression or memory.[92] The Asia connection was culturally managed and transformed to become part of the normative and patriotic implementation of 'improvement'. The wider lesson to draw from the example of the metropolitan provinces is that returning empire materially remade society but did not always appear to do so. This seemingly contradictory cultural dynamic means that the 'maximalist' and 'minimalist' positions are in some ways both correct, but for very different reasons.

Notes

1 Richard Price, 'One Big Thing: Britain, Its Empire, and Their Imperial Culture', *Journal of British Studies*, 45 (2006), 602–27.
2 Stephen Howe, 'Empire and Ideology', in Stockwell, *The British Empire*, p. 164; Hall and Rose, 'Introduction', p. 14; Hall, 'Culture and Identity', pp. 202–5.
3 Porter, *The Absent-Minded Imperialists*, pp. ix, 5–12; Marshall, 'Imperial Britain', 392–3; Thompson, *The Empire Strikes Back?*, pp. 238–42; Price, 'One Big Thing', 609–11.
4 Hall and Rose, 'Introduction', pp. 16–17, 19–20, 29–30; Thompson, *The Empire Strikes Back?*, p. 8, fn. 54.
5 Porter, 'Further Thoughts on Imperial Absent-Mindedness', 108–12; John M. MacKenzie, 'Comfort and Conviction: A Response to Bernard Porter', *The Journal of Imperial and Commonwealth History*, 36 (2008), 665–6.
6 John M. MacKenzie, 'Empire and Metropolitan Cultures', in Andrew Porter (ed.), *The Oxford History of the British Empire, Vol. III: The Nineteenth Century* (Oxford: Oxford University Press, 1998), p. 271; Wilson, 'Introduction: Histories, Empires, Modernities', pp. 14–15; Hall and Rose, 'Introduction', pp. 21–2; Catherine Hall and Keith McClelland, 'Introduction', in Catherine Hall and Keith McClelland (eds), *Race, Nation and Empire: Making Histories, 1750 to the Present* (Manchester: Manchester University Press, 2010), p. 5.
7 Porter, *Absent-Minded Imperialists*, p. 147; Bernard Porter, 'Further Thoughts on Imperial Absent-Mindedness', 102; Andrew Thompson, 'Empire and the British State', in Stockwell, *The British Empire*, p. 51.
8 T. M. Devine, 'The Spoils of Empire', pp. 102–8; McGilvary, *East India Patronage*, pp. 185–202; A. Mackillop, 'The Highlands and the Returning Nabob:

Sir Hector Munro of Novar, 1770–1807', in Harper, *Emigrant Homecomings*, pp. 233–61; McGilvary, 'Return of the Scottish Nabob', pp. 90–108.

9 Alistair Mutch, *Tiger Duff: India, Madeira and Empire in Eighteenth-Century Scotland* (Aberdeen: Aberdeen University Press, 2017), pp. 145–66; Ellen Filor, 'The Intimate Trade of Alexander Hall: Salmon and Slaves in Scotland and Sumatra, c.1745–1765', and Alistair Mutch, 'Connecting Britain and India: General Patrick Duff and Madeira', in Finn and Smith, *The East India Company at Home*, pp. 318–32, 333–54.

10 Whatley, *Scottish Society*, pp. 66–7; Devine, *Scotland's Empire*, pp. 326–45; McGilvary, *East India Patronage*, pp. 184–202.

11 Bartlett, '"This Famous Island Set in a Virginian Sea"', pp. 253–75; Dickson, *Old World Colony*, pp. 120–3; Evans, 'Wales, Munster and the English South West', pp. 45–6.

12 Thompson, *The Empire Strikes Back?* p. 241.

13 IOR, B/52, p. 2; www.historyofparliamentonline.org/ [Steuart, William (1686–1768), of Weyland and Seatter, Orkney].

14 McGilvary, *East India Patronage*, pp. 38–67; NRS, GD24/1/464(e)/146.

15 Sutherland, *The East India Company in Eighteenth Century Politics*, pp. 79–89; Bowen, *Revenue and Reform*, pp. 30–42.

16 www.historyofparliamentonline.org/ [Clive, Richard (c.1693–1771), of Styche Hall, nr. Market Drayton, Salop]; PRAI, Vol 213, No.s 139946–47, pp. 95–7; Barnard, *A New Anatomy of Ireland*, p. 202.

17 Smith, *Slavery, Family and Gentry Capitalism*, pp. 197–204.

18 IOR, J/1/1, p. 151; MS Eur/Photo Eur 109, pp. 1–146; B/79, p. 281; B/80, p. 50; B/85, p. 117; *A Letter to the Proprietors of East India Stock from John Johnstone*, pp. 1–10; Rothschild, *The Inner Lives of Empires*, pp. 182–5; Riddy, 'Warren Hastings', p. 52.

19 Rosalind Carr, 'The Gentleman and the Soldier: Patriotic Masculinities in Eighteenth-Century Scotland', *Journal of Scottish Historical Studies*, 28 (2008), 102–21.

20 Hall and Rose, 'Introduction', pp. 16–17, 19–20, 29–30.

21 NRS, RS62/19: 30 August 1773 and 13 December 1776; W. Ferguson, 'The Electoral System in the Scottish Counties Before 1832', The Stair Society, Miscellany II, 35 (1984), 261–94. www.historyofparliamentonline.org/ [Pulteney, William (1729–1805), of Westerhall, Dumfries]

22 Bowen, 'The "Little Parliament"', 861–5; *The Scots Magazine*, 29 (1767), pp. 665–9.

23 PRONI, D/2432/2/1, pp. 8, 18; D/2433/A/3/1: London, 23 September 1776: D/2433/A/3/2: Dublin, 11 May 1777; Dublin, 1 December 1777; D/2433/A/91/2/1.

24 NAI, MS2533, p. 418; PRAI, Register of Deeds, Vol. 114, No. 797743, pp. 80–6; Vol. 115, No. 79488, pp. 84–91; Vol. 116, No. 79742, pp. 118–25; PRONI, D654/B1/2A, pp. 13–14; PRONI, D572/19/64, 73, 84, 91, 94, 110; PRONI, D/2432/5/3/4; D/2433/A/3/2: Caledon, 20 November 1782; TCD, MS3767/95.

25 Mackillop, 'The Highlands and the Returning Nabob', pp. 241–2.
26 Bowen, 'Asiatic Interactions', pp. 179–80.
27 Cullen, 'Scotland & Ireland', p. 242.
28 www.historyofparliamentonline.org/research/constituencies/constituencies-1754-1790 [Anglesey]; [Clackmannan]; [Ross-shire]; Johnston, *History of the Irish Parliament*, vol. II, p. 382.
29 Philips, *The East India Company*, pp. 309–11.
30 Devine, *Scotland's Empire*, pp. 236–9; McGilvary, *East India Patronage*, p. 207.
31 www.historyofparliamentonline.org/research/constituencies/constituencies-1754-1790 [Inverness Burghs]; [Ross-shire]; www.historyofparliamentonline.org/ [Grant, Charles I (1746–1823), of Battersea Rise, Clapham, Surr.; 40 Russell Square, Mdx.; and Waternish, Skye, Inverness]; [Grant, Charles II (1778–1866)]; NRS, GD46/17/4, pp. 74–5; IOR, P/416/98 [1782], pp. 51–6.
32 Brown, 'Henry Dundas', pp. 83–5, 215; Sunter, *Patronage and Politics*, pp. 3–7, 132–7.
33 Sunter, *Patronage and Politics*, pp. 8–9.
34 NRS, GD51/3/37; GD51/3/39/2; NLS, MS14828, fos. 22–3, 30.
35 NLS, MS19298, fos. 21–6, 28–31; MS14828, fo. 30.
36 NLS, MS1074, fo. 100.
37 Cullen, 'Scotland and Ireland', pp. 231–43; Jackson, *The Two Unions*, pp. 138–40.
38 PRONI, D572/19/79; NLS, MS1074, fo. 148.
39 Marshall, *East Indian Fortunes*, pp. 234, 255–6.
40 Marshall, *East Indian Fortunes*, pp. 229–55; McGilvary, *East India Patronage*, p. 200; Devine, 'The Spoils of Empire', p. 106.
41 S. G. Checkland, *Scottish Banking: A History, 1695–1973* (London: Collins, 1975), p. 142; C. H. Lee, 'The Establishment of the Financial Network', in Devine, Lee and Peden, *The Transformation of Scotland*, pp. 105–7.
42 I. B. Watson, 'Yale, Elihu (1649–1721), merchant and administrator in India and benefactor', *Oxford Dictionary of National Biography*: https://doi-org.ezproxy.lib.gla.ac.uk/10.1093/ref:odnb/30183.
43 Finlay McKichan, *Lord Seaforth: Highland Landowner, Caribbean Governor* (Edinburgh: Edinburgh University Press, 2018), pp. 17–94.
44 Nechtman, *Nabobs*, pp. 156–7; Mackillop, 'The Highlands and the Returning Nabob', pp. 244–7.
45 NLS, MS1171, fo. 271.
46 IOR, B/57, pp. 198, 284, 325; B/59, p. 31; B/61, pp. 231, 346, 523, 538; B/62/p. 122, 406, 422; B/65. p. 408; Farrington, *Biographical Index*, p. 510; NLS, MS588/1365, fos. 197–8.
47 Stephanie Barczewski, *Country Houses and the British Empire, 1700–1930* (Manchester: Manchester University Press, 2014), pp. 52–5.
48 George McGilvary, 'Return of the Scottish Nabob', p. 101; Barczewski, *Country Houses*, pp. 52–7, 256–61.
49 Stephanie Barczewski, 'Scottish Landed-Estate Purchases, Empire and

Union, 1700–1900', in Berczewski and Farr, *The MacKenzie Moment*, pp. 171–88.
50 Devine, *Scotland's Empire*, pp. 332–3; T. M. Devine, 'Did Slavery Make Scotia Great? A Question Revisited', in Devine, *Recovering Scotland's Slavery Past*, pp. 238–9.
51 Devine, 'The Colonial Trades', p. 13.
52 IOR, L/MIL/9/85 [1754], pp. 64–5; Hodson, *List of the Officers of the Army of Bengal*, vol. II, p. 314; NRS, GD248/227/1/32; *The Statistical Account of Scotland*: https://stataccscot.edina.ac.uk: 443/link/osa-vol11-p604-parish-perth-callander.
53 NLS, MS1169, fos. 151, 153; MS1368, fo. 35.
54 NRS, GD248/52/1/2–3, 6, 45, 56–7, 69–70; GD248/51/3/20–5; GD248/227/2/77; NRS, GD23/9/18.
55 NRS, GD29/2067/12; GD393/6/1, fos. 99–102; NLS, MS10947, fos. 23–4; MS6360, pp. 113–15; KH, Box 16/32; Edinburgh, 16 May 1778; PRONI, D/2432/1/2: London, 20 November 1764. DCA, Wedderburn of Pearsie, Box 7/15/3: London, 18 June 1813: George Constable to Charles Wedderburn.
56 PRAI, Register of Deeds, Vol. 223, No. 147708, pp. 144–7.
57 NRS, RS62/20: 20 September 1777; Registers of Sasines, Perth (6635).
58 IOR, B/71, pp. 528–32, 552; B/55, p. 517; B/61, p. 394; B/63, pp. 409, 488; B/67, p. 482; P/416/78, pp. 184–6; B/91, pp. 31–2; L/AG/34/29/186 [1783–84], pp. 192–211; PRAI, Register of Deeds, Vol. 114, No. 797743, pp. 80–6; Vol. 115, No. 79488, pp. 84–91; Vol. 116, No. 79742, pp. 118–25; Vol. 223, No. 147708, pp. 144–7; PRONI, D/2432/5/4/2; Norman Gash, 'Wellesley, Arthur, first duke of Wellington (1769–1852)', *Oxford Dictionary of National Biography*: https://doi-org.ezproxy.lib.gla.ac.uk/10.1093/ref:odnb/29001; C. A. Bayly, Wellesley, Richard, Marquess Wellesley', *Oxford Dictionary of National Biography*: https://doi-org.ezproxy.lib.gla.ac.uk/10.1093/ref:odnb/29008.
59 NLS, MS10920, fos. 145–6; NLS, MS19298, fos. 85–94; NLS, MS1256, fos. 139–41; NRS, GD1/594/1: Edinburgh 31 March 1796; NRS, GD128/1/4/2; NRS, GD116/2/57; BC, Box 1/ London, 1 March 1790; AUL, MS2253/8/3/8; IOR, P/328/62 [1768], pp. 36–9.
60 NLS, MS3946, fos. 18–110; MS3947, fos. 5–110; MS3971, fos. 1–103; MS3973, pp. 3–22.
61 DCM, 3/70/1–4; NLS, MS2958, fos. 77–84; NRS, SC70/1/12, pp. 421–35; NRS, Registers of Sasines, Lothian (12160) (16581); Argyll (1134) (1177); Inverness (657) (691) (847).
62 CSAS, Duncan Papers, No 31, p. 26; NLS, MS6360, pp. 117–18; NLS, MS1256, fo. 209; NRS, Register of Sasines, Peebles (389) (606); Roxburgh (4254); Haddington (1205); Lothian (6666).
63 NRS, CC3/5/5, pp. 294–300; Hodson, *List of the Officers of the Army of Bengal*, vol. I, p. 417; vol. II, p. 332.
64 Paul Henderson Scott, 'Galt, John (1779–1839): *Oxford Dictionary of National Biography*: https://doi-org.ezproxy.lib.gla.ac.uk/10.1093/ref:odnb/10316.
65 PRAI, Register of Deeds, Vol. 295, No, 195406, pp. 164–6.

66 C. W. Munn, *The Scottish Provincial Banking Companies, 1747–1864* (Edinburgh: Donald, 1981), pp. 23–58.
67 NRS, Register of Sasines, Lanark (1842–43) (1872) (3708–10).
68 Lawson and Phillips, '"Our Execrable Banditti"', 226–34; P. J. Marshall, 'Burke and Empire', in S. Taylor, R. Connors and C. Jones (eds), *Hanoverian Britain and Empire* (Woodbridge: Boydell, 1998), pp. 296–8.
69 PRONI, D/2433/A/3/2: Caledon, 1 January 1779; NRS, RHP 42696; GD508/3/2/2–5; GD508/3/26; HL, Pulteney Papers, Box 4: Westerhall, 13 December 1764. *The Statistical Account of Scotland*. https://stataccscot.edina.ac.uk:443/link/osa-vol18-p586-parish-fife-leuchars. For smaller properties see NLS, MS6360, pp. 47–8, 134–136; NRS, GD128/1/3: September 1776; GD1/398/61; HAC, Novar Papers, D/538/39; DCA, Wedderburn of Pearsie, Box 7/25/17: Pearsie, 29 March 1778; PKA, MS115/Bundle 4: June 1806 to February 1808.
70 Devine, *Scotland's Empire*, p. 327.
71 *The Statistical Account of Scotland*. https://statascot.edina.ac.uk:443/link/osa-vol10-p365-inverness-harris; NLS, EMS.s.646: William Bald, 'Map of Harris', [1805].
72 *Statues Passed in the Parliaments Held in Ireland*, vol. IX (Dublin: George Geirson, 1799), pp. 472–4; W. Fitz Patrick (ed.), *HMC, Fortescue MSS*, Vol. I (London: HMSO, 1892): Dublin, 23 November 1783.
73 PRONI, D/2433/A/3/2: 12 August 1782; PRAI, Registry of Deeds, Vol. 352, No. 236829, p. 104; Vol. 357, No. 241112 p. 375; Vol. 385, No. 254654, pp. 152–4; Vol. 218, No. 144443, p. 481; IOR, L/MIL/10/131; TNA, PROB 11/1120. p. 333; Hodson, *List of the Officers of the Army of Bengal*, vol. I, p. 216.
74 NLI, MS29767/3: 10 August 1791; *Names of the proprietors of Grand Canal stock, and the amount, as it stood in the Company's ledger on the 1st day of June, 1800* (Dublin: n.p. 1800).
75 Devine, *Scotland's Empire*, pp. 331–2; NRS, SC36/48/6, pp. 275–7; GD393/6/1, fos. 99–102; Registers of Sasines, Ayr, Vol. I (2221) (8846–47) (9004); *The Statistical Account of Scotland*: https://stataccounscot.edina.ac.uk:443/link/osa-vol20-p165-parish-ayrshire-sorn.
76 B. Watters, *Where Iron Runs Like Water: A New History of Carron Iron Works, 1759–1982* (Edinburgh: John Donald, 1998), pp. 41–5, 183; *The Statistical Account of Scotland:* https://stataccscot.edina.ac.uk:443/liml/osa-vol1-p212-parish-edinburgh-crammond.
77 Devine, 'The Colonial Trades', pp. 1–13.
78 NRS, GD9/3, pp. 431–9.
79 A. Mackenzie, *History of the Munros of Fowlis* (Inverness: Mackenzie, 1908), p. 535; TNA, PROB 11/1651, pp. 99–104.
80 HAC, HHB/1/1/1, 'Minutes of Committee of Subscribers for the Northern Infirmary, 1799–1804'; HHB/1/2/1, pp. 2–10.
81 Jessica Hanser, *Mr Smith Goes to China: Three Scots in the Making of Britain's Global Empire* (New Haven, CT, and London: Yale University Press, 2019), pp. 166–7.

82 Peter John Anderson, *Officers and Graduates of the University and King's College, Aberdeen, 1495–1860* (Aberdeen: New Spalding Club, 1893), pp. 244, 358; TNA, PROB 11/1514, pp. 186–91. For other educational bursaries, see, IOR, L/AG/34/29/209, pp. 1–6.
83 *The Statistical Account of Scotland*: https://stataccscot.edina.ac.uk:443/link/osa-vol16-p511-parish-roxburgh-morebattle_and_mow; TNA, PROB 11/549, pp. 211–13.
84 *The Statistical Accounts of Scotland*: https://stataccscot.edina.ac.uk:443/link/nsa-vol13-p5-parish-elgin-elgin; NRS, SC26/38/1/101–113: Elgin, 14 December 1824; NLS, EMS.s.759: Robert Ray, 'Plan of the Burgh of Elgin from actual survey' (Edinburgh: Leith & Smith, 1838).
85 Dundee Art Galleries and Museums Collection (Dundee City Council), Alexander Nasmyth (1758–1840), 'Castle Huntly', *c*.1800.
86 *The Statistical Account of Scotland.* https://statascot.edina.ac.uk:443/link/osa-vol10-p365-inverness-harris; NLS, William Bald, 'Map of Harris', [Edinburgh: W. Ballantyne, 1805]: EMS.s.646.
87 'Rowadill in Harris, 1819', in William Daniell, *A Voyage around Great Britain, 1814–1825*. Image at: www.tate.org.uk/art/artworks/daniell-rowadill-in-harris-t02837.
88 Price, 'One Big Thing', 602–27; Hall, *Civilising Subjects*, pp. 4, 11–12; Hall and Rose, 'Introduction', pp. 13–14, 32–4.
89 NRS, GD155/1326/2: *Rules of the Edinburgh East India Club with a list of the members, and when admitted. 27 January 1815* (Edinburgh: Oliver & Boyd, 1815); NRS, GD29/2067/33.
90 Bob Harris, *The Scottish People and the French Revolution* (London: Pickering and Chatto, 2008), p. 125.
91 Finn and Smith, 'Introduction', p. 3.
92 Mackillop, 'The Highlands and the Returning Nabob', pp. 242–52.

Conclusion
'Poor' Europe's pathways to empire and globalisation

In 1821, eight years after the termination of the English East India Company's India monopoly and at the end of the era covered by this book, Sir Walter Scott penned one of his typically memorable phrases. Conjuring up the essence of his own country's now substantial links with Britain's Eastern Empire, he noted that India was 'the corn chest for Scotland where we poor gentry must send our youngest sons as we send our black cattle to the South'.[1] For all its obvious attempts to paint the imperial connection in the homely imagery of the ancient cattle trade with England, Scott's characterisation finds support in the analysis offered here. His observation is nothing less than a description of an economy of high-value human capital in action. It was another Scots Borderer, John Maxwell of Broomholm, who captured the far less sentimental reality when he thanked his patron in 1762 for efforts to place his son in India, adding 'I looked on sending him sooner than sixteen, as making a sacrifice of him for the bread of the rest.'[2] This understudied form of provincial economy, which treated people as capital and migration as an investment and development strategy, lies at the heart of this book. As a mode of expansion it constituted the primary means by which the metropolitan provinces of the pre-1815 British and Irish Isles accessed the eastern hemisphere of England and later Britain's world empire.

The emergence of this economy of human capital and its capacity to accumulate financial surpluses offers a number of interpretative perspectives. Firstly, it provides a holistic understanding of the scale of Ireland, Scotland and Wales's participation in a part of the British Empire that is far less well studied in the histories of these societies compared to the Atlantic world.[3] Although less influential in the socio-economic and migration experience of all three countries before the 1820s, the Company's commerce and colonialism should be integrated more consistently into assessments of early modern Scottish, Irish and Welsh histories. The starting point for an informed awareness of this Asia dimension is the matter of numbers. The Company's embarkation lists, muster rolls and censuses between c.1753 and the end of the India monopoly in 1813 make it clear that a minimum of about 17,000 and perhaps as many as 20,000 Irishmen migrated to Asia in this period. By contrast, calculations for departures to North America between 1700 and 1800 fall into a capacious band of between 110,000 to over 200,000.[4] The same quantitative uncertainty and numeric disparity applies to assessments of Scottish mobility. Suggestions of about 86,000 crossing to North America between about 1700 and 1800 have been augmented by the 17,000 or so moving to the Caribbean in the second half of the century.[5] The likely amount departing for Asia in the same period underlines the much greater scale of human involvement in the Atlantic Empire. The Company's records point to a robust but conservative estimate of around 10,000 Scottish civil servants, military and marine officers, doctors and enlisted men in the British and Company armies from the early 1750s to about 1813 or trading in Asia on their own account. In the same period Welsh involvement amounted to 1,200–1,300.

At one level these figures can be analysed as part of the well-known migration histories of Ireland and Scotland. But they can also be read in a radically different way, as an expression of how the comparatively disadvantaged, finance constrained areas of Europe mobilised social assets to exploit empire and its associated global economies. Viewing these movements as something more than migration and as transhemispheric investments of human capital involves a fundamental reconceptualising of migrants and their social networks. People constituted the most mobile form of wealth available to large swathes of 'poor' early modern Europe. This reformulation warns against defining 'capital' too narrowly, as a purely monetary phenomenon. To do so risks relegating the role of human mobility to a reactive manifestation of the socio-economic displacement brought about by finance capital's deployment and market influence.[6] The boundaries between people and capital overlapped. One of the key effects of empire in Asia was to amplify the productive potential of this entanglement. The wider value of early modern Ireland and Scotland to debates on the nature of global expansion is that they reveal how the boundaries between people and wealth, and between economic development and migration, were blurred and mutually constitutive. This perspective moves societies like Ireland and Scotland out of the imprecise category of 'semi-peripheries' attached to them by World Systems models.[7] Instead they can be put in a more precise demarcation of countries that were 'poor' in terms of monetary capital but compensated for this disadvantage through a relative reliance on human and social wealth. These 'poor' societies collapsed the distinction between people and venture finance and used human capital as a proxy. It is in this more exact sense that Scotland and Ireland can be understood as exemplars of 'poor' Europe. Through this framing their sojourning economies become a case study of the historically crucial role of human capital in European colonialism and global expansion. One of the most significant lessons to be drawn from the cycles of departure to and return from Asia outlined here is that people provided 'poor' Europe with highly effective pathways into proto-globalisation.

There are major implications in this reconfiguration and its emphasis on the plurality of routes into empire and the global economic system.[8] Not the least of these is the need to rethink the place of London and the metropolitan provinces in the long eighteenth-century phase of British expansion and empire. How are concepts of gentlemanly and gentry capitalism to be configured if migrants were a mode of investment which was more mobile in many ways than the monetary assets that defined the City's economic dominance? Another benefit of connecting societies like Ireland and Scotland to London and to transnational institutions like the United English East India Company is that the variations of gentlemanly capitalism become clearer. To the original City-centric formulation can be added a mode of provincial gentry capitalism which traded in venture finance where these were available but also relied heavily on social assets and human wealth. Brokers of human capital like Laurence Sulivan, John Drummond of Quarrell or David Scott of Dunninald were adept at extending London's influence into the localities while simultaneously embedding local interests in the metropole, the Company and its operations in Asia.

This multicentred version of pre-1815 provincial gentry capitalism forces a reconsideration of assumptions that Ireland, Scotland and Wales simply slotted into London's pre-existing frameworks of finance and commerce from a position of dependency.[9] Human capital meant the provinces were not as impoverished as assessments based on conventional monetary resources might suggest.[10] The relationship between province and City was less defined by hegemony and dependency than by mutual interaction and the blending of metropolitan and provincial variants of wealth. Another effect of incorporating the Eastern hemisphere into an understanding of the Irish, Scots and Welsh role in empire is that London looms larger than is the case when the frame of reference is the Atlantic world. Connections with the Western half of the Empire are usually studied in terms of direct, bilateral contact between colonies and dynamic provincial ports like Belfast, Cork, Swansea or Glasgow. Foregrounding Asia brings the metropolis more fully into the socio-economic and migration histories of Ireland, Scotland and Wales.

If the prism of human capital offers fundamentally new interpretative possibilities, it is equally important to understand that not all human capital had the same value or, crucially, the same capacity to generate monetary wealth. A rank-and-file recruit to the European regiments at Bombay,

Calcutta or Madras might, if life and luck continued, make a considerable amount of money. But the chances of moving beyond salary subsistence to secure sustained capital accumulation were remote. This is why ordinary soldiers and seamen can be conceived of as high-volume/low-value human capital. These descriptions apply only in terms of the potential for creating surplus monetary capital and are not intended to rob these individuals of their human agency and personal dignity. The high-volume attribution refers to the fact that the EIC employed thousands of such personnel every year. The single most significant connection between Irish society and the Company consisted of exporting substantial amounts of low-value human capital. This was paralleled by a smaller, more socially and regionally specific input of low-volume/high-value individuals. This elite branch of pre-1815 Irish mobility to Asia has been compiled for the first time in the SIWA database. The findings reveal 128 civil servants, 102 merchant marine officers, 46 surgeons and 1,256 military officers between 1690 and 1813. All but fifty-four of these were appointed after 1750. Human wealth leaving Ireland for Asia did so in a highly distinctive configuration. The vast bulk, probably in the order of 15,000–17,000 men between 1750 and the early 1810s, were high-volume/low-value soldiers. By contrast, the addition of the known number of private merchants and mariners means only 1,796 confirmed Irish individuals in the same period consisted of the low-volume/high-value variant of sojourner.

Welsh interactions followed a radically different path. Indeed, the contrast is such that it highlights the inability of empire, no matter how pervasive 'at home', to overcome some of the metropolitan provinces' pre-existing social, economic and cultural configurations. Scotland, Ireland and Wales were exposed to exactly the same empire influences after $c.1750$ and yet interacted and reacted in remarkably different ways. With its consistent pattern of under representation within the Company's European workforce, the case of Wales provides unique insights. The relative Welsh absence from empire in Asia in terms of direct human involvement is a telling example of an early modern society adjusting to global forces in ways directly determined by its own pre-existing geographic, linguistic and socio-economic condition.[11] The country's experience is an example of glocalism's capacity to generate radically different modes of interaction with, and partial disconnection from, seemingly generic and homogenising imperial dynamics.

If Irish society increasingly developed a high-volume/low-value human capital export economy, Scotland's interactions with the Company evolved as a low-volume/high-value paradigm. A consistent feature of the Scottish presence in pre-1815 Asia was a pattern of overrepresentation in key areas of the elite workforce, especially military officers, medical personnel and free merchants/mariners. The acquisition of posts in the civil service and merchant marine was less sustained but reached levels at, or not far below, the country's share of population by the early 1750s and 1760s. By the 1790s and 1800s the tendency towards an enhanced share was also evident in these prestigious and profitable sectors. While approximately 6,000–6,500 Scots served as soldiers from the 1750s to 1810s, 4,013 can be traced to higher-level positions at the same time. Only around 10–12 per cent of Irish sojourners in this period were 'high-value' migrants: in the case of Scots it was about 40 per cent. In conventional migration terms the Scottish numbers can seem trifling, but they are the demographic indicators of a society mobilising and exporting its high-value human capital.

The marked differences between Wales, Ireland and Scotland warn against emphasising only the Empire's capacity to integrate or assimilate the British and Irish Isles.[12] If empire worked its influence upon locality, region and nation, these in turn shaped the functioning nature of British expansion and imperialism. A key consequence of this interactive dynamic was the development of new internal divergences within and between the metropolitan provinces. One manifestation of this trend towards new differences was the variation in rates of wealth creation. A key attraction of the Eastern Empire for cash-poor societies like Ireland and Scotland was that it acted as an exchange mechanism converting human capital into its monetary counterpart. In this context the precise configuration of human wealth exported under the Company's aegis enabled Scottish society to benefit more broadly than the other two metropolitan provinces. The scale of returning profits was such that only 8.6 per cent of the 4,013 Scottish and 5 per cent of the 1,796 Irish sojourners traced in this book accrued over £5.5 million and £2.1 million respectively. One way of contextualising these sums is to note they are equivalent to 'real price', conservative estimates in 2019 of £670.2 million and £261.5 million.[13] Both the historic and contemporary figures underline the previously unappreciated capacity of sojourning human capital to generate significant levels of primitive capital accumulation. The amounts may not seem especially impressive if viewed from the developed regions of what historians of globalisation call 'comparatively advantaged' Europe.[14] But in 'comparatively disadvantaged', 'poor Europe', the transformative potential of such sums cannot be underestimated.

Another way of putting these profits into context is to compare them with figures used in debates over the role of overseas surpluses in the development of Britain's capitalist and industrialising economy. Both Dadabhai Naoroji's 'drain theory' (more usually applied to nineteenth- and early twentieth-century India) and Eric Williams's famous thesis relating to the role in the English economy of slavery-derived capital have found supporters and detractors.[15] Both concepts take on a different significance and new relevance when viewed from the perspective of pre-1815 Ireland or

Scotland. In an attempt to quantify the importance of Company-era transfers from South Asia back to Britain, one deliberately conservative estimate has posited a total of between £30–38 million in the period 1758 to 1815.[16] Viewed in this light, Irish accumulation derived from the export of its human capital was well below its share of the British and Irish Isles' population. By contrast, the £5.5 million traced to 347 Scottish sojourners suggests either these individuals secured a minimum of 14 per cent of all British returns or, more likely, that the overall amount remitted to Britain was actually larger. Scottish evidence suggests that the marginalisation of 'drain' from Asia in explanations of pre-1815 Britain's economic performance needs reconsideration and revisiting. East Indies profits may not have materially influenced the already affluent and diverse economy of large parts of England. But the case for a more central role for imperial wealth is much stronger when it comes to Scotland during the long eighteenth century.[17] The new evidence of the scale and dispersal of returning capital from the Eastern Empire makes this case even stronger still. Set against the national banking sector's entire stock of £2 million or the average capital assets of the provincial banks, the £5.5 million and the lending shown in Appendix 7.1 represent major, country-wide injections of new wealth. Eastern profits unquestionably augmented Scotland's capital stock and credit circulation and were especially significant in buttressing the solvency of the landed order as it implemented large-scale, transformative agrarian 'improvement'.[18] The confirmed totals also mean that the Asian hemisphere of the Empire needs to be placed firmly alongside the tobacco trade and the slave compensation scheme of 1834 as a key driver in the crucial process of Scotland's primitive capital accumulation.[19] Asia was central in turning 'poor' early modern Scotland into a 'richer' country in monetary capital terms.

The uneven pattern of capital accumulation in Ireland and Scotland highlights one of the great ironies of the Eastern Empire's impact on the metropolitan provinces. Despite sending out greater numbers of people, Irish society did not accrue profits in proportion. This is because connections to the Company evolved in a unique fashion. Ireland became the key supplier of high-volume/low-value manpower for the corporation's strategically vital European regiments in the armies of Bengal, Bombay and Madras. Alongside this human 'drain' was a parallel economy in service-gentry officers which drew overwhelmingly from established Protestant families and regions. This left the majority community in Ireland in a low-profit nexus with the Company, with wealth-generating opportunities largely, although not entirely, restricted to the country's most affluent communities. The operating realities of the British Empire in Asia meant that while Ireland was rich in people, her people could not make Ireland rich. It was a diametrically opposite dynamic in Scotland. With high-value/low-volume human capital forming such a significant element in migration to Asia, Scottish society, despite its relatively low population reserves, found that a small number of people made the country significantly richer.

These broad patterns played out in regionally nuanced and complex ways. Both Wales and Ireland exhibited similar clustering in terms of the geographic and social origins of those joining the Company's civil elite, its merchant marine and military services. The provinces of Leinster and Ulster dominated in an Irish context while in Wales the anglicised, urbanised and commercially developing southern and eastern counties supplied the vast bulk of such personnel. The debate over whether the structure of Scotland's Atlantic commerce resulted in profits coalescing in geographically and economically limited 'enclaves' has largely been settled through a greater appreciation for the wide regional dispersal of profits.[20] Ironically, a theory originally developed in relation to west-central Scotland rather better explains trends in Ireland and Wales. With a fuller understanding of the Irish contribution to the Empire in Asia it is possible to argue that Ireland in the long eighteenth century evolved at least three distinct regionally orientated branches of interaction with British imperialism. Ulster's linen industry drove commercial and migratory connections to the ports and hinterlands of the eastern seaboard of North America and the Caribbean. In the south-west, provisioning of Royal Navy, slaving-related and EIC shipping shaped agricultural, market and port economies. Meanwhile, Ulster and Leinster in particular evolved sustained connections to the Empire's two separate military forces, supplying disproportionate numbers of officers and men for the British army and EIC.[21] An intriguing question, outside the scope of this book, is the extent to which these three modes of involvement shaped nineteenth-century Ireland's trajectory within the Union and its status as a 'sub-metropolitan' part of the wider empire.[22]

The pattern of evidence derived from Asia also raises significant questions about imperialism's uneven effects on Ireland's relationship with the British union state. Irish Protestant gentry and middling orders were in receipt of high levels of corporate military patronage between around 1750 and 1780. In these decades they secured approximately 20 per cent of all commissioned posts. Yet even as they participated disproportionately in a key sector of global expansion, or perhaps because of this, Protestant communities felt confident enough to challenge British interference in their domestic political and commercial liberties. Inordinate involvement in empire did not mean accepting the hegemony of the British parliament. An important lesson for historians of Britain and Britishness to be drawn from the high Irish profile in the EIC's military is that it points to the clear limits of the Empire's assimilative influence upon the largest and most populous of the metropolitan provinces.

The contradictory dynamics between emerging empire in South Asia and evolving state formation in the British and Irish Isles continued into the era of union. It has been argued that the prospect of full involvement in imperial affairs became a primary means of persuading a sceptical Protestant political nation in the 1790s of the benefits of an incorporating union.[23] Yet at exactly the same time as the kingdom obtained full access to the British Atlantic system after 1780, existing patterns of over representation in the officer-levels of the EIC's military complex went into relative decline. Ireland's age of union and empire between the 1780s and the early 1800s was characterised by profoundly ambiguous dynamics that worked across each other.[24] Free trade gains in the Atlantic were offset by three previously unappreciated trends in the Eastern Empire. These involved a reduced share of the Company's military officer corps, the increasing emergence of the low-value export economy in manpower, and a marginal profile in the dynamic country trade. The capacity of Britain's global empire under these circumstances to deliver substantial and socially dispersed wealth into Ireland in ways that might have helped secure the Union was limited and, crucially, becoming more from the 1780s. These contradictory trends point to how empire simultaneously facilitated and stymied the expansion of Britishness across the British and Irish Isles. If the domestic unions terminated the older 'ancient' and independent 'kingdoms', one effect of overseas expansion and imperialism was to drive the evolution of 'metropolitan provinces' which integrated with but also diverged from English society and each other in new ways.[25] One of the Empire's most significant domestic effects was to shape the Scottish and Irish unions so that they acted as management mechanisms for internal differences rather than as the means of creating a genuinely assimilated unitary state and society.

Regional engagement also characterised Scottish society's intersection with the Company. However, unlike Ireland or Wales, patterns of involvement were broadly distributed in a social and geographic sense, spreading the influence of the eastern empire throughout the country. This distribution meant that while the number of sojourners involved was relatively small, the effect of the Asia connection was evident across almost all regions and localities. The only exception was the far north, in Caithness, Orkney and Shetland. A possible reason for this lack of engagement may be that these areas developed a highly effective human capital economy with another of London's global corporations, the Hudson's Bay Company.[26] Meanwhile, aristocracy, gentry and leading tenants from the Scottish Highlands committed substantial reserves of high-value human capital to the Asian half of the Empire, supplying more military officers per capita to the Company in this period than any other part of Britain and Ireland. The extent of this involvement underscores how the region reacted to imperial and global opportunities with a mixture of dynamism and the adaptation of social assets such as familial and kin networks.[27]

Major outward movement was matched with the arrival back of people and profits. Few if any other parts of Scotland felt the returning impact as directly and intensely as large parts of Ross-shire, Argyllshire and Inverness-shire. Nabob wealth played out in these localities in conspicuous and arbitrary ways. Financially embattled noble families were able to retain their estates while imperial profits provided 'improving' service gentry with the capacity and security to begin evictions, as at Novar, or major resettlement schemes in areas of Skye, Harris and Kinlochmoidart.[28] It was in rural districts such as these, lacking reserves of capital and economic diversity, that returning imperial wealth seemed to make the most demonstrable impact and leave the easiest-to-trace legacies.

The same dynamic played out across the rest of Scotland to varying degrees. One of the most surprising lessons to be drawn from how Scots moved into the Company is the heightened profile of parts of the country not strongly associated with the pre-1815 phase of empire. The role and profile of Edinburgh is transformed once empire in Asia is factored in. The city secured over 10 per cent of all traceable Scottish civil servant and military officers (Tables 3.2 and 4.3). The established emphasis on the rise of Glasgow through its Atlantic connections needs to be balanced with an awareness of Edinburgh and its Lothian hinterland's strong links to Asia. Eighteenth-century Scotland had two imperial cities, not one. The rebalancing of where and how society engaged with empire can be extended to the whole of the eastern seaboard. Counties like Stirling, Perth, Fife and Angus witnessed substantial numbers departing as sojourners and a considerable clustering of returning Asia wealth in the form of credit and estate purchases (Map 7.2 and Appendix 7.1). If the Atlantic world underpinned the rise of west-central Scotland, the Company's empire materially sustained east-central Scotland.

When all these developments are brought together, the truly pervasive extent of Scottish society's engagement with British expansion becomes clear. Involvement developed a pronounced set of regional emphases in a manner similar to Ireland. Four major modes of intersection with pre-1815 British imperialism can be delineated and which between them covered the entire country and encompassed all of its social hierarchy. The first of these, the case of Orkney, has already been mentioned. In many ways the wholly disproportionate profile of Orcadians in the Hudson's Bay Company provides a revealing example of glocalism in the age of early modern expansion. So too does the supply of manpower to the British army which emerged in the Scottish Highlands between the battles of Culloden and Waterloo.[29] This was a niche economy of high-volume/low-value soldiers and high-value/low-volume officers. These features match exactly the pattern which developed between Irish society and the EIC, with the crucial distinction that in Scotland the landed classes used their proprietary control over tenantry to negotiate advantageous conditions of state as opposed to corporate employment. The manpower supply chain in the Highlands delivered state salaries and social status to officer gentry and access to substantial amounts of land for enlisted men, either on their home estates or in North America.[30]

To these two northern regional economies needs to be added the well-known history of west-central Scotland's commercial expansion into the slavery-based tobacco, sugar and, later, cotton trades.[31] Now that the lineaments of involvement in Asia can be traced for Scotland, the fourth major branch can be included. This sojourner economy of high-value human capital emerged across the entire country but tended to be concentrated around Edinburgh, the east-central counties, the north-east and the Highlands. Highland gentry and leading tenantry joined the officer corps of the Company's forces in ways that paralleled their high profile within the British army. The existence of these four major branches of engagement meant that every region of pre-1815 Scotland became deeply immersed in and reshaped by empire.

The picture of differently configured regional aligned economies emerging across Ireland, Scotland and to a lesser extent Wales, points to the wider usefulness of these provincial societies when conceptualising early modern Europe's global expansion. The polycentric, diversified nature of Irish and Scottish participation in empire echoes the new emphasis on the pluralistic pathways to 'modernity' and the multiple configurations of proto-globalisation.[32] The key asset used by the 'poor' provinces of the British and Irish Isles to achieve this involvement also highlights the need to think holistically about the spectrum of resources used to exploit colonial expansion. Arguably the single most striking feature of Irish and Scottish (though not Welsh) involvement in the EIC's trade and empire was the central place of people and their mobility. Faced with how to access global expansion while surmounting the related need for investment finance, the metropolitan provinces threw their people at the problem. The sharp contrasts between the three provincial societies also reveals how proto-global forces worked inside the colonising 'core' to produce new patterns of assimilation and interconnection but also new forms of distinctiveness. Even as empire created powerful integrative forces across the British and Irish Isles it generated uneven levels of involvement and inequalities of primitive capital accumulation of the sort more usually associated with colonial societies. Alongside the demonstration they provide of 'poor' Europe's sophisticated use of people as venture capital, these complexities at the 'core' are a key lesson to be drawn from Ireland, Scotland and Wales's diverse trajectories within early British imperialism in Asia.

The impact and legacies of these variegated patterns of participation, especially those of the more numerically significant Irish and Scots, goes well beyond the national histories of these societies or that of Britain and its empire. Involvement in the Company meant two small Northern European countries contributed disproportionately to a process of conquest between c.1750 and c.1820 that brought tens of millions of people under the corporation's rule and which altered the course of world history.[33] 'Poor' Europe, just as surely as 'comparative advantaged' Europe, lay at the cutting edge of some of the most expansionist and coercive forms of pre-1815 empire. Yet does a better understanding of the innately composite character of the coloniser matter? In some ways, no. If viewed from the perspective of those in India and elsewhere in Asia on the receiving end of corporate imperialism, the Scots, Irish and Welsh would have seemed largely indistinguishable from the wider British or European colonial community.[34] But the influx of metropolitan provincials into the English East India Company and its associated country trades was important. It deepened and diversified the human, social and cultural make-up of the colonising presence. Alongside the formal institutional, economic and financial power of the Company was added a welter of familial, local, regional and national networks with diverse priorities and adaptable practices. The metropolitan provincials helped make early British colonialism in Asia a many-headed hydra. In doing so they made it more complex, multifaceted, and difficult to anticipate and resist. In this, at least, the presence of the Irish and Scots did matter to the early modern history of Asia's peoples and communities.

Yet perhaps the most apt concluding point is to stress that the connections with Asia outlined here were always protean and subject to change. By the time of Sir Walter Scott's observation, metropolitan provincial interactions were already undergoing a slow but ultimately seminal reconfiguration. Although Ireland continued for another two to three decades to supply high-volume/low-value soldiers, its links with the Eastern Empire after about 1830 began to resemble aspects of the high-value/low-volume human capital nexus so characteristic of Scottish society of c.1720– c.1820. Increasing numbers of Irishmen (both Catholic and Protestant) entered the Company's and then the Raj's civil, military and medical divisions up until the twentieth century. Running parallel and counter to this were growing Irish and Indian nationalist interactions and co-operations that sought to end British power in both countries.[35] While Irish society developed new modes of imperial involvement and mutually constitutive political and cultural dynamics with South Asia, Scotland's trajectory remained in a more obviously colonial configuration. The export of high-value human wealth and its resultant financial returns had materially aided the country's primitive capital accumulation during the long eighteenth century. By the 1820s colonialism in Asia had facilitated transformative processes of 'improvement' and helped turn 'poor' Scotland into a richer society with far greater levels of monetary capital and liquidity. By the 1830s Scottish reliance on people as the key mode of investment shifted towards a greater emphasis on imperial, commercial, industrial and commodity links defined by financial and technological assets.[36] One age and one form of capital gave way to another and in doing so helped define both Scotland and Ireland's enduring, if always tellingly different, immersions in Britain's empire in Asia up until the onset of decolonisation in 1947.

Notes

1 Bryant, 'Scots in India', 22.
2 HL, Pulteney Papers, Box 4: Broomholm, 4 July 1762.
3 H. V. Bowen, 'Introduction', in Bowen, *Wales and the British Overseas Empire*, pp. 10–11; Truxes, *Irish-American Trade*, pp. 46–50; Devine and Rössner, 'Scotland and the Atlantic Economy', pp. 30–53.
4 Patrick Fitzgerald and Brian Lambkin, *Migration in Irish History, 1607–2007* (Basingstoke: Palgrave, 2008), pp. 113–48 (figure 2).
5 James Horn, 'British Diaspora: Emigration from Britain, 1680–1815', in Marshall, *The Oxford History of the British Empire*, vol. II, p. 32; Cullen, 'The Irish Diaspora', pp. 98, 104; Smout, Landsman and Devine, 'Scottish Emigration in the Seventeenth and Eighteenth Centuries', pp. 140–1; Hamilton, *Scotland, the Caribbean and the Atlantic World*, p. 23.
6 de Vries, 'The Limits of Globalisation', 713–14; Parthasarathi, *Why Europe Grew Rich*, pp. 264–8.
7 Wallerstein, *The Modern World-System II*, pp. 251–4.
8 de Vries, 'The Limits of Globalisation', 711–14.
9 Dumett, 'Exploring the Cain/Hopkins Paradigm', pp. 8–9.
10 Colley, *Britons*, pp. 123–4; Langford, 'South Britons' Reception of North Britons', pp. 143–69.
11 Nussbaum, 'Introduction', pp. 8–10; Natalie Zemon Davis, 'Decentering History: Local Stories and Cultural Crossing in a Global World', *History and Theory*, 50 (2011), 190–1; Neil Evans, 'Writing Wales into the Empire: Rhetoric, Fragments – and Beyond?', in Bowen, *Wales and the British Overseas Empire*, pp. 31–3.
12 Colley, *Britons*, p. 375; Jackson, *The Two Unions*, pp. 338–44.
13 Estimates for the contemporary value of these historic profits are drawn from the Measuring Worth.Com calculator and use the most conservative, 'real price' calculation, taking 1790 as the benchmark. See www.measuringworth.com/calculators/ppoweruk/.

14 Bayly, *The Birth of the Modern World*, pp. 60–4; Pomeranz, *The Great Divergence*, pp. 24, 285–7.
15 Tirthanker Roy, *How British Rule Changed India's Economy: The Paradox of the Raj* (Basingstoke: Palgrave Macmillan, 2019), pp. 103–5; Sutapa Bose, 'The Problem of Primitive Accumulation', *Economic and Political Weekly*, 23 (1988), 1169–74; Furber, *John Company at Work*, pp. 304–10; Stanley L. Engerman, 'Slave Trade and British Capital Formation in the Eighteenth Century: A Comment on the Williams Thesis', *The Business History Review*, 46 (1972), 430–43; Joseph E. Inikori, *Africans and the Industrial Revolution in England: A Study in International Trade and Development* (Cambridge: Cambridge University Press, 2002), pp. 479–81.
16 Javier Cuenca Esteban, 'The British Balance of Payments, 1772–1820: India Transfers and War Finance', *The Economic History Review*, 54 (2001), 60, 66.
17 Devine, *Scotland's Empire*, pp. 326–8; Devine, 'Did Slavery Make Scotia Great?', pp. 232–4.
18 T. M. Devine, *The Transformation of Rural Society: Social Change and the Agrarian Economy, 1660–1815* (Edinburgh: Edinburgh University Press, 1994), pp. 60–5.
19 Draper, 'Scotland and Colonial Slave Ownership', pp. 179–82; Devine, 'Did Slavery Make Scotia Great?', pp. 229–38.
20 Devine, *Scotland's Empire*, pp. 330–5.
21 Dickson, *Old World Colony*, pp. 120–3; Truxes, *Irish-American Trade*, pp. 46–50; Cookson, *The British Armed Nation*, pp. 153–81.
22 Crosbie, *Irish Imperial Networks*, pp. 17–23.
23 Bartlett, 'An Union for Empire', pp. 53–7.
24 Jackson, *The Two Unions*, pp. 185–7.
25 Livesey, *Civil Society and Empire*, pp. 18–23, 214–18; Landsman, 'The Provinces and Empire', pp. 246–50.
26 Rigg, *Men of Spirit and Enterprise*, pp. 11–37, 174–5.
27 Taylor, *The Wild Black Region*, pp. 248–60.
28 Mackillop, 'The Highlands and the Returning Nabob', pp. 246–56.
29 Rigg, *Men of Spirit and Enterprise*, pp. 174–5; Mackillop, 'More Fruitful than the Soil', pp. 234–44.
30 Mackillop, 'More Fruitful than the Soil', pp. 182–90; Dziennik, *The Fatal Land*, pp. 220–8; Mackillop, '"As Hewers of Wood"', pp. 23–45.
31 Devine, *The Glasgow Tobacco Lords*, pp. 171–3; Richards, 'Scotland and the Uses of the Atlantic Empire', pp. 68–114.
32 Bayly, *The Birth of the Modern World*, pp. 44–5; Phillips, 'The Global Transformation, Multiple Early Modernities', 481–8.
33 Bayly, *The Making of the Modern World*, pp. 88–91; Pomeranz, *The Great Divergence*, pp. 199–200; Andrew Phillips and J. C. Sharman, *Outsourcing Empire: How Company States Made the Modern World* (Princeton, NJ: Princeton University Press, 2020), pp. 136–49.
34 Gulfishan Khan, *Indian Muslim Perceptions of the West during the*

Eighteenth Century (Oxford and New Delhi: Oxford University Press, 1998), pp. 55–203.
35 Cook, 'The Irish Raj', 507–23; Bayly, 'Ireland, India and the Empire', 377–97; M. Silvestri, *Ireland and India: Nationalism, Empire and Memory* (Basingstoke: Palgrave Macmillan, 2009), pp. 4–12.
36 T. M. Devine, *To the Ends of the Earth: Scotland's Global Diaspora* (London: Allen Lane, 2011), pp. 56–84, 291; Jim Tomlinson, *Dundee and the Empire: 'Juteopolis' 1850–1939* (Edinburgh: Edinburgh University Press, 2014), pp. 24–34.

Appendices

Appendix 2.1 Metropolitan regionalism: patterns of patronage, 1791–1813

Director/ Govt Minister	Regional Origin	Total Scots, Irish and Welsh Clients (dates)	Own Nationality	Region
Sweny Toone	Munster	34 (1800–1813)	18 (52.9%)	Leinster = 9 (50%) Ulster = 3 (16.6%) England = 3 (16.6%) Munster = 2 (11.1%) Connacht = 1 (6.2%)
Lord Castlereagh	Ulster	61 (1802–1812)	53 (86.8%)	Ulster = 35 (67.3%) Leinster = 8 (13.1%) Munster = 6 (11.5%) Connacht = 4 (7.6%)
William F- Elphinstone	Central	78 (1791–1811)	72 (92.3%)	West-Central = 21 (29.1%) Central = 14 (19.4%) Edinburgh = 12 (15.3%) Lothians = 6 (8.3%) Borders = 4 (5.1%) Highlands = 3 (4.1%) Scotland = 11 (15.4%) England = 1 (1.3%)
Charles Grant	Highlands	101 (1799–1813)	93 (92%)	Highlands = 50 (51%) NE = 11 (11.8%) West-Central = 7 (7.5%) Edinburgh = 7 (7.5%) Central = 6 (6.4%) Borders = 3 (3.2%) Lothians = 2 (2.1%) England = 2 (2.1%) Atlantic Empire = 2 (2.1%) Northern Isles = 1 (1%) Bengal = 1 (1%) Unknown = 1 (1%)

(Source: SIWA: IOR, J/1/13–28; L/MIL/9/107–125; L/MIL/12/86; L/MIL/9/358–365).

Appendix 4.1 High- and low-value human capital: military embarkations, 1753–1813

1753–1763	Total	Scots	Irish	Welsh
Officers	87	22 (25.2%)	14 (14.5%)	0 (0%)
Cadets	290	19 (6.5%)	65 (22.4%)	13 (4.4%)
Rank and File	7,268	618 (8.5%)	889 (12.2%)	170 (2.3%)

1775–1781	Total	Scots	Irish	Welsh
Cadets	928	190 (20.4%)	193 (20.7%)	14 (1.5%)
NCOs	172	22 (12.7%)	69 (40.1%)	0 (0%)
Privates	4,949	170 (3.4%)	1,302 (26.3%)	66 (1.3%)

1782–1786	Total	Scots	Irish	Welsh
Privates	5,056	328 (6.4%)	790 (15.6%)	95 (2.4%)

1792–1793	Total	Scots	Irish	Welsh
NCOs	19	6 (31.5%)	2 (10.5%)	1 (8.3%)
Privates	2,821	159 (6.2%)	716 (25.3%)	50 (2.5%)

1795	Total	Scots	Irish	Welsh
NCOs	7	0	0	1 (14.2%)
Privates	537	19 (3.5%)	128 (23.5%)	11 (2%)

1810	Total	Scots	Irish	Welsh
NCOs	56	1 (1.7%)	25 (44.6%)	1 (1.7%)
Privates	688	12 (1.7%)	400 (58.1%)	12 (1.7%)

1812	Total	Scots	Irish	Welsh
NCOs	123	14 (11.3%)	54 (43.9%)	1 (0.77%)
Privates	1,780	70 (3.9%)	847 (47.5%)	35 (1.9%)

(Source: IOR, L/MIL/9/85, L/MIL/9/90; L/MIL/9/95, L/MIL/9/96; L/MIL/9/98; L/MIL/9/104).

Appendix 6.1 The Graham meso-network: Scotland, London, Lisbon, Bengal, Madras, Dacca and Benkulen

London
Thomas Cheap of Sauchie - Scot (EIC director)
Hugh Inglis - Scot (EIC director)
William Fullerton-Elphinstone - Scot (EIC director)
William Bensley - English (EIC director)
William Lushington - English (EIC director)
Robert, John & William Mayne - Scots (merchant/finance/patronage)
Henry Streachy - English
Hugh Cleghorn - Scot
James Macpherson - Scot (patronage)
Lauchlin Macleane - Irish (patronage)
Henry Dundas - Scot (patronage)

Scotland
Robert Burt of Barns, Fife
Advocate Cullen and Dr Cullen - Edinburgh
John Johnstone of Alva
Park of Balingry
George Brown, Leith
Adam Ferguson, Edinburgh
Henry Halket, Edinburgh
A. J. Douglas, Edinburgh
Margaret Wordie, Edinburgh
Spottiswoode of Dunipace
Crauford Bruce of Stenhouse
Sir John Murray-MacGregor of Lanrick (EIC)
David Anderson (EIC civil servant)
Col. William Duncan, Kelso (EIC army)
Sir John Cumming, Altyre (EIC army)
Col. Clephane

Lisbon
Thomas Mayne - Scots (merchant)
Thomas Mayne Brown - Scot (merchant)
John Fleetwood - English (merchant)
De Mesquita & Co.

The Graham Brothers
John Graham - Bengal civil servant
Thomas Graham - Bengal civil servant
George Graham - Bengal free mariner
Robert Graham - Bengal free merchant

Madras
Sir Hector Munro - Scot (army)
Col. Charles Cathcart - Scot (army)
Lt-Col. John Malcolm - Scot (army)
Alexander Pringle - Scot (civil servant)
Patrick Pringle - Scot (medic)
Alexander Cockburn - Scot (free merchant)
George Ramsay - Scot (civil servant)
Sir Eyre Coote - Irish (army)
Sir John Burgoyne - English (army)

Bengal
'Nobokisein' - South Asian financier
Sir John Murray-MacGregor - Scot
Sir Robert Abercrombie - Scot
Col. Robert Stuart - Scot
Alexander Elliot - Scot (civil servant)
Day Hort MacDowell - Scot (civil servant)
Dr James Burns - Scot (chaplain)
Dr John Watson - Scot (medic)
Thomas Lyon - Scot (medic)
John Henderson - Scot (medic)
John Wordie - Scot (free merchant)
Capt. Peter Murray - Scot
Capt. Robert Bruce - Scot
Maj. Patrick Duff - Scot
Lt. John Brown - Scot
Ensign Colin Monteith - Scot
Lt. William Duncanson - Scot
Cadets Cullen & James Hume - Scot
Lt. William Moncrieff - Scot
Capt. James Stewart - Scot
Cadet George Clephane - Scot
David Scott & Co. - Scot (free merchants)
Fairlie & Co. - Scot (free merchants)
Gov-Gen. Warren Hastings - English
Col. Parker - English
Nathaniel Middleton - English (civil servant)
Joseph Fowke - English (civil servant)
Richard Barwell - English - (civil servant)
Thomas Motte - English - (civil servant)
Cromellin & Dacre & Co. - English (free merchants)
Cockerell, Frail, Palmer & Co. - English (free merchants)
Thomas Pattle - English (civil servant)
Thomas Larwell
John Townson
George Templer
Richard Johnson
Col. Grainger Muir - Irish
Lt. Stephen Read - Irish
Capt. Edward Shewen - Welsh

East Indiaman Officers
Capt. Alexander Lennox - Scot
Capt. James Rattray - Scot (the *Duke of Atholl*)
Capt. Thomas Robertson - Scot (the *Busbridge*)
Capt. William Agnew - Scot (the *Vansittart*)
Monteith - Scot (4th mate, the *Triton*)

Dacca
James Crawford - Scot (free mariner)
James Hunter - Scot (surgeon)
Alexander Duncanson - Scot

Benkulen (S-E Asia)
Maj. Alexander Murray - Scot

(Source: Kinross House, '2nd Series, vols. 14 & 57; Bundles 53, 57; Ledger 2; NRS, GD29/1865, 2055–57, 2061, 2063, 2066–69, 2075–76, 2080, 2083, 2088, 2102, 2108, 2021, 2136–37, 2140, 2144, 2146).

Appendix 6.2 Arthur Cole's meso-network: Ireland, London, Calcutta and Madras, 1801–1813

London

Castlereagh - Down (patronage)
Charles Croggan - finance - Irish
Martin A. Shee - portrait - Irish
John Bligh, fourth earl of Darnley - Meath
Thomas Reynall - Irish
John Kennedy - Irish
W. C. Faulkner - Irish
Guy Lenox Prendergast - Tipperary
James Armstrong - Fermanagh
Henry Dundas - patronage - Scot
Robert Hobart, fourth earl of Buckingham - English (former governor of Madras) - patronage
Jane Boyd, Lady Carhampton - Irish (social networks)
Elizabeth Bingham, Lady Lucan - Anglo-Irish (social networks)

Madras

Sir John Craddock - English (c-in-c Madras: A.C. joined his household)
Col. John Malcolm - Scot (A.C. seconded as his secretary)
Thomas Packenham - Kildare (civil servant: joined A.C.s household)
John Sulivan - London-Irish (civil servant)
Lt. Thomas Smyth - Fermanagh
Capt. Thomas Stewart - Fermanagh
Lt. Charles Kennedy - Down
Lt. Ralph Gore - Wicklow
William R. Irwin - Longford (civil servant)
Sir William Bentinck - English
Andrew Barclay - Scot (civil servant)
Brig-Maj. Campbell - Scot

Ireland

Francis Balfour (sister) - Louth
Anne Lowry-Corry (mother) - Tyrone
John Cole (brother) - second earl of Enniskillen - Fermanagh
Guy Lenox Prendergast - Tipperary

Arthur Cole - Fermanagh
Madras civil servant

Voyage to India

Col. Davis
John Van Agnew - Scot (civil servant - shared household in Calcutta with A.C.)
Lushington - English (civil servant)
Cadet Cox (shared cabin with A.C.)

Bombay

Guy Lenox Prendergast - Tipperary (civil servant)

Bengal

Sir William Dunkin - Antrim (lawyer)
Francis MacNaghtan - Antrim (lawyer)
James Armstrong - Fermanagh (ADC to A. Wellesley)
Sir Arthur Wellesley - Meath (A.C. joined his household)
Capt. Montgomery - Irish (introductions/advice)
John Savage - Antrim (civil servant)
Longford Kennedy - Down (civil servant)
Capt. Benjamin Sydenham - English
Gen. Gerrard Lake - English
Arthur Annesley - Anglo-Irish (A.C. joined his household)
Gen. Sir James Craig - Scot
Sally Caulfield - Irish

(Source: TCD, Townley Hall Papers, MS3767/1–108; MS3768/109–113).

Appendix 7.1 Imperial profits, estates, and landed credit, 1781–1813

Region	Number of Parishes*	Parishes Affected by Credit and %	Lending	Estates Owned with Links to Asia Profits
Borders	172	79 (45.9%)	£269,715	52
Lothians	70	35 (50%)	£217,811	44
West-Central	123	65 (52.8%)	£403,139	60
Central	172	79 (45.9%)	£402,809	92
North-East	183	44 (24%)	£130,845	31
Highlands	146	63 (43.1%)	£250,072	63
North	40	4 (10%)	£8,360	5
TOTAL	906	369 (40.7%)	£1,682,751	347

(Source: Minute Books of the General Register of Sasines, RS62/18–20; Register of Sasines (Printed Abridgements, 1781–1813): Aberdeen [1–3991]; Angus [1–7184]; Argyll [1–2319]; Ayr [1–11223]; Banff [1–338]; Berwick [1–3249]; Bute [1–190]; Caithness [1–572]; Clackmannan [1–1865]; Dumfries [1–3071]; Dunbarton [1–2383]; Fife [1–9985]; Glasgow Barony [1–9259]; Haddington [1–1561]; Inverness [1–1428]; Kincardine [1–1054]; Kinross [1–1388]; Kirkcubright [1–3063]; Lanark [1–6911]; Linlithgow [1–2044]; Lothian [1–16692]; Moray & Nairn [1–871]; Orkney & Shetland [1–973]; Peebles [1–637]; Perth [1–8311]; Renfrew [1–10964]; Ross & Cromarty [1–1169]; Roxburgh [1–4305]; Selkirk [1–309]; Stirling [1–7455]; Sutherland [1–182]; Wigton [1–1036]).
* Based on Old Statistical Account returns.

Appendix 7.2 Asia-derived wealth and manufacturing investment, Scotland

Venture	Location	Investor	Amount
Stanley Mills	Stanley, Perthshire	George Dempster & Co.	–
Portobello Brick & Tile Co.	Portobello, Lothian	Andrew Hunter, EIC	£857
Soap and Candle works	South Leith, Lothian	George Neilsen, EIC	Owner
Todd, Shortbridge & Co., manufacturers	Glasgow	Col. David Muirhead, EIC	£2,000
Lanark Twist Co. (cotton)	Glasgow	Claud Alexander, EIC	£11,029
Robert F. Alexander, manufacturer	Glasgow	Trustees, John Alexander, EIC	£1,450
Cudbear manufactory	Glasgow	Trustees, Mj John Munro, EIC	£600
William Alexander, manufacturer	Paisley	Trustees, John Alexander, EIC	£550
Lindsay, Smith & Co., printmill	Dunbartonshire	John Lennox of Woodhead	£6,000

Appendix 7.2 Continued

Venture	Location	Investor	Amount
Glassent coal mines	Stirlingshire	John Lennox of Woodhead	–
Greenock Cooperage	Renfrew	John Lennox of Woodhead	£600
Edinburgh glass works	Lothian	Col. Patrick Ross	£1,000
Cannonmills distillery	Lothian	Capt. Thomas Blair, EIC	£1,500
Dunfallandie linen mill	Perth	Col. Archibald Fergusson, EIC	–
Lochore coal mines	Fife	Capt. Alexander Park, EIC	£2,000
Annfield coal mines	Fife	John Balfour of Balbirnie, EIC	£2,200
Duncancroy Mills	Inverness-shire	Capt. John Baillie of Dunain	£393
Catrine Cotton Mills	Catrine, Ayrshire	Claud Alexander, EIC	–
Oil mill	East Cadder	Archibald Stirling	£400
McNiven, Davidson & Co., Cotton mill	Kilbride, Lanarkshire	Gen. James Stuart, EIC	–
Spinningdale cotton mill	Sutherland	George Dempster & Capt John Hamilton Demspter, EIC	–
Newton Point, textiles/distribution	Sutherland	Capt. John Hamilton Dempster, EIC	–
Lurach slate quarry	Argyll	George Hay, EIC	–

(Source: NRS, Registers of Sasines [Abridgements], Perth (6598); Midlothian (4400); (10592) (13327); Glasgow (1767) (1915) (3175) (5767) (6124); Renfrew (5372); Lothian (6524–25); Sutherland (99–100, 118, 121); NRS, GD1/398/61; NRS, GD29/2063/70; NRS, GD288/98–112/28; NRS, GD128/2/3, 'State of the affairs of Dunain, 10 July 1801'; NRS, SC36/48/6, pp. 275–7; CC8/8/142, pp. 3–19: GCA, T-LX 3/26/2: Woodhead, January 1805; T-LX3/12/1; T-LX 5/27; GCA, T-SK 15/7 [1782], pp. 6–7; NLS, MS5335, fo. 39; MS14828, fo. 14; J. F. Wood, *Skibo* (Oxford: Oxford University Press, 1984), pp. 24–6)).

Appendix 7.3 Asia-derived wealth and educational/poor relief

Donator	Parish	Donation	Annual Poor Fund/No. of poor
Major William Hemmings	Finglas, Dublin	£100 [1809]	–
James Tobin	Kilkenny Catholic Church, Kilkenny	£400 [1732]	–
Lt-Col. Francis Robertson	Donegal, Donegal	£20 [1792]	–
Lt-Col. Francis Robertson	Gartan, DonegalColraine,	£20 [1792]	–
Dr James Allen	L'derry	£50 [1791]	–
Lawrence James	Kirkwall, Shetland	£200 [1813]	–
Col. James Duff	Forglen, Banff	'handsome sum'	–
Sgt-Maj. James Grant	Kirkmichael, Banff	£20 [1795]	£7 [1794]: 32 poor
George Smith	Fordyce, Banff	£1,000 [1790]	Education: 50 children
James Pyper	Episcopal Church, Turriff, Aberdeen	£5 [1780]	–
Capt. Alexander Forbes	Strathdon, Aberdeen	£10 [1806]	£17 [1794]: 40 poor
John Mather	Foveran & Fyvie, Aberdeen	£55 [1809]	Education: 8 children
John Mather	Foveran, Aberdeen	£25 [1809]	£20 [1793]: 40 poor
Maj. George Philips	Fyvie, Aberdeen	£600 [1806]	–: 24 poor
James Lyon	Glamis, Angus	£100 [1763]	£26 [1792]: 20 poor
Capt. John Ramsay	Dundee, Angus	£200 [1774]	£823 [1794]: 243 poor
Lt-Col. John Murray	Cortachy, Angus	£100	£10: 7 poor
Francis Seton	Episcopal Church, Haddington	£160 [1722]	–
William Fraser	Inverness burgh	£50 [1715]	SSPCK School
William Fraser	Petty, Inverness	£5 [1715]	£6 [1792]
Capt. Lt. John MacGowan	Kilmallie, Inverness	£10 [1766]	£20 [1791]
Capt. Norman Macleod	Bracadale, Inverness	£10 [1795]	–: [1792] 170 poor

Appendix 7.3 Continued

Donator	Parish	Donation	Annual Poor Fund/No. of poor
John Stuart	Cromdale, Inverness	£200 [1805]	£15 [1793]: 30 poor
Capt. Hugh Mackay	Lairg, Sutherland	£500 [1803]	£37 [1845]
James Wishart	Kirkcaldy, Fife	'Residue' [1788]	£63 [1796]
Lt-Col. John Murray	Longforgan, Perth	£100 [1799]	£26 [1797]
George Patterson	Longforgan, Perth	£3 p. ann [1797]	Education: 12 children
David Scott	Methven, Perth	£50 [1761]	£78 [1775]: 36 poor
John Moore	Morebattle, Roxburgh	£1,600 [1753]	Poor of several parishes
William Wordie	St Ninians, Stirling	£1,000 [1786]	£210 [1786]: 111 poor.
John Ferguson	Burgh of Ayr	£1,000 [1790]	£290
John Ferguson	Burgh of Ayr	£2,000 [1790]	Education: 230 children
Lt-Col. Sam'l Kilpatrick	Campbeltown, Argyll	£100 [1781]	£39 [1794]: 160 poor
John Clark	Campbeltown, Argyll	£200 [1804]	£39 [1794]: 160 poor
Surgeon Arthur Sinclair	Thurso, Caithness	£50 [1786]	£25 [1798]
Capt. Lt. John MacGowan	Old Kirk, Edinburgh	£10 [1766]	–

(Source: IOR, L/AG/34/29/22, pp. 537–41; L/AG/34/29/209, pp. 1–6; L/AG/34/29/185 [1780], pp. 164–5; L/AG/34/29/205 [1806], pp. 36–9; L/AG/34/29/341 [1788], pp. 108–9; L/AG/34/29/201, LAG/34/29/187 [1786], pp. 117–19, 128–30; L/AG/34/29/6 [1786], 1; L/AG/34/29/7 [1792], 21, 47; L/AG/34/29/9/5; IOR, P/416/90, pp. 24–5; TNA, PROB 11/1058: pp. 273–4; TNA, PROB 11/549, pp. 211–13; TNA, PROB 11/672, pp. 173–4; PROB 11/630, pp. 119–21; NRS, CC/3/3/12, pp. 72–86; The Statistical Accounts of Scotland, 1791–1845: https://stataccscot.edina.ac.uk/static/statacc/dist/home).

Bibliography

Archives

Aberdeen City and Aberdeenshire Archives, Aberdeen
Propinquity Book, 1637–1705; Propinquity Book, 1706–1733

Aberdeen University Library, Aberdeen
Forbes and Hay of Seaton Papers
MS2253/8/3/8

Ross of Arnage Papers
MS3346; Box 8

Skene Papers
MS38/45

British Library, London
India Office Records
B/40–B/95: Minutes of the Court of Directors, April 1690–April 1780
H/74; H/78; H/85, H/121: Home Correspondence (Miscellaneous)
J/1/1–19, 21–26: Writers' Petitions, 1749–1813
L/AG/14/5/1: East India Stockholders, 1710
L/AG/34/29/4–22, 185–210, 341–343; P/328/60–64; P/416/77–98: Bengal, Bombay and Madras Wills, 1740–1813
L/F/10/1–5; L/F/10/111–113: Bengal and Madras Civil Servant Lists, 1707–1797
L/MIL/5/159: Correspondence relating to Seringapatam prize money, 1800
L/MIL/9/85, 90, 95–96, 98, 104: Military Embarkations, 1753–1813
L/MIL/9/107–127: Cadet Applications, 1791–1813
L/MIL/9/256–59: Cadet Lists, 1775–1790
L/MIL/9/358–365: Surgeon Applications, 1805–1813
L/MIL/10/130–131; L/MIL/11/109: Bengal and Madras Army Muster Rolls
MSS Eur. D.1087: Patronage Letter Book of David Scott
MSS Eur. E276: Letter Book of Claud Russell, Vols. I–III
MSS Eur. F/5/19: Lord Castlereagh, India Board of Control
MSS Eur. F128: Papers of Brigadier-General John Carnac
MSS Eur. F164: Robert Francis Mudie Collection
MSS Eur. F291/83/1 & 2: Papers of Sir John Macpherson
MSS Eur. Photo 109: John Johnstone Letter Book

O/1/1: Bonds and Agreements, 1741–91
O/5/26–27: European Inhabitants, Bengal, 1793–1812
O/5/30–31: European Inhabitants, Madras, 1702–1828
P/1/1/PT2 and PT3: Bengal Public Consultations

Brodie Castle, Forres
Brodie of Brodie Papers
Box 1

Centre for South Asian Studies, Cambridge
Boileau Papers, Box 1/1
Duncan Papers, No 31
Hunter-Blair Papers, Box 1/1; Box 1/4
MacPherson Papers, Microfilm 9/T1–3

Dundee City Archive, Dundee
Wedderburn of Pearsie
GD131/30; Box 7/15/3; Box 7/25/1 & 16–17; Box 7/26/8

Dunvegan Castle Muniments, Dunvegan, Isle of Skye
DCM, 3/70/1–4

Edinburgh University Library, Edinburgh
Murchison Papers
MS2263/3/1–10
Sir Archibald Campbell of Inverneil (Madras Papers)
Mic M. 920

Glasgow City Archive, Mitchell Library, Glasgow
Bogle Papers
Bo. 2: Letter Book of George Bogle of Calcutta; Bo. 7/2; Bo. 12/2–3; Bo. 12/5; Bo. 12/8, 12 & 14; Bo. 20/14 & 17; Bo. 25

Campbell of Succoth Papers
TD219/5/83; TD219/8/1, 4; TD219/10/1; TD219/10/152

Lennox of Woodhead
T-LX3/12/17; T-LX3/13/24; T-LX3/16/1 & 2; T-LX3/18/1; T-LX3/22/3; T-LX3/26/2

Stirling of Keir and Cawdor
T-SK 11/2; T-SK 15/11

Glasgow University Library, Glasgow
Allen Thomson Medical Papers
MS GEN 1476A/123

MS Cullen/141

MS Hunter 73 (T.3.11.)
MS50. T.2.8

Guildhall Library, London
Michie Papers
MS5881

Highland Archive Centre, Inverness
Northern Infirmary Records
HHB/1/1/1; HHB/1/2/1

Novar Papers, D/538/39

Huntington Library, Pasadena, CA
Loudon (Scottish) Papers
LO1120; LO1345(5); LO1384(2); LO1391; LO1683(1); LO2529(1 & 5); LO2533(4); LO3936(1); LO4011(1); LO4012(1); LO4068(2); LO7569; LO/9964

Pocock Collection
PO 1032

Pulteney Papers
Boxes 3–26

Stowe Collection
HL, ST 34; ST 57/30; ST 58/1 & 4; ST/68; ST/71 & 74; ST 80

Kinross House Papers, Kinross
Graham Papers, 2nd Series, 51–126/57; Box 16/32

London Metropolitan Archives
LMA/4365/A/001–2: Session Books of the Scots-Church in Swallow St., Westminster, 1735–1806

National Archive of Ireland, Dublin
MS2533: 'Hints towards a Typographical History of the Counties of Sligo[e], Donegal, Fermanagh and Lough Earne.'

National Library of Ireland, Dublin
Hibernian Mining Company Papers
MS29767

Conwell Papers
MS14337

Townley Hall Papers
MS10242

National Library of Scotland, Edinburgh
Airth Papers
MS10802; MS10872; MS10919; MS10920; MS10921; MS10947; MS10953

Crawford (Balcarres) Papers
Acc 9769/30/3–4; Acc 9769/30/5/1, 3, 5, 16; Acc 9769/30/5/9/1–2; Acc 9769/30/5/16–17

Fletcher of Saltoun Papers
MS16536; MS16538; MS16549

George Johnstone Letters
MS9246

Mackenzie of Delvine Papers
MS1169; MS1170; MS1171; MS1256; MS1328; MS1336; MS1337; MS1142; MS1367; MS1368

Mackintosh of Raigmore
MS6360

Macpherson-MacAulay Letters
MS2958

Macleod of Geanies Papers
MS19298; MS19300

Melville Papers
MS49; MS50; MS52; MS56; MS360; MS1055; MS1060; MS1062; MS1073; MS1074; MS1078; MS1091; MS3385; MS3387

Minto Papers
MS11005; MS11020; MS11041

Robert Ray, 'Plan of the Burgh of Elgin from actual survey' (Edinburgh: Leith & Smith, 1838)
EMS.s.759

Robertson-Macdonald Papers
MS3946; MS3947; MS3971; MS3973

Stuart Stevenson Papers
MS8207; MS8220; MS8434; MS8437; MS8250; MS8252; MS8257; MS833

Walker of Bowland Papers
MS13775

Watson Collection
MS588

William Bald, 'Map of Harris', [1805]
EMS.s.646

Yester Papers
MS14828; MS14439; MS14528

National Records of Scotland, Edinburgh
Abercairney Muniments
GD24/1/463; GD24/1/464/D/47; GD24/1/464/E/49; GD24/1/464 (c) (d) (e) & (n);
    GD 24/1/484; GD 24/1/495; GD 24/3/296, 302, 304–5, 313, 337, 346, 360, 362;
    GD24/1/484/62 & 121

Baillie of Culterallers Papers
GD1/1155/69

Balfour of Balbirnie Papers
GD288/322

British Fisheries Society Papers
GD9/3/431–440

Boyd Alexander Papers
GD393/6/1 [Photocopy of British Library Add MS45424]

Breadalbane Muniments
GD112/52/601/13; GD112/74/852

Bught Papers
GD23/1/312/15; GD23/6/261; GD23/9/18

Cameron of Fassifern
GD1/736/5

Campbell of Duntroon
GD116/2/57

Campbell of Inverneil Muniments
RH4/121/1, 6–7

Clerk of Penicuik
GD18/5218; GD18/5368

Cochrane of Rochsoles
GD1/594/1

Cromartie Papers
GD305/1/162/190 & 260

Cunningham-Graham Muniments
GD22/2/145/2

Dalguise Muniments
GD38/2/8

Gordon Castle Muniments
GD44/23/33/2; GD44/43/205

Fergusson of Dunfallundy Papers
GD1/398/54 & 61

Fraser-Mackintosh Collection
GD128/1/1 & 3; GD128/1/2/1; GD128/1/4/1 & 2

Grant of Monymusk
GD345/1155/2, 5, 7, 9–10; GD345/1157/1; NRS, GD345/1173/1; GD345/1175/2; GD345/1195

Hamilton Dalrymple of North Berwick
GD110/975; GD110/987/2; GD110/1021/12

Messrs Hope, Todd and Kirk
GD246/46/1

Innes of Stow
GD113/5/365A/6

Journal of Lieutenant Gordon, 89th Highland Regiment in India, 1761–63
RH4/136/1/84-V2

Kinross House Papers
GD29/1876; GD 29/2055; GD29/2056; GD29/2057; GD29/2058; GD29/2063; GD29/2067; GD29/2069; GD29/2122; GD29/2127; GD29/2132; GD29/2136; GD29/2144

Letter Book of Sir John Lindsay, 1770–71
RH4/51

Macpherson of Cluny Papers
GD80/904/1; GD80/904/2; GD80/914/11; GD80/913/2

Mackay of Bighouse
GD87/1/34/1–2

Maxtone Graham of Cultoquhey
GD155/1326/2

Melville Castle Muniments
GD51/3/3, 14, 16, 37, 39, 53, 58, 85, 99, 164, 305; GD51/4/1–4, 16, 43, 88, 89–91, 167–169

Miscellaneous Papers
GD1/768/10

Patterson of Huntly Castle
GD508/3/2/2–5; GD508/3/26

Register of Sasines
RS27/133 & 135; RS62/19–20

Printed Abridgements, 1781–1813: Aberdeen [1–3991]; Angus [1–7184]; Argyll [1–2319]; Ayr [1–11223]; Banff [1–338]; Berwick [1–3249]; Bute [1–190]; Caithness [1–572]; Clackmannan [1–1865]; Dumfries [1–3071]; Dunbarton [1–2383]; Fife [1–9985]; Glasgow Barony [1–9259]; Haddington [1–1561]; Inverness [1–1428]; Kincardine [1–1054]; Kinross [1–1388]; Kirkcudbright [1–3063]; Lanark [1–6911]; Linlithgow [1–2044]; Lothian [1–16692]; Moray & Nairn [1–871]; Orkney & Shetland [1–973]; Peebles [1–637]; Perth [1–8311]; Renfrew [1–10964]; Ross & Cromarty [1–1169]; Roxburgh [1–4305]; Selkirk [1–309]; Stirling [1–7455]; Sutherland [1–182]; Wigton [1–1036]

RHP 42696: Map of the Novar Estate, 1788

Robertson of Lude Muniments
GD132/768

Robertson Preston of Woodford Papers
GD 1/453/Boxes 1–3

Rosslyn Muniments
GD164/1698/5(1–6); GD164/1699/1–2; GD164/1700/1–4; GD164/1709/1–11

Scott of Raeburn Muniments
GD104/297/2

Scottish Wills and Testaments
CC1/6/56, 59, 74, 133: Aberdeen Commissary Court
CC3/3/12, 15; CC3/4/32; CC3/5/2, 5, 6, 15: Brechin Commissary Court
CC8/8/83–84, 90, 105, 110, 112–113, 116, 118–136, 138–142, 144–146: Edinburgh Commissary Court
CC9/7: Glasgow Commissary Court
CC10/5: Hamilton Commissary Court
CC16/4; Moray Commissary Court
CC18/4: Peebles Commissary Court
CC20/7/4: St Andrew's Commissary Court
CC21/7/9: Stirling Commissary Court
SC36/48/6–7: Glasgow Sheriff Court Inventories
SC70/1/3–4, 6–7, 12–14, 17, 22–23; Edinburgh Sheriff Court Inventories

Scrymgeour-Wedderburn Muniments
GD137/1134; GD137/1136

Seafield Muniments
GD248/49/1; GD248/51/1 & 3; GD248/52/1-3; GD248/60/3/28; GD248/179/1; GD248/179/3; GD248/226/2 & 5; GD248/227/1 & 2; GD248/413

Seaforth Muniments
GD46/1/10/122; GD46/17/11

Shairp of Houston Muniments
GD30/1597

Perth and Kinross Archive, Perth
Stuart of Annat Papers
MS115/Bundle 4

Property Registration Authority of Ireland, Dublin
Registry of Deeds
Vols. 114–16; Vol. 213; Vol. 218; Vol. 223; Vol. 295; Vol. 337; Vol. 352; Vol. 357; Vol. 385

Public Record Office of Northern Ireland, Belfast
Caledon Papers
D2432/1/2-4 & 7; D/2432/5/3/4; D/2432/5/4/2; D/2433/A/3/1 & 2; D/2433/A/91/2/1

Londonderry Papers (Papers of Robert Cowan)
D654/B1/2A

McCartney Papers
PRONI, D/572/19/15, 40, 64, 72–73, 79, 84, 87–88, 91, 94–95, 103, 110–12, 124

Royal College of Physicians and Surgeons of Glasgow Library, Glasgow
GB 250 70/3

The National Archives, Kew, London
PROB 11/401–1903: Probate Court of Canterbury wills, 1688–1837

WO17/1738: 'Present State of HM Troops under the Command of Major General James Stuart, 1 Sept 1783.'
WO120/5: Royal Hospital, Chelsea, Regimental Registers for 72nd and 73rd Highland Regiments

Trinity College Dublin Library, Dublin
MS1576; Khulāsat-al-Hikma or Epitome of Medicine by Hakim Hamid of Dībāfoūr
MS1612: Persian and Hindustani Dictionary (Presented by Captain Richard Long of County Tipperary)

Papers of John George Bellingham
MS11414

John Maxwell Stone Correspondence
MS3551/1 & 2

Townley Hall Papers
MS3767; MS3768

Printed primary material

Ainslie, Whitelaw, *Materia medica of Hindoostan and artisan's and agriculturalist's nomenclature* (Madras: n.p., 1813).

A Letter to the Proprietors of East India Stock from John Johnstone, Esq (London: n.p., 1766).

A Letter to the R.H. Lord North on the East India Bill now Depending in Parliament (London: n.p., 1772).

A list of the names of the members of the United-Company of Merchants of England, Trading to the East-Indies, who are also members of the general society, the 7th of April, 1709 (London: s.n., 1709).

A List of the Hon and United East India Company's civil and military servants on the Bengal establishment, 1785 (Calcutta: n.p., 1785).

A List of the Names of those Members of the United Company of Merchants of England ... 13th of April 1790 (London: n.p., 1790).

A Summary of the View of the Rise, Constitution, and Present State of the Charitable Foundation of King Charles the Second, commonly called the Scots Corporation (London: n.p., 1738).

A Summary View of the Rise, Constitution, and present state of the Charitable Foundation of King Charles the Second commonly called the Scots Corporation in London (London: W. Strahan, 1761).

A Vindication of the Conduct of the English Forces, Employed in the Late War, under the Command of Brigadier General Mathews against Nabob Tippoo Sultaun (London: J. Walter, 1787),

An Account of the Institution, Progress, and Present State of the Scottish Corporation in London (London: n.p. 1806).

An Account of the Rise, Progress and Present State of the Most Honourable and Loyal Society of Ancient Britons (London: n.p., 1800).

An Act for assuring to the English company trading to the East-Indies, on account of the united stock, a longer time in the fund and trade (London: n.p., 1707).

An address to the College of Physicians, and to the Universities of Oxford and Cambridge; occasion'd by the late swarms of Scotch and Leyden physicians, &c. (London: M. Copper, 1747).

Anon., *Administration of justice in Bengal. The several petitions of the British inhabitants of Bengal* (London: n.p., 1780).

Anon., *A List of the Names of those Members of the United Company of Merchants of England, Trading to the East Indies who stood qualified as voters on the Company's Books the 13th of April 1790* (London: n.p., 1790).

Answers for James Ker of Crummock, surgeon in the service of the East India Company (Edinburgh: n.p., 1768).

Bryce, James, *An Account of the Yellow Fever, with a successful method of cure ...* (Edinburgh: W. Creech, 1796).

Clark, John, *Observations on the diseases in long voyages to hot countries, and particularly on those which prevail in the East Indies* (London: G. Nicol & D. Wilson, 1773).
Clark, Thomas, *Observations on the Nature and Cure of Fevers, and of the Diseases of the West and East Indies and of America* (Edinburgh: n.p., 1801).
Dodwell, Edward & Miles, *Alphabetical List of the Officers of the Indian Army ...* (London: Longman, Orme, Brown & Co., 1838).
The East India Kalendar, or, Asiatic register for 1791 to 1800 (London: J. Debrett, 1791–1800).
The East-India Register & Directory for 1813 (London: W. H. Allen, 1813).
Hardy, Charles, *A Register of Ships, Employed in the Service of the Honorable the United East India Company* (London: W. Heseltine, 1811).
Holwell, J. Z., *Important facts regarding the East-India Company's affairs in Bengal, from the year 1752 to 1760* (London: T. Becket & P. A. De Hondt, 1764).
——, *An account of the manner of inoculating for the small pox in the East Indies* (London: T. Becket & P. A. de Hondt, 1767).
——, *A review of the original principles, religious and moral, of the ancient Bramins* (London: T. Vernor, 1779).
Mackenzie, R., *A Full and Exact Account of the Proceedings of the Court of Directors and Council-General of the Company of Scotland Trading to Africa and the Indies with relation to the Treaty of Union now under Parliament's Consideration* (Edinburgh: n.p., 1706).
Maclean, Charles, *To the British Inhabitants of India* (Calcutta: n.p., 1798).
Medical and Philosophical Commentaries. By a Society in Edinburgh (London: J. Murray, 1774).
Medical and Philosophical Commentaries, I–VI (1773–1779).
Medical Commentaries, VII–X; I–VIII (1780–1793).
Medical Commentaries for the year 1785 (London: J. Murray, 1786).
Medical Commentaries for the Year 1792, VII (Edinburgh: Peter Hill, 1793).
Names of the proprietors of Grand Canal stock, and the amount, as it stood in the Company's ledger on the 1st day of June, 1800 (Dublin: n.p. 1800).
Price, Joseph, *The Saddle put on the Right Horse: or, an Enquiry into the Reason why certain Persons have been denominated Nabobs, with Arrangement of those Gentlemen into their proper Classes or Real, Spurious, Reputed, or Mushroom Nabobs* (London: J. Stockdale, 1783).
——, *Some Observations and Remarks on a Late Publication Entitled Travels in Europe, Asia and Africa* (London: n.p., 1783).
Reasons why the East-India Company ought to pay the equivolent agreed to be paid the Scots Company by the articles of union: and also some cautions offer'd with respect to the renewal of their grant (London: n.p., 1708).
Rules of the Edinburgh East India Club with a list of the members, and when admitted. 27 January 1815 (Edinburgh: Oliver & Boyd, 1815).
The Scots Magazine, 1–52 (Edinburgh: Murray & Cochran, 1739–1790).
Scott, Helenus, *The adventures of a rupee* (London: J. Murray, 1782).
Statues Passed in the Parliaments Held in Ireland, vol. IX (Dublin: George Geirson, 1799).
Thomson, Thomas, (ed.), *A Biographical Dictionary of Eminent Scotsmen*, vol. II (Glasgow, Edinburgh and London: Blackie, 1855).

——, *The Acts of the Parliaments of Scotland*, 9 (Edinburgh: n.p., 1822).
Toone, Wolfe, *An address to the people of Ireland, on the present important crisis* (Belfast: n.p., 1796).
Wilson's Dublin directory, for the year 1778 (Dublin: W. Wilson, 1778).
Woodrow, R. *Analecta: or, materials for a History of Remarkable Providences; mostly relating to Scotch Ministers and Christians*, vol. III (Edinburgh: Maitland Club, 1843).

Secondary sources

Addison, W. Innes (ed.), *A Roll of the Graduates of the University of Glasgow from 31 December 1727 to 31 December 1897* (Glasgow: James Maclehose & Co., 1898).
Alavi, Seema, *The Sepoys and the Company: Tradition and Transition in Northern India, 1770–1830* (New Delhi: Oxford University Press, 1998).
——, 'Introduction', in S. Alavi (ed.), *The Eighteenth Century in India* (New Delhi: Oxford University Press, 2002).
Allan, D., *Scotland in the Eighteenth Century* (London: Longman, 2002).
Allen, Richard B., 'Satisfying the "Want for Labouring People": European Slave Trading in the Indian Ocean, 1500–1850', *Journal of World History*, 21 (2010), 45–73.
——, 'Ending the History of Silence: Reconstructing European Slave Trading in the Indian Ocean', *Dossiê O Tráfico De Escravos Africanos: Novos Horizontes*, 23 (2017), 295–313.
Anderson, Peter John, *Officers and Graduates of the University and King's College, Aberdeen, 1495–1860* (Aberdeen: New Spalding Club, 1893).
—— (ed.), *Records of the Marischal College and University of Aberdeen*, vol. II (Aberdeen: Aberdeen University Press, 1898).
Anheier, Helmut K., Gerhards, Jurgen and Romo, Frank P., 'Forms of Capital and Social Structure in Cultural Fields: Examining Bourdieu's Social Topography', *The American Journal of Sociology*, 100 (1995), 859–903.
Anon, *The House of Binny* (Madras: Associated Printers, 1969).
Armitage, David, 'Greater Britain: A Useful Category of Historical Analysis', *American Historical Review*, 102 (1999), 427–45.
——, *The Ideological Origins of the British Empire* (Cambridge: Cambridge University Press, 2000).
——, 'Three Concepts of Atlantic History', in D. Armitage and M. J. Braddick (eds), *The British Atlantic World, 1500–1800* (Basingstoke: Palgrave, 2002), pp. 11–30.
Armitage, D. and Braddick, M. J., 'Introduction', in D. Armitage and M. J. Braddick (eds), *The British Atlantic World, 1500–1800* (Basingstoke: Palgrave, 2002), pp. 1–10.
Arnold, D. 'India's Place in the Tropical World, 1770–1930', *Journal of Imperial and Commonwealth History*, 26 (1998), 1–21.
Aslanian, Sebouh, 'Social Capital, "Trust" and the Role of Networks in Julfan Trade: Informal and Semi-Formal Institutions at Work', *Journal of Global History*-, 1 (2006), 382–402.
Bailey, C., 'Metropole and Colony: Irish Networks and Patronage in the Eighteenth-Century Empire', *Immigrants & Minorities*, 23 (2005), 161–81.

——, 'The Nesbitts of London and their Networks', in David Dickson, Jan Parmentier and Jane Ohlmeyer (eds), *Irish and Scottish Mercantile Networks in Europe and Overseas in the Seventeenth and Eighteenth Centuries* (Ghent: Academia Press, 2007), pp. 231–50.

——, *Irish London: Middle-Class Migration in the Global Eighteenth Century* (Liverpool: Liverpool University Press, 2013).

Bailey, Peter, 'Irish Men in the East India Company Army', *Irish Family History*, 17 (2001), 84–92.

Bailyn, B., *Voyagers to the West: Emigration from Britain to America on the Eve of the Revolution* (London: I.B.Tauris, 1987).

Bailyn, Bernard and Morgan, Philip D., 'Introduction', in Bernard Bailyn and Philip D. Morgan (eds), *Strangers within in the Realm: Cultural Margins of the First British Empire* (Chapel Hill, NC, and London: University of North Carolina Press, 1991), pp. 1–31.

Ballantyne, Tony, 'Empire, Knowledge and Culture: from Proto-Globalisation to Modern Globalisation', in A. G. Hopkins (ed.), *Globalisation in World History* (London: Pimlico, 2002), pp. 115–40.

Barber, W. J., *British Economic Thought and India, 1600–1858* (Oxford: Clarendon Press, 1975).

Barczewski, Stephanie, *Country Houses and the British Empire, 1700–1930* (Manchester: Manchester University Press, 2014).

——, 'Scottish Landed-Estate Purchases, Empire and Union, 1700–1900', in Stephanie Barczewski and Martin Farr (eds), *The MacKenzie Moment and Imperial History: Essays in Honour of Professor John MacKenzie* (Cham: Palgrave Macmillan, 2019), pp. 171–88.

Barnard, T. C., 'The Gentrification of Eighteenth-Century Ireland', *Eighteenth-Century Ireland/Iris an dá chultúr*, 12 (1997), 137–55.

——, *A New Anatomy of Ireland: The Irish Protestants, 1649–1770* (New Haven, CT: Yale University Press, 2004).

Bartlett, T. (ed.), *McCartney in Ireland, 1768–1772* (Belfast: PRONI, 1978).

——, '"A People Made Rather for Copies than Originals": The Anglo-Irish, 1760–1800', *International History Review*, 12 (1990), 11–25.

——, 'The Origins and Progress of the Catholic Question in Ireland, 1690–1800', in T. P. Power and Kevin Whelan (eds), *Endurance and Emergence: Catholics in Ireland in the Eighteenth Century* (Blackrock: Irish Academic Press, 1990), pp. 1–19.

——, *The Fall and Rise of the Irish Catholic Nation: The Catholic Question, 1690–1830* (Dublin: Gill & Macmillan, 1992).

——, 'The Irish Soldier in India, 1750–1947', in Michael Holmes and Denis Holmes (eds), *Ireland and India: Connections, Comparisons, Contrasts* (Limerick: Blackwater Press, 1997), pp. 12–28.

——, '"This Famous Island Set in a Virginian Sea": Ireland in the British Empire, 1690–1801', in P. J. Marshall (ed.), *The Oxford History of the British Empire, II: The Eighteenth Century* (Oxford: Oxford University Press, 1998), pp. 253–75.

——, 'An Union for Empire': the Anglo-Irish Union as an Imperial Project', in M. Brown, P. M. Geoghan, and J. Kelly (eds), *The Irish Act of Union, 1800: Bicentenial Essays* (Dublin: Four Courts, 2001), pp. 50–7.

——, *Ireland: A History* (Cambridge: Cambridge University Press, 2010).

Bartlett, T. and Jeffery, K., 'An Irish Military Tradition', in T. Bartlett and K. Jeffery (eds), *A Military History of Ireland* (Cambridge: Cambridge University Press, 1996), pp. 1–25.

Basset, D. K., 'Early English Trade and Settlement in Asia, 1602–1690', in P. Tuck (ed.), *The English East India Company, 1600–1858* (London: Routledge, 1998), pp. 1–28.

Bayly, C. A., *Indian Society and the Making of the British Empire* (Cambridge: Cambridge University Press, 1988).

——, *Imperial Meridian: The British Empire and the World, 1780–1830* (London: Longman, 1989).

——, 'The British Military-Fiscal State and Indigenous Resistance: India, 1750–1820', in Lawrence Stone (ed.), *An Imperial State at War: Britain from 1689–1815* (London: Routledge, 1994), pp. 322–54.

——, 'The First Age of Global Imperialism c.1760–1830', *Journal of Imperial & Commonwealth Studies*, 26 (1998), 28–47.

——, 'The Second British Empire', in R. W. Winks (ed.), *The Oxford History of the British Empire, V: Historiography* (Oxford: Oxford University Press, 1998), pp. 54–72.

——, *Empire and Information: Intelligence Gathering and Social Communication in India, 1780–1870* (Cambridge: Cambridge University Press, 1999).

——, 'Ireland, India and the Empire: 1780–1914', *Transactions of the Royal Historical Society*, sixth series, 10 (2000), 377–97.

——, '"Archaic" and "Modern" Globalisation in the Eurasian and African Arena, c.1750–1850', in A. G. Hopkins (ed.), *Globalisation in World History* (London: Pimlico, 2002), pp. 47–73.

——, *The Birth of the Modern World, 1780–1914* (Oxford: Blackwell, 2004).

Becker, G. S., *Human Capital: A Theoretical and Empirical Analysis*, 3rd edn (Chicago: University of Chicago Press, 1993).

Belich, James, *Replenishing the Earth: The Settler Revolution and the Rise of the Anglo-World, 1783–1939* (Oxford: Oxford University Press, 2011).

Benton, Lauren, 'Colonial Law and Cultural Difference: Jurisdictional Politics and the Formation of the Colonial State', *Comparative Studies in Society and History*, 41 (1999), 563–88.

Bose, Sutapa, 'The Problem of Primitive Accumulation', *Economic and Political Weekly*, 23 (1988), 1169–74.

Bourdieu, Pierre, 'The Forms of Capital', in John G. Richardson (ed.), *Handbook of Theory & Research for the Sociology of Education* (New York: Greenwood Press, 1986), pp. 241–58.

Bowen, H. V., 'The East India Company and Military Recruitment in Britain, 1763–1771', *Bulletin of the Institute of Historical Research*, 59 (1986), 78–89.

——, 'A Question of Sovereignty? The Bengal Revenue Issue, 1765–67', *Journal of Imperial and Commonwealth History*, 16 (1988), 155–76.

——, 'Investment and Empire in the Late Eighteenth Century: East India Stockholding, 1756–1791', *Economic History Review*, second series, 42 (1989), 186–206.

——, '"The Little Parliament": The General Court of the East India Company, 1750–1784', *The Historical Journal*, 34 (1991), 857–72.

——, *Revenue and Reform: The Indian Problem in British Politics, 1757–1773* (Cambridge: Cambridge University Press, 1991).

——, *Elites, Enterprise and the Making of the British Overseas Empire, 1688–1775* (London: Palgrave Macmillan, 1996).
——, 'British India, 1765–1813: The Metropolitan Context', in P. J. Marshall (ed.), *The Oxford History of the British Empire, II: The Eighteenth Century* (Oxford: Oxford University Press, 1998), pp. 530–51.
——, *The Business of Empire: The East India Company and Imperial Britain, 1756–1833* (Cambridge: Cambridge University Press, 2006).
——, 'Privilege and Profit: Commanders of East Indiamen as Private Traders, Entrepreneurs and Smugglers, 1760–1813', *International Journal of Maritime History*, 19 (2007), 43–88.
——, 'Asiatic Interactions: India, the East India Company and the Welsh Economy, c.1750–1830', in H. V. Bowen (ed.), *Wales and the British Overseas Empire, 1650–1830* (Manchester: Manchester University Press, 2011), pp. 168–92.
——, 'Introduction', in H. V. Bowen (ed.), *Wales and the British Overseas Empire, 1650–1830* (Manchester: Manchester University Press, 2011), pp. 1–14.
Bowen, H. V., Mancke, Elizabeth and Reid, John G., 'Introduction: Britain's Oceanic Empire', in H. V. Bowen, Elizabeth Mancke and John G. Reid (eds), *Britain's Ocean Empire: Atlantic and Indian Ocean Worlds, c.1550–1850* (Cambridge: Cambridge University Press, 2012), pp. 1–12.
Bowie, Karin, 'Cultural, British and Global Turns in the History of Early Modern Scotland', *The Scottish Historical Review*, 92 (2013), 38–48.
Braddick, Michael J. and Walter, John, 'Introduction. Grids of Power: Hierarchy and Subordination in Early Modern Society', in Michael J. Braddick and John Walter (eds), *Negotiating Power in Early Modern Society: Order, Hierarchy, and Subordination in Britain and Ireland* (Cambridge: Cambridge University Press, 2003), pp. 1–42.
Brockliss, Laurence, 'The Professions and National Identity', in Laurence Brockliss and David Eastwood (eds), *A Union of Multiple Identities: The British Isles, 1750–1850* (Manchester: Manchester University Press, 1997), pp. 9–28.
Broadie, Alexander, *The Scottish Enlightenment* (Edinburgh: Birlinn, 2001).
Brooks, C., 'Apprenticeship, Social Mobility and the Middling Sort, 1550–1800', in J. Barry and C. Brooks (eds), *The Middling Sort of People: Culture, Society and Politics in England, 1550–1800* (London: Macmillan, 1996), pp. 52–83.
Brotherstone, T., Clark, A. and Whelan, K., 'Rethinking the Trajectory of Modern British History: An Ireland-Scotland approach', in T. Brotherstone, A. Clark and K. Whelan (eds), *These Fissured Isles: Ireland, Scotland and British History, 1798–1848* (Edinburgh: John Donald, 2005), pp. 1–42.
Brotherstone, T., Clark, A. and Whelan, K. (eds), *These Fissured Isles: Ireland, Scotland and British History, 1798–1848* (Edinburgh: John Donald, 2005), 43–60.
Brown, C. G., *The Social History of Religion in Scotland since 1730* (London: Methuen, 1987).
Brown, Hilton, *Parrys of Madras: A Story of British Enterprise in India* (Madras: Parry & Co., 1954).
Brown, Keith M. and Kennedy, Allan, 'Land of Opportunity? The Assimilation of Scottish Migrants in England, 1603–c.1762', *Journal of British Studies*, 57 (2018), 709–35.
——, '"Their Maxim Is Vestigia nulla restrorsum": Scottish Return Migration and Capital Repatriations from England, 1603–c.1760', *Journal of Social History*, 52 (2018), 1–25.

——, 'Becoming English: The Monro Family and Scottish Assimilation in Early-Modern England', *Cultural and Social History*, 16 (2019), 125–44.
Brumwell, S., *Redcoats: The British Soldier and Wars in the Americas, 1755–1763* (Cambridge: Cambridge University Press, 2002).
——, 'The Scottish Military Experience in North America, 1756–1783', in Edward M. Speirs, Jeremy A. Crang and Matthew J. Strickland (eds), *A Military History of Scotland* (Edinburgh: Edinburgh University Press, 2012), pp. 383–406.
Bryant, G., 'Officers of the East India Company's Army in the Days of Clive and Hastings', *The Journal of Imperial and Commonwealth History*, 6 (1978), 203–27.
——, 'Scots in India in the Eighteenth Century', *The Scottish Historical Review*, 64 (1985), 22–41.
Bulley, Anne, *The Bombay Country Ships, 1790–1833* (Abingdon: Routledge, 2000).
Burgess, Glenn, 'Introduction: The New British History', in G. Burgess (ed.), *The New British History: Founding a Modern State, 1603–1715* (London: I.B.Tauris, 1999), pp. 2–32.
Burley, E. I., *Servants of the Honourable Company: Work, Discipline, and Conflict in the Hudson's Bay Company, 1770–1870* (Oxford: Oxford University Press, 1997).
Burke, Bernard, *A Genealogical and Heraldic History of the Landed Gentry of Ireland* (London: Harrisons & Sons, 1912).
Burton, Antoinette, 'Who Needs the Nation? Interrogating "British" History', *Journal of Historical Sociology*, 10 (1997), 227–48.
Burton, John Hill *The Scots Abroad*, vols. I–II (Edinburgh: William Blackwood, 1864).
Cadell, P. 'Irish Soldiers in India', *The Irish Sword*, 1 (1949–53), 75–9.
Cage, R. A., 'The Scots in England', in R. A. Cage (ed.), *The Scots Abroad: Labour, Capital, Enterprise, 1750–1914* (London: Croom Helm, 1985), pp. 29–45.
Cain, P. J. and Hopkins, A. G., *British Imperialism: Innovation and Expansion, 1688–1914* (London: Longman, 1993).
——, 'Afterword: The Theory and Practice of British Imperialism', in R. E. Dumett (ed.), *Gentlemanly Capitalism and British Imperialism: The New Debate on Empire* (London: Longman, 1999), pp. 196–220.
Cairns, John W., *Law, Lawyers, and Humanism: Selected Essays on the History of Scots Law, Volume I* (Edinburgh: Edinburgh University Press, 2015).
Cairns Craig, Robert, 'An Empire of Intellect', in John M. MacKenzie and T. M. Devine (eds), *The Oxford History of the British Empire: Scotland and the British Empire* (Oxford: Oxford University Press, 2011), pp. 84–117.
Callahan, R. *The East India Company and Army Reform 1783–1798* (Cambridge, MA: Harvard University Press, 1972).
Cameron, Charles A., *History of the Royal College of Surgeons in Ireland* (Dublin: Fannin, 1886).
Cameron, George G. *The Scots Kirk in London* (Oxford: Becket, 1979).
Campbell, Duncan, *Records of Clan Campbell in the Military Service of the Honourable East India Company, 1600–1858* (London: Longman's, Green and Co., 1925).
Canny, N. (ed.), *The Oxford History of the British Empire, I: The Origins of Empire* (Oxford: Oxford University Press, 1998).

Caputo, Sarah, 'Scotland, Scottishness, British Integration and the Royal Navy, 1793–1815', *The Scottish Historical Review*, 97 (2018), 85–118.

Carr, Rosalind, 'The Gentleman and the Soldier: Patriotic Masculinities in Eighteenth-Century Scotland', *Journal of Scottish Historical Studies*, 28 (2008), 102–21.

Catterall, D., 'At Home Abroad: Ethnicity and Enclave in the World of Scottish Traders in Northern Europe c.1600–1800', *Journal of Early Modern History*, 8 (2004), 319–57.

Chakrabarti, Shubhra, 'Collaboration and Resistance: Bengal Merchants and the English East India Company, 1757–1833', *Studies in History* 10 (1994), 105–29.

Chatterjee, Idrani, 'Colouring Subalternity: Slaves, Concubines, and Social Orphans in Early Colonial India', in Ranajit Guha, Partha Chatterjee and Gyanendra Pandey (eds), *Subaltern Studies, X: Writings on South Asian History and Society* (Delhi: Oxford University Press, 1982), pp. 49–97.

Chaudhuri, K. N., *The Trading World of Asia and the English East India Company, 1660–1760* (Cambridge: Cambridge University Press, 1978).

Checkland, S. G., *Scottish Banking: A History, 1695–1973* (London: Collins, 1975).

Cheong, W. E., *Mandarins & Merchants, Jardine Matheson & Co., A China Agency of the Early Nineteenth Century* (London: Curzon, 1979).

Clark, J. C. D., *English Society, 1688–1832* (Cambridge: Cambridge University Press, 2000).

Codell, J. F. and Macleod, D. S., 'Orientalism Transposed: the "Easternisation" of Britain and Interventions to Colonial Discourse', in J. F. Codell and D. S. Macleod (eds), *Orientalism Transposed: The Impact of the Colonies on British Culture* (Aldershot: Ashgate, 1998), pp. 1–14.

Cohn, Bernard, S., 'Recruitment and Training of British Civil Servants in India, 1600–1860', in Ralph Braibanti (ed.), *Asian Bureaucratic Systems Emergent from the British Imperial Tradition* (Durham, NC: Duke University Press, 1966), pp. 87–140.

Coleman, J. S., 'Social Capital in the Creation of Human Capital', *American Journal of Sociology*, 94 (1988), 95–120.

Colley, L., *Britons: Forging the Nation, 1707–1837* (London: Pimlico, 1992).

——, *Captives: Britain, Empire and the world, 1600–1850* (London: Jonathan Cape, 2002).

Collins, Randall, 'The Micro Contribution to Macro Sociology', *Sociological Theory*, 6 (1988), 242–53.

Colt, George Frederick Russell, *History & Genealogy of the Colts of that Ilk and Gartsherrie, and of the English & American Branches of that Family* (Madison, WI: n.p., 1887).

Connolly, S. J., 'Varieties of Britishness: Ireland, Scotland and Wales in the Hanoverian State', in Alexander Grant and Keith J. Stringer (eds), *Uniting the Kingdom? The Making of British History* (London: Routledge, 1995), 193–207.

——, *Religion, Law and Power: The Making of Protestant Ireland* (Oxford: Clarendon Press, 1995).

——, 'Introduction', in S. J. Connolly (ed.), *Kingdoms United? Great Britain and Ireland since 1500: Integration and Diversity* (Dublin: Four Courts Press, 1998), pp. 9–12.

Conway, Stephen, *The British Isles and the War of American Independence* (Oxford: Oxford University Press, 2002).

——, 'The Scots Brigade in the Eighteenth Century', *Northern Scotland* 1 (2010), 30–41.

——, *Britain, Ireland and Continental Europe in the Eighteenth Century* (Oxford: Oxford University Press, 2011).

——, *Britannia's Auxiliaries: Continental Europeans and the British Empire, 1740–1800* (Oxford: Oxford University Press, 2017).

Cook, Scott B., 'The Irish Raj: Social Origins and Careers of Irishmen in the Indian Civil Service, 1855–1914', *Journal of Social History*, 20 (1987), 508–29.

Cookson, John, *The British Armed Nation, 1793–1815* (Oxford: Oxford University Press, 1997).

Cotton, Julian James, *List of Inscriptions on Tombs or Monuments in Madras*, vols. I–III (Madras: Government Press, 1905).

Crawford, D. G., *A History of the Indian Medical Service, 1600–1913*, vols. I–II (London: Thacker, 1914).

——, *Roll of the Indian Medical Service, 1615–1930* (London: Thacker, 1930).

Cressy, D., 'Kinship and Kin Interaction in Early Modern England', *Past & Present*, 113 (1986), 38–69.

Crosbie, Barry, 'Ireland, Colonial Science and the Geographic Construction of British Rule in India, c.1820–1870', *Historical Journal*, 52 (2009), 963–87.

——, *Irish Imperial Networks: Migration, Social Communication and Exchange in Nineteenth-Century India* (Cambridge: Cambridge University Press, 2012).

Cullen, L. M., *Anglo-Irish Trade, 1600–1800* (New York: A. M. Kelley, 1968).

——, 'Merchant Communities Overseas, the Navigation Acts and Irish and Scottish Responses', in L. M. Cullen and T. C. Smout (eds), *Comparative Aspects of Scottish and Irish Economic History, 1600–1900* (Edinburgh: John Donald, 1977), pp. 165–76.

——, 'Economic Development, 1750–1800', in T. W. Moody and V. E. Vaughan (eds), *A New History of Ireland* (Oxford: Clarendon Press, 1986), pp. 159–95.

——, *An Economic History of Ireland since 1660* (London: Batsford Press, 1987).

——, 'Scotland & Ireland, 1600–1800: Their Role in the Evolution of British Society', in R. A. Houston (ed.), *Scottish Society, 1500–1800* (Cambridge: Cambridge University Press, 1989), pp. 226–44.

——, 'The Irish Diaspora of the Seventeenth and Eighteenth Centuries', in N. Canny (ed.), *Europeans on the Move: Studies in European Migration, 1500–1800* (Oxford: Clarendon Press, 1994), pp. 113–52.

——, 'Alliances and Misalliances in the Politics of The Union', *Transactions of the Royal Society*, sixth series, X (2000), 221–41.

——, 'Apotheosis and Crisis: The Irish Diaspora in the Age of Choiseul', in T. O'Connor and M. A. Lyons (eds), *Irish Communities in Early-Modern Europe* (Dublin: Four Courts, 2006), pp. 6–31.

——, 'The Two Fitzgeralds of London, 1718–1759', in David Dickson, Jan Parmentier and Jane Ohlmeyer (eds), *Irish and Scottish Mercantile Networks in Europe and Overseas in the Seventeenth and Eighteenth Centuries* (Ghent: Academia Press, 2007), pp. 251–70.

Dalrymple, William, *The Anarchy: The Relentless Rise of the East India Company* (London: Bloomsbury, 2019).

Davis, Natalie Zemon, 'Decentering History: Local Stories and Cultural Crossing in a Global World', *History and Theory*, 50 (2011), 188–202.

Devine, T. M., 'The Colonial Trades and Industrial Investment in Scotland, c.1700–1815', *Economic History Review*, 29 (1976), 1–13.
——, *The Glasgow Tobacco Lords* (Edinburgh: John Donald, 1976).
——, 'The Union of 1707 and Scottish Development', *Scottish Economic and Social History*, 5 (1985), 23–40.
——, *The Transformation of Rural Society: Social Change and the Agrarian Economy, 1660–1815* (Edinburgh: Edinburgh University Press, 1994).
——, 'The Golden Age of Tobacco', in T. M. Devine and Gordon Jackson (eds), *Glasgow, Volume I: Beginnings to 1830* (Manchester: Manchester University Press, 1995), pp. 139–83.
——, *The Scottish Nation, 1700–2000* (London: Penguin, 1999).
——, *Scotland's Empire, 1600–1815* (London: Allen Lane, 2003).
——, 'Industrialisation', in T. M. Devine, C. H. Lee and G. C. Peden (eds), *The Transformation of Scotland: The Economy since 1700* (Edinburgh: Edinburgh University Press, 2005), pp. 34–70.
——, 'Scottish Elites and the Indian Empire, 1700–1815', in T. C. Smout (ed.), *Anglo-Scottish Relations, 1600–1900* (Oxford: Oxford University Press, 2005), pp. 213–29.
——, 'The Spoils of Empire', in T. M. Devine (ed.), *Scotland and the Union, 1707–2007* (Edinburgh: Edinburgh University Press, 2008), pp. 91–108.
——, *To the Ends of the Earth: Scotland's Global Diaspora* (London: Allen Lane, 2011).
——, 'Did Slavery Make Scotia Great? A Question Revisited', in T. M. Devine (ed.), *Recovering Scotland's Slavery Past: The Caribbean Connection* (Edinburgh: Edinburgh University Press, 2015), pp. 225–45.
——, 'A Scottish Empire of Enterprise', in T. M. Devine and Angela McCarthy (eds), *The Scottish Experience in Asia, c.1700 to the Present: Settlers and Sojourners* (Cham: Palgrave Macmillan, 2017), 23–49.
Devine, T. M. and McCarthy, Angela, 'Introduction: The Scottish Experience in Asia, c.1700 to the Present: Settlers and Sojourners', in T. M. Devine and Angela McCarthy (eds), *The Scottish Experience in Asia, c.1700 to the Present: Settlers and Sojourners* (Cham: Palgrave Macmillan, 2017), pp. 1–21.
Devine, T. M., and Rössner, Philip R., 'Scotland and the Atlantic Economy, 1600–1800', in John M. MacKenzie and T. M. Devine (eds), *The Oxford History of the British Empire: Scotland and the British Empire* (Oxford: Oxford University Press, 2011), pp. 30–53.
de Vries, Jan, 'The Limits of Globalisation in the Early Modern World', *Economic History Review*, 63 (2010), 710–33.
Dickson, D., *New Foundations: Ireland 1660–1800* (Dublin: Criterion Press, 1987).
——, *Cork: Old World Colony: Cork and South Munster 1630–1830* (Cork: Cork University Press, 2005).
——, '1857 and 1908: Two Moments in the Transformation of Irish Universities', in David Dickson, Justyna Pyz and Christopher Shepard (eds), *Irish Classrooms and British Empire: Imperial Contexts in the Origins of Modern Education* (Dublin: Four Courts, 2012), pp. 184–205.
Dickson, Tony, *Scottish Capitalism: Class, State and Nation from Before the Union to the Present* (London: Laurence & Wishart, 1980).
Dingwall, Helen M., *A History of Scottish Medicine* (Edinburgh: Edinburgh University Press, 2003).

Dirks, N. B., *The Scandal of Empire: India and the Creation of Imperial Britain* (London: Harvard University Press, 2006).
Ditchburn, D., *Scotland and Europe: The Medieval Kingdom and Its Contacts with Christendom, c.1215–1545* (East Linton: Tuckwell, 2000).
Draper, Nicholas, 'Scotland and Colonial Slave Ownership: The Evidence of the Slave Compensation Records', in T. M. Devine (ed.), *Recovering Scotland's Slavery Past: The Caribbean Connection* (Edinburgh: Edinburgh University Press, 2015), pp. 166–86.
Drayton, Richard, 'Empire and Knowledge', in P. J. Marshall (ed.), *The Oxford History of the British Empire, II: The Eighteenth Century* (Oxford: Oxford University Press, 1998), pp. 231–52.
——, *Nature's Government: Science, Imperial Britain and the 'Improvement' of the World* (New Haven, CT: Yale University Press, 2000).
Drayton, Richard and Motade, David, 'The Futures of Global History', *Journal of Global History*, 13 (2018), 1–21.
Dumett, R. E., 'Exploring the Cain/Hopkins Paradigm. Issues for Debate; Critique, and Topics for New Research', in R. E. Dumett (ed.), *Gentlemanly Capitalism and British Imperialism: The New Debate on Empire* (London: Longman, 1999), 1–43.
Dziennik, Matthew P., 'Through an Imperial Prism: Land, Liberty, and Highland Loyalism in the War of American Independence', *Journal of British Studies*, 50 (2011), 332–58.
——, *The Fatal Land: War, Empire, and the Highland Soldier in British America* (New Haven, CT: Yale University Press, 2015).
——, 'The Fiscal-Military State and Labour in the British Atlantic World', in Aaron Graham and Patrick Walsh (eds), *British Fiscal Military States, 1660–1783* (London: Routledge, 2016), pp. 159–78.
Eacott, Jonathan, *Selling Empire: India and the Making of Britain and America, 1600–1830* (Williamsburg, VA: University of North Carolina Press, 2016).
Ebaugh, H. Rose and Curry, M., 'Fictive Kin as Social Capital in New Immigrant Communities', *Sociological Perspectives*, 43 (2000), 189–209.
Emerson, Roger L., 'Science and the Origins and Concerns of the Scottish Enlightenment', *History of Science*, 26 (1988), 333–66.
——, *Essays on David Hume, Medical Men and the Scottish Enlightenment* (Farnham: Ashgate, 2009).
Engerman, Stanley L., 'Slave Trade and British Capital Formation in the Eighteenth Century: A Comment on the Williams Thesis', *The Business History Review*, 46 (1972), 430–43.
Esteban, Javier Cuenca, 'The British Balance of Payments, 1772–1820: India Transfers and War Finance', *The Economic History Review*, 54 (2001), 58–86.
Evans, Chris, 'Wales, Munster and the English South West: contrasting articulations with the Atlantic World', in H. V. Bowen (ed.), *Wales and the British Overseas Empire, 1650–1830* (Manchester: Manchester University Press, 2011), pp. 40–61.
Evans, Neil, 'Writing Wales into the Empire: Rhetoric, Fragments – and Beyond?', in H. V. Bowen (ed.), *Wales and the British Overseas Empire, 1650–1830* (Manchester: Manchester University Press, 2011), pp. 15–39.
Farr, James, 'Social Capital: A Conceptual History', *Political Theory*, 32 (2004), 6–33.

Farrington, A., *A Biographical Index of East India Company Maritime Service Officers, 1600–1834* (London: British Library, 1999).
Feldbæk, Ole, *India Trade under the Danish Flag, 1772–1808: European Enterprise and Anglo-Indian Remittance and Trade* (Odense: Studentlitteratur, 1969).
Ferguson, W. 'The Electoral System in the Scottish Counties Before 1832', *The Stair Society, Miscellany II*, 35 (1984), 261–94.
——, *Scotland: 1689 to the Present* (Edinburgh: Mercat, 1997).
Field, J., *Social Capital* (London: Routledge, 2003).
Filor, Ellen, 'The Intimate Trade of Alexander Hall: Salmon and Slaves in Scotland and Sumatra, c.1745–1765', in Margot Finn and Kate Smith (eds), *The East India Company at Home, 1757–1857* (London: University College London Press, 2018), pp. 318–32.
Fine, B., *Social Capital versus Social Theory* (London: Routledge, 2001).
Finlay, R. J., 'Caledonia or North Britain? Scottish Identity in the Eighteenth Century', in D. Brown, R. J. Finlay and M. Lynch (eds), *Image and Identity: The Making and Remaking of Scotland through the Ages* (Edinburgh: John Donald, 1998), pp. 143–56.
Finn, Margot, 'Anglo-Indian Lives in the Later Eighteenth and Early Nineteenth Centuries', *Journal for Eighteenth-Century Studies*, 33 (2010), 49–65.
——, 'Family Formations: Anglo-India and the Familial Proto-State', in David Feldman and Jon Lawrence (eds), *Structures and Transformations in Modern British History* (Cambridge: Cambridge University Press, 2011), pp. 100–17.
——, 'Material Turns in British History: I. Loot', *Transactions of the Royal Historical Society*, 28 (2018), 5–32.
——, 'The Female World of Love & Empire: Women, Family & East India Company Politics at the End of the Eighteenth Century', *Gender & History*, 31 (2019), 7–24.
Finn, Margot and Smith, Kate, 'Introduction', in Margot Finn and Kate Smith (eds), *The East India Company at Home, 1757–1857* (London: University College London Press, 2018), pp. 1–24.
Fitzgerald, Patrick '"Come Back, Paddy Reilly": Aspects of Irish Return Migration, 1600–1845', in Marjory Harper (ed.), *Emigrant Homecomings: The Return Movement of Emigrants, 1600–2000* (Manchester: Manchester University Press, 2005), pp. 32–51.
Fitzgerald, Patrick and Lambkin, Brian, *Migration in Irish History, 1607–2007* (Basingstoke: Palgrave, 2008).
Fitz Patrick, W. (ed.), *HMC, Fortescue MSS*, Vol. I (London: HMSO, 1892).
Foggatt, P., 'The Irish Connection', in Derek A. Dow (ed.), *The Influence of Scottish Medicine* (Carnforth: Parthenon, 1988), pp. 63–76.
Fraser, T. G., 'Ireland and India', in K. Jeffery (ed.), *An Irish Empire? Aspects of Ireland and the British Empire* (Manchester: Manchester University Press, 1996), pp. 77–93.
Fry, Michael, *The Dundas Despotism* (Edinburgh: Edinburgh University Press, 1992).
——, *The Scottish Empire* (East Linton: Tuckwell Press, 2001).
Furber, H., *Rival Empires of Trade in the Orient, 1600–1800* (Minneapolis, MN: University of Minnesota Press, 1976).
——, *John Company at Work: A Study of European Expansion in India in the Late Eighteenth Century* (New York: Octagon, 1970).

Ghosh, Durba, *Sex and the Family in Colonial India: The Making of Empire* (Cambridge: Cambridge University Press, 2006).

Gibb, Andrew Dewar, *Scottish Empire* (Glasgow: A. Maclehose, 1937).

Girwood, R. H., 'The Influence of Scotland on North American Medicine', in Derek A. Dow (ed.), *The Influence of Scottish Medicine* (Carnforth: Parthenon, 1988), pp. 31–42.

Glaisyer, N., 'Networking: Trade and Exchange in the Eighteenth-Century British Empire', *The Historical Journal*, 47 (2004), 451–76.

Gould, Eliga H., 'A Virtual Nation: Greater Britain and the Imperial Legacy of the American Revolution', *The American Historical Review*, 104 (1999), 476–89.

Graham, Eric. J., *A Maritime History of Scotland 1650–1790* (East Linton: Tuckwell, 2002).

Grant, Eric and Mutch, Alistair, 'Indian Wealth and Agricultural Improvement in Northern Scotland', *Journal of Scottish Studies*, 35 (2015), 25–44.

Griffin, P., *The People with No Name: Ireland's Ulster Scots, America's Scots Irish and the Creation of a British Atlantic World, 1689–1764* (Princeton, NJ: Princeton University Press, 2001).

Guerrani, Anita, 'A Scotsman on the Make: The Career of Alexander Stuart', in Paul Wood (ed.), *The Scottish Enlightenment: Essays in Reinterpretation* (Rochester, NY: University of Rochester, 2000), pp. 157–76.

——, 'Scots in London Medicine in the Early Eighteenth Century', in Stana Nenadic (ed), *Scots in London in the Eighteenth Century* (Lewisburg, PA: Bucknell University Press, 2010), 165–85.

Hall, Catherine, 'Introduction: Thinking the Postcolonial, Thinking the Empire', in Catherine Hall (ed.), *Cultures of Empire: Colonisers in Britain and the Empire in the Nineteenth and Twentieth Centuries* (Manchester: Manchester University Press, 2000), pp. 1–36.

——, *Civilising Subjects: Metropole and Colony in the English Imagination, 1830–1867* (Cambridge: Polity Press, 2002).

Hall, Catherine, 'Culture and Identity in Imperial Britain', in Sarah Stockwell (ed.), *The British Empire: Themes and Perspectives* (Oxford: Blackwell, 2010), pp. 199–217.

Hall, Catherine and McClelland, Keith, 'Introduction', in Catherine Hall and Keith McClelland (eds), *Race, Nation and Empire: Making Histories, 1750 to the Present* (Manchester: Manchester University Press, 2010), pp. 1–11.

Hall, Catherine and Rose, Sonya, O., 'Introduction: Being at Home with the Empire', Catherine Hall and Sonya O. Rose (eds), *At Home with the Empire: Metropolitan Culture and the Imperial World* (Cambridge: Cambridge University Press, 2006), pp. 1–31.

Halpern, D., *Social Capital* (Cambridge: Polity, 2003).

Hamilton, D. J., *Scotland, the Caribbean and the Atlantic World, 1750–1820* (Manchester: Manchester University Press, 2005).

——, 'Scotland and the Eighteenth Century Empire', in T. M. Devine and Jenny Wormald (eds), *The Oxford Handbook of Modern Scottish History* (Oxford: Oxford University Press, 2012), pp. 423–38.

——, 'Brothers in Arms: Crossing Imperial Boundaries in the Eighteenth-Century Dutch West Indies', in Stephanie Barczewski and Martin Farr (eds), *The MacKenzie Moment and Imperial History: Essays in Honour of Professor John MacKenzie* (Cham: Palgrave Macmillan, 2019), pp. 287–309.

Hancock, D., *Citizens of the World: London Merchants and the Integration of the British Atlantic Community, 1735–1785* (Cambridge: Cambridge University Press, 1995).
——, 'Combining Success and Failure: Scottish Networks in the Atlantic Wine Trade', in D. Dickson, J. Parmentier and J. Ohlmeyer (eds), *Irish and Scottish Mercantile Networks in Europe and overseas in the Seventeenth and Eighteenth Centuries* (Ghent: Academia Press, 2007), pp. 5–38.
Hanser, Jessica, *Mr Smith Goes to China: Three Scots in the Making of Britain's Global Empire* (New Haven, CT, and London: Yale University Press, 2019).
Harper, M., 'Introduction', in M. Harper (ed.), *Emigrant Homecomings: The Return Movement of Emigrants, 1600–2000* (Manchester: Manchester University Press, 2005), pp. 1–14.
Harrington, Peter, 'The Scottish Soldier in Art', in Edward M. Speirs, Jeremy A. Crang and Matthew J. Strickland (eds), *A Military History of Scotland* (Edinburgh: Edinburgh University Press, 2012), pp. 608–705.
Harris, R., 'The Scots, the Westminster parliament and the British State in the Eighteenth Century', in J. Hoppit (ed.), *Parliaments, Nations and Identities in Britain and Ireland* (Manchester: Manchester University Press, 2003), pp. 124–45.
——, *The Scottish People and the French Revolution* (London: Pickering & Chatto, 2008).
Harrison, Mark, 'Tropical Medicine in Nineteenth-Century India', *The British Journal for the History of Science*, 25 (1992), 299–318.
——, *Medicine in an Age of Commerce and Empire: Britain and Its Tropical Colonies* (Oxford: Oxford University Press, 2010).
——, 'Networks of Knowledge: Science and Medicine in Early Colonial India, c.1750–1820', in Douglas M. Peers and Nandini Gooptu (eds), *The Oxford History of the British Empire: India and the British Empire* (Oxford: Oxford University Press, 2012), pp. 191–211.
Hasan, Farhat, 'Indigenous Cooperation and the Birth of a Colonial City: Calcutta, c.1698–1750', *Modern Asian Studies*, 26 (1992), 65–82.
Hayes, James, 'Scottish Officers in the British Army, 1714–1763', *The Scottish Historical Review*, 37 (1958) 22–33.
Hechter, M., *Internal Colonialism: The Celtic Fringe in British National Development, 1536–1966* (London: Routledge and Kegan Paul, 1975).
Hedström, P., Sandell, R. and Stern, C., 'Meso-Level Networks and the Diffusion of Social Movements: The Case of the Swedish Social Democratic Party', *The American Journal of Sociology*, 106 (2000), 145–72.
Henshaw, Victoria, *Scotland and the British Army, 1700–1750: Defending the Union* (London: Bloomsbury, 2014).
Hodson, V. C. P., *List of the Officers of the Army of Bengal, 1754–1834*, I–IV (London: Longman, Orme, Brown & Co., 1927).
Holmes, Michael and Holmes, Denis, 'Ireland and India: A Distant Relationship', in Michael Holmes and Denis Holmes (eds), *Ireland and India: Connections, Comparisons, Contrasts* (Limerick: Blackwater Press, 1997), pp. 1–7.
Holzman, J. M., *The Nabobs in England: A Study of the Returned Anglo-Indian, 1760–1785* (New York: P.P., 1926).
Hopkins, A. G., 'Introduction: Globalisation – An Agenda for Historians', in A. G. Hopkins (ed.), *Globalisation in World History* (London: Pimlico, 2002), pp. 1–10.

——, 'The History of Globalisation – and the Globalisation of History?', in A. G. Hopkins (ed.), *Globalisation in World History* (London: Pimlico, 2002), pp. 11–46.

Hoppit, Julian, 'Scotland and the Taxing Union, 1707–1815', *The Scottish Historical Review*, 98 (2019), 45–70.

Horn, James, 'British Diaspora: Emigration from Britain, 1680–1815', in P. J. Marshall (ed.), *The Oxford History of the British Empire, II: The Eighteenth Century* (Oxford: Oxford University Press, 1998), pp. 28–52.

Horwitz, H., 'The East India Trade: The Politicians and the Constitution: 1689–1702', *Journal of British Studies*, 17 (1977), 1–18.

Houston, R. A., 'The Demographic Regime', in T. M. Devine and Rosalind Mitchison (eds), *People and Society in Scotland, 1760–1830, vol. 1* (Edinburgh: John Donald, 1988), pp. 9–26.

Hunter, Jim, *'A Dance Called America': The Scottish Highlands, the United States and Canada* (Edinburgh: Mainstream, 1994).

Inikori, Joseph E., *Africans and the Industrial Revolution in England: A Study in International Trade and Development* (Cambridge: Cambridge University Press, 2002).

Insh, G. P., *Scottish Colonial Schemes, 1620–1686* (Glasgow: Maclehose, Jackson & Co., 1922).

——, 'The Founding of the Company of Scotland Trading to Africa and the Indies', *The Scottish History Review*, 22 (1924), 288–95.

Irving-Stonebraker, Sarah, 'Disease and Civilization: A Scottish Atlantic Network of Physicians in the Enlightenment', *Britain and the World*, 10 (2017), 197–216.

Jackson, Alvin, *The Two Unions: Ireland, Scotland and the Survival of the United Kingdom, 1707–2007* (Oxford: Oxford University Press, 2012).

Jasanoff, Maya, 'The Other Side of Revolution: Loyalists in the British Empire', *The William and Mary Quarterly*, 65 (2008), 205–32.

Jenkins, P., *The Making of a Ruling Class: The Glamorgan Gentry, 1640–1790* (Cambridge: Cambridge University Press, 1983).

Johnston, E. M. (ed.), *History of the Irish Parliament, 1695–1800*, 6 vols (Belfast: Ulster Historical Foundation, 2002).

Jones, C., 'Collectors of Natural Knowledge: The Edinburgh Medical Society and the Associational Culture of Scotland and the North Atlantic World in the 18th Century', *Journal of the Royal College of Physicians, Edinburgh*, 48 (2018), 155–64.

Jones, D. W., *War and Economy in the Age of William III and Marlborough* (London: Blackwell, 1988).

Jones, E., 'The Age of Societies', in E. Jones (ed.), *The Welsh in London* (Cardiff: University of Wales, 2001), pp. 54–87.

Karras, Alan, *Sojourners in the Sun: Scottish Migrants in Jamaica and the Chesapeake, 1740–1800* (Ithaca, NY, and London: Cornell University Press, 1992).

Karsten, Peter, 'Irish Soldiers in the British Army, 1792–1922: Suborned or Subordinate?', *Journal of Social History*, 17 (1983), 31–64.

Kaufman, Matthew H., *Medical Teaching in Edinburgh during the Eighteenth and Nineteenth Centuries* (Edinburgh: RCSE, 2003).

Kehoe, Karly, 'Accessing Empire: Irish Surgeons and the Royal Navy, 1840–1880', *Social History of Medicine*, 26 (2013), 204–24.

Kelly, James, *Prelude to Union: Anglo-Irish Politics in the 1780s* (Cork: Cork University Press, 1992).

——, 'The Emergence of Scientific and Institutional Medical Practice in Ireland, 1650–1800', in Greta Jones and Elizabeth Malcolm (eds), *Medicine, Disease and the State in Ireland, 1650–1940* (Cork: Cork University Press, 1999), pp. 21–39.

Khan, Gulfishan, *Indian Muslim Perceptions of the West During the Eighteenth Century* (Oxford and New Delhi: Oxford University Press, 1998).

Knox, S. J., *Ireland's Debt to the Huguenots* (Dublin: Alexander Thom, 1959).

Kochhar, Rajesh, 'Smallpox in the Modern Scientific and Colonial Contexts, 1721–1840', *Journal of Biosciences*, 36 (2011), 761–8.

Kolff, Dirk, *Naukar, Rajput and Sepoy: the Ethnohistory of the Military Labour Market in Hindustan, 1450–1850* (Cambridge: Cambridge University Press, 1990).

Konickx, C., *The First and Second Charter of the Swedish East India Company, 1731–1766* (Kortrijk: Van Ghemmert, 1980).

Koniordos, S. M., 'Introduction', in S. M. Koniordos (ed.), *Networks, Trust & Social Capital: Theoretical and Empirical Investigations from Europe* (Aldershot: Ashgate, 2005), pp. 3–14.

Laidlaw, Z., *Connecting Colonies: Metropole and Professions, 1815–1845* (Manchester: Manchester University Press, 2003).

Landsman, N. C., 'The Provinces and the Empire: Scotland, the American Colonies and the Development of British Provincial Identity', in Lawrence Stone (ed.), *An Imperial State at War: Britain from 1689–1815* (London: Routledge, 1994), pp. 258–87.

——, 'The Legacy of the British Union for the North American Colonies: Provincial Elites and the Problem of Imperial Union', in John Robertson (ed.), *A Union for Empire: Political Thought and the British Union of 1707* (Cambridge: Cambridge University Press, 1995), pp. 297–317.

Langford, Paul, 'South Britons' Reception of North Britons, 1707–1820', in T. C. Smout (ed.), *Anglo-Scottish Relations, 1600–1900* (Oxford: Oxford University Press, 2005), pp. 143–69.

Lawson, P., *The East India Company: A History* (London: Longman, 1993).

Lawson, Philip and Philips, Jim, '"Our Execrable Banditti": Perceptions of Nabobs in Mid-Eighteenth Century Britain', *Albion*, 16 (1984), 225–41.

Lee, C. H., 'The Establishment of the Financial Network', in T. M. Devine, C. H. Lee and G. C. Peden (eds), *The Transformation of Scotland: The Economy since 1700* (Edinburgh: Edinburgh University Press, 2005), pp. 100–27.

Lee, Wayne E., 'Subjects, Clients, Allies, or Mercenaries? The British Use of Irish and Amerindian Military Power, 1500–1800', in H. V. Bowen, Elizabeth Mancke and John G. Reid (eds), *Britain's Ocean Empire: Atlantic and India Ocean Worlds, c1550–1850* (Cambridge: Cambridge University Press, 2012), pp. 179–217.

Lenman, Bruce, *An Economic History of Modern Scotland 1660–1976* (London: B.T. Batsford, 1977).

Lester, Alan, 'Imperial Circuits and Networks: Geographies of the British Empire', *History Compass*, 4 (2006), 124–41.

Lin, Nan, *Social Capital: A Theory of Social Structure and Action* (Cambridge: Cambridge University Press, 2003).

——, 'Building a Network Theory of Social Capital', in Nan Lin, Karen Cook and Ronald S. Burt (eds), *Social Capital: Theory and Research* (New Brunswick, NJ: Aldine Transaction, 2005), pp. 3–29.
Livesey, James, *Civil Society and Empire: Ireland and Scotland in the Eighteenth-Century Atlantic World* (New Haven, CT, and London: Yale University Press, 2009).
Lougheed, Kevin, 'National Education and Empire: Ireland and the geography of the national education system', in David Dickson, Justyna Pyz and Christopher Shepard (eds), *Irish Classrooms and British Empire: Imperial Contexts in the Origins of Modern Education* (Dublin: Four Courts, 2012), pp. 5–17.
Love, H. D. (ed.), *Vestiges of Old Madras, 1640–1800*, vols. I–III (London: John Murray, 1913).
Lyons, M. A. 'The Emergence of an Irish Community in Saint-Malo, 1550–1710', in T. O'Connor and M. A. Lyons (eds), *Irish Communities in Early-Modern Europe* (Dublin: Four Courts, 2006), pp. 107–26.
Macinnes, A. I., 'Union Failed, Union Accomplished: The Irish Union of 1703 and the Scottish Union of 1707', in D. Keogh and K. Whelan (eds), *Acts of Union: The Causes, Contexts, and Consequences of the Act of Union* (Dublin: Four Courts, 2001), pp. 67–94.
——, *Union and Empire: The Making of the United Kingdom in 1707* (Cambridge: Cambridge University Press, 2007).
Mackenzie, A., *History of the Munros of Fowlis* (Inverness: Mackenzie, 1908).
MacKenzie, J. M., 'On Scotland and the Empire', *International History Review*, 15 (1993), 714–39.
——, *Orientalism: History, Theory and the Arts* (Manchester: Manchester University Press, 1995).
——, *Empires of Nature and the Nature of Empires: Imperialism, Scotland and the Environment* (East Linton: Tuckwell Press, 1997).
——, 'Empire and National Identities: The Case of Scotland', *Transactions of the Royal Historical Society*, sixth series, 8 (1998), 215–31.
——, 'Empire and Metropolitan Cultures', in Andrew Porter (ed.), *The Oxford History of the British Empire, Vol. III: The Nineteenth Century* (Oxford: Oxford University Press, 1998), pp. 270–93.
——, 'Irish, Scottish, Welsh and English Worlds?' A Four-Nation Approach to the History of the British Empire', *History Compass*, 6 (2008), 1244–63.
——, 'Comfort and Conviction: A Response to Bernard Porter', *The Journal of Imperial and Commonwealth History*, 36 (2008), 659–68.
MacKenzie J. M. with Dalziel, N. R., *The Scots in South Africa: Ethnicity, Identity, Gender and Race, 1772–1914* (Manchester, Manchester University Press, 2007).
Mackillop, A., *'More Fruitful than the Soil': Army, Empire and the Scottish Highlands, 1715–1815* (East Linton: Tuckwell, 2000).
——, 'Accessing Empire: Scotland, Britain, Europe and the Asia Trade, c.1690–1750', *Itinerario*, 29 (2005), 7–30.
——, 'The Highlands and the Returning Nabob: Sir Hector Munro of Novar, 1770–1807', in Marjory Harper (ed.), *Emigrant Homecomings: The Return Movement of Emigrants, 1600–2000* (Manchester: Manchester University Press, 2005), pp. 233–61.

——, 'Europeans, Britons and Scots: Scottish Sojourning Networks and Identities in Asia, c.1700–1815', in A. McCarthy (ed.), *A Global Clan: Scottish Migrant Networks and Identities since the Eighteenth Century* (London: I.B.Tauris, 2006), pp. 19–47.

——, 'A Union for Empire: Scotland, The English East India Company and the British Union', *The Scottish Historical Review*, 87 (2008), 116–34.

——, 'Dundee, London and the Empire in Asia', in Christopher Whatley, Charles MacKean and Bob Harris (eds), *Dundee: A History* (Dundee: Dundee University Press, 2009), pp. 161–85.

——, '"A Reticent People?": The Welsh in Asia, 1700–1815', in H. V. Bowen (ed.), *Wales and the British Overseas Empire, 1650–1830* (Manchester: Manchester University Press, 2011), pp. 143–67.

——, 'Locality, Nation and Empire: the Scots in Asia, c.1695–1813', in John M. MacKenzie and T. M. Devine (eds), The *Oxford History of the British Empire: Scotland and the British Empire* (Oxford: Oxford University Press, 2011), pp. 54–83.

——, '"As Hewers of Wood and Drawers of Water": Scotland as an Emigrant Nation, c.1600–c.1800', in Angela McCarthy and John M. MacKenzie (eds), *Global Migrations: The Scottish Diaspora since 1600* (Edinburgh: Edinburgh University Press, 2016), pp. 23–38.

——, 'Military Scotland in the Age of Proto-Globalisation', in David Forsyth and Wendy Ugolini (eds), *A Global Force* (Edinburgh: Edinburgh University Press, 2016), pp. 13–28.

——, '"Subsidy State" or "Drawback Province": Scotland and the British Fiscal-Military Complex', in Aaron Graham and Patrick Walsh (eds), *British Fiscal Military States, 1660–1783* (London: Routledge, 2016), pp. 179–200.

Mackillop, A. and Murdoch, Steve, 'Introduction', in A. Mackillop and Steve Murdoch (eds), *Military Governors & Imperial Frontiers, c.1600–1800: A Study of Scotland and Empires* (Leiden: Brill, 2003), pp. xxv–li.

Macpherson, B. H., 'Scots Law in the Colonies', *Juridical Review* (1995), pt. 1, 191–207.

Magee, Gary B. and Thompson, Andrew S., *Empire and Globalisation: Networks of People, Goods and Capital in the British World, c.1850–1914* (Cambridge: Cambridge University Press, 2010).

McAleer, John, 'This "Ultima Thule": The Cape of Good Hope, Ireland and Global Networks of Empire, 1795–1815', *Eighteenth-Century Ireland/Iris an dá chultúr*, 29 (2014), 63–84.

McCulloch, J. H., *The Scot in England* (London: Hurst & Blackett, 1935).

McDougall, Warren, 'Charles Elliot's Medical Publications and the International Book Trade', in Paul Wood and Charles W. J. Withers (eds), *Science and Medicine in the Scottish Enlightenment* (East Linton: Tuckwell Press, 2002), pp. 215–54.

McDowell, R. B., *Ireland in the Age of Imperialism and Revolution, 1760–1801* (Oxford: Clarendon Press, 1991).

McGilvary, G., *Guardian of the East India Company: The Life of Laurence Sulivan* (London: I.B.Tauris, 2006).

——, *East India Patronage and the British State: The Scottish Elite and Politics in the Eighteenth Century* (London: I.B.Tauris, 2011).

——, 'The Return of the Scottish Nabob', in M. Varricchio (ed.), *Back to Caledonia: Scottish Homecomings from the Seventeenth Century to the Present* (Edinburgh: John Donald, 2012), pp. 90–108.

——, 'Scottish Agency Houses in South East Asia, c.1760–1813', in T. M. Devine and Angela McCarthy (eds), *The Scottish Experience in Asia, c.1700 to the Present: Settlers and Sojourners* (Cham: Palgrave Macmillan, 2017), pp. 75–96.

McGrath, Charles Ivar, *Ireland and Empire, 1692–1770* (London: Pickering & Chatto, 2012).

McKichan, Finlay, *Lord Seaforth: Highland Landowner, Caribbean Governor* (Edinburgh: Edinburgh University Press, 2018).

McLaren, Jennifer, 'An Irish Surgeon in Barbados and Demerara: Vexation, Misery and Opportunity', in D. S. Roberts and J. J. Wright (eds), *Ireland's Imperial Connections, 1775–1947* (Cambridge: Cambridge University Press, 2019), pp. 251–72.

McLaren, M., *British India and British Scotland, 1780–1830* (Akron, OH: Akron Press, 2001).

McNally, P., *Parties, Patriots & Undertakers: Parliamentary Politics in Early Hanoverian Ireland* (Dublin: Four Courts Press, 1997).

Marshall, P. J., *Problems of Empire: Britain and India, 1757–1813* (London: George Allen and Unwin, 1968).

——, 'Economic and Political Expansion: The Case of Oudh', *Modern Asian Studies*, 9 (1975), 465–82.

——, *East Indian Fortunes: The British in Bengal in the Eighteenth Century* (Oxford: Clarendon Press, 1976).

——, 'Masters and Banians in Eighteenth-Century Calcutta', in Blair B. Kling and M. N. Pearson (eds), *The Age of Partnership: Europeans in Asia before Dominion* (Honolulu, HI: University of Hawaii Press, 1979), pp. 191–213.

——, 'Early British Imperialism in India', *Past & Present*, 106 (1985), 164–73.

——, 'Empire and Authority in the Later Eighteenth Century', *Journal of Imperial and Commonwealth History*, 15 (1987), 105–22.

——, 'Private British Trade in the Indian Ocean before 1800', in A. Das Gupta and M. N. Pearson (eds), *India and the Indian Ocean, 1500–1800* (Calcutta: Oxford University Press, 1987), pp. 276–300.

——, *Bengal: The British Bridgehead: Eastern India, 1740–1828* (Cambridge: Cambridge University Press, 1990).

——, 'The Whites of British India, 1780–1830: A Failed Colonial Society?', *International History Review*, 12 (1990), 26–44.

——, 'The Eighteenth-Century Empire', in J. Black (ed.), *British Politics and Society from Walpole to Pitt* (Basingstoke: Palgrave, 1990), pp. 177–200.

——, 'Imperial Britain', *Journal of Imperial & Commonwealth History*, 23 (1995), 379–94.

——, 'A Nation Defined by Empire', in Alexander Grant and Keith J. Stringer (eds), *Uniting the Kingdom? The Making of British History* (London: Routledge, 1995), pp. 208–22.

——, 'British Society in India under the East India Company', *Modern Asian Studies*, 31 (1997), 89–108.

——, 'Burke and Empire', in S. Taylor, R. Connors and C. Jones (eds), *Hanoverian Britain and Empire* (Woodbridge: Boydell, 1998), pp. 288–98.

——, 'Private British Investment in Eighteenth Century Bengal', in P. Tuck (ed.), *The East India Company, IV: Trade, Finance and Power* (London: Routledge, 1998), pp. 127–41.
——, 'The English in Asia to 1700', in N. Canny (ed.), *The Oxford History of the British Empire, I: The Origins of Empire* (Oxford: Oxford University Press, 1998), pp. 264–85.
—— (ed.), *The Oxford History of the British Empire, II: The Eighteenth Century* (Oxford: Oxford University Press, 1998).
——, *The Making and Unmaking of Empires: Britain, India and America c.1750–1783* (Oxford: Oxford University Press, 2005).
Marwick, James David (ed.), *Extracts from the Records of the Convention of the Royal Burghs of Scotland, 1759–79* (Edinburgh: H. & J. Pillans & Wilson, 1868).
Mentz, Søren, *The English Gentleman Merchant at Work: Madras and the City of London 1660–1740* (Copenhagen: Museum Tusculanum Press, 2005).
Mukherjee, R., 'Trade and Empire in Awadh, 1765–1804', *Past & Present*, 94 (1982), 85–102.
Müller, L., 'Scottish and Irish Entrepreneurs in Eighteenth-Century Sweden', in David Dickson, Jan Parmentier and Jane Ohlmeyer (eds), *Irish and Scottish Mercantile Networks in Europe and Overseas in the Seventeenth and Eighteenth Centuries* (Ghent: Academia Press, 2007), pp. 147–74.
Munn, C. W., *The Scottish Provincial Banking Companies, 1747–1864* (Edinburgh: Donald, 1981).
Murdoch, Alex, *British History, 1660–1832: National Identity and Local Culture* (Basingstoke: Macmillan, 1998).
——, 'Scotland and the Idea of Britain in the Eighteenth Century', in T. M. Devine and J. R. Young (eds), *Eighteenth Century Scotland: New Perspectives* (East Linton: Tuckwell Press, 1999), pp. 106–21.
Murdoch, Steve, 'Introduction', in Steve Murdoch (ed.), *Scotland and the Thirty Years' War* (Leiden: Brill, 2001), pp. 1–26.
Murtagh, Harman, 'Irish Soldiers Abroad, 1600–1800', in T. Bartlett and K. Jeffery (eds), *A Military History of Ireland* (Cambridge: Cambridge University Press, 1996), pp. 294–314.
Mustakeem, Sowande, '"I Never Have Such a Sickly Ship Before": Diet, Disease, and Mortality in 18th-Century Atlantic Slaving Voyages', *Journal of African American History*, 93 (2008), 474–96.
Mutch, Alistair, *Tiger Duff: India, Madeira and Empire in Eighteenth-Century Scotland* (Aberdeen: Aberdeen University Press, 2017).
——, 'Connecting Britain and India: General Patrick Duff and Madeira', in Margot Finn and Kate Smith (eds), *The East India Company at Home, 1757–1857* (London: University College London Press, 2018), 333–54.
Nash, R. C., 'Irish Atlantic Trade in the Seventeenth and Eighteenth Centuries', *The William and Mary Quarterly*, 42 (1985), 329–56.
Nechtman, Tillman W., *Nabobs: Empire and Identity in Eighteenth-Century Britain* (Cambridge, Cambridge University Press, 2010).
Neild-Basu, Susan, 'The Dubashes of Madras', *Modern Asian Studies*, 18 (1984), 1–31.
Nenadic, Stana, 'Introduction', in Stana Nenadic (ed.), *Scots in London in the Eighteenth Century* (Lewisburg, PA: Bucknell University Press, 2010), pp. 13–48.

Nightingale, P., *Fortune and Integrity: A Study of Moral Attitudes in the India Diary of George Paterson, 1769–1774* (Oxford: Oxford University Press, 1985).

Nussbaum, F. A. 'Introduction', in F. A. Nussbaum (ed.), *The Global Eighteenth Century* (Baltimore, MD: John Hopkins University Press, 2003), pp. 1–20.

Ohlmeyer, J. H., 'A Laboratory for Empire? Early Modern Ireland and English Imperialism', in K. Kenny (ed.), *Ireland and the British Empire* (Oxford: Oxford University Press, 2004), pp. 26–60.

——, 'Eastward Enterprises: Colonial Ireland, Colonial India', *Past & Present*, 240 (2018), 83–118.

Osterhammel, Jürgen, *Unfabling the East: The Enlightenment's Encounter with Asia* (Princeton, NJ: Princeton University Press, 2018).

Parker, J. G., 'Scottish Enterprise in India, 1750–1914', in R. A. Cage (ed.), *The Scots Abroad: Labour, Capital, Enterprise, 1750–1914* (London: Croom Helm, 1985), pp. 191–219.

Parmentier, J., 'Irish Mercantile Builders in Ostend, 1690–1790', in T. O'Connor and M. A. Lyons (eds), *Irish Communities in Early-Modern Europe* (Dublin: Four Courts, 2006), pp. 376–82.

Parthasarathi, Prasannan, *Why Europe Grew Rich and Asia Did Not: Global Economic Divergence, 1600–1850* (Cambridge: Cambridge University Press, 2011).

Peers, Douglas, 'State, Power, and Colonialism', in Douglas M. Peers and Nandidi Gooptu (eds), *The Oxford History of the British Empire: India and the British Empire* (Oxford: Oxford University Press, 2012), pp. 16–43.

Pentland, Gordon, '"We Speak for the Ready": Images of Scots in Political Prints, 1707–1832', *The Scottish Historical Review*, 90 (2011), 64–95.

Phillips, Andrew, 'The Global Transformation, Multiple Early Modernities, and International Systems Change', *International Theory*, 8 (2016), 481–91.

Phillips, Andrew and Sharman, J. C., *Outsourcing Empire: How Company States Made the Modern World* (Princeton, NJ: Princeton University Press, 2020).

Phillips, C. H., *The East India Company, 1784–1834* (Manchester: Manchester University Press, 1961).

Poliakov, L., 'Racism from the Enlightenment to the Age of Imperialism', in R. Ross (ed.), *Racism and Colonialism: Essays on Ideology and Social Structure* (The Hague: M. Nijhoff, 1982), pp. 55–64.

Pomeranz, Kenneth, *The Great Divergence: China, Europe, and the Making of the Modern World Economy* (Princeton, NJ, and Oxford: Princeton University Press, 2000).

Pomeranz, Kenneth and Topik, Steven, *The World that Trade Created: Society, Culture and the World Economy, 1400 to the Present* (London and New York: Routledge, 2018).

Porter, A., '"Gentlemanly Capitalism" and Empire: The British Experience of 1750', *Journal of Imperial and Commonwealth History*, 18 (1990), 265–95.

Porter, B., *The Absent-Minded Imperialists: Empire, Society and Culture in Britain* (Oxford: Oxford University Press, 2004).

——, 'Further Thoughts on Imperial Absent-Mindedness', *Journal of Imperial and Commonwealth History*, 36 (2008), 101–17.

Portes, A., 'The Two Meanings of Social Capital', *Sociological Forum*, 15 (2000), 1–12.

Powell, Martyn J., *Britain and Ireland in the Eighteenth-Century Crisis of Empire* (Basingstoke: Palgrave Macmillan, 2003).
——, *The Politics of Consumption in Eighteenth-Century Ireland* (London: Palgrave Macmillan, 2005).
Price, Richard, 'One Big Thing: Britain, Its Empire, and Their Imperial Culture', *Journal of British Studies*, 45 (2006), 602–27.
Quiley, Geoffrey, 'The East India Company's Patronage of Eighteenth-Century Art', in Huw V. Bowen and Nigel Rigby (eds), *The Worlds of the East India Company* (London: Boydell & Brewer, 2004), pp. 183–99.
Raj, Kapil, 'Colonial Encounters and the Forging of New Knowledge and National Identities: Great Britain and India, 1760–1850', in Roy Macleod (ed.), 'Nature and Empire: Science and the Colonial Enterprise', *Osiris*, second series, 15 (2000), pp. 119–34.
——, *Relocating Modern Science: Circulation and the Construction of Scientific Knowledge in South Asia and Europe* (New Delhi: Permanent Black, 2006).
——, 'Mapping Knowledge Go-Betweens in Calcutta, 1770–1820', in Simon Schaffer, Lissa Roberts, Kapil Raj and James Delbourgo (eds), *The Brokered World: Go-Between and Global Intelligence, 1770–1820* (Sagamore Beach, MA: Science History Publications, 2009), pp. 105–50.
Rees, Ann Lowri, 'Welsh Sojourners in India: The East India Company, Networks and Patronage, c.1760–1840', *The Journal of Imperial and Commonwealth History*, 45 (2017), 165–87.
Rice, C. D., 'Scottish Enlightenment, American Revolution and Atlantic Reform', in O. D. Edwards and G. Shepperson (eds), *Scotland, Europe and the American Revolution* (Edinburgh: Edinburgh University Student Publications, 1976), pp. 75–82.
Richards, Eric, 'Scotland and the Uses of the Atlantic Empire', in B. Bailyn and Philip D. Morgan (eds), *Strangers within the Realm: Cultural Margins of the First British Empire* (Chapel Hill, NC, and London: University of North Carolina Press, 1991), pp. 67–114.
——, *Britannia's Children: Emigration from England, Scotland, Wales and Ireland since 1600* (London: Cambridge University Press, 2004).
Riddy, J., 'Warren Hastings: Scotland's Benefactor?', in G. Carnall and C. Nicolson (eds), *The Impeachment of Warren Hastings* (Edinburgh: Edinburgh University Press, 1989), pp. 30–57.
Riello, Giorgio, *Cotton: The Fabric that Made the Modern World* (Cambridge: Cambridge University Press, 2013).
Rigg, Suzanne, *Men of Spirit and Enterprise: Scots and Orkneymen in the Hudson's Bay Company, 1780–1821* (Edinburgh: John Donald, 2011).
Risse, Guenter, B., *New Medical Challenges during the Scottish Enlightenment* (New York: Rodopi B.V., 2005).
Robertson, John, 'The Scottish Contribution to the Enlightenment', in Paul Wood (ed.), *The Scottish Enlightenment: Essays in Reinterpretation* (Rochester, NY: Rochester University Press, 2000), pp. 37–62.
——, 'Empire and Union: Two Concepts of the Early Modern European Political Order', in John Robertson (ed.), *A Union for Empire: Political Thought and the British Union of 1707* (Cambridge: Cambridge University Press, 1995), pp. 3–36.
Rogers, Nicholas, 'Money, Land and Lineage: The Big Bourgeoisie of Hanoverian London', *Social History*, 4 (1979), 437–54.

Rosenband, L. N., 'Social Capital in the Early Industrial Revolution', *Journal of Interdisciplinary History*, 29 (1999), 435–57.
Roseveare, H. G., 'Jacob David: A Huguenot London Merchant of the Late Seventeenth Century & His Circle', in I. Scouloude (ed.), *Huguenots in Britain and Their French Background, 1550–1800* (Basingstoke: Macmillan, 1987), pp. 72–88.
Ross, Peter, *The Scots in America* (New York: Raeburn, 1896).
Rotger, Neus, Roig-Sanz, Diana and Puxan-Oliva, Marta, 'Introduction: Towards a Cross-Disciplinary History of the Global in the Humanities and the Social Sciences', *Journal of Global History*, 14 (2019), 325–34.
Rothschild, Emma, *The Inner Lives of Empires: An Eighteenth-Century History* (Princeton, NJ: Princeton University Press, 2011).
Roy, Tirthanker, *How British Rule Changed India's Economy: The Paradox of the Raj* (Basingstoke: Palgrave Macmillan, 2019).
Rubinstein, W. D., 'The End of "Old Corruption" in Britain 1780–1860', *Past & Present*, 101 (1983), 55–86.
Ryder, S., 'Ireland, India and Popular Nationalism in the Early Nineteenth Century', in T. Foley and M. O'Connor (eds), *Ireland and India: Colonies, Culture and Empire* (Dublin: Irish Academic Press, 2006), pp. 12–25.
Saddle, D. J., 'Migration as a Strategy of Accumulation: Social and Economic Change in Eighteenth-Century Savoy', *Economic History Review*, 50 (1997), 1–20.
Said, E. W., *Orientalism* (London: Penguin, 2003).
Schwarz, Suzanne, 'Scottish Surgeons in the Liverpool Slave Trade in the Late Eighteenth and Early Nineteenth Centuries', in T. M. Devine (ed.), *Recovering Scotland's Slavery Past: The Caribbean Connection* (Edinburgh: Edinburgh University Press, 2015), pp. 145–65.
Sebastiani, Silvia (translated by Jeremy Carden), *The Scottish Enlightenment: Race, Gender, and the Limits of Progress* (New York: Palgrave Macmillan, 2013).
Sen, S. P., *The French in India, 1763–1816* (New Delhi: M. Manoharlal, 1971).
Shaw, J. S., *The Political History of Eighteenth-Century Scotland* (Basingstoke: Macmillan, 1999).
Shepard, Christopher, 'Cramming, Instrumentality and the Education of Irish Imperial Elites', in David Dickson, Justyna Pyz and Christopher Shepard (eds), *Irish Classrooms and British Empire: Imperial Contexts in the Origins of Modern Education* (Dublin: Four Courts, 2012), pp. 172–83.
Sher, Richard, 'Science and Medicine in the Scottish Enlightenment: The Lessons of Book History', in Paul Wood (ed.), *The Scottish Enlightenment: Essays in Reinterpretation* (Rochester, NY: University of Rochester Press, 2000), pp. 99–156.
Sheridan, R. B., 'The Role of the Scots in the Economy and Society of the West Indies', in V. Rubin and A. Tuden (eds), *Comparative Perspectives on Slavery in New World Plantation Societies* (New York: New York Academy of Sciences, 1977), pp. 94–106.
——, *Doctors and Slaves: A Medical and Demographic History of Slavery in the British West Indies, 1680–1834* (Cambridge: Cambridge University Press, 1985).
Silvestri, M., *Ireland and India: Nationalism, Empire and Memory* (Basingstoke: Palgrave Macmillan, 2009).

Singh, S. B., *European Agency Houses in Bengal* (Calcutta: Firma K.L. Mukhopadhyay, 1966).
Smail, J., 'Credit, Risk and Honor in Eighteenth-Century Commerce', *Journal of British Studies*, 44 (2005), 439–56.
Smith, S. D., *Slavery, Family and Gentry Capitalism in the British Atlantic: The World of the Lascelles, 1646–1834* (Cambridge: Cambridge University Press, 2006).
Smout, T. C., Landsman N. C. and Devine, T. M., 'Scottish Emigration in the Seventeenth and Eighteenth Centuries', in N. Canny (ed.), *Europeans on the Move: Studies in European Migration, 1500–1800* (Oxford: Clarendon Press, 1994), pp. 76–112.
Sramek, Joseph, 'Rethinking Britishness: Religion and Debates about the "Nation" among Britons in Company India, 1813–1857', *Journal of British Studies*, 54 (2015), 822–43.
Starkey, Janet, *The Scottish Enlightenment Abroad: The Russells of Braidshaw in Aleppo and on the Coast of Coromandel* (Leiden: Brill, 2018).
Steengaard, N., 'The Companies as a Specific Institution in the History of European Expansion', in L. Blussé and F. Gaastra (eds), *Companies and Trade: Essays on Overseas Trading Companies during the Ancien Régime* (Leiden: Leiden University Press, 1981), pp. 245–64.
Stern, P. J., 'British Asia and the British Atlantic: Comparisons and Connections', *William and Mary Quarterly*, 63 (2006), 693–712.
——, 'History and Historiography of the English East India Company: Past, Present, and Future!', *History Compass*, 7 (2009), 1146–80.
——, *The Company State: Corporate Sovereignty and the Early Modern Foundations of the British Empire in India* (Oxford: Oxford University Press, 2011).
——, 'Seeing (and Not Seeing) Like a Company-State: Hybridity, Heterotopia, Historiography', *Journal of Early Modern Cultural Studies*, 17 (2017), 105–20.
Steven, Margaret, *Merchant Campbell 1769–1846: A Study in Colonial Trade* (Melbourne: Oxford University Press, 1965).
Stone, L., 'Literacy and Education in England, 1640–1900', *Past & Present*, 42 (1969), 69–139.
Subrahmanyam, Sanjay, *Europe's India: Words, People, Empire, 1500–1800* (Cambridge, MA: Harvard University Press, 2017).
Subrahmanyam, Sanjay and Bayly, C. A., 'Portfolio Capitalists and the Political Economy of Early Modern India', *The Indian Economic and Social History Review*, 25 (1988), 401–24.
Sunter, R., *Patronage and Politics in Scotland, 1707–1832* (Edinburgh: John Donald, 1986).
Sutherland, L., *The East India Company in Eighteenth Century Politics* (Oxford: Clarendon Press, 1962).
Sutton, Jean, *Lords of the East: The East India Company and Its Ships* (London: Conway Maritime Press, 1981).
——, *The East India Company's Maritime Service, 1746–1834: Masters of Eastern Seas* (Woodbridge: Boydell Press, 2010).
Tabili, Laura, 'An Homogeneous Society? Britain's Internal "Others", 1800–Present', in Catherine Hall and Sonya O. Rose (eds), *At Home with the Empire: Metropolitan Culture and the Imperial World* (Cambridge: Cambridge University Press, 2006), pp. 53–76.

Taylor, David, *The Wild Black Region: Badenoch, 1750–1800* (Edinburgh: John Donald, 2016).

Taylor, J., *A Cup of Kindness: The History of the Royal Scottish Corporation, 1603–2003* (East Linton: Tuckwell, 2003).

Teissier, Beatrice, 'Asia in Eighteenth-Century Edinburgh Institutions: Seen or Unseen?', *Proceedings of the Societies of Antiquaries of Scotland*, 134 (2004), 499–556.

Teltscher, Kate, 'Writing Home and Crossing Cultures: George Bogle in Bengal and Tibet, 1770–1775', in K. Wilson (ed.), *A New Imperial History: Culture, Identity, and Modernity in Britain and the Empire, 1660–1840* (Cambridge: Cambridge University Press, 2004), pp. 281–96.

——, *The High Road to China: George Bogle, the Panchen Lama and the First British Expedition to Tibet* (London: Bloomsbury, 2007).

Thompson, Andrew, *The Empire Strikes Back? The Impact of Imperialism on Britain from the Mid-Nineteenth Century* (Harlow: Pearson Longman, 2005).

——, 'Empire and the British State', in Sarah Stockwell (ed.), *The British Empire: Themes and Perspectives* (Oxford: Blackwell, 2008), pp. 39–61.

Tilly, C., 'Transplanted Networks', in V. Yans-McLaughlin (ed.), *Immigration Reconsidered: History, Sociology, and Politics* (Oxford: Oxford University Press, 1990), pp. 79–95.

Tomlinson, B. R., 'From Campsie to Kedgeree: Scottish Enterprise, Asian Trade and the Company Raj', *Modern Asian Studies*, 36 (2002), 769–92.

Tomlinson, Jim, *Dundee and the Empire: 'Juteopolis' 1850–1939* (Edinburgh: Edinburgh University Press, 2014).

Turner, J. H., 'The Formation of Social Capital', in P. Dasgupta and I. Serageldin (eds), *Social Capital: A Multifaceted Perspective* (Washington, DC: World Bank, 2000), pp. 94–146.

——, 'Toward a General Sociological Theory of the Economy', *Sociological Theory*, 22 (2004), 229–46.

Truxes, T. M., *Irish–American Trade, 1660–1783* (Cambridge: Cambridge University Press, 2004).

——, 'London's Irish Merchant Community and North Atlantic Commerce in the Mid-Eighteenth Century', in David Dickson, Jan Parmentier and Jane Ohlmeyer (eds), *Irish and Scottish Mercantile Networks in Europe and Overseas in the Seventeenth and Eighteenth Centuries* (Ghent: Academia Press, 2007), pp. 271–310.

van Gelder, R., *Het Oost-Indisch avantuur: Duitsers in dienst can de VOC, 1600–1800* (Nijmegen: Sun, 1997).

van Lottum, Jelle and van Zanden, Jan Luiten, 'Labour Productivity and Human Capital in the European Maritime Sector of the Eighteenth Century', *Explorations in Economic History*, 53 (2014), 83–100.

van Lottum, Jelle, Brock, Aske and Sumnall, Catherine, 'Mobility, Migration and Human Capital in the Long Eighteenth Century: The Life of Joseph Anton Ponsaing', in Maria Fusaro, Bernard Allaire, Richard Blakemore and Tijl Vanneste (eds), *Law, Labour, and Empire: Comparative Perspectives on Seafarers, c.1500–1800* (London: Palgrave Macmillan, 2015), pp. 158–76.

Vance, S., 'A Man for all Regions – Patrick Copland and Education in the Stuart World', in Allan Macinnes and Arthur H. Williamson (eds), *Shaping the*

Stuart World, 1603–1714: The Atlantic Connection (Leiden: Brill, 2005), pp. 55–78.
Varricchio, Mario, 'Introduction: The Other Side of Leaving', in Mario Varricchio (ed.), *Back to Caledonia: Scottish Homecoming from the Seventeenth Century to the Present* (Edinburgh: John Donald, 2012), pp. 1–33.
Veevers, David, '"Inhabitants of the Universe": Global Families, Kinship Networks, and the Formation of the Early Modern Colonial State in Asia', *Journal of Global History*, 10 (2015), 99–121.
Vicziany, Markia, 'Imperialism, Botany and Statistics in Early Nineteenth-Century India: The Surveys of Francis Buchanan (1762–1829)', *Modern Asian Studies*, 20 (1986), 625–60.
Vidal, Jean-Pierre, 'The Effect of Emigration on Human Capital Formation', *Journal of Population Economics*, 11 (1998), 589–600.
Wagner, Joseph, 'The Scottish East India Company of 1617: Patronage, Commercial Rivalry, and the Union of the Crowns', *Journal of British Studies*, 59 (2020), 582–607.
Wallerstein, Immanuel, *The Modern World-System I: Capitalism Agriculture and the Origins of the European World-Economy in the Sixteenth Century* (Berkeley and LA, CA: University of California Press, 2011).
——, *The Modern World-System II: Mercantilism and the Consolidation of the European-World Economy, 1600–1750* (Berkeley and LA, CA: University of California Press, 2011).
Walsh, Patrick, 'The Fiscal State in Ireland', *Historical Journal*, 56 (2013), 629–56.
Washbrook, D. A. 'Orients and Occidents: Colonial Discourse Theory and the Historiography of the British Empire', in R. W. Winks (ed.), *The Oxford History of the British Empire, V: Historiography* (Oxford: Oxford University Press, 1998), pp. 596–611.
——, 'South India, 1770–1840: The Colonial Transition', *Modern Asian Studies*, 38 (2004), 479–516.
Watt, D., *The Price of Scotland: Darien, Union and the Wealth of Nations* (Edinburgh: Luath, 2007).
Watters, B., *Where Iron Runs Like Water: A New History of Carron Iron Works, 1759–1982* (Edinburgh: John Donald, 1998).
Watson, Ian Bruce, *Foundation for Empire: English Private Trade in India, 1659–1760* (New Delhi: Vikas, 1980).
——, 'Fortifications and the "Idea" of Force in Early English East India Company Relations with India', *Past & Present*, 88 (1980), 70–87.
Webster, A., 'The Political Economy of Trade Liberalization: The East India Company Charter of 1813', *Economic History Review*, second series, 43 (1990), 404–19.
——, *The Twilight of the East India Company: The Evolution of Anglo-Asian Commerce and Politics, 1790–1860* (Woodbridge: Boydell, 2009).
Wetherell, C., Plakan, A. and Wellman, B., 'Social Networks, Kinship and Community in Eastern Europe', *Journal of Interdisciplinary History*, 24 (1994), 639–63.
Whatley, C. A., *The Industrial Revolution in Scotland* (Cambridge: Cambridge University Press, 1997).
——, *Scottish Society, 1707–1830* (Manchester: Manchester University Press, 2000).
Whelan, K., 'An Underground Gentry? Catholic Middlemen in Eighteenth-Century Ireland', *Eighteenth-Century Ireland/Iris an dá chultúr*, 10 (1995), 7–68.

—, 'Ireland, Scotland and Britain in the Long Eighteenth Century', in T. Wickremesekera, Channa, *'Best Black Troops in the World'*: *British Perceptions and the Making of the Sepoy, 1746–1805* (New Delhi: Manohar, 2002).
Wilkinson, Theon, *Two Monsoons* (London: Duckworth, 1976).
Williams, G. A., *When Was Wales?: A History of the Welsh* (London: Penguin, 1991).
Wilson, Jon E., *The Domination of Strangers: Modern Governance in Eastern India, 1780–1835* (London: Palgrave Macmillan, 2008).
Wilson, K., *The Sense of the People: Politics, Culture and Imperialism in England, 1715–1785* (Cambridge: Cambridge University Press, 1998).
—, *The Island Race: Englishness, Empire and Gender in the Eighteenth Century* (London: Routledge, 2003).
—, 'Introduction: Histories, Empires, Modernities', in K. Wilson (ed.), *A New Imperial History: Culture, Identity, and Modernity in Britain and the Empire, 1660–1840* (Cambridge: Cambridge University Press, 2004), pp. 1–26.
—, 'Empire, Gender, and Modernity', in Philippa Levine (ed.), *Gender and Empire* (Oxford, Oxford University Press, 2004), pp. 14–45.
Winks, R. W., 'The Future of Imperial History', in R. W. Winks (ed.), *The Oxford History of the British Empire, V: Historiography* (Oxford: Oxford University Press, 1998), pp. 653–68.
Withers, Charles W. J., *Placing the Enlightenment, Thinking Geographically about the Age of Reason* (Chicago: University of Chicago Press, 2007).
Withington, P., *The Politics of Commonwealth: Citizens and Freemen in Early Modern England* (Cambridge: Cambridge University Press, 2005).
Wood, J. F., *Skibo* (Oxford: Oxford University Press, 1984).
Wood, Paul, 'The Scientific Revolution in Scotland', in Roy Porter and Mikuláš Teich (eds), *The Scientific Revolution in National Context* (Cambridge: Cambridge University Press, 1992), pp. 263–87.
Wood, Paul and Withers, Charles, W. J., 'Introduction: Science, Medicine and the Scottish Enlightenment: An Historiographical Overview', in Paul Wood and Charles W. J. Withers (eds), *Science and Medicine in the Scottish Enlightenment* (East Linton: Tuckwell Press, 2002), pp. 1–16.
Woodhead, J. R., *The Rulers of London, 1660–1689* (London: Arrowsmith, 1965).
Wrightson, Keith, 'Kindred Adjoining Kingdoms: An English Perspective on the Social and Economic History of Early modern Scotland', in R. A. Houston (ed.), *Scottish Society, 1500–1800* (Cambridge: Cambridge University Press, 1989), pp. 245–60.
Wrigley, E. A., 'A Simple Model of London's Importance in Changing English Society and Economy 1650–1750', *Past & Present*, 37 (1967), 44–70.
Wyman, Mark, 'Emigrants Returning: The Evolution of a Tradition', in Marjory Harper (ed.), *Emigrant Homecomings: The Return Movement of Emigrants, 1600–2000* (Manchester: Manchester University Press, 2005), pp. 16–31.

Unpublished theses

Brown, D. J., 'Henry Dundas and the Government of Scotland' (PhD dissertation, University of Edinburgh, 1989).
Bryant, G. J., 'The East India Company and Its army, 1600–1778' (PhD dissertation, King's College, 1975).

McGilvary, G. K., 'East India Patronage and the Political Management of Scotland, 1720–1774' (PhD dissertation, The Open University, 1989).
Parker, J. G., 'The Directors of the East India Company, 1754–1790' vols. I and II (PhD dissertation, University of Edinburgh, 1977).

Websites

British Museum, Satirical Prints: Newton, Richard, 'Progress of an Irishman (London: n.p., 1794), image at: www.britishmuseum.org/collection/object/P_ 1948-0214-372; Newton, Richard, 'Progress of a Scotsman' (London: William Holland, 1794), image at: www.britishmuseum.org/collection/object/P_1868-06 12-1247.
The History of Parliament: www.historyofparliamentonline.org/.
Measuring Worth.Com: www.measuringworth.com/calculators/ppoweruk/.
Oxford Dictionary of National Biography: www.oxforddnb.com.
The Statistical Accounts of Scotland: https://stataccscot.edina.ac.uk/.
Tate Art: Daniell, William, *A Voyage around Great Britain, 1814–1825*, image at: www.tate.org.uk/art/artworks/daniell-rowadill-in-harris-t02837.

Index

Aberdeen (burgh and county) 36–7, 41, 67, 94, 97, 112, 122, 141, 162–3, 177, 210, 227, 244
Ainslie, Whitelaw (EIC surgeon) 159
Alexander, Claud (EIC civil servant) 203, 243
Alexander, James (first earl of Caledon) 63, 202–3, 214, 225, 232–4, 237–8, 240, 241–2
'ancien régime' empire 2, 7, 11, 59, 77, 138, 195
Anglesey 138, 226
Antrim 71, 199, 225–6, 271
Armagh 138, 202, 225, 234
Asian merchants 85, 88, 192, 201–2, 205
Austrians (Austrian Netherlands) 1, 101
Aungier, Gerald (EIC governor) 35, 40
Awadh 120, 123, 201

Ballantyne, Ninian (EIC surgeon) 47, 165–6, 173
banks and banking 6, 42, 61, 68, 230, 240, 259
Belfast 13, 256
Bengal 5, 36, 46, 63, 66, 68, 85, 88, 108, 120–1, 123, 141–3, 163, 177, 196, 200
 army 129, 132, 138, 141, 259
Benkulen 41, 46, 48, 65, 108, 200, 206, 210
Board of Control 66, 74, 93
Bogle, George, of Daldowie (EIC civil servant) 44, 59, 88, 209

Bombay 11, 40, 43, 48, 65, 68, 86, 88, 109, 121, 134, 142, 160, 177, 184, 192, 195, 200, 206
 army 128–9, 138, 259
Borders (Scotland) 74, 234, 236, 254
Brecon 75, 138
British and Irish Isles 1–4, 6–7, 17, 31, 36, 71–4, 76, 87, 94, 108–13, 125, 147–9, 220–1, 226, 254
British Army 58, 87, 91, 101, 109–10, 120–2, 124, 127, 131–2, 134–5, 148, 167, 169, 172, 260–2
British Empire 4, 11, 50, 57–8, 60, 65, 67, 76–7, 84, 87, 101, 110, 220–2
 Atlantic Empire 4, 6, 8–9, 11, 30, 34, 37, 39–40, 49, 58, 62, 65–6, 86, 88–9, 92, 97, 106, 108, 111, 119, 124, 126, 131, 134, 140, 171, 196, 212–13, 256, 260
 domestic impact 5–6, 8, 220–48
 Eastern Empire 3, 7–8, 12–13, 17, 30, 39, 47, 49–50, 58, 61, 65, 70, 75, 86–9, 91, 106, 111–12, 126, 212–13, 221, 232, 241
British fiscal military state 15, 33, 63, 97, 120
British Fisheries Society 243–5
British identity 7, 30, 34, 70, 72, 74, 84, 91, 101–2, 110, 125, 195, 206, 209, 211
British imperialism and expansion (definitions) 4, 6
Brooke, Robert (of Prosperous) 124, 126, 242

Cairns, Henry (merchant) 37, 46
Calcutta 57, 59, 65, 68, 86, 88, 134, 142, 162, 169, 184, 192, 196, 200, 203, 206, 210
Campbell, Archibald (earl of Ilay, third duke of Argyll) 93, 139
Campbell, Archibald (of Inverneil) 60, 206, 227, 233
capital
   human capital 1, 10, 13–14, 35, 39, 44–5, 47–8, 58–9, 62, 65, 68–9, 73, 76–7, 83–4, 88, 94–6, 109–12, 119–21, 125, 128, 139, 144, 147–9, 158–84, 200–1, 203, 214, 222, 232, 247, 255–6
   monetary capital 2, 10, 13–14, 35, 44–5, 48, 58–9, 62, 64, 68, 76–7, 85, 87–9, 96, 109–12, 142, 147–9, 200, 214, 247
   social capital 13–14, 35, 39, 44–5, 50, 58–9, 64, 70, 76–7, 83, 89, 94–9, 109–12, 121, 128, 158–84
Camacs, of Lurgan 144, 243
Caribbean 9, 58, 87, 95, 108, 126, 136, 171, 176, 182, 196, 223, 244, 255, 260
Carnacs, of Dublin (John and Scipio) 86, 145
China 5, 31, 33–4, 42, 80, 109, 184, 192, 200
   Canton 65, 192, 200–1, 206–8
Clerk, John (of Penicuik) 45, 161
Clive, Robert 85, 140, 144, 223
Cockburn, James (EIC director) 67, 71, 73, 128
Cole, Arthur, of Enniskillen (EIC civil servant) 86–7, 205, 209–11, 271
College of Surgeons (Edinburgh and Glasgow) 166, 181–3
College of Surgeons (Ireland) 167, 172
colonial knowledge 156–84
Company of Scotland trading to Africa and the Indies 1, 31, 36, 41–3
comparative history 8–9, 11, 91–4, 120
Connacht 12, 94, 106, 135, 145
Coote, Eyre (Lieutenant general) 140–1, 144, 232, 238, 240

Cork 13, 46, 49, 68, 135, 138, 142, 200, 239, 256
Corporation of Surgeons (London) 161–3, 166, 182
'country trade' (private trade) 42, 65, 89, 192–214, 261
Cowan, Robert (EIC governor) 74, 88, 235
credentialism (securities) 33–5, 40–1, 45–50, 63–4, 69–70, 76, 97, 110, 161–2, 165, 194

Danish East India Company (Danes) 1, 197, 207–8
Dempster, George (MP) 224, 227, 272–3
directors (English East India Company) 32–5, 43, 45, 48, 50, 62, 64–7, 69–74, 76, 89, 91, 94, 122, 125–8, 139, 162, 169, 172
   Irish 40, 58, 67–9, 72–3
   Scots 43, 48, 58, 67–9, 72–3, 172
   Welsh 58, 67–9, 72–3
Drummond, John, of Quarrell (EIC director) 33, 43, 45, 68–9, 73, 85, 93, 161, 181, 222, 227, 256
Drummonds (bank) 33, 68, 97, 102
Dublin 14, 35, 46, 61, 63, 70, 72, 86, 94, 96–7, 126, 135, 162–3, 167, 171, 180, 238
Dundas, Henry (first viscount Melville) 63, 66, 73, 75, 84, 93, 126, 139, 199, 228
Dundas, Robert (second viscount Melville) 93
Dundee 13, 37, 63, 66, 97, 108, 239
Dutch East India Company (VOC), 29, 65, 120, 122

East Central (Scotland) 73, 94, 228, 236, 262
East Indiaman 45, 48, 60, 65, 98–9, 101, 103–11, 164, 173, 176–7, 227–8, 236
   commander 60, 98, 100–3, 106–10, 112, 173, 177, 227
East India Club (of Edinburgh) 247

East India Company House (Leadenhall Street) 36, 43, 46–50, 64, 68, 73, 75, 102, 223, 228
Edinburgh 14, 63–4, 67, 71, 87, 96–7, 99–100, 103, 112, 126, 144, 159, 166, 177, 181–2, 262
education (professional training) 13, 15, 38, 45–6, 50, 83, 87, 96–8, 107, 135, 157, 159–67, 199
Elgin 245
England 3, 5, 10, 44, 96–7, 123, 158
English East India Company (EIC) ('Old', 'New', 'United') 1, 8–10, 15, 17, 30–1, 34, 36, 39, 41, 49, 59, 69, 71, 76, 83, 101
English East India Company (EIC) (personnel)
 civil servants and merchants 32–3, 41, 43–4, 46–8, 65–6, 68, 70–1, 73–6, 83–4, 87–98, 111–13, 121, 201, 230–2, 256–7
 maritime officers 45, 65–6, 68, 73–6, 83–4, 89, 98–113, 121, 256–7
 medical officers 63, 65–6, 73–6, 83, 89, 157–84, 230–2, 256–7
 military officers 32, 48, 65–6, 68, 71, 73–6, 84, 89, 91, 113, 119–49, 230–2, 256–7
English East India Company (EIC) (structure)
 armed forces 8, 91, 119–49
 colonial government 8, 65–6, 83, 85, 88, 160, 163, 165, 167, 176, 264
 monopoly 1, 2, 10, 31, 36, 59, 98, 192, 213
English law 38, 199
Englishness 34, 84, 86, 109, 195
Enlightenment
 medical 157–84
 Scottish 9, 158–60, 167, 173, 180–4
Equivalent, the 36, 140
established churches
 Ireland 63, 92
 Scotland 63, 138, 229
Europe 1, 4, 13, 29, 43, 85, 87, 108, 123–4, 207
 comparatively advantaged, 'rich Europe' ('core') 5, 15–17, 44, 111–13, 123, 263
 comparatively disadvantaged, 'poor Europe' ('semi-periphery') 2, 5, 10, 15–17, 44, 111–13, 120, 123, 147, 149, 237, 255–6, 258, 263–4
European identity 72, 123, 205–6, 211

family (identities and networks) 4, 14–15, 64, 72–3, 77, 83–4, 91, 98, 102, 109–10, 174, 193, 199, 211–12
Ferguson, Fairlie & Co. (Calcutta) 197–9, 200, 244
Fife 106, 135
Firth of Forth 38, 106, 112
France 1, 3, 5, 123, 131, 158, 183, 201, 207
 French East India Company 29, 120
Fraser, William (EIC governor) 40, 45, 61, 245
Fraser, Simon (EIC director) 67, 69, 74
free merchants and mariners 2, 32, 68–9, 76, 84, 89, 109, 192–214, 257
Fullerton-Elphinstone, William (EIC director) 68–9, 72–4, 103

gentlemanly capitalism 7, 10, 17, 57, 60–1, 68–9, 76, 98–100, 123, 192
gentry 10, 61, 85, 88, 96, 124, 174
gentry capitalism 10, 17, 57–8, 62, 64, 76, 99–100, 109, 127, 147, 223, 241, 256
Glamorgan 35, 94, 141
Glasgow 13, 49, 67, 96–7, 100, 126, 148, 163, 236, 256, 262
 tobacco trade 58, 67, 106, 148, 235–6, 259, 263
global history 3, 4, 17, 119, 139, 147
 'Great Divergence' 4
 World Systems 4, 17, 255
glocalism 13, 17, 72–4, 77, 124, 139, 204, 214, 257, 262
Graham of Airth 99, 108
Grahams of Kinross, 208, 211, 214, 270

George (free mariner) 60, 201, 211
John (EIC civil servant) 63, 201, 211
Thomas (EIC civil servant) 60, 201, 211, 237
Grant, Charles (EIC director) 68–9, 72–4, 77, 109–10, 227
Grant, Hugh (Colonel) 236–7
Grant, James, of Grant 88, 127, 236
Gray's Inn (London) 38, 46
Gregory, Robert (EIC director) 68–9, 71, 197, 200

Hastings, Warren (Governor-General) 59, 244
high- and low-value human capital 13, 65, 119–49, 158–9, 230–4, 254, 256–60, 264–5, 269
Highland Clearances 9, 242
Highland regiments 130, 133–4, 140, 142, 148, 227, 239
Highlands (Scotland) 12–13, 94, 130, 135, 142, 146, 148, 228, 234, 242, 261–3
Holwell, John Zephaniah (EIC surgeon) 162
Hudson's Bay Company 40, 58, 171, 261–2
Huguenots (Ireland) 61, 144, 210
human mobility (migration) 1, 2, 4, 9, 14, 16, 37–8, 41, 44, 49, 59, 62, 68, 84, 86, 88, 106, 126, 146–9, 158–84, 181, 232, 236, 354–5, 259
Humberston-Mackenzie, Francis (earl of Seaforth) 227, 233, 239
Hume, Abraham, of Ayton and Wormleybury 33, 102–3, 173
Hume, Alexander, of Ayton and Wormleybury, (EIC director) 33, 43, 70, 101–3

'improvement' (agrarian and civic) 99, 139, 184, 240, 242–8, 259, 265, 272–3
Indian rising (1857) 31
Inglis, Hugh, (EIC director) 67, 69, 71

internal colonialism 3
Inverness (burgh and county) 37, 67, 97, 135, 139, 227–8, 236–7, 239, 244, 262
investment (manufacturing) 242–4
Ireland 6, 7, 15–17, 36–7, 74, 97, 111, 121–3, 158, 172, 213, 221, 238, 255–9
  economy 34, 49, 61, 100, 112, 229
  politics 11–12, 30, 38, 63–4, 71, 97, 112, 138–9, 172, 222–9, 247
  society 10–11, 15–16, 49, 76, 91, 94–6, 112, 120, 123, 135, 229, 232
Ireland (counties and provinces) 4, 11–12, 17, 29, 46, 61, 67, 71, 84, 91–2, 94–6, 106, 124, 135, 144, 148, 174–5, 260
Irish identities 71–5, 84, 110, 195, 204, 206, 210
Ivory, Patrick (EIC surgeon) 110, 174, 244

James, William (EIC director) 75
Johnstone, John of Westerhall (EIC civil servant) 85, 223–4, 240
Jones, William (EIC director) 68

Kildare 138, 141
Kilpatrick, James (Major) 144–5, 232
Kilpatrick, Samuel (Major) 144
kin and kinship 10, 14–15, 17, 35, 37, 40, 43, 47, 63, 68, 71, 74, 77, 83, 98–9, 110, 193, 199, 204, 211–12, 264

landed estates
  Ireland xvi, 141, 174, 223, 225, 233–41, 247
  Scotland xvii, 9, 108, 127, 139, 141, 174, 209, 224, 233–42, 247, 272
  Wales xviii, 223, 226, 235
Leinster 86, 94, 106, 112, 135, 148, 260
Lennox, of Woodhead 98, 233
Lincoln's Inn (London) 45–6
Lindsay, Robert, of Leuchars (EIC civil servant) 203, 209, 238, 242

linen 36, 63
London 2, 4, 10, 12, 14, 34, 42–3, 46, 59, 72, 76–7, 83, 87, 96, 112, 144, 159, 161, 174, 177, 192, 200–1, 237, 256
  Irish migrants in 29–30, 37, 41, 44–6, 49–50, 58, 60–2, 71–2, 74, 76, 97, 102, 112, 159
  Scottish migrants in 29–30, 33, 37, 41, 44–50, 58, 60–2, 72, 76, 93–4, 102, 159
  Welsh migrants in 29–30, 37, 41, 44–5, 49–50, 58, 60–2, 92, 111
Londonderry (county and town) 63, 163, 165, 202, 225
loot (prize money) 139–42, 146
Lord Lieutenant of Ireland 63, 66, 71, 229
Lothians 91, 96, 100, 106, 110–12, 135, 236, 262

McCartney, George (first earl) 71, 73–4, 199, 225
Mackenzie, John (Lord Macleod) 227, 239
Macky, Robert (EIC civil servant) 46
Macleod, Alexander (of Harris) 102, 173, 236, 242, 246
Macleod, Donald, of Geanies, 89, 228–9
Macleod, Norman, of Dunvegan (Major General) 236, 239, 244
Macpherson, John (Governor-General) 181, 244
Madras 40, 46, 48, 57, 65, 68, 71–3, 86, 88, 91, 108, 123, 134, 142, 165, 177, 184, 192, 196, 206
  army 129, 138, 140–1, 145, 176–7, 259
Matheson, James 235
Mayne, Robert and William (London and Lisbon) 63, 207, 211
Medical Commentaries (Edinburgh periodical) 176, 182
metropole (metropolis) 6, 10, 17, 30, 35–6, 38, 44, 46, 57–60, 64, 68–9, 76–7, 99–100, 103–4, 112, 122, 125, 147, 161–2, 182–3, 201, 223, 237, 256
metropolitan provinces 4, 10, 15, 17, 32, 34–6, 41, 44, 48, 57–8, 60, 62, 64, 67, 69, 75–7, 83–4, 87, 96–7, 99–100, 111–12, 119, 125, 127–8, 197, 258, 261
  definition 3
  distinctiveness 7, 8, 12, 30, 64, 72–3, 75, 77, 109–12, 128, 134, 139, 147, 258–9, 261
  integration 7, 12, 30, 49, 58, 68–9, 72–3, 75, 77, 94, 109–12, 120, 139, 147, 197, 261
middling social order (middle and professional classes) 10, 38, 50, 85, 88, 96, 106, 136, 138, 158, 162
military recruitment 65, 83, 89, 119–49, 256–7
  Ireland 8, 122–4, 126, 129, 134, 147, 259
  Scotland 122, 124, 126, 130–1, 133–4, 147
  Wales 124, 126, 130, 132, 134, 148
Moffat, Andrew (London) 47–8, 103, 112
Moffat, James (EIC director) 48, 103
Montrose 37, 64, 67, 112
Munro, Hector, of Novar (Major General) 140, 227, 242, 244, 262
Munster 67, 71, 148, 221
Murchison, Kenneth (EIC surgeon) 163–4, 174

nabobs 74, 145–6, 148, 223–7, 232, 234–6, 239–40, 242–5, 262
  definition 46
Naoroji, Dadabhai 258–9
Nesbitt, Albert and Arnold (merchants) 37, 46, 102
Netherlands 1, 3, 5, 38–9, 123, 133, 158, 183, 207–8
networks 17, 30, 33, 59, 83–4, 110
  macro- 14–15, 47–8

meso- 14–15, 37, 39, 47–8, 50, 69, 71–2, 76, 99, 102–3, 200, 203–4, 208, 264
micro- 14–15, 39, 41, 47–8, 50, 69, 71, 99, 103, 112, 200, 203–4, 264
new imperial history 3, 4
non-commissioned officers (sergeants and corporals) 91, 129–30, 134, 142
north-east (of Scotland) 37, 73, 94, 106, 110, 174, 208
North (Scotland) 94, 261–2
North Sea 37–8, 106, 112, 174

opium 202, 235
'Orient' (Orientalist scholarship and 'Orientalism') 48, 86–7, 89, 98, 140, 180–3, 223, 240, 245
Ostend 29, 101–2

parliament 14, 31
British 60, 224–9
Irish 12, 36, 71, 224–9
Scottish 31, 36, 42, 45
Parry, Thomas (Madras) 197, 200, 204, 212, 214
patronage 12, 44–6, 50, 60, 63–6, 68, 70, 72–6, 93, 96, 100, 108, 110–12, 138, 172, 226–9, 268
Patterson, George (of Castle Huntly) 238, 242, 245
Penal Laws (Ireland) 9, 11, 100–2, 123, 159
Perth (burgh and county) 37, 41, 112, 210, 222, 224, 227–8, 238–9, 262
Pitt India Act (1784) 66, 86, 202
poor relief 244–5, 274–5
Popham, Stephen 199–200, 232
Portugal (Portuguese) 1, 3, 201, 207
Preston, Robert, of Woodford and Valleyfield (shipping interest) 99, 109, 112, 173
Price, Joseph 197, 210
primitive capital accumulation 142–3, 147, 214, 230–4, 237, 240, 247, 254, 258–9

Probate Court of Canterbury 168–9
proprietary court (English East India Company) 59–60, 62, 64, 67
share/stockholders 50, 58–63, 67–8, 76, 87, 89, 100, 112
proto-globalisation 1, 5, 15, 17, 32, 44, 58, 76–7, 112, 119–21, 123, 127, 135, 147, 159, 193, 213–14, 256, 263
provincial gentry capitalism 11, 17, 58, 64, 99–100, 109, 123, 127, 240–1, 256
provincial/subsidiary metropole 9, 63, 94, 96–7, 100

race 65, 72, 83, 87, 176–7, 195, 205–6, 241
Regulating Act (1773) 59, 202
religion 11, 94, 138, 205
Catholicism 16, 63, 93, 100–1, 111–12, 120, 123, 125–6, 131, 138, 174, 244, 259, 264
Presbyterianism 11, 33, 38, 45, 92
Protestants (Ireland) 16, 40, 50, 61, 63, 72, 74, 86, 91–3, 98, 102, 112, 120, 125–6, 131, 142, 199, 259, 264
Roscommon 141, 238, 240
Ross, Hugh (London) 47–8
Ross-shire 86, 89, 174, 226, 228, 233, 262
Rotterdam 43, 61
Royal Navy 33, 58, 87, 91, 101, 108, 110, 167, 169, 260

sailors 41, 83, 89, 102, 109
Saint Helena 42, 65, 136, 200
Scotland 1, 6, 11, 32, 49, 75, 120, 133, 146, 158, 182, 213, 221, 225, 232, 240, 254, 257, 263–5
economy 37, 41, 49, 112
politics 9, 11–12, 36, 39, 60–1, 63–4, 97, 112, 139, 222–9, 247
society 10–11, 15, 49, 76, 91, 94–6, 112, 123, 229

Scotland (counties and regions) 4, 11–13, 17, 37, 64, 67, 70, 72–3, 76–7, 84, 91, 94–6, 110, 135, 163, 174–5, 228, 247, 260
Scott, David, of Dunninald (EIC director) 67–9, 73–7, 97, 109–10, 197, 211, 228, 256
Scottish Corporation of London 38–9, 42–3, 46–9, 194
Scottish identities 72–3, 75, 84, 86, 98, 110, 195, 204, 206, 210
Scottish law 38, 99–100, 103, 199
   Scottish courts (Commissary and Sheriff) 92, 232
Scott, Walter (Sir) 254, 264
Seringapatnam 140
shipping interest 32–3, 48, 84, 98–112
slavery 10, 58, 108–9, 140, 148, 176–7, 182, 259–60, 263
Society of Ancient Britons 38–9
sojourning 2, 4, 9, 45, 84, 106, 158, 161, 200, 205, 230
   return 46, 65, 67, 85–6, 165, 220–48
South Asia (India) 2–3, 8, 31, 65–7, 71, 74, 83, 86–8, 93, 120–1, 123, 139–40, 148, 192, 205, 264
Spain (Spaniards) 1, 3, 101, 131, 140, 207
Speedwell (Company of Scotland vessel) 42–3
Stewart, Robert (first viscount Castlereagh) 73–5, 110, 225, 238
Stone Maxwell, John (EIC civil servant) 202, 206–7
Stuart, James, of Torrance (Major general), 128, 141
Stuarts (court patronage) 36, 38–40
Sulivan, Laurence (EIC director) 29, 48, 68–9, 71–4, 76–7, 91, 193, 223, 256
supercargo 33, 42, 65
Surat 43, 48
surnames (as method for identifying origins) 62, 92, 104, 194
Swansea 70, 257
Sweden (Swedes) 1, 29, 207–8

tenant farmers and tacksman 10, 71, 138–9
Tibet 59
Tobin, James (merchant marine officer) 101–2
Tod, Thomas (lawyer) 71, 99
Toone, Sweny (EIC director) 68, 71–3, 91
Trinity Inn (London) 38, 46
Tyrone 110, 169, 225

Ulster 12, 46, 67, 72–3, 87–8, 94, 106, 110, 112, 124, 133, 135, 144–5, 148, 174, 202, 221, 235, 260
union
   Anglo-Scottish (1707) 6, 31, 34, 36–7, 94, 140
   British-Irish (1800) 7, 11–12, 31, 34, 60, 71, 93–4, 133, 183, 213, 260–1
   corporate (1702–1709) 31, 34, 36
universities 63, 157, 161, 172, 179
   Aberdeen (Marischal and King's colleges) 163, 174, 180–1, 244
   Edinburgh 161–3, 166, 179, 182–3
   Glasgow 163, 183
   Trinity College Dublin 161, 167, 172, 180, 183
   Maynooth 244

Wales 1, 3, 9, 12, 35, 61, 75, 92, 110–11, 124, 126, 133, 172, 199, 223, 232, 235, 257, 260
   economy 9, 12, 49, 58, 112
   politics 35, 38, 64, 112, 223–5
   society 10–11, 15, 29, 35, 49, 76, 91, 94–6, 112, 172, 232
Wales (counties and regions) 4, 11–12, 17, 35, 58, 67, 72–3, 75, 84, 91–2, 94–6, 106, 112, 135, 174–5, 260
   East 94, 135, 226
   North/West 94, 106, 135
   South 94, 174, 260
Waterford 13, 97, 100, 124
Wellesleys 40, 209, 238
   Arthur (Sir) 144

Richard (second earl of Mornington, Governor-General) 74, 144, 226
Welsh identities 84, 195, 204, 206, 210
West Central (Scotland) 96, 235–6, 243, 260, 262
Wigram, Robert (EIC surgeon and shipping interest) 102
Wigram, William (EIC director) 68

Williams, Eric 258–9
wills and testaments 92, 94, 104, 134, 141–4, 168–9, 171, 196, 200, 205, 230, 232

Yeshe, Lobsang Palden (Panchen Lama) 59

EU authorised representative for GPSR:
Easy Access System Europe, Mustamäe tee 50,
10621 Tallinn, Estonia
gpsr.requests@easproject.com

www.ingramcontent.com/pod-product-compliance
Lightning Source LLC
Chambersburg PA
CBHW071827230426
43672CB00013B/2780